D1637039

# FROM CONSULTATION TO CONFRONTATION

# FROM CONSULTATION
# TO CONFRONTATION

A study of the Muslim League in British Indian Politics,
1906–1912.

Matiur Rahman, M.A., Ph.D.(London)

LUZAC & COMPANY LTD.
46 Great Russell Street,
LONDON, W.C.1.

1970

DS
480.5
R3

PRINTED IN ENGLAND BY
STEPHEN AUSTIN AND SONS, LIMITED, HERTFORD, HERTS.

DEDICATED TO MY MOTHER

# FOREWORD

Muslims of British India formally entered all-India politics, as Muslims, by forming the All-India Muslim League and acquired, through the grant of separate electorates, their own constitutional identity within four years of the departure in 1905 of a British Viceroy, Curzon, who had hoped to end all Indian political activity and to deny all Indians and not only Muslims any effective constitutional identity. A policy of administrative reform, of state action to improve the lot of India's toiling millions—fondly believed or pretended by British officials to be Britain's silent 'block vote' in India—would isolate the miniscule minority of would-be politicians and reveal them as a noisy irrelevance to India's true welfare. But Curzon found that India was not to be treated as though she were a dominion of packages rather than a dominion of men and he left India with not only the politically-minded minority raw and smarting but with that minority, in Bengal at least, in closer rapport with the non-political majority than ever before. Curzon bequeathed a situation where the British were obliged to play politics—and to play politics openly—in order to defuse a political time bomb. After Curzon, British India could never appear as an administrative state again, as a British 'possession' and this, let it be recalled, nearly a decade before that first great European war of the twentieth century which so weakened the white man's credibility as the selected rulers of creation.

But in that decade the British in India were still able to play politics from strength or at least to choose the kind of politics they would play. The politics they wished to play were those of 'balance and rule' or of encouraging a babble of voices in India so that no one strong single voice could be heard above the din which might rivet the attention of all upon its call to depose the British from their ruling position. One of the voices the British wished to join the babble was that of Muslims.

Many have alleged that any Muslim voice in India in the first decade of the twentieth century was that of the British ventriloquist. It is one of Dr. Matiur Rahman's important contributions that he adds further data to that accumulated in recent years (by Dr. S. R. Wasti for example), which militates against the validity of this allegation. He shows that there was major disagreement among Muslim spokesmen from the different provinces of British India about the contents of the

vii

Simla deputation's address to Lord Minto and that the concern of
Muslim leaders in Bengal over threats to Curzon's partition of Bengal
were not equally shared by, for example, Muslim spokesmen from the
Punjab. Dr. Rahman reveals the careful diplomacy needed to arrive at
the highest common factor of agreement among Muslims from the
different provinces, provinces which, so far as Muslims were concerned,
were at varying stages of political development. If the Simla deputation
had been a command performance, it would be surprising to find the
players arguing so much about their script. However, I hope Dr.
Rahman would agree that the members of the Simla deputation knew in
advance that they would not, to say the least, meet with a hostile
reception from Lord Minto, and that this fore-knowledge powerfully
influenced the requests they made and the manner in which they made
them. But the early political activity of the Indian National Congress
had germinated under equally favourable atmospheric conditions so far
as officialdom was concerned.

   Dr. Matiur Rahman carefully documents the stages in the story of the
formation of the All-India Muslim League in the months after the Simla
deputation, bringing out the leading role of Nawwab Salimullah and the
decisive importance of Bengali Muslim hostility towards the anti-
partition movement. He also shows however how fearful Muslim leaders
in other provinces were lest they be identified with any anti-Hindu
political movement as such. Dr. Rahman shows that by 1906 the
question was not whether Muslims would have an all-India political
organisation, but whether they would have a cautious and conservative
or a radical political organisation. As Sir Harcourt Butler was to note
later, there was never any question of any 'splendid loyalty' of Muslims
to the British, but how rather to prevent the younger and predominantly
English-educated Muslim of the professional classes from abandoning
the curriculum of the 'Anglo-Muhammadan' school of politics, favoured
by such as Sir Muhammad Shafi, a curriculum which by and large
suited the interests of the higher Muslim landed classes. The British
policy seems to me to have been one of divide and rule within the
Muslim community, a policy of trying to keep Muslims away not only
from Congress politics but also from the militancy displayed by those
Muslims whom Minto's successor, Hardinge, was elegantly to describe
in official correspondence as 'Mahomed Ali and his gang'. It is this
British policy that helps to explain the success of Muslim agitation
against Lord Morley's electoral college scheme, once the British realised
the strength of this agitation (amply documented by Dr. Rahman) and

that that agitation was mainly led by Muslims with whom it should be possible to work on a conservative basis in the enlarged Provincial Councils.

Dr. Rahman's chapter 'The Elaboration of a Party Platform' does underline, in a manner not previously attempted, the inadequacy of the conservative members of the Muslim League in 1909 for electioneering on a common political platform and indeed the difficulties facing the League in its earliest days in devising any common political platform. If members of the League were in the event elected in the separate Muslim electorates under the first elections to be held after the Morley-Minto reforms, it was by reason of their personal local and provincial prestige and not by reason of any subscription to a League programme— which indeed in 1909 did not exist. Indeed, after those first elections the League continued for nearly two years to present the appearance not only of leaders in search of followers but also of leaders in search of some goal towards which to lead. No doubt it was tacit British appreciation of these difficulties of the League that explains why anxiety over a possible League response did not enter into British calculations before the revocation of the partition of Bengal.

Dr. Rahman effectively depicts the galvanic effect of the revocation of the partition of Bengal upon Muslim politics. Henceforth for Muslims too there were to be no 'settled facts' and no reluctance to put pressure upon a government apparently now revealed as so vulnerable to pressure. It was irrelevant that in 1910 the Muslim League had been a debating society many of whose members seemed to have more important things to do. What mattered now was that it existed as a ready-made arena for the display of Muslim gladiatorial talents. Dr. Rahman shows that not only young Muslims of the professional classes, led by Muhammad Ali, Shaukat Ali, Fazl al-Haq, Mazhar al-Haq and Fazl-i-Husain, *inter alios,* assumed leadership by the League session of December 1912, but that many Muslim members of Congress also joined the League but not to the exclusion of their Congress membership. The 'objectives resolution' of December, 1912, with its demand for self-government in a 'suitable' form for India, its proclamation of loyalty not, as hitherto, to the British government but to the British crown, and its call to promote national unity by fostering public spirit among the people of India and by co-operating with other communities spoke, after just over six years, a very different language from that of the Simla deputation which had begged 'most respectfully' to approach Lord Minto with an address for his 'favourable consideration'.

In the Cawnpore Mosque incident of 1913, Hardinge's bowing to the storm of Muslim protest, however graceful, revealed how sensitive the Government of India had become to any possibility of an alliance between the younger Muslim leadership and the advanced wing of Congress. The government knew very well the weakness of the conservative Muslim when faced with the cry of 'religion in danger'. By 1914 the Muslim League, against the background of Muslim suspicion of Britain over the Balkan wars, over her developing association with Russia and France, countries with recent records of imperialist attacks upon parts of the hitherto independent Muslim world, was becoming more Muslim and less a league of gentlemen for preserving their gentility. The Lucknow pact of 1916 surely signified that although the League may have begun its life as an army of all officers and no privates, in so far as it was now raising the banner of Islam it was drawing in the privates, and must be accepted by others as a serious political force.

Dr. Rahman's careful and dispassionate history of the formative phase of Muslim political life in British India, a political life conducted in the liberal constitutional idiom of public meetings, conferences, resolutions and newspaper editorials, deserves to stand as authoritative at least until such time as the early Muslim League records, now in the care of the University of Karachi, are fully available to students. His work should also be of interest to students of British politics in the age of Asquith for it introduces an episode of 'pressure group' politics in the London political world of 1909, conducted by the London branch of the Muslim League led by Sayyid Amir Ali. It would be interesting to know how far the domestic political repercussions of Lloyd George's famous Budget of 1909 made Morley and other members of the Liberal government amenable to Indian Muslim representations. I have the greatest personal pleasure in commending Dr. Rahman's monograph to the attention of students and of general readers alike.

P. Hardy,
Reader in the History of Islam
in South Asia in the University
of London.

# PREFACE

The inauguration of the All-India Muslim League at Dacca in December, 1906, heralded a new era in the history of Muslims of India. Earlier currents within the Muslim community circumscribed by self-absorption and nostalgia and rising only to a national level in the *Tariqa-i-Muhammadiya* had been only marginally political. The transition from heirarchical religio-social movements in which the *ulama* were the dominant force, to the British-Indian legalistic politics was greatly facilitated by the efforts of Abdul Latif, Ameer Ali, Syed Ahmad Khan and others. However, it was not until 1906 that the change was fully effected. Soon after its inception the League, working within an alien structure, achieved separate Muslim electorates. Although this had partially vindicated the Muslims' claim to a separate identity, within five years of its establishment the League had perforce helplessly to witness the liquidation of the Province of Eastern Bengal and Assam, the maintenance of the integrity of which was one of its *raisons d'etre.* Eventually, however, after much heart-searching and against tremendous odds it succeeded in establishing a separate Muslim State—Pakistan— though in a 'mutilated' and 'truncated' form.

The rise and growth of the Muslim League from being a loyalist, narrowly-based, conservative body to becoming the spokesmen of an overwhelming majority of the Muslims of the sub-continent should be a fascinating study. While a complete analysis of this metamorphosis of the League must await the release of its official papers and of the relevant records and documents preserved by the then governments of the British-Indian provinces, the importance of the subject requires that some attempts should be made towards a comprehensive research in the early history of the League. The present work is an humble attempt towards that end. It traces the circumstances leading to the formation of the League, examines the evolution of the League's constitution and policy, analyses its reaction to British policy and evaluates the League's contribution in British-Indian politics between 1906 and 1912. In analysing the subject I have endeavoured to be objective. To avoid complications and for clearer exposition sometimes events have been discussed in detail.

This study has been based on a variety of sources including private papers, official records and proceedings, newspapers, native newspaper reports, official publications of the League, pamphlets and published books. In transliteration the pronunciation in Pakistan has been given preference over the original forms. Except in a few instances like Muhammad and Ahmad, names have generally been spelled according to the forms used by the persons concerned.

This book evolved out of my thesis—The All-India Muslim League in Indian Politics, 1906–1912—approved for the degree of Doctor of Philosophy by the University of London. But for the constant help, inspiration and guidance I received from my supervisors Dr. P. Hardy and Dr. R. J. Moore of the School of Oriental and African Studies this study could not have been completed. Both Dr. Hardy and Dr. Moore have spent a good deal of their time in going through the chapters and in suggesting various improvements. My gratitude to them is as sincere as it is deep. I also gratefully acknowledge the honour done to me by Dr. Hardy in writing the Foreword to this book.

I was initiated into historical research by my former teacher Dr. Abdul Majed Khan, who also supervised my M.A. dissertation on the history of the Muslim League at the University of Dacca. It so happened that at the initial stage of the present work, Dr. Khan was present in London and took a kindly interest in its progress. My interest in the history of the Muslim League was sustained by Prof. A. B. M. Habibullah of the University of Dacca, who undertook to supervise my proposed study of the Pakistan Movement from 1940–47. Several factors including the lack of source materials in Pakistan resulted in my abandoning that project after about two years. I am indebted to Prof. Habibullah and Dr. Khan for their kind interest in my study of the League.

In the preparation of this book, I have been helped by a number of friends all of whose names it will not be possible to mention here. Dr. A. M. Wahiduzzaman kindly read the manuscript with me and suggested certain improvements. Dr. S. Z. H. Zaidi and Dr. A. H. M. Habibur Rahman have made certain source materials available to me which otherwise it would have been difficult for me to obtain. My young friend Mr. M. Suleman Ali of the School of Oriental and African Studies has been a great help in preparing the press copy as well as the index. The publication of this book would have been much delayed but for the kind and active interest of a friend who prefers to remain anonymous. I take this opportunity to thank him and all others mentioned above.

A scholarship from the Government of East Pakistan enabled me to undertake this study. The governing body of the Bangla College, Dacca, also facilitated the work by sanctioning my leave of absence from the College. My thanks are due to them. A considerable part of the financial burden involved in the writing of the book has been cheerfully shouldered by my wife Dr. Razia Rahman who interrupted her own research work to take up teaching. She has also been a source of constant encouragement and useful advice over the years spent on this study.

I should like to thank the librarians and staff of the India Office Library, the British Museum, the School of Oriental and African Studies Library, the Senate House Library, the National Library of Scotland, the University of Cambridge Library and the Kent Archives Offices for the ungrudging help rendered to me. My grateful thanks are due to Her Majesty the Queen for her kind permission to publish extracts from the correspondence of H.M. King George V. I am also thankful to Mr. H. Reynolds, Managing Director of Luzac & Co., Ltd., for accepting the manuscript for publication.

Matiur Rahman

15, Chesham Place,
London, S.W.1.

# TABLE OF CONTENTS

# ABBREVIATIONS

| | |
|---|---|
| A.I.M.L. | All-India Muslim League. |
| B.P. | Butler Papers. |
| C.N.M.A. | Central National Mahomedan Association. |
| Corr. India. | Correspondence with Persons in India. |
| Corr. England and Abroad. | Correspondence with Persons in England and Abroad. |
| C.P. | Curzon Papers. |
| G.G. | Governor General. |
| H.P. | Hardinge Papers. |
| I.N.C. | Indian National Congress. |
| J. & P. | Judicial and Public Department Papers. |
| L.C. | Legislative Council. |
| Min. P. | Minto Papers. |
| Mor. P. | Morley Papers. |
| N.N.R. | Native Newspaper Reports. |
| Parl. Debates. | Parliamentary Debates. |
| Proc. | Proceedings. |

# BACKGROUND

For several centuries the Muslims have lived in the Indo-Pakistan sub-continent side by side with the Hindus. The two communities met at a thousand points and profoundly influenced each other in various walks of life. But religious taboos, social conventions and the fact that the Muslims were the rulers over the greater part of the country while the Hindus were the ruled, prevented the merging of the two communities. In almost every Indian village and town Hindus and Muslims lived in different and distinct quarters. They rarely shared their food and drink, intermarried or mixed with each other at the social level.

With the beginning of British rule in India, the conditions of the Muslims as well as their relations with the Hindus underwent enormous changes. Both communities were now subjects of a sovereign who had little in common with them. But while for the Hindus the advent of the British was merely a change of masters, for the Muslims it meant the loss of power, position, wealth and dignity. Consequently, the reactions of the two communities towards British rule were different. 'Hindus were on the side of the Government and the Muslims arrayed against it.'[1]

With the consolidation of British rule, the Muslims were adversely affected. The Muslim officials and institutions were replaced by British officials and institutions with educated Hindu coadjutors. By the time the Muslims had reconciled themselves to British rule and its institutions, the Hindus under favourable circumstances had made long strides in every direction.[2] The newly acquired material prosperity of the Hindu landed aristocracy and middle class was accompanied by the discovery of ancient Hindu civilisation under the British patronage. 'The very first result of this renaissance was a progressive de-Islamisation of the Hindus of India and a corresponding revival of Hindu traditions. Throughout the nineteenth century the culture of the Hindus of India was taken back to its ancient Sanskritic foundations.'[3]  From Ram

[1] Ram Gopal, *Indian Muslims: A Political History*, p. 20.
[2] M. Noman, *Muslim India: Rise and Growth of the All-India Muslim League*, p. 47.
[3] N. C. Chaudhuri, *The Autobiography of an Unknown Indian*, p. 226.

1

Mohan Roy to Rabindranath Tagore all the Hindu thinkers and reformers ignored the Islamic trends and traditions in the Indian society.[4]

The leaders of this Hindu revivalist movement did not make a secret of their religio-political motives. Ram Mohan Roy, who is often regarded as 'the father of Indian nationalism,'[5] did not hesitate to name his pioneering English institution the 'Hindu College'. Nabagopal Mitra, who has been called 'the father of Nationalism in Bengal,'[6] named his political gathering the 'Hindu Mela'. Joy Kissen Mukherjee's Land Holders' Society—an apparently non-communal organisation—styled its organ *'The Hindoo Patriot'*. Eventually some of these leaders started calling themselves nationalists. But the change of name did not indicate any change in their concept which was essentially Hindu. Inspired by the Hindu Mela, for which Rabindranath Tagore had written two songs,[7] Rajnarain Bose who claimed to be the 'grandfather of Nationalism in Bengal'[8] established the 'National Society' in 1870. Its aim was to promote unity and national feeling among the Hindus.[9] On being asked why a Hindu association was styled as national, the *National Paper,* the organ of the Hindu Mela asserted: 'We do not understand why our correspondent takes exception to the Hindus who certainly form a nation by themselves, and as such, a society established by them can very properly be called a national society.'[10]

Side by side with the religio-political activities of the Hindu leaders, a section of the educated Muslims too came forward to organise their co-religionists on exclusive lines. The first Muslim organisation—the Mohammedan Association—was founded on 31 January, 1856, at Calcutta, with Fazlur Rahman and Muhammad Muzher as president and secretary respectively.[11] It had several branches including one at Agra. It is noteworthy that the establishment of the Mohammedan Association did not cause any surprise to the Hindu leaders. On the contrary it was welcomed by the British Indian Association.[12] Evidently, the enlightened leaders of the two communities had considered it natural that they

---

[4] *Ibid.*

[5] A. K. Majumdar, *Advent of Independence*, p. 39.

[6] B. B. Majumdar, *Indian Political Associations and Reform of Legislature (1818–1917)*, p. 94.

[7] A. K. Majumdar, *Advent of Independence*, pp. 39–40.

[8] B. B. Majumdar, *Indian Political Associations, op.cit.*, p. 94.

[9] A. K. Majumdar, *Advent of Independence*, p. 40.

[10] Quoted in A. K. Majumdar, *Advent of Independence*, p. 40.

[11] B. B. Majumdar, *Indian Political Associations, op.cit.*, p. 22.

[12] *Ibid.*

should have different but not antagonistic socio-political associations. The latter-day theory of Muslim separatism having been the product of British imperialism—*divide et impera*—had not yet come to the fore.

The second important Muslim organisation—the Mahomedan Literary Society—was established at Calcutta in 1863 by Abdul Latif. The Society's main purpose was cultural but it played an important part in the growth of political consciousness among the Muslims.[13]

The first political organisation of the Indian Muslims was established in 1878 by Syed Ameer Ali (later member of the Judicial Committee of the Privy Council), then a young man of twenty-eight years only. Significantly enough, the organisation was styled the National Mahomedan Association. This was later changed to Central National Mahomedan Association. The formation of the Association was due to a keen awareness of the necessity for a '*bona fide* political body among the Mahomedans, to represent faithfully and honestly to Government from a loyal but independent standpoint, the legitimate wants and requirements of the Mussulman community'.[14] Non-Muslims were eligible for membership of the organisation but were not entitled to vote on purely Muslim matters.[15] Through correspondence and extensive tours by Ameer Ali, the Central National Mahomedan Association had, within a short time, set up fifty-three branches all over India. Of them twelve were in Bengal; eleven in Bihar; eight in the Punjab; seven in the U.P.; five in Madras; three in Bombay; and one each in Assam, Delhi, Orissa and Rajasthan.[16] Through the persuasion of the Association, the Government of India had on 15 July, 1885, issued an important resolution relating to Muslim education and employment. In 1888 Ameer Ali had convened an all-India Muslim political convention in order to finally transform the Association to a really all-India political party.[17] The date of the meeting was later shifted to 1889. But due to opposition from Syed Ahmad Khan, the lack of educated workers among the Muslims, and Ameer Ali's elevation to a judgeship of the Calcutta High Court in 1890, the proposed convention could not be held, and eventually the Central National Mahomedan Association became moribund.

---

[13] *Ibid.*, pp. 222–223.

[14] *Report of the Committee of the Central National Mahomedan Association, 15 April, 1883*, pp. 1–2.

[15] '*The Memoirs of Right Honourable Syed Ameer Ali.*' *The Islamic Culture*, Hyderabad, Deccan, vol. vi, No. 1, p. 9.

[16] B. B. Majumdar, *Indian Political Associations, op.cit.*, p. 225.

[17] *Source Material for a History of the Freedom Movement in India, Vol. II* (1885–1920) Bombay, 1959, pp. 64–65.

The meagre political activities among the Muslims during the nineteenth century were primarily due to the Muslim backwardness in education and Syed Ahmad Khan's opposition to their participation in politics. Syed Ahmad wanted the Muslims to concentrate wholly on educational development and did not support Ameer Ali's plea for a political party.[18] However, the United Indian Patriotic Association formed by him to combat the Congress, albeit in a limited sense, was a political body. In 1893, consequent upon a serious Hindu-Muslim riot in Bombay and a general anti-Muslim movement in various parts of the country, Syed Ahmad Khan had established another organisation—the Mohammadan Defence Association—at Aligarh.[19] Neither of the organisations was a success, for Syed Ahmad did not devote much time to them. It was through the two non-political institutions, the Aligarh College and the All-India Mahomedan Educational Conference, founded in 1877 and 1886 respectively, that Syed Ahmad exercised his great influence over the Indian Muslims.

The question of the Hindus and the Muslims forming one political organisation did not become an issue until the foundation of the Indian National Congress in 1885. Of the seventy-two delegates attending the first session of the Congress, only two were Muslims.[20] This was interpreted by *The Times* as the deliberate abstention by 'the entire Mohammedan population of India' from the Congress movement.[21] The Congress leaders took serious note of this criticism and sought to bring as many Muslims as possible to the Calcutta session of the Congress held in 1886. Their attempts were largely thwarted by the refusal of the Central National Mahomedan Association and the Mahomedan Literary Society to send delegates to the session.[22] Henceforward the Congress leaders tried their best to attract the Muslims to join the party but attained only limited success. Between 1885 and 1905 the Muslim delegates formed only ten per cent of the total number of Congress delegates.[23] Moreover, a majority of the Muslim delegates were political

---

[18] *'The Memoirs of Right Honourable Syed Ameer Ali.' The Islamic Culture*, Hyderabad, Deccan, vol. v, No. 4, p. 541.

[19] A. H. Albiruni, *Makers of Pakistan and Modern Muslim India*, pp. 45–46.

[20] *Report of the I.N.C. for 1885*, pp. 4–5.

[21] *The Times'* article has been reproduced in *Appendix C of the Report of the I.N.C. for 1885*.

[22] I. M. Jones, The Origin and Development to 1892 of the Indian National Congress. London University unpublished M.A. thesis, p. 455.

[23] This has been calculated on the basis of the incomplete series of the Reports of the I.N.C. between 1885 and 1905 available at the India Office Library.

nobodies and came mostly from those provinces or cities where the session had taken place.

There were several reasons for Muslim opposition towards the Congress. In the first place, the Congress demands for open competition as the basis for state employment and the introduction and extension of representative institutions were thought to be against the interests of the Muslims who were educationally backward, economically impoverished and numerically in a minority over a greater part of the country.[24] Secondly, Muslim Leaders like Syed Ahmad Khan and Abdul Latif thought that the Muslims were not yet fully prepared for political activities and that their participation in the Congress movement would create an unfavourable reaction among the rulers of the country.[25] Thirdly, the anti-Muslim activities of some Congress leaders, particularly Tilak,[26] had convinced a large number of Muslims that their interests would suffer in the hands of the Congress. The Muslim opposition to the Congress was so intense that in 1888 Badruddin Tyabji, president of the Congress, asked Hume, the founder-secretary of the party, to suspend its activities for five years.[27] Tyabji noted: 'The fact exists and whether we like it or not, we must base our proceedings upon the fact that an overwhelming majority of Mahomedans are against the movement... If then the Mussalman community as a whole is against the Congress—rightly or wrongly does not matter—it follows that the movement *ipso facto* ceases to be a general, or National Congress.'[28]

Tyabji's advice was not accepted by the Congress leaders who continued their efforts to persuade the Muslims to join the movement. But even among the relatively few Muslim members of the Congress, there were some who were as zealous about the separate identity and interests of the Muslims as Ameer Ali or Syed Ahmad Khan had been. At the Allahabad session of the Congress held in 1889 Hidayet Rasul had demanded that the number of Muslims in the Legislative Councils should always be equal to that of the Hindus.[29] He maintained: 'We

---

[24] The *Mahomedan Observer,* Calcutta, quoted in A. Seal, *The Emergence of Indian Nationalism: Competition and Collaboration in the Later Nineteenth Century,* p. 315.

[25] R. A. Zakaria, Muslims in India: A Political Analysis (1885—1906), London University unpublished Ph.D. thesis, pp. 55, 58—62.

[26] Sir V. Lovett, *A History of the Indian Nationalist Movement,* pp. 47—48.

[27] *Source Material For a History of the Freedom Movement in India, Vol. II.,* op.cit., p. 81.

[28] *Ibid.*

[29] *Report of the I.N.C., 1889,* pp. 32—33.

have not joined this Congress movement to sell our freedom of speech, we will support the movement only so long as our National Honour is not injured.'[30]    While supporting Hidayet Rasul, another member, Wahid Ali Rizvi remarked that the Congress had no right to style itself as 'National'.[31]

During the last few years of the nineteenth century the introduction of a public Ganapati festival and Shivaji celebrations by Tilak and the Hindu agitation against cow slaughter had caused Hindu-Muslim relations to deteriorate.  The situation took a grave turn when in April, 1900, A. Macdonnell, the Lieutenant-Governor of the U.P., accepted Hindi as an official language. This greatly shook the Muslims of the U.P. who started organising a counter agitation in defence of Urdu.[32] Mohsin-ul-Mulk, the then secretary of the Aligarh College and the All-India Mahomedan Educational Conference, took a leading part in this agitation.  But Macdonnell took a serious view of Mohsin-ul-Mulk's activities.  Descending upon Aligarh, he threatened to stop all assistance to the College unless Mohsin-ul-Mulk dissociated himself from the movement.[33]    Mohsin-ul-Mulk wanted to resign the secretaryship of the College in order to continue the agitation but was finally persuaded by some Muslim leaders to sever his connection with the Urdu Defence Association.[34]

Macdonnell's high-handedness had convinced the Aligarh Muslim leaders of the necessity for a political organisation to look after their interests.  Now the initiative was taken by Mushtaq Husain Viqar-ul-Mulk, a colleague of Syed Ahmad Khan and a former high official of the Nizam's Government.  Through his efforts, the Mahomedan Political Association was established at Lucknow in 1901.[35] The Association, however, limited its activities to the U.P., and did not even attempt to set up branches in other provinces.

In 1905 the readjustment of provincial boundaries in Bengal and the creation of Eastern Bengal and Assam gave rise to a serious Hindu agitation, particularly in Bengal.  A large majority of the Muslims of Eastern Bengal and Assam supported the new province.[36] The Eastern

[30] *Ibid.*, p. 32.

[31] *Ibid.*, p. 35.

[32] A. H. Albiruni, *Makers of Pakistan, op.cit.*, p. 88.

[33] *Ibid.*

[34] *Ibid.*, p. 89.

[35] A. H. Albiruni, *Makers of Pakistan and Modern Muslim India*, p. 104.

[36] Fuller to Minto, 26 November, 1905.  Min. P. Corr. India, 1905–6, vol. I. Also Hare to Minto, 20 and 31 October, 1906, *ibid.*, vol. II.

Bengal and Assam Provincial Mahomedan Association, founded on 16 October, 1905, on the initiative of Nawab Salimullah, started a vigorous campaign to defend the province's existence.[37] This brought down upon Bengali Muslims the wrath and hatred of the Hindu leaders.[38]

The anti-partitionists scored their first major victory in July, 1906, when, as a result of his differences with the Government of India over two Hindu-managed schools at Sirajganj, Sir Bampfylde Fuller, Lieutenant-Governor of the new province, resigned.[39] The Muslims strongly resented the acceptance of his resignation.[40] For the first time, they realised that unless the anti-partition agitation, which had through the efforts of the Congress spread all over India, could be combatted on an all-India basis, the future of the province would not be secured. Thereafter they became active in enlisting support and sympathy of the Muslim leaders from outside the two Bengals,[41] and took steps to organise an all-India Muslim political party.

[37] The *Bengal Times,* 21 October, 1905.

[38] N. C. Chaudhuri, *The Autobiography of an Unknown Indian,* p. 229.

[39] S. R. Wasti, *Lord Minto and the Indian Nationalist Movement, 1905–1910.* pp. 38–39.

[40] *The Mihir-o-Sudhakar,* 17 and 31 August, 1906. *Vide* the Bengal N.N.R., 1906; J. & P. 2876/1906, vol. 773.

[41] The Muslim public meeting held at Dacca during the first week of August, 1906, to protest against the acceptance of Fuller's resignation was attended by a few Muslim leaders from outside the two Bengals. *Vide* the *Englishman,* 7 August, 1906.

Chapter I

# THE SIMLA DEPUTATION AND THE FORMATION OF THE ALL-INDIA MUSLIM LEAGUE

On 1 October, 1906, thirty-five Muslim leaders from all over British India gathered in the Viceregal Lodge at Simla to present an address to Lord Minto. They were led by His Highness Sultan Muhammad Shah Aga Khan, a former member of the Viceroy's Legislative Council. Of the forty-two members selected at a meeting of Muslim leaders held at Lucknow to compose the deputation,[1] Nawab Salimullah, member, Eastern Bengal and Assam Legislative Council, Syed Zain-al-Edros, member, the Bombay Presidency Legislative Council, Nawab Fateh Ali Khan Qazilbash, member, the Punjab Legislative Council, Nawabzada Nasrullah Khan, barrister, Bombay, Qazi Ghiyasuddin Peerzada, Nasik, Raja Jahandad Khan, Hazara, and Shaikh Shahid Husain, barrister, Lucknow, were unable to proceed to Simla either because of illness or for other reasons.[2]

The Simla deputation was composed of members drawn from the Muslim nobles, jagirdars, zamindars, *taluqdars,* lawyers, merchants and retired officials. Members of the legal profession, some of whom were of landholding families, formed the largest single group,[3] followed by landed and titled aristocrats. Two members of the pre-British ruling families of Mysore and the Carnatic represented the old ruling aristocracy; two retired high officials of the Hyderabad State service, the Foreign Minister of Patiala and three Nawabs came from the higher officials and social groups; and the ten barristers, one retired sub-judge, two honorary magistrates, one special magistrate, were drawn from the English educated upper middle class.

The Simla deputation was unique in that for the first time the Muslims of India were not only prepared but also anxious to take their full share in the political activities of the country as a distinct identity. The address presented by the deputation was signed by 1,461,183

---

[1] The *Times of India Mail,* 29 September, 1906.

[2] The *Bombay Gazette,* 3 October, 1906.

[3] Among the forty-two members selected for the deputation twelve were barristers but ultimately only ten were present at Simla.

Muslims,[4] individuals, as well as groups, representing Muslim associations and *Anjumans* and particularly the Muslim dominated urban areas from Peshawar to Madras.[5]   They included among others seven members and eleven ex-members of the Supreme and Provincial Legislative Councils, ten C.I.E.s, one K.C.S.I., three Nawabs, nine Shams-ul-ulama, forty-five Khan Bahadurs, eighty-nine honorary magistrates and municipal commissioners, one hundred and eighteen barristers and pleaders, three hundred and eighty-nine zamindars, one hundred and fifty-five merchants, forty-nine public servants, thirteen mukhtars, sixteen editors of journals, and twelve members of the pre-British ruling families of Arcot, Mysore, Oudh, and of the late Mughal emperors of Delhi.[6]   The support extended to the deputation by Sardar Muhammad Yakub Khan, the minister of Khairpur State, Sardar Yar Muhammad Khan, the minister of Jaora State, and His Highness Nawab Amiruddin Khan of Rampur State, who were prevented on 'political grounds' from joining the deputation,[7] showed that the influential Muslim leaders of the Native States shared equally the views of the leaders who met the Viceroy at Simla.

An important feature of the deputation was that most of its members were closely connected with the Aligarh movement through the Mahomedan Educational Conference.   The contact already existing between the members of the deputation had greatly facilitated the preparation and presentation of the address.   The address was drafted by Syed Husain Bilgrami,[8] a former president of the Mahomedan Educational Conference and a staunch supporter of Syed Ahmad Khan. He was assisted by Nawab Mohsin-ul-Mulk who had succeeded Syed Ahmad as the secretary of the M.A.O. College, Aligarh, and of the Mahomedan Educational Conference.   The leader of the deputation, the Aga Khan, was himself a former president of the Educational Conference.   So was Muhammad Shah Din—another member of the deputation. Among other deputationists Viqar-ul-Mulk, Muzammil Ullah Khan, Haji Ismail Khan, Syed Nabiullah, Munshi Ihtisham Ali, Muhammad Shafi, Nawab Ali Choudhury, Naseer Husain Khan Kheyal and Aftab Ahmad Khan were prominent members of the Educational Conference.

[4] Muhammad Noman, *Muslim India: Rise and Growth of the All-India Muslim League,* p. 72.
[5] The *Times of India Mail,* 6 October, 1906.
[6] *Ibid.*
[7] Mehdi Ali Mohsin-ul-Mulk's article in the *Aligarh Institute Gazette,* 23 October, 1906, *vide* the *U.P. N.N.R.,* 1906).
[8] *Infra,* p. 21.

A considerable number of the deputationists were associated with various political and semi-political parties and *Anjumans*. They included Sahebzadah Bakhtiar Shah, president of the Mahomedan Literary Society, Calcutta, Nawab Syed Amir Husain, formerly secretary of the Central National Mahomedan Association, Nawab Ali Choudhury, vice-president of the Eastern Bengal and Assam Provincial Mahomedan Association, Malik Omar Hayat Khan, Muhammad Shah Din and Muhammad Shafi of the *Anjuman*-i-Islamia, Lahore, Khawaja Yusuf and Ghulam Sadiq of the *Anjuman*-i-Islam, Amritsar, and Viqar-ul-Mulk, Syed Sharfuddin, and Syed Ali Imam of the Mahomedan Political Association. Among them Sharfuddin and Ali Imam had earlier played an important role as members of the Indian National Congress.[9]

Critics questioned the representative character of the Simla deputation. A few Congress newspapers in Bengal and the U.P. interpreted the absence of Nawab Syed Muhammad of Madras from the deputation as the sign of lack of unity amongst the Muslim leaders.[10]    Syed Muhammad was a prominent Congress member and was hoping to be accepted as an all-India national leader through the Congress platform. Differences between him and the organisers of the Simla deputation could be expected. But even he was sympathetic to the deputation. In fact Mohsin-ul-Mulk had caused certain verbal alterations to be made in the deputation's address in response to some of Syed Muhammad's suggestions.[11] The reason why he did not join the deputation appears to be as Minto said—'a little personal jealousy on account of the Aga Khan being selected' to lead the same 'instead of himself'.[12]

Other criticisms against the deputation were that the deputationists came mainly from the Punjab and Bengal (possibly including Eastern Bengal),[13] that the *taluqdars* of Oudh were ill-represented in the deputation,[14] that Sind, a predominantly Muslim area, was poorly

---

[9] Sharfuddin had been one of the very few Muslims who attended the early sessions of the Congress. At the Allahabad sessions of the Congress held in 1888 he claimed that 'the great bulk of the Mahomedans, as the great bulk of the Hindus, Jews, Parsees, and Indian Christians, are everywhere for, and not against, the Congress'. *Vide, Report of the fourth I.N.C. held at Allahabad*, p. 30.

[10] The *Bengalee*, 3 October, 1906; the *Amrita Bazar Patrika*, 4 October, 1906 (*vide* the *Bengal N.N.R.*, 1906); and the *Oudh Akhbar*, 5 October, 1906 (*vide* the *U.P. N.N.R. 1906*.

[11] Mohsin-ul-Mulk's article in the *Aligarh Institute Gazette*, 23 October, 1906 (*vide* the *U.P. N.N.R.*, 1906).

[12] Minto to Morley, 4 October, 1906, Mor. P., vol. 9.

[13] The *Oudh Akhbar*, 12 October, 1906. *Vide* the *U.P. N.N.R.*, 1906.

[14] *Ibid.*

represented and, 'although the vizier of Khairpur, the recognized leader of the Mussulmans, was at Simla, he did not identify himself with the movement'.[15] These opinions are hardly justified. We have already noted that the wazir of Khairpur, despite his support for the deputation, could not join the same on political grounds. But Sind was represented by Syed Allahdad Shah, vice-president of the Zamindars' Association of Khairpur. From the point of view of the numerical strength of the Muslims, not only Sind but also Eastern Bengal and Assam was inadequately represented. However, the fact remains that the deputationists were not selected strictly on the basis of the numerical proportion of Muslim population. And the members selected from Sind and Eastern Bengal and Assam, being prominent leaders of the Zamindars' Association, Khairpur, and Mahomedan Association of Eastern Bengal and Assam respectively, did enjoy the support of a considerable proportion of their co-religionists in the areas concerned. The allegation about the excessive number of members from the Punjab and Bengal is not fair. While the Punjab and two Bengals had ten and nine members respectively, the U.P. and Bombay had twelve and seven members respectively among the deputationists. As for the under-representation of the *taluqdars* of Oudh, two *taluqdars* were, perhaps, an adequate representation of a single interest of a part of a province in an all-India body of forty-two members.

Despite the objections to and criticism against the composition of the Simla deputation, the truth was, as the *Bengalee*, one of the violent critics of the exclusive Muslim movement, admitted, that it was 'as thoroughly representative and influential as could be desired'.[16] The Muslim press in general reacted favourably to the deputation[17] and there was very little criticism from any section except the hostile Hindu press, and an aggrieved minority of Muslim opinion, mostly born out of disappointment at being excluded from it.[18]

[15] M. N. Das, *India under Morley and Minto*, p. 173.

[16] The *Bengalee*, 29 September, 1906.

[17] Among the numerous Muslim newspapers endorsing the deputation mention may be made of the *Union Gazette*, 7 December, 1906; the *Sahifa*, 12 December, 1906; the *Dabdaba-i-Sikandari*, 1 October, 1906; the *Naiyar-e-Azam*, 12 October, 1906; and the *Rohilkhand Gazette*, 1 November, 1906 (*vide* the *U.P. N.N.R.*, 1906). Even the radical *Urdu-i-Mualla* (October, 1906) did not dispute the representative character of the deputation (*vide* the *U.P. N.N.R.*, 1906).

[18] The *Express* (15 November, 1906) of Lucknow questioned the representative character of the deputation on the ground of the absence of journalists at the Lucknow meeting held in September, 1906. *Ibid.*

The address presented by the Simla deputation demanded that a due proportion of Muslims should find employment in the Government service, that Muslim judges should be appointed to the High Courts and Chief Courts of Judicature, that in case of the appointment of Indians to the Viceroy's Executive Council, the claims of the Muslims should not be overlooked, and that the Government should take steps towards the creation of a Muslim university.[19]  The address was, however, mainly concerned with the proposed extension of the elective elements in the viceregal and provincial councils.  The deputationists sought to impress upon the Viceroy that the interests of the Muslims could not be safeguarded under a European system of open election. They cited the difficulties Muslims had suffered in obtaining representation on various elective bodies operating under Ripon's Local Self-government Act and the Government of India Act of 1892. 'Even in the provinces,' they observed, 'in which the Mohammedans constitute a distinct majority of the population, they have too often been treated as though they were inappreciably small political factors, that might, without unfairness be neglected.'[20]  They pointed out that 'this has been the case, to some extent in the Punjab; but in a marked degree in Sind and Eastern Bengal'.  They were, therefore, apprehensive that it was 'most unlikely that the name of any Mohammedan candidate will ever be submitted for the approval of Government by the electoral bodies as now constituted unless he is in sympathy with the majority in all matters of importance'.[21]

The deputationists were possibly on the safest ground when they complained about the failure of the system of mixed electorates in securing them the representation due even on account of their numerical strength.  Though the Muslims formed about twenty-three per cent of the population of British India they had obtained only twelve per cent representation in the Imperial Legislative Council.[22]  In the provincial legislative councils their representation was still poorer.  The Muslims of Bengal who comprised more than half of the Indian Muslims had a little over ten per cent representation in the provincial council.[23]

[19] The address of the Simla deputation, enclosed with Minto to Morley, 4 October, 1906, Mor. P., vol. 9.

[20] *Ibid.*

[21] *Ibid.*

[22] Government of India Home (Public) Department letter, 24 August, 1907. India Home (Public) Proc. May–August, 1907, vol. 7588.

[23] R. A. Zakaria, Muslims in India: A political Analysis 1885–1905, London University Ph.D. thesis, 1948 (unpublished), p. 155.

Furthermore, the Muslim members of the councils, except in a few cases, were either political nonentities nominated by the Government, or Congressmen like Nawab Syed Muhammad and Rahimatullah Sayani, who did not represent the views and aspirations of the bulk of the educated Muslims. The picture of Muslim representation in the municipalities and district boards except in the U.P. was much more dismal. Even in overwhelmingly Muslim areas like Sind and Eastern Bengal the number of elected Muslim members was either nil or negligible.[24]

However, the deputationists did not ask for the abolition of the elective system, which they applauded as the special gift of England, but rather separate representation of the Muslims as well as of the Hindus. The system of separate electorates, they observed, had already been in operation in Aligarh and some of the Punjab municipalities. They wanted the extension of this system over the whole of India, and in all elective bodies, including the Senates and Syndicates of the universities, with the provision that the number of Muslim and Hindu representatives to all these bodies should be statutorily determined in consideration of 'the numerical strength, social status, local influence, and special requirements of either community'.[25]

The deputationists suggested the election of Muslim representatives by distinct electoral colleges constituted separately for provincial and central legislative councils. They proposed that important Muslim landowners, lawyers, merchants and representatives of other important interests, along with the Muslim members of district boards and municipalities and Muslim graduates of a certain standing, should form electoral colleges for the provincial councils. As for the central legislative council, the deputationists recommended the formation of electoral colleges consisting of Muslim landowners, lawyers, merchants and representatives of other interests as well as Muslim members of the provincial councils and Muslim Fellows of the universities. The deputationists demanded that the number of Muslim representatives in all the councils should be determined in such a proportion that in no case should they be an ineffective minority.[26]

The deputationists urged special consideration of the claims of the Muslims on grounds of their numerical strength (which was more numerous than the population of any of the first class European states

---

[24] The *Sind Gazette,* 24 November, 1908. *The Bombay N.N.R.,* 1908.
[25] The address of the Simla deputation. Mor. P., vol. 9.
[26] *Ibid.*

except Russia), their contribution to the army and the defence of the Empire as well as their political importance. The members of the deputation did not elaborate the political importance of the Muslims, perhaps with a view to avoiding controversy,[27] but they were well aware 'of the position they occupied in India a little more than a hundred years ago', traditions of which 'have naturally not faded from their minds'.[28]

The cautious conservatism of the deputationists was underlined by their careful avoidance of any criticism of the policy pursued by the Government towards the Muslims. They used very temperate language in placing their grievances before the Viceroy. They were, on the other hand, loud in appreciating 'the incalculable benefits conferred by British rule', and expressed their gratitude 'for the peace, security, personal freedom, and liberty of worship'[29] enjoyed by the Indians. In this respect they distinctly differed from a section of the younger generation of the English-educated Muslims who considered the 'encomiums heaped on Government at the outset of the Address' to be 'unmerited' for the most part.[30] This difference in attitude was, however, frankly admitted by the deputationists, who felt concerned for 'recent events', which had 'stirred up feelings, especially among the younger generation of Mohammedans, which might, in certain circumstances and under certain contingencies, easily pass beyond the control of temperate counsel and sober guidance'.[31] The members of the deputation themselves were content with the 'excellent and time-honoured tradition' of placing implicit faith in the sense of justice and fair dealing of the Government. They were proud of the fact that the Muslims had refrained from pressing their claims by methods that might have proved embarrassing to authorities.[32] They hoped that the younger generation of Muslims might be kept under control if the

---

[27]It was a well-known belief with the Muslims that the Englishmen were received as guests by the Mughals whose heirs they became and for both these reasons as well as for the Muslims' affiliations with their co-religionists outside India they claimed special treatment by the British Government (*vide* Hafiz Ghulam Sarwar's letter to the *Civil and Military Gazette,* 6 October, 1906).

[28]The address of the Simla deputation, enclosed with Minto to Morley, 4 October, 1906, Mor. P., vol. 9.

[29]*Ibid.*

[30]The *Urdu-i-Mualla,* October, 1906. The *U.P. N.N.R.,* 1906.

[31]The address of the Simla deputation, enclosed with Minto to Morley, 4 October, 1906. Mor. P., vol. 9.

[32]*Ibid.*

aspirations of the community as set forth in the memorial to the Viceroy were satisfied.

The Simla deputation has often been called 'a command performance',[33] which was manoeuvred 'from Simla'[34] as the consequence of a 'conspiracy between the British and the Muslims'.[35] The only direct evidence advanced in support of this allegation[36] has been a letter written by A. J. Archbold, Principal of the Aligarh College, on 10 August, 1906, to Mohsin-ul-Mulk, informing the latter of the Viceroy's consent to receive the Muslim deputation. Extracts from this letter, first published by Tufail Ahmad Manglori in *Musalmanon-ka Roshan Mustaqbil,* and translated into English by Mehta and Patwardhan in *The Communal Triangle in India*[37], have been quoted by several authors. The contents of this letter have also been vouchsafed by Dr. Syed Mahmud who claims to have acted as one of Mohsin-ul-Mulk's secretaries in those days.[38] But neither Dr. Mahmud nor Tufail Ahmad cared to disclose the fact that this letter had been a reply from Archbold to Mohsin-ul-Mulk's letter of 4 August, 1906. On that day the secretary of the Aligarh College had asked Principal Archbold, then enjoying his summer holiday at Simla, to 'inform' him whether it would be advisable 'to submit a memorial from the Mohammedans to the Viceroy and to request His Excellency's permission for a deputation to wait on His Excellency to submit the views of Mohammedans on the matter?'[39] The withholding of any reference to Mohsin-ul-Mulk's letter of 4 August, 1906, while publishing Archbold's reply to the same purporting to show the latter's initiative in organising the Simla deputation has resulted in the gross misrepresentation of the origin of the deputation and thus of the Muslim politics in the early twentieth century. Even a well-known Indian historian like R. C. Majumdar has

[33] Muhammad Ali's presidential speech at the Coconada Congress. *Congress Presidential Addresses,* Natesan & Co., vol. II, p. 620.

[34] A. M. Khan, *The Communalism in India—its origins and growth,* p. 23.

[35] R. C. Majumdar, *History of the Freedom Movement in India,* vol. II, p. 227.

[36] a) *Ibid.,* pp. 224–227.
 b) Mehta and Patwardhan, *The Communal Triangle in India,* pp. 29–30.
 c) Sachin Sen, *The birth of Pakistan,* pp. 52–53.
 d) R. Prashad, *India Divided,* pp. 106–7.
 e) R. Gopal, *Indian Muslims—A Political History,* p. 97.
 f) B. M. Chaudhari, *Muslim Politics in India,* pp. 15–16.

[37] Mehta and Patwardhan, *The Communal Triangle in India,* pp. 29–30.

[38] Syed, Mahmud, *Hindu-Muslim Cultural Accord,* p. 72.

[39] Mohsin-ul-Mulk to Archbold, 4 August, 1906, enclosed with Minto to Morley, 8 August, 1906. Mor. P., vol. 9.

fallen prey to this distortion of facts when on the authority of Archbold's letter of 10 August, 1906, he emphatically declares: 'It is now definitely known that the whole of this [Simla] deputation was engineered by the Government or at least by Englishmen under official inspiration'.[40]

However, after the recent publication of Mohsin-ul-Mulk's letter of 4 August, 1906, along with certain other evidence regarding the spontaneity of the Simla deputation,[41] it could be expected that the myth of the deputation being engineered by the Government had been demolished. But some authors still doubt whether or not Archbold's part had been limited to that of an emissary of Mohsin-ul-Mulk,[42] and whether Mohsin-ul-Mulk's advisers on the matter were 'Muslim Indians or Englishmen'.[43] A careful analysis of the circumstances and evidence should, it is hoped, convince any observer that the deputation was initiated and organised by Muslims and by Muslims alone.

Morley's declaration in Parliament in July 1906 about the extension of the Legislative Councils in India had revived the old Muslim fear of being swamped by the Hindus in the various elective bodies. This apprehension had been repeatedly pronounced by various Muslim leaders since the days of Ripon's Local Self-Government Act. On 3 March, 1883, speaking on the local self-government Bill in the Bengal Legislative Council, Muhammad Yusuf, a leading member of the Central National Mahomedan Association, pointed out that 'when there is party spirit and angry feeling between the two classes of people, it is necessary to reserve power for the representation of the minority'.[44] He knew that the Government intended to safeguard Muslim interests through nomination. But 'it would be an advantage and a more fit recognition of the claims' of the Muslims if provision could be made 'for the election of Mohammedans by reserving a certain number of memberships for that community'. The following month in a speech in the Imperial Legislative Council, Syed Ahmad Khan had pleaded with the Viceroy that 'in a country like India, where caste distinctions still flourish, where there is no fusion of the various races, where religious distinctions are still violent, where education in its modern sense has

[40] R. C. Majumdar, *—History of the Freedom Movement in India,* vol. II, p. 224.
[41] S. R. Wasti, *Lord Minto and the Indian Nationalist Movement 1905–1910,* pp. 61–68.
[42] B. L. Grover, *British Policy Towards Indian Nationalism,* pp. 80, 81 and 86.
[43] S. A. Wolpert, *Morley and India, 1906–1910,* p. 186.
[44] Proc. Bengal L.C., 3 March, 1883, p. 65.

not made an equal or proportionate progress among all the sections of the population' the introduction 'of the principle of election, pure and simple for various interests' would be attended with evils of greater significance than purely economic considerations.[45] He had warned the Viceroy that in case the principle of election was accepted as the only means of representation, the majority community would totally over-ride the interests of the Muslims and that the Government would be held responsible for any such eventuality. Again in 1890, when the proposals of the Government of India Act, 1892, were being discussed, the Mahomedan Literary Society had, in a memorial to the Secretary of State for India, pointed out that 'should election form the basis of any contemplated legislation on the subject of the Indian councils the Mahomedan community though numbering some fifty millions, will be at the mercy of a strong and compact Hindu majority, whose notions of right and wrong are so different on so many vital points, from those entertained by the Mahomedans'.[46] The same year the Indian Patriotic Association sent to the British Parliament a petition signed by nearly 40,000 Muslims from about seventy different cities and towns of India strongly opposing Bradlaugh's Bill of 1889 on grounds of its advocacy of elective councils.[47] After the promulgation of the Government of India Act, 1892, the Central National Mahomedan Association told the then Viceroy, Lansdowne, that under the electoral system envisaged in the Act the Muslims would have no chance of being returned by any one of the recommending bodies,[48] and also urged him to reserve three seats for the Muslims in the Supreme Council, but to no avail.

In 1896, the Anglo-Oriental Defence Association, Aligarh, brought forward a memorial asking for reservation of seats, weightage and separate Muslim electorates in the Legislative Council and the local self-governing bodies in the North Western Provinces.[49] The Muslim leaders of Aligarh, some of whom played a significant role in organising the Simla deputation in October, 1906, had thus formulated the demands for separate electorates and weightage as early as 1896. The memorial of 1896, however, was not formally submitted to the Government, possibly because of the pre-occupation of the Aligarh leaders

[45] Proc. of the Council of the Governor-General of India, 1883, Vol. 22, pp. 19–20.

[46] Mahomedan Literary Society's memorial to the Secretary of State for India, April, 1890, Public and General letters from India and Bengal, vol. I, 1890.

[47] R. A. Zakaria, *op. cit.,* p. 145.

[48] Home (Public) Proc. no. 52, October, 1893.

[49] The *Pioneer,* 22 December, 1896.

with the embezzlement of the college funds,[50] and also possibly due to the lack of favourable response from the few Englishmen to whom it was sent for advice and support.[51]

The repeated and strong protests against the introduction of the British system of election having had no effect upon the Government, the Muslims had gradually fallen back on the provision of nomination as the main means of their representation. Morley's declaration of the extension of elective elements had, therefore, caused a serious repercussion among their leaders. Their reaction was so prompt and sharp that even before the publication of the full text of the Secretary of State's budget speech in India, Syed Husain Bilgrami wrote to C. S. Bayley, the British Resident at Hyderabad: 'I see that Mr. Morley is going ahead in a most reckless manner. Ministers who know nothing of the conditions of life in India and yet wish to carry out their theories at any hazard can only bring about the ruin of the country. . . I am afraid Mr. Morley knows more about Voltaire and eighteenth century literature than the condition of contemporary India.'[52]

Thus, to safeguard the Muslim interests in the reformed councils the idea of a deputation to the Viceroy was first suggested on 30 July, 1906, by Haji Muhammad Ismail Khan, *raees* of Aligarh, and afterwards a member of the Simla deputation, to Mohsin-ul-Mulk.[53] By about the same time Khawaja Yusuf Shah of Amritsar, another member of the Simla deputation, had telegraphically alerted Mohsin-ul-Mulk to the bad consequences of Fuller's resignation for the Muslims of Eastern Bengal and Assam,[54] and Mohsin-ul-Mulk had already been in communication with Syed Husain Bilgrami. Besides Ismail Khan, Yusuf Shah and Syed Husain Bilgrami, several other Muslim leaders including Nawab Ali Choudhury[55] and Viqar-ul-Mulk[56] approached Mohsin-ul-Mulk

---

[50] M. S. Jain, *The Aligarh Movement—Its Origin and Development 1858–1906*, p. 129.

[51] Copies of the memorandum were sent to, among others, Strachey and Colvin, former Lieutenant-Governors of North-Western provinces, *ibid*.

[52] Syed Husain Bilgrami to C. S. Bayley, 24 July, 1906, enclosed with Bayley to Dunlop Smith, 25 July, 1906. Min. P., Corr. India 1906, vol. 2.

[53] Mohsin-ul-Mulk's article in the *Aligarh Institute Gazette*, 23 October, 1906. The *U.P. N.N.R.*, 1906.

[54] Butler to Harry Richards, 25 September, 1906, B.P. Folio 57.

[55] Extracts from Nawab Ali Choudhury's letter were quoted by Mohsin-ul-Mulk in his letter to Archbold on 18 August, 1906. *Vide* Min. P., Corr. India 1906, vol. 2.

[56] Viqar-ul-Mulk's letter to Mohsin-ul-Mulk cannot be traced but the latter's reply to the same has been quoted in Albiruni's *Makers of Pakistan and Modern Muslim India*, p. 92.

with suggestions for safeguarding the Muslim interests at this critical juncture.

It was these demands for positive action that caused Mohsin-ul-Mulk to fear that the Aligarh leadership was in danger of being ignored by the politically conscious section of the Muslims if it did not act.[57] He was determined to assert the Aligarh leadership, and, therefore, to voice the concern of the Muslims to the Viceroy. One can get a clear picture about his activities in connection with the deputation from his letter to Viqar-ul-Mulk in which he stated: 'Immediately on the receipt of your first letter, I addressed some selected people about the matter in question, and in particular wrote to Mr. Archbold to inquire from the Viceroy as to whether he would receive a deputation for the submission of a Muslim memorial'.[58] Mohsin-ul-Mulk could have hardly imagined that Archbold's reply to his query would be utilised by interested persons to show him as a pawn[59] in the hands of the Government.

Had the Government had any hand in organising the Muslim deputation, Mohsin-ul-Mulk's request for its reception as put forward by Archbold would certainly have had an immediate response in its favour. But the Viceroy took time to consider the matter. On 8 August, 1906, he told Morley that he was as 'yet undecided whether to receive the deputation or not'.[60] On 9 August, 1906, Archbold again entreated Dunlop Smith, private secretary to the Viceroy, to get Minto's consent for receiving the deputation.[61] While referring to the 'present excited state' of Muslim leaders, Archbold, on his own responsibility, assured the Government that any proposed memorial that might be presented by the deputation would not contain anything 'disloyal or objectionable'.[62]

---

[57] '. . . there is still a general complaint on their part that we [Aligarh people] take no part in politics, and do not safeguard the political rights of Mohammedans . . . It has also been proposed that a memorial be submitted to His Excellency the Viceroy to draw the attention of Government to a consideration of the rights of Mohammedans.'

'I feel it is a very important matter, and, if we remain silent, I am afraid, people will leave us to go their own way and act up to their own personal opinions.' Mohsin-ul-Mulk to Archbold, 4 August, 1906, enclosed with Minto to Morley, 8 August, 1906. Mor. P., vol. 9.

[58] Quoted in Albiruni's *Makers of Modern Muslim India and Pakistan*, p. 92.

[59] R. Gopal, *Indian Muslims, A Political History*, p. 97.

[60] Minto to Morley, 8 August, 1906. Mor. P., vol. 9.

[61] Archbold to Dunlop Smith, 9 August, 1906. Min. P., Corr. India, 1906, vol. 2.

[62] *Ibid.*

He further assured Dunlop Smith that the deputation would consist of representative Muslims from various parts of India and that since all of them were 'very well known' the number of the deputationists was not likely to be very large.

On 10 August, 1906, Ibbetson, a member of the Viceroy's executive council, advised Minto to receive the deputation.[63] The same day Dunlop Smith told Archbold that the Viceroy had decided to receive the deputation 'if it is offered'.[64] Dunlop Smith also asked Archbold to inform Mohsin-ul-Mulk that a formal application must be made seeking the deputation and that a copy of the proposed memorial was to be sent to him at least two days before the agreed date of the reception of the deputation.[65] Consequently, the formal petition for the permission to receive the deputation was forwarded by Mohsin-ul-Mulk on 7 September, 1906[66] and on 13 September he was informed that the deputation would be received by the Viceroy on 1 October, 1906, at 11 a.m.[67]

Meanwhile on 10 August, 1906, while communicating the Viceroy's private consent to the projected deputation, Archbold had given his own suggestions about the matter as Mohsin-ul-Mulk had asked for them. Archbold proposed that the deputationists should give assurance of a deliberate aloofness from political agitation in the future.[68] Personally he believed that 'it would be wise of the Muslims to support nomination, as time to experiment with elections has not yet come. In election it will be very difficult for the Muslims to secure their share.'[69] Archbold's suggestions clearly disclosed that despite his sympathy for the Muslims he had been entirely out of touch with their aspirations and that he had no knowledge of the Muslim leaders' demands for separate electorates and weightage.

The memorial submitted by the deputation, as has been seen, preferred

---

[63] Denzil Ibbetson to Dunlop Smith, 10 August, 1906. Min. P., Corr. India, 1906, vol. 2.

[64] Archbold to Mohsin-ul-Mulk, 10 August, 1906, quoted in Albiruni, *Makers of Pakistan and Modern Muslim India*, p. 93.

[65] *Ibid.*

[66] Mohsin-ul-Mulk to Dunlop Smith, 7 September, 1906, referred to in Dunlop Smith's letter to Mohsin-ul-Mulk, 13 September, 1906. Min. P., Corr. India, 1906, vol. 2.

[67] Dunlop Smith to Mohsin-ul-Mulk, 13 September, 1906. *Ibid.*

[68] Archbold to Mohsin-ul-Mulk, 10 August, 1906. *Vide The Communal Triangle in India* by Mehta and Patwardhan, p. 62.

[69] *Ibid.*

election to nomination and did not give any undertaking of Muslim aloofness from politics. Moreover, it was concerned not merely with the question of the electoral system but also with other issues which vitally affected the interests of the community. The memorial had been the outcome of private consultations among Muslim leaders from different parts of India. The first draft was drawn by Syed Husain Bilgrami[70] on the basis of suggestions received from various Muslim leaders. The draft, marked 'strictly prohibited', was printed and circulated 'for private perusal and approval' by those leaders who were expected to be the members of the deputation.[71] It was liable to be 'altered or amended later on before final presentation'.[72]

On 13 September, 1906, a 'Revised' and 'Confidential' draft of the memorial was circulated among the probable members of the deputation.[73] The revised draft made certain verbal alterations in the original and slightly moderated its tone. It also differed from the original in one important aspect. The original draft, while referring to the possible appointment of Indians to the Viceroy's executive council and to the council of the Secretary of State, had recommended Ameer Ali for the latter.[74] The revised draft omitted the reference to the Secretary of State's council as well as the demand for Ameer Ali's appointment to the same and limited itself to the claim for a Muslim in the Viceroy's council.[75]

The revised memorial was discussed for hours together at a meeting of the Muslim leaders from different parts of India held at Lucknow on 15 and 16 September, 1906, under the presidency of Rafiuddin Ahmad, a Bombay barrister.[76] A most notable addition in the memorial at this stage was the question of the establishment of a Muslim University. Indeed, the Muslim leaders attending the Lucknow meeting appear to have been more concerned with the foundation of the Muslim University than Mohsin-ul-Mulk and Syed Husain Bilgrami, two stalwarts of the Aligarh movement who had been the chief organisers of the deputation.

[70] A printed copy of the first draft of the memorial bearing Syed Husain Bilgrami's name is available in the Butler Papers, folio. 57. See Appendix I.

[71] The copy of the memorial drafted by Syed Husain Bilgrami. *Ibid.*

[72] *Ibid.*

[73] The 'Revised' and 'Confidential' draft of the memorial available in the Butler Papers, *ibid.*

[74] The copy of the memorial drafted by S. H. Bilgrami. B.P. Folio 57.

[75] Revised and Confidential draft of the memorial, *Ibid.*

[76] Mohsin-ul-Mulk's article in the *Aligarh Institute Gazette,* 23 October, 1906. The *U.P. N.N.R.,* 1906. Also the *Times of India Mail,* 29 September, 1906.

There were, however, grave differences of opinion among the leaders as regards the inclusion of a particular demand in the memorial and on the emphasis to be laid on certain claims. Salimullah and Nawab Ali Choudhury insisted that the question of the partition of Bengal be definitely mentioned and that an assurance be sought on the stability of Eastern Bengal and Assam.[77] Muhammad Shafi and Shah Din, on the other hand, strongly opposed this demand. The two Punjab leaders considered the issue as 'controversial' and threatened to dissociate themselves if it was included in the memorial.[78] Doubtless, the partition of Bengal was a controversial question, but an overwhelming majority of the Muslims of Eastern Bengal and Assam had considered it as a matter of supreme interest and their standpoint had been endorsed by Muslims of different parts of the country including the Punjab.[79] However, a majority of the delegates attending the Lucknow meeting thought it proper to avoid a head-on clash with the Hindus who had been decrying the proposed deputation as the handiwork of the frustrated Muslim leaders of Eastern Bengal and Assam.[80] Furthermore, they believed that since 'the Mahomedans had already in each province passed resolutions in favour of the partition, it was not necessary to mention the subject in the address of the deputation'.[81] In the event, the question was referred to in the memorial as 'recent events' (meaning the circumstances leading to and following Fuller's resignation).[82]

Another significant point on which the participants at the Lucknow meeting differed amongst themselves was the nature of stress to be laid upon the demands for separate electorates and government service. Mohsin-ul-Mulk and Bilgrami had been primarily concerned with securing separate electorates and weightage in representation. But others, particularly the lawyers and members of the professional classes, considered the question of more employment as vital for the progress of the Muslim community and wanted it to get precedence over the claim for separate electorates.[83] Eventually, the language of the memorial was slightly changed and additional sentences were added

---

[77] M. Noman, *Muslim India*, pp. 74–75.

[78] *Ibid.*, p. 75.

[79] The *Englishman*, 5 September, 1906; also, 7–9, 11, 13, 15, 18 and 25 August, 1906, etc.

[80] The *Bengalee*, 9 September, 1906.

[81] Rafiuddin Ahmad's letter to the *Englishman*, 25 December, 1906.

[82] The address of the Simla deputation, enclosed with Minto to Morley, 4 October, 1906. Mor. P., vol. 9.

[83] Butler to H. Richards, 16 September, 1906. B.P., Folio 57.

so as to make the demand for more employment almost as important as that of separate electorates.[84]    The Lucknow meeting was thus eminently successful in adopting the memorial as well as selecting the members of the deputation unanimously.

The Lucknow meeting was held behind closed doors[85] and although the names of the participants and those selected for the deputation were released to the press, the proceedings were not published. The Government of India, however, got some information about the discussions through Harcourt Butler, Commissioner of Lucknow.[86]    Butler had received the information from Mohsin-ul-Mulk who considered him as evincing 'a kindly interest in matters connected with the Mohamedans'.[87]

Butler's testimony and his own role in connection with the Simla deputation provide additional evidence about the absolute baselessness of the allegation of the deputation being engineered by the Government. On 16 September, 1906, Butler told H. E. Richards, Law Member of the Government of India, that the 'whole business, from Fuller's retirement to now, has been organized by Mohsin-ul-Mulk and Imadul Mulk [Syed Husain Bilgrami] in a hurry'.[88]    Butler kept the Law Member informed about the inner developments in Muslim politics and the activities of the leaders assembled for the Lucknow meeting. He was the first to have supplied the Viceroy's office with a copy of the draft memorial whose contents were earlier unknown to it.[89]    Besides posting the Government with useful information, Butler also sought to influence the Muslim leaders in formulating their policy towards the Government and the Hindus. He was opposed to any measure that would create division among the Hindu and Muslim landholders of Oudh. He told Richards that the 'big Mah [omedan] Talukdars of Oudh will not take part in the discussions, as the majority of the Talukdars are Hindus and they do not want a Hindu-Mah [omedan] split. This is partly on my advice.'[90]    However, to the disappointment of Butler and despite their

---

[84] A comparison between the revised confidential draft and the final address adopted at the Lucknow meeting reveals this discrepancy between the two groups. Also Butler to H. Richards, 16 September, 1906. *Ibid.*

[85] The *Advocate,* 16 September, 1906. *Vide* B.P. Folio 57.

[86] Butler wrote a series of letters to Dunlop Smith and H. Richards intimating the discussions that took place among the Muslim leaders at Lucknow. Some of these letters are available in folio 57 of the Butler Papers.

[87] Mohsin-ul-Mulk to Butler, 2 September, 1906. B.P. Folio 57.

[88] Butler to H. Richards, 16 September, 1906, *ibid.*

[89] Dunlop Smith to Butler, 20 September, 1906, *ibid.*

[90] Butler to Richards, 16 September, 1906, *ibid.*

agreement with him, the two biggest landholders of Oudh, the Rajas of Jahangirabad and Mahmudabad, eventually attended the meeting on 16 September, 1906.[91]

Butler also failed in his attempt to dissuade the Muslim leaders from raising the question of employment of the Muslims in the memorial. He had advised Mohsin-ul-Mulk that the Muslims would 'do much better to take this question up in instalments by provinces, so as not to unite the Hindus'.[92]    Although Mohsin-ul-Mulk himself was inclined to accept Butler's suggestions, a majority of his colleagues preferred 'to "go the whole hog"' in the matter.[93]

Butler thought that despite his friendly relations with certain Muslim leaders he was not apprised as to all the facts about the Lucknow meeting.[94]    Butler was pleased to note that the Hindus and Muslims were as 'unable to take concerted action as Orangemen and Catholics in Ireland'.[95]    But he objected to the most important of the Muslim demands—the demand for separate electorates.    He remarked that 'separate electorates would mean constant irritation and excitement'.[96] He did not believe that any scheme for it 'w[oul]d ever get through the Sec[retary] of State, even if it got so far wh[ich] I gather is unlikely'.[97]

The Government of India's lack of information about the exact nature of the Muslim demands until they received a copy of the draft memorial through Butler, together with Minto's assurance to Morley that his reply would vindicate 'entire and resolute impartiality between races and creeds',[98] clearly demonstrate that the Government had no ulterior motive in receiving the deputation.    Of the six Muslim demands Minto was either silent or evasive with regard to five.    And the most positive note in his reply concerned the fate of Eastern Bengal and Assam— a point which the deputationists had referred to only by implication. Minto asked the Muslim leaders to believe that the course the Government had pursued in connection with the affairs of Eastern Bengal and

[91] Butler to Richards, 25 September, 1906, *ibid.*

[92] Butler to Richards, 16 September, 1906, *ibid.*

[93] *Ibid.*

[94] Butler told Richards that he did not know if 'there was any Pan-Islamic talk [in the Lucknow meeting], but I sh[oul]d not get information of this, if there had been any for some time'.    Butler to Richards, 25 September, 1906, *ibid.*

[95] *Ibid.*

[96] *Ibid.*

[97] *Ibid.*

[98] Minto to Morley (tel.), 31 August, 1906 and (letter) 29 August, 1906, Mor. P., vol. 9.

Assam—the future of which he thought to have been assured—was dictated solely by a regard for the interests of its inhabitants.[99]

Minto's reply regarding Eastern Bengal and Assam was mainly based on the suggestions of Hare, Lieutenant-Governor of the province. The Government of India itself believed that the deputationists were 'sure to allude to the idea of their co-religionists in Bengal that they have been thrown over by Government',[100] and hence Hare had been asked to give his opinion which the Viceroy used freely in his reply.[101]

Minto frankly told the deputationists that the points raised by them were before the committee lately appointed by him 'to consider the question of representation' and that he could merely forward their memorial to the committee.[102] Here the Viceroy seems to have overlooked the fact that the said committee was solely concerned with the question of representation of Indians in the Provincial and Supreme Legislative Councils and that the deputationists' demands for adequate representation in the local self-governing bodies, the Senates and Syndicates of the universities, not to speak of their claim for more employment, were outside the jurisdiction of the committee.

However, without 'in any way forestalling the committee's report', Minto proceeded to declare that the 'pith of your address as I understand it is a claim that in any system of representation—whether it affects a Municipality, a District Board, or a Legislative Council in which it is proposed to introduce or increase an electoral organisation—the Mahomedan community should be represented as a community. . . . and you justly claim that your position should be estimated not merely on your numerical strength but in respect to the political importance of your community and the services it has rendered to the Empire. I am entirely in accord with you.'[103] He was as firmly convinced as the deputationists themselves that 'any electoral representation in India would be doomed to mischievous failure which aimed at granting a personal enfranchisement regardless of the beliefs and traditions of the communities composing the population of this continent'.[104] These were significant words and were tantamount to accepting the Muslim

[99]Minto's reply to the Simla deputation, enclosed with Minto to Morley, 4 October, 1906, Mor. P., vol. 9.

[100]Dunlop Smith to Hare, 24 August, 1906, Min. P. Corr. India, 1906, vol. 2.

[101]Minto to Hare, 1 October, 1906, and Dunlop Smith to Hare, 2 October, 1906, *ibid.*

[102]Minto's reply to the Simla deputation, *op. cit.*

[103]*Ibid.*

[104]*Ibid.*

demands for separate electorates and weightage *in toto*. Later on the Muslim leaders fixed on this part of Minto's speech, construing it as a pledge that their demands for separate electorates and representation in excess of their numerical strength would be fulfilled; Minto was unsuccessful in wholly extricating himself from such an interpretation.

Muslim reactions to the Viceroy's reply were mixed. The organisers of the deputation called it a success, as possibly they had to do in order to mollify the younger generation of the community. Mohsin-ul-Mulk, for example, expressed his gratitude to the Viceroy for 'a clear and sympathetic recognition of the rights of the Mohammedans of India, as a distinct community' and for his appreciation of their political importance.[105]  *Al-Bashir,* published from Etawah, Mohsin-ul-Mulk's home-town, and usually a staunch supporter of the Aligarh leadership, went a step further maintaining that the Viceroy's reply gave more satisfaction than could have been anticipated.[106]

The response from other quarters, however, was not as uncritical. The *Nasim-i-Agra* remarked that the Viceroy's reply whilst appearing *a priori* to encourage very high hopes would be seen, on closer examination, as leading to no practical results.[107]  The *Observer,* Lahore, while appreciating the historical references in Minto's speech regretted that 'habitual political reserve in speech mastered the Viceroy so far as not to allow him to give us a better reply'.[108]  This influential English language bi-weekly paper was particularly disappointed at Minto's silence over the demands for more employment in the services and the judiciary. It further noted that out of a long list of requests presented by the deputation, 'the sole point singled out for reply is referred to in a vague general manner' thus offering 'a poor reward for the waiting and expectation of weeks'.[109]  The *Moslem Patriot,* Madras, considered Minto's silence on the ideal of a Muslim university as 'disappointing in the extreme'.[110]  'It was afraid that the Viceroy's assurance of safe-guarding the interests of the Muslims as a community in administrative reorganisation was 'too vague and too indefinite to be assuring in the slightest degree'. The paper wondered if Minto's guarantee would 'not share the same fate which more definite viceregal pronouncements and more satisfactory government orders' on Muslim questions had suffered

[105]Mohsin-ul-Mulk to Dunlop Smith, 7 October, 1906, Min. P., Corr. India, vol. 2.

[106]*Al-Bashir,* 9 October, 1906, the *U.P. N.N.R.,* 1906.

[107]The *Nasim-i-Agra,* 15 October, *ibid.*

[108]The *Observer,* 6 October, 1906, cutting in the Minto Papers.

[109]*Ibid.*

[110]The *Moslem Patriot,* 5 October, *op. cit.*

in the past. The *Moslem Patriot* thought that the Viceroy had deliberately overlooked the demand for more employment as well as the questions of Muslim representation in the local self-governing bodies and in the universities. The newspaper, therefore, looked upon the deputation as a 'failure'.[111]

Minto's pronouncement about the permanence of the province of Eastern Bengal and Assam had, however, given great satisfaction, particularly to the Muslim leaders of the province, who had been disappointed at the drafting of the memorial. Nawab Salimullah made this point clear when he publicly declared that he had hoped that the address to the Viceroy would have urged 'a definite policy to be enunciated by his Excellency and particularly as regards the growing unrest on the question of the partition of Bengal', but it was deemed advisable not to put anything contentious in the address, and 'disappointed as we were at this we can not adequately express our joy and satisfaction at his Excellency's going out of his way to lay down a policy of sympathy and encouragement'.[112]  The language of Salimullah's speech was moderate but its tone was unmistakably bitter against those Muslim leaders who had been responsible for the exclusion of the issue of the partition of Bengal from the Simla memorial.

The opposition to the direct mentioning of the Bengal question in the memorial had considerably lessened Salimullah's enthusiasm for the deputation as such. About the time when his brother delegates were gathering at Simla, Salimullah was undergoing an eye operation for removal of a cataract[113]—an operation which perhaps could have been deferred if he had been enthusiastic about joining the deputation. However, he was not inactive. The disappointment at Lucknow had roused his determination for the establishment of an all-India Muslim political organisation so as to overcome the difficulties created by certain Muslim leaders who hesitated to face the challenge thrown open by the opponents of the new province. He had, therefore, sent his 'notes' to the deputationists requesting them to consider formation of a Muslim political party on all-India basis.[114]  The notes were discussed at an informal meeting of Muslim leaders at Simla and it was decided to postpone decision on the matter until the meeting of the All-India Mahomedan Educational Conference, scheduled to meet at Dacca towards the last week of December, 1906.[115]

[111] *Ibid.*
[112] The *Times of India Mail,* 27 October, 1906.
[113] The *Englishman,* 27 September, 1906.
[114] The *Bengalee,* 14 October, 1906.
[115] *Ibid.*

The proposal for a central organisation was appealing to Muslims and could not be brushed aside, though, according to Salimullah's information, there were three distinct opinions about it amongst the delegates at Simla.[116] First, the majority favoured Salimullah's proposal. Second, a small group held it unnecessary as 'it would cripple and starve the local Associations'. The third group saw it as a threat to the Aligarh leadership.

The leader of the Simla deputation, the Aga Khan, did not subscribe to any of the above groups. It may be noted here that the Aga Khan had little political background. It was his high prestige with the Government[117] that had earned him the membership of the Imperial Legislative Council. His association with the Aligarh movement dated from 1901, when Mohsin-ul-Mulk had persuaded him to preside over the All-India Mahomedan Educational Conference held that year at Delhi. Since then the Aga Khan had become a personal friend of Mohsin-ul-Mulk and a patron of the Aligarh College. He was away from India when, through Mohsin-ul-Mulk's influence, the Muslim leaders had selected him as leader of the Simla deputation.

The Aga Khan's opinion on the question of the all-India Muslim political association was given in his letter of 2 October, 1906, to Mohsin-ul-Mulk. The Aga Khan thought that the matter should 'be left to the judgement of the future leaders of the community'[118]—a clever suggestion to knock out Salimullah's proposition. He had, however, his own proposal on the subject. He advised the Muslim leaders to constitute the Simla deputation into a permanent committee[119]—perhaps without changing its leader—until the demands set forth in the memorial were realised. The question of a central Muslim political organisation

[116]*Ibid.*

[117]The Aga Khan's grandfather Muhammad Hasan Aga Khan, the forty-sixth Imam of the Ismaili Shias was a claimant to the Persian throne. On being defeated in his bid for the succession, he escaped to India and greatly assisted General Napier in his campaign against the Amirs of Sind. Consequently, he was awarded with the hereditary title of His Highness and a pension of seventy-five pounds per month. Muhammad Hasan was succeeded by his son Fatih Ali Shah Aga Khan, the father of Sultan Muhammad Shah Aga Khan III. The Aga Khan III assumed the Imamship of the Ismaili community at an early age. He greatly impressed Lord Elgin on the occasion of Queen Victoria's Diamond Jubilee Celebrations. Subsequently he visited England as the guest of the Queen and since then he had maintained a cordial relationship with the Royal family.

[118]The Aga Khan to Mohsin-ul-Mulk, 2 October, 1906, translated by Alam Kuli Khan and published in the *Times of India Mail,* 5 January, 1907.

[119]*Ibid.*

thus brought the clash between the Aga Khan and a section of the Aligarh leadership on the one hand, and the more militant Bengal leadership on the other to the surface, though no conflict was openly admitted.

The difference of opinion between the Aga Khan and Salimullah centred round the question of the partition of Bengal. The Aga Khan did not support the adjustment of the boundary of Bengal and the creation of the new province[120] though it was true that he did not join the anti-partitionists after the matter was settled by the Government. On the eve of the reception of the Muslim deputation by the Viceroy, Nawab Ali Choudhury, right hand man of Salimullah, had stressed that the Aga Khan should ascertain the opinion of the delegates on the question of the partition of Bengal so that he could correctly inform Minto or any other member of the Government if and when the matter was raised. Consequently, on 1 October, 1906, the Aga Khan was definitely told by individual members of the deputation that they all supported the continuation of the province of Eastern Bengal and Assam though they did not include the issue in the memorial.[121] The unanimity of the delegates did not change the Aga Khan's mind on the question but he had been shrewd enough to tell the Viceroy that although he had been personally opposed to the partition of Bengal, 'now that the thing had been done, any attempt to undo it would be full of very serious risk'.[122]

Salimullah, on the other hand, was much more committed on the partition issue. In fact it was he who had been leading the movement of the Bengal Muslims against the more vocal anti-partitionists. He had staked his political future,[123] and even his personal fortune,[124] in advocating the cause of the supporters of the new province.

It is evident that the difference in the viewpoints of the Aga Khan and Salimullah as well as their respective supporters on the partition issue greatly determined their attitude towards the question of the central organisation. Salimullah sought to establish a broad-based

[120]Minto to Morley, 4 October, 1906, Mor. P.,.vol. 9.

[121]Rafiuddin Ahmad to the *Englishman,* 25 December, 1906.

[122]Minto to Morley, 4 October, 1906, Mor. P., vol. 9.

[123]Salimullah was being constantly vilified by the Hindu newspapers for his support to the new province. *Vide* the *Bengalee,* 22 December, 1906.

[124]The *Bengalee* called upon Salimullah's co-sharers to partition their property and advised the money-lenders to put pressure on them. *Vide* the *Bengalee,* 22 December, 1906. Also Hare to Minto, 22 September, 1906. Min. P. Corr. India, 1906, vol. 2.

organisation to ensure large support for the new province and incident-ally to oppose the Congress which had strengthened the anti-partitionists. As he admitted later on, he had viewed the foundation of the all-India Muslim association primarily as a means to furthering the political object of the Muslims of Eastern Bengal and Assam.[125] The Aga Khan had fully realised the implications of the Salimullah scheme. But his apathy towards the Bengal issue and aversion to any popular movement had prompted him to suggest the perpetuation of the Simla deputation as a committee. His attempt to keep the initiative with the Simla deputation seems to have been also motivated by the consider-ation of his own position as its leader. The Aga Khan had asked Mohsin-ul-Mulk to circulate his letter of 2 October, 1906, only to the members of the deputation[126] —a subtle move to confine the discussion on the matter to a limited number of people. He revealed himself wholly when he told Mohsin-ul-Mulk that 'a small committee would work better, but this may be enlarged if considered necessary'.[127] The Aga Khan's letter to Mohsin-ul-Mulk had also contained a hint about absentee members and as Salimullah had been a prominent absentee, this could be said to have some reference to him. The Aga Khan considered that 'Failure of a member to attend or absence of interest on a member's part in the work ought not to prevent the committee from continuing its work. This would not mean his resigna-tion, but would only signify his temporary absence from work. Every member would be considered permanent till he resigns or is made to resign his seat.'[128]

The Aga Khan's bid to perpetuate the Simla deputation certainly did not satisfy Salimullah. On 11 November, 1906, Salimullah went to the press with his scheme.[129] The move appears to have been designed not only to win support for the scheme but also to bring to public knowledge the manoeuvres for which the Aga Khan had been respon-sible behind the scenes. Whether Salimullah was bringing his clash with the Aga Khan into the open cannot be decided with certainty, but since he had been aware of the Aga Khan's motives in designating

[125] Salimullah's presidential address at the A.I.M.L. session held at Calcutta in March 1912. *Vide* the *Englishman,* 4 March, 1912.

[126] The Aga Khan to Mohsin-ul-Mulk, 2 October, 1906. The *Times of India Mail,* 5 January, 1907.

[127] *Ibid.*

[128] *Ibid.*

[129] The *Bengalee,* 14 December, 1906. (Extracts of the Salimullah scheme were published in the English language daily papers all over India.)

the Simla deputation as a committee, his overture to the press was at the very least aimed at preventing the Aga Khan from accomplishing his plan. Salimullah was not content with merely approaching the press; he circulated his scheme to various associations and individuals all over India,[130] urging them to discuss the matter and to send delegates to the conference to be held at Dacca in December, 1906.

In the event, Salimullah foiled the Aga Khan's plan and accelerated the process of forming a central organisation. Salimullah's proposed central body was tentatively to be termed the 'Moslem All-India Confederacy'.[131] All the local Muslim associations in different parts of India were to form its units and it was to carry on its work somewhat on the lines of the various chambers of commerce, the British Indian Association etc. Membership of the Confederacy was to be offered to those Muslims who would pay ten rupees as annual subscription or one hundred rupees for life membership. Patrons were required to subscribe at least one thousand rupees, while the members of the executive committee other than the president and secretary would pay thirty rupees only as annual fee.[132]

The objects of the Moslem All-India Confederacy were stated by Salimullah as first, 'to protect the cause and advance the interests' of Muslims all over India; second, 'whenever possible', to support all measures emanating from the Government; third, to controvert the influence of the 'so-called Indian National Congress', which had a tendency to misrepresent and subvert the British rule in India; and fourth, to enable young Muslims of education, who for want of such an association as the Confederacy 'have joined the Congress camp, to find scope on account of their fitness and ability for public life'.[133]

Salimullah's hostility towards the Congress is understandable but it was extremely impolitic for him to suggest that the proposed Confederacy should seek to counteract the influence of the Congress. Similarly, his proposition to support all measures taken by the Government, though qualified by 'whenever possible', was impracticable. This object, if accepted, would have severely restricted the freedom of action by the Confederacy. However, Salimullah was cognizant of the limitations in his scheme and had considered it tentative. He had also

[130] *Ibid.*
[131] *Ibid.*
[132] *Ibid.*
[133] *Ibid.*

invited alternative proposals or schemes to be sent either directly to him or through Mohsin-ul-Mulk.[134]

Mohsin-ul-Mulk was, it appears, at this stage playing a difficult role. The Aga Khan relied on him to support his plan and had already proposed him as secretary to the permanent committee of the Simla deputation.[135] Salimullah also counted on his assistance and claimed to have had communication with him.[136] Mohsin-ul-Mulk's inner sympathy went to the Aga Khan's plan, as possibly was shown by his acceptance of the secretaryship of the Simla deputation committee. But circumstances compelled him to appear favourable towards the Salimullah scheme or some such widely based political organisation. Not only had a majority of the delegates at Simla supported the proposal for a central organisation but Mohsin-ul-Mulk's closest colleagues like Viqar-ul-Mulk and Aftab Ahmad Khan were pressing for the realisation of such an association.[137] Moreover, Mohsin-ul-Mulk himself was under duress from the Pan-Islamic publicists and their young supporters. His earlier public stand in the Urdu-Hindi controversy, when, in order to retain his secretaryship of the Aligarh College, he had resigned from the Urdu Defence Association, condemned him before the eyes of some supporters of Urdu.[138] His interpretation of the institution of Khilafat, questioning the right of the Ottoman Sultan to be regarded as Khalifa,[139] had made him obnoxious to a powerful section of the Muslim community who called him 'a traitor to the national cause'[140] and even threatened to stop contributions to the Aligarh College unless he changed his policy.[141] Mohsin-ul-Mulk could not but take note of the atmosphere, if not so much for the future of his own leadership at least for the future of the Aligarh College.

Apart from Salimullah's efforts, by 1906, the establishment of an all-India Muslim political organisation was widely regarded as necessary.

[134] The *Madras Weekly Mail*, 22 December, 1906.

[135] The Aga Khan to Dunlop Smith, 29 October, 1906, Min. P., Corr. India, 1906, vol. 2.

[136] The *Madras Weekly Mail*, 22 December, 1906.

[137] While Viqar-ul-Mulk had already established several branches of the Mahomedan Political Association between 1901 and 1903, it was in 1903 that Aftab Ahmad Khan publicly asserted in favour of an exclusively Muslim Political party (*vide* M. S. Jain, *The Aligarh Movement*, p. 151).

[138] Hafiz Raziuddin Ahmed Barelvi to the *Civil and Military Gazette*, 26 May, 1906.

[139] The *Bombay Gazette Weekly English News Supplement*, 14 July, 1906.

[140] The *Bombay Gazette Summary*, 4 August, 1906.

[141] Abdur Rahman Khan to the *Civil and Military Gazette*, 22 June, 1906.

From London Ameer Ali had renewed his appeal to the Muslims to unite for 'a concerted action to prevent the future decline of their people, to promote their advancement, to place before Government their concerted views in public matters or to obtain relief from the misunderstanding of their laws and customs'.[142] The question was also taken up by a number of Muslim newspapers and periodicals in India. The *Shifa-ul-Mulk* observed that as the state of things had greatly changed, the Muslims could hardly expect to gain their object by relying on the Government and that it was high time for them to take steps to bring their grievances to the notice of the Government 'respectfully but fearlessly' through 'a separate political association of their own'.[143] The *Asrar-e-Jadid* held that the Muslims would not get 'their rights in the shape of responsible and lucrative appointments, seats in the Legislative Councils or in the University', without agitating for them through a political organisation.[144] Among other newspapers and journals which urged similar views were the *Qulqul*,[145] the *Zulqarnain*,[146] the *Al-Aziz*,[147] and the *Urdu-i-Mualla*,[148] the last named even being a pro-Congress journal. Besides the newspaper editors, individual Muslim correspondents drew the attention of the community to the urgency of a separate all-India political party. On 8 November, 1906, a correspondent of the *Mufid-e-Aam*, Agra, pointed out that the importance given to 'cow-worship' by the *Gorakshini Sabha*, the celebration of the anniversary of Shivaji, and the consequent attack on Aurangzeb, the attempts to minimise the importance of Urdu as a vernacular, and the resentment expressed at the partition of Bengal had left no other alternative for the Muslims but to organise themselves in a political party.[149]

The Simla deputation, which was designed partly to keep in check these radical views, had failed to obtain any positive commitment from the Viceroy except on one issue. This apparent failure had further discredited the method of petitioning for redress of grievances. As the *Moslem Patriot* wrote on 5 October, 1906, 'The younger men in the

---

[142] 'India and the New Parliament', an article by Ameer Ali in the *Nineteenth Century*, August, 1906, p. 257.

[143] The *Shifa-ul-Mulk*, June, 1906. The *U.P. N.N.R.*, 1906.

[144] The *Asrar-e-Jadid*, September, 1906, *ibid.*

[145] The *Qulqul*, 28 May, 1906, *ibid.*

[146] The *Zulqarnain*, 7 September, 1906, *ibid.*

[147] The *Al-Aziz*, September, 1906, *ibid.*

[148] The *Urdu-i-Mualla*, January, 1906, *ibid.*

[149] The *Mufid-e-Aam*, 8 November, 1906, *ibid.*

community were anxious to set up a popular agitation for safeguarding their rights and interest;  but the older leaders were still averse to abandon the time-honoured methods of making respectful representations to Government and getting their grievances quietly redressed'.[150] In the event the newspaper thought that 'the bitter disappointment' the Muslims had suffered at the hands of Minto should urge them on to action. They should 'determine to agitate, agitate and agitate until their united representations are heard in full and their just and moderate demands are granted in entirety'.[151]

Except perhaps in the old and higher ranks of the leadership of the Indian Muslims, the mood had definitely turned in favour of concerted action and constitutional agitation.  Political associations had been springing up in various parts of India to safeguard the interest of the community and to develop political instincts among them.[152]  The existing local associations had also been taking increasing interest in the political activities.  At the provincial level, the Mahomedan Political Association of the U.P. and the Provincial Mahomedan Association of Eastern Bengal and Assam had been engaged in furthering the special interests of the Muslims of the respective provinces. In February, 1906, Fazl-i-Husain, a barrister, formed a 'Muslim League' in Lahore with a view to advance political culture among the Muslims.[153]  In November, 1906, Syed Ameer Husain established the 'Mahomedan Vigilance Committee' at Calcutta to 'prevent cases of oppression' by Hindus towards Muslims.[154]  During the second half of 1906, the Muslim leaders of Bombay and Madras also showed abundant interest in forming political associations both at provincial as well as all-India levels.[155]

On the basis of their pre-occupations the advocates of an all-India Muslim political party may broadly be divided into four groups not necessarily exclusive of each other.  The first came mostly from Bengal and Eastern Bengal and Assam under the leadership of Salimullah and Nawab Ali Choudhury.  Their primary interest in seeking to establish a central organisation, as has already been noted, was to combat the anti-partition agitation.  The second group consisted mainly of those

---

[150] The *Moslem Patriot,* 5 October, 1906, *op. cit.*

[151] *Ibid.*

[152] The *Moslem Patriot,* 12 October, 1906, quoted in the *Indian Spectator,* 20 October, 1906.

[153] A. Husain.  *Fazl-i-Husain–A Political Biography,* p. 96; also the *Oudh Akhbar,* 20 August, 1906, the *U.P. N.N.R.,* 1906.

[154] The *Pioneer Mail,* 30 November, 1906.

[155] The *Moslem Patriot,* 12 October, *op. cit.*

English-educated young men who believed that the Muslim demands for appointments, separate electorates, etc., could not be achieved without agitation. Among them were Yakub Hasan and Hamid Hasan, proprietor and editor, respectively, of the *Moslem Patriot*,[156] Madras, Abdul Aziz, editor, the *Observer*,[157] Lahore, Ghulam Muhammad,[158] a barrister of Rajkote, Khawaja Ghulam-us-Saqlain,[159] pleader and journalist, Lucknow, Muhammad Ali, an Oxford graduate currently in the Baroda civil service and several others. The third group comprised some traditionalists whose chief concern had been the protection and promotion of the Urdu language and such other special interests of the Muslims. Viqar-ul-Mulk, Aftab Ahmad Khan, a barrister of Aligarh, Abdullah Jan, pleader, Saharanpur, Muhammad Yusuf, zamindar, Patna, and the editors of the *Qulqul,* the *Shifa-ul-Mulk,* the *Zulqarnain* and a few others belonged to this group. The last group included those radicals who canvassed the establishment of a Muslim political party for discussing and safeguarding peculiarly Muslim interests and for co-operating with the Congress in matters of general interest. Fazlul Hasan Hasrat,[160] better known as Hasrat Mohani, editor of the *Urdu-i-Mualla,* and Fazl-i-Husain,[161] barrister, Lahore, were leading members of this group. It may be noted here that most of the members of these four groups joined the All-India Muslim League within a short time of its foundation.

The activities of the above groups and of the existing and recently formed local associations greatly facilitated the task of Salimullah and his supporters. Salimullah's Confederacy scheme came up at the All-India Mahomedan Educational Conference held at Dacca from 27 December to 30 December, 1906. The first three days of the conference, which was attended by nearly 3,000 delegates and about 1,000 officials and observers[162] (some delegates coming even from Natal and

---

[156] The *Moslem Patriot,* 5 and 12 October, 1906, *op. cit.*

[157] The *Observer,* 26 September, 1906. The *Punjab N.N.R.,* 1906.

[158] Ghulam Muhammad's scheme for an all-India Muslim political party. *Vide* the *Times of India Mail,* 29 December, 1906.

[159] The *Asrar-e-Jadid,* September, 1906. The *U.P. N.N.R.,* 1906.

[160] The *Urdu-i-Mualla,* January, 1906. The *U.P. N.N.R.,* 1906.

[161] Fazl-i-Husain had been much concerned with pan-Islamic developments. He had cautioned the Government that in the event of any conflict between the British Government and the Ottoman Sultan ninety-five per cent of the Indian Muslims would not be able to subordinate their religious interests to their loyalty. *Vide* the *Paisa Akhbar,* 11 June, 1906. The *Punjab N.N.R.,* 1906.

[162] The *Englishman Weekly Summary,* 3 January, 1907, and the *Bengalee,* 30 December, 1906.

Somaliland),[163] were devoted to the discussion of educational problems. However, while the educational conference was going on, the Salimullah scheme, together with other drafts, was thrown open to informal discussion among delegates. Every point was discussed minutely and unanimity was sought. Where no agreement appeared feasible, the disputed points were referred to a special committee.[164] The phraseology of parts of the Salimullah scheme and the term 'Confederacy' did not seem quite happy to the majority of delegates but the 'spirit' and the 'essence' of the scheme was approved.[165]

On 30 December, 1906, the session of the Educational Conference being over, the question of the formation of a central Muslim political organisation was formally taken up. Students and government officials were excluded from this meeting.[166] The meeting opened with a brief speech by Mohsin-ul-Mulk, who confined himself to thanking Salimullah for his splendid hospitality[167] and to appreciating the enthusiasm of the people of Eastern Bengal and Assam, who 'were bound to go far and fare well' under the new conditions.[168] Viqar-ul-Mulk who was proposed to the chair by Salimullah, spoke of the necessity of the Muslims uniting 'in support of one another and working in loyal unison' with the Government.[169] He warned the Muslims of the danger of their being 'submerged by the enormous Hindu flood', at the same time appealing to them not to be unreasonably bitter or hostile to any other community or party.[170] Their motto was to be defence not defiance. Viqar-ul-Mulk was sceptical about the wisdom of the 'too hot, too frothy' youth's participating in politics and cautioned against the revolutionary tendencies that existed in the country. He urged the Muslims to be prepared 'to fight and die for the Government if necessary'.[171]

Salimullah, chairman of the reception committee of the Educational Conference and convenor of the political meeting, made a lengthy

[163] Rafiuddin Ahmad's interview to the representative of the *Englishman*, 4 January, 1907.

[164] Mazhar-ul-Haque to the editor, the *Englishman*, 25 January, 1907.

[165] Rafiuddin Ahmad's interview to the *Englishman*, 4 January, 1907.

[166] Syed Naseer Husain to the editor, *Englishman*, 4 January, 1907.

[167] Salimullah had arranged accommodation and food for all the delegates from his own resources. *Vide* the *Madras Weekly Mail*, 10 January, 1907.

[168] The *Englishman Weekly Summary*, 3 January, 1907.

[169] *Ibid.*

[170] *Ibid.*

[171] *Ibid.*

speech in proposing the creation of a central organisation, named the All-India Muslim League. He said that India was on the eve of a new era and that the Muslims were awakening from the coma into which they had fallen. But while appreciating the increasing political activities among the Muslims, Salimullah made it abundantly clear that the movement for the establishment of an all-India political party had been forced on his co-religionists. He maintained that had 'the party now in power in England been familiar with the position of Moslems, and had Indian public men represented justly Moslem claims, the movement might perhaps not have been heard of, but quiet unobtrusive work was now at a discount and those who cried loudest had a chance of being heard'.[172] As regards the feeble opposition from a small section of the Muslim leaders against the establishment of a central organisation, Salimullah observed that the last twenty years had wrought a vast change in the position of the Muslims. They were no longer 'uneducated with passions still unrestrained, spirit of caution lacking, loyalty in places undeveloped'. The Muslims were now fully prepared to enter into a political career 'as a community united, enlightened, loyal and law-abiding'.[173]

Salimullah's irrevocable opposition to the Congress as expressed in the Confederacy scheme was remarkably moderated in his speech at the conference. He affirmed that he had no prejudice against the members of other communities, and the resolution he was going to move was aimed at the protection and furtherance of political rights and interests of the Muslims of India without prejudice to their rulers and to their neighbours.[174] He was distinctly more accommodating towards other communities and parties when he announced that 'those interests which we have in common with other communities will be advanced by us in common with them, and those additional interests which are exclusively ours will be advanced exclusively by us, though we shall advance them both through our own League'.[175] He then moved that 'this meeting composed of Mussalmans from all parts of India, assembled at Dacca, decide that a political Association be formed, styled the All-India Muslim League, for the furtherance of the following objects:—

[172] *Ibid.*
[173] *Ibid.*
[174] *Ibid.*
[175] Quoted in an article by Edward E. Lang in the *Contemporary Review,* September 1907, p. 351.

*a)* To promote among the Mussalmans of India, feelings of loyalty to the British Government, and to remove any misconception that may arise as to the intention of Government with regard to any of its measures.

*b)* To protect and advance the political rights and interests of Mussalmans of India, and to respectfully represent their needs and aspirations to the Government.

*c)* To prevent the rise among the Mussalmans of India of any feeling of hostility towards other communities, without prejudice to the aforementioned objects of the League.'[176]

Hakim Ajmal Khan of Delhi seconded the resolution and it was supported by Zafar Ali Khan, Muhammad Ali and a few others. After a short debate it was carried with acclamation.[177]

The conference then resolved to appoint a 'provisional committee' consisting of 56 members including Mohsin-ul-Mulk and Viqar-ul-Mulk as joint secretaries with power of co-option.[178] The committee was asked to frame a constitution for the League within four months from the date of its appointment. The committee was also authorised to convene a representative meeting of the Muslims of India 'at a suitable time and place' and to submit the constitution before that body for final consideration and adoption.[179] The provisional committee was composed of Muslim leaders from different parts of India. All the provinces of British India and some of the native states were represented on it. More than fifty per cent of its members were lawyers by profession.[180] Others came from the titled aristocracy, the land-holding class, journalism and the business community. Among the total number of fifty-six, twenty had been members of the Simla deputation. A few members of the Simla deputation seem to have been included in the committee in their absence. One very notable exception was the Aga Khan. His hostility towards the foundation of a broadly-based central organisation was possibly so well-known to the Muslim leaders as to exclude him from the committee of the League. But, curiously enough, the Aga Khan later claimed to be the prime mover

---

[176] Home (Public) Proceedings, February, 1907, vol. 7587.

[177] *Ibid.* and the *Englishman Weekly Summary*, 3 January, 1907.

[178] Home (Public) Proceedings, February, 1907, vol. 7587.

[179] *Ibid.*

[180] The occupation of a large majority of the members of the provisional committee is available from the list of members supplied to the Government of India by Viqar-ul-Mulk. Home (Public) Proc., February, 1907, vol. 7587.

behind the birth of the League.[181] The Aga Khan's belated assertion, though absolutely bogus, has found recognition in many publications.[182] However, the fact remains that not only did the Aga Khan and his supporters oppose the foundation of a political party like the League, but even after its establishment some of his supporters persisted in their opposition and demanded that the League should be 'kept distinct' from the work of the Simla deputation committee.[183]

It is significant to note that while almost all the members of the provisional committee of the League were connected with the Muslim associations and *Anjumans* in their respective areas, about a third of them had already gathered political experience as members of the Central National Mahomedan Association, the Mahomedan Anglo-Oriental Defence Association, the Mahomedan Political Association (U.P.), and the Provincial Mahomedan Association of Eastern Bengal and Assam. The committee also included four prominent Congress or ex-Congressmen. They were Ali Imam, Hasan Imam, and Mazhar-ul-Haque, barristers of Bihar, and Hamid Ali Khan, barrister, Lucknow. This was the beginning of a process that was to win over most of the Congress Muslims into the fold of the League in about three years' time.

The last resolution of the conference related to the new province of Eastern Bengal and Assam. The resolution was proposed by Professor Ghulam Saqlain of Lucknow and seconded by Khawaja Ghulam Sadiq of Amritsar, supported by several others and carried unanimously. The resolution, 'in view of the clear interests' of the Muslims of Eastern Bengal, considered that 'partition is sure to prove beneficial to the Mahomedan community which constitutes the vast majority of that province'. The resolution also discouraged and strongly condemned all agitation against the partition of Bengal including boycott.[184]

Thus the Muslim leaders from all over India reaffirmed their support for the province of Eastern Bengal and Assam, thereby rectifying the calculated omission of the issue from the memorial of the Simla deputation and endorsing Salimullah's primary motive behind the establishment of the League. Salimullah might have felt his efforts amply rewarded. But his initiative and singleness of purpose in founding

---

[181] The Aga Khan's speech at the Delhi session of the League, held at Delhi in January 1910. Proc. Third Annual Sessions of the A.I.M.L., pp. 13 and 14.

[182] J. Nehru, *The Discovery of India,* pp. 366 and 375.

[183] Alam Kuli Khan to the editor, the *Times of India Mail,* 5 January, 1907.

[184] Home (Public) Proceedings, February, 1907, vol. 7587.

the League made him the butt of the adversaries of this new-born party, some of whom went so far as to call it Nawab Salimullah's latest fad,[185] and the Salimullah League.[186]

It has been suggested that the All-India Muslim League was started 'under the inspiration of the British Government and the leadership of one of its chief supporters, the Aga Khan'.[187] We have already noted how the Aga Khan had opposed the formation of the League and thus the hollowness of the second part of the allegation has already been exposed. The first part of the accusation is equally untenable and has never been substantiated. It was either politically motivated or made on the analogy of the Government's inspiration towards the foundation of the Indian National Congress. But unlike the Congress, which had been fortunate in having its father and 'godfather'[188] in the persons respectively of A. O. Hume and Lord Dufferin, the League was started at the initiative of and by the Muslim leaders themselves.

Indeed, the Government seem to have discouraged the movement for such an organisation as the All-India Muslim League. While the Viceroy, the provincial Governors and Lieutenant-Governors were stark silent on this important event, certain individual Englishmen and officials known to have been sympathetic towards the Muslims did not conceal their disapproval of the Muslims organising themselves into a separate political party. Principal Archbold, considered by some to have immense influence over Muslim politics, told Dunlop Smith on 15 December, 1906, that he and his colleagues were 'preparing for the Mahomedan Educational Conference at Dacca. We are most anxious to keep politics out of it, but it may not be easy'.[189] As late as 21 December, 1906, Archbold had no definite information about the move for the establishment of the League. By that date he could only

---

[185] The *Bengalee*, 10 January, 1907.

[186] *Ibid.*, 18 January, 1907.

[187] J. Nehru, *The Discovery of India*, p. 366.

[188] R. P. Masani, *Dadabhai Naoroji: The Grand Old Man of India*, p. 303. Recently doubts have been raised regarding Dufferin's encouragement of the project for the Congress (*vide* Anthony Parel, "Hume, Dufferin and the Origins of the Indian National Congress", *Journal of the Indian History*, vol. 42, 1964, p. 724). But the first generation of Congress leaders, including Hume, W. C. Bonerjee, Wedderburn, S. N. Banerjea, and D. E. Wacha, some of whom knew Dufferin, proudly asserted that the Congress was blessed by Dufferin. The arguments against their testimony do not appear to be convincing.

[189] Archbold to Dunlop Smith, 15 December, 1906. Min. P., Corr. India, 1906, vol. 2.

inform Dunlop Smith about the possibility of a Muslim meeting to be held at Dacca on 30 December, 1906, 'to deal with the Political Association matter'.[190]

Dunlop Smith had kept his reactions towards the Muslim activities to himself. On 10 September, 1906, he had noted in his diary: 'What I want to stop is these young Mohammedans forming small societies all over India. Once they start that game they can make us really anxious. The Bengalis are a low-lying people . . . [but] It's the Mussulman with the green flag calling for blood and the Mahratta Brahmin—*not* the Mahratta but the Brahmin—whom we have to watch.'[191] Similar apprehension regarding the organised activities by the Muslims was entertained by Hare, who had 'advised the Mohammedans so far that it was unnecessary to organise counter demonstrations [against the anti-partitionists]. If these are started, the fat will be in the fire, and we do not know where it will end.'[192]

The dejection of at least a considerable section of government officials at the Muslim enterprise for the foundation of an all-India political organisation was definitely conveyed to the Muslim leaders by Harcourt Butler. On a later occasion Butler told Fraser that he 'was in at the birth of the Moslem League'.[193] Recapitulating his conversation with Mohsin-ul-Mulk on the eve of the establishment of the League, Butler wrote that Mohsin-ul-Mulk came to see him at Lucknow and 'told me that they could no longer hold the young men and that they would join the Hindus if they were not given some political organisation of their own. I remember asking him then whether the leaders would be able to hold them when they got their own political organisation, as I much doubted this, having such experience of the inner history of Aligarh.'[194] Mohsin-ul-Mulk did not deny the probability but regarded the danger as remote. Butler told another correspondent that those Muslim leaders who discussed the formation of the League with him in 1906 'were quite frank . . . there never was any splendid loyalty . . . It was purely in their own interests that they formed the Moslem League'.[195]

As for the British Government's attitude towards the establishment of the League nothing is known. The India Office did not take any note

[190] Archbold to Dunlop Smith, 21 December, 1906, *ibid.*
[191] M. Gilbert, *Servant of India,* p. 56.
[192] Hare to D. Smith, 1 September, 1906, Min. P. Corr. India, 1906, vol. 2.
[193] Butler to Fraser, 8 April, 1913, B.P., folio 57.
[194] *Ibid.*
[195] Butler to Allen, 6 April, 1913, *ibid.*

of the event. But if the reactions of the influential British newspapers at the birth of the League is any index of the Government's feeling in the matter then it can be safely said that they did not favour the new party. The British newspapers either ignored or coldly received the League. *The Times* observed that 'despite the eminently pacific language of its [the League's] founders, there seems room for doubt whether its establishment will make for peace'.[196] It drew prominent attention to the League's making the prevention of the growth of hostility towards other communities conditional on the safety of its other objects.[197] The *Morning Post* was still louder in its warnings and commented that should the League overstep its defensive role, the situation would require 'the most drastic intervention of the British rulers'.[198] The *Spectator*, while noting the soundness of the objects of the League, confessed that 'we do not like this feeling among Muslims that they must organise in a camp by themselves'.[199]

The fiction of the Muslim League being the handmaiden of the Government has persisted due to errors and the political motivations of certain writers. Most historians have neglected the fact that the clamour for the central Muslim organisation had been the inevitable outcome of the social exclusiveness of the two communities and that long before the establishment of the League a large number of exclusively Hindu and Muslim organisations existed (at the lower levels) all over India. Moreover, important Hindu associations like the Hindu Mela of Bengal and the Hindu Sabha of Madras had set the example before the Muslims to organise themselves on a wider basis. Thus, in 1906, the movement for the foundation of an all-India Muslim association did not introduce any new element in Indian politics, except that the movers had certain specific political ends in view and that they sought to integrate the numerous existing Muslim associations into one central body and to form new associations on the model, more or less, of the existing ones. Even the movement for a central organisation was not an innovation. The Central National Mahomedan Association with its fifty-three branches in different parts of the country can, in a limited sense, be called the first central organisation of the Muslims of India. If Ameer Ali's plan for the All-India Mahomedan Convention had been successful then the Indian Muslims would have got their real and fully-fledged all-India political party as early as 1888.

[196] *The Times,* 2 January, 1907.
[197] *Ibid.*
[198] The *Morning Post,* 19 January, 1907.
[199] The *Spectator,* 5 January, 1907.

Taking into account the Hindu sense of physical pollution at the touch of a Muslim,[200] the Muslim apprehensions of Hindu domination, the conflict of interests between the two communities on the questions of language, representation in the elective bodies, the share in the government service, etc., the chauvinism of certain Congress leaders especially evident during the anti-cow killing movement and the Ganapati and Shivaji celebrations, as well as the activities of the local communal associations, the formation of a Muslim central organisation had been a question only of time, initiative and a common programme. The zero hour arrived towards the end of 1906, when the anti-partition agitation threatened the existence of Eastern Bengal and Assam as a separate province and when the proposed reforms were said to have aimed at the extension of the mixed electorates. The initiative came from Eastern Bengal. And the demands set forth in the memorial of the Simla deputation along with that of the demand for the permanence of the new province provided a minimum working programme.

However, the most important factor behind the Muslims forming themselves into an all-India political party was the awakening of the community from its slumber. The Congress was started thirty years after the establishment of the Calcutta University. After the lapse of almost the same period from the foundation of the Aligarh College,[201] the Muslims brought into being their fully-fledged all-India party. The political awakening among the Muslims had been in direct proportion

---

[200] It was repeatedly pointed out that since even the enlightened Hindus did not treat the Muslims as equals and never admitted them into their socio-economic institutions it was impossible for the Muslims to trust the Hindus or to co-operate with them politically. *Vide* the *Madras Weekly Mail,* 11 October, 1906, (letter to the Editor), and the *Express,* 17 May, 1906, (editorial) quoted in the *U.P. N.N.R.,* 1906 etc.

[201] The following table showing the number of Muslim graduates from different Indian universities and from the Aligarh College gives us an idea of the important part played by the latter in the spread of English education among the Muslims.

| Years | University of Calcutta | University of Madras | University of Bombay | University of the Punjab | University of Allahabad | Aligarh College | Total |
|---|---|---|---|---|---|---|---|
| 1882–87 | 80 | 12 | 7 | 11 | – | 10 | 110 |
| 1888–92 | 90 | 9 | 7 | 44 | 53 | 17 | 203 |
| 1893–97 | 107 | 31 | 18 | 77 | 165 | 77 | 398 |
| 1898–1902 | 121 | 18 | 24 | 123 | 192 | 116 | 478 |

In 1882 the percentage of Aligarh graduates to the total number of Muslim graduates in India was only 9.09, in 1902 it had risen to more than 27.

to the spread of education in the community.[202] But for this transformation in the Muslim society Salimullah's efforts might have met the
fate of Ameer Ali's earlier move towards the same direction.

To sum up, the All-India Muslim League was no mushroom growth.
Nor was it the creation of any individual or group of individuals. It was
the inevitable product of the forces, on the one hand of Hindu exclusiveness and revivalism, and on the other of the educational and political
activities of the Muslims starting with the foundations of the Aligarh
College and of the Central National Mahomedan Association.

[202]The following table shows the increase in the number of Muslim students
in various institutions from 1886 to 1907. (The percentages refer to the proportion of Muslim students to the total number of pupils in India.)

| Year | Arts Colleges | Professional Colleges | Secondary Schools |
|------|---------------|----------------------|-------------------|
| 1886–87 | 338 (4.2%) | 139 (5.1%) | 58,644 (13.7%) |
| 1891–92 | 736 (5.9%) | 246 (7.5%) | 66,652 (14.0%) |
| 1896–97 | 939 (6.6%) | 291 (6.7%) | 75,976 (14.2%) |
| 1901–02 | 1,259 (7.3%) | 345 (6.4%) | 55,487 (14.4%) |
| 1906–07 | 1,469 (8.1%) | 471 (7.5%) | 70,614 (14.8%) |

(*Vide* Progress of Education in India, 1st–5th Quinquennial Review).

## Chapter II

## THE CONSOLIDATION OF THE CENTRAL ORGANISATION

During the first two years after its formation the All-India Muslim League was principally engaged in strengthening its base through the formation of provincial organisations. In the matter of policy the League's primary concern was to hold the Government to what it regarded as a pledge of separate electorates. Both of these pre-occupations will be the subject of analysis in later chapters. First, however, it is necessary to consider reactions within India to the formation of the League, internal conflicts over its purpose and its framing of a constitution.

While the Muslims of India had generally welcomed the birth of the All-India Muslim League,[1] the hostility of a prominent section of the Hindu leaders to the new party was vehement. One of the earliest Hindu reactions to the formation of the League was an attempt to form and publicise a counter organisation of the Indian Muslims. On 9 January, 1907, the *Bengalee* reported the establishment of an All-India Mahomedan Association at Calcutta on 31 December, 1906.[2] The main purposes of this Association were 'to join the members of the other communities in their attempts for the political and economic advancement of the Indian people', to ventilate 'the special grievances' of the Muslims, and to ensure that the interests of the Muslims were safeguarded.[3]

Whether any such meeting was held or any such organisation was ever formed is open to serious doubt. When he was asked about it, Syed Muhammad, who was declared to be the president of the Association, denied any knowledge of the very organisation and categorically stated that his name had been used without any authority.[4] What casts further doubt on the whole report is its appearance some nine days after the alleged event, whereas a meeting held in Calcutta on 5

[1] The *Indian Daily Telegraph,* 1 January, 1907, and the *Tafrih,* 14 January, 1907 (*vide* the *U.P. N.N.R.,* 1907).

[2] The *Bengalee,* 9 January, 1907.

[3] *Ibid.*

[4] Mazhar-ul-Haque's letter to the editor, the *Englishman,* 25 January, 1907.

January, 1907, under the auspices of the Bengal Mahomedan Association, which was said to be the sponsor and host of the so-called All-India
Mahomedan Association, was reported in the *Bengalee* on the following
day.[5]   This evidence as well as the fact that none of the persons
reported as members of the alleged All-India Mahomedan Association
ever asserted its formation, suggests that the Association was probably
manufactured in the editorial office of the *Bengalee.*

The counter-move against the Muslim League having failed, the
*Bengalee* and a section of the Hindu press started a campaign of abuse
and personal attack against the founders of the League and particularly
against Salimullah.   Headlining Salimullah's speech at the Munshiganj
League meeting as 'Nawabi Nonsense', the *Bengalee* compared the
Nawab with a 'tradesman' soliciting 'public patronage', and further
depicted him as 'a wandering dervish holding his pilgrim staff in one
hand and his begging bowl[6] in the other'.[7]   The newspaper even trans-
gressed the limits of journalistic decency and decorum when, in the
same article, it remarked that Salimullah was 'not fit to unloose the
latchets of their [his opponents' i.e. the anti-partitionists'] shoes.'[8]
This growling against Salimullah, however, showed that the *Bengalee*
and its supporters were mainly concerned with the Nawab's role as the
spokesman of the new province of Eastern Bengal and Assam.

Every attempt to strengthen the League and its branches during the
early months of 1907 was subjected to inflammatory criticism by the
*Bengalee,* its editor, Surendranath Banerjea and their supporters.  Nawab
Ali Choudhury's visit to Sirajganj in connection with the League work
was regarded by Surendranath Banerjea as an attempt to cause a rupture
between Hindus and Muslims.[9]   The news of Salimullah's visit to
Comilla in March, 1907, where an attempt was made on his life and
where his private secretary was beaten up, was headlined: 'Divide et
impera . . . Order by Dacca Nawab to Loot Hindu Shop'.[10]   On this

___

[5] The *Bengalee,* 6 January, 1907.

[6] The *Bengalee* was possibly referring to the Nawab's application for a loan
from the Government which it had adversely criticised on 1 and 15 February,
1907.  It is significant to note that while the Hindu press all over India created a
hue and cry over the proposed loan to Salimullah a large number of newspapers,
including the *Bengalee* (3 March, 1907), strongly advocated a much bigger loan
to the Maharani of Ajodhia.

[7] The *Bengalee,* 22 January, 1907.

[8] *Ibid.*

[9] Salimullah's speech at the public meeting held at Dacca on 12 March,
1907, *vide* the *Englishman Weekly Summary,* 28 March, 1907.

[10] The *Bengalee,* 5 March, 1907.

occasion another Hindu newspaper remarked: 'It is also a noteworthy fact that the Hindus have at last learnt to take the law into their own hands. Who can blame them if they really gave a beating to someone in the employ of the Nawab.'[11]

Besides using provocative language, the *Bengalee* and several other Calcutta newspapers also indulged in various sorts of insinuation against the League and its leaders.[12] Commenting on the foundation of the Benares League at a public meeting presided over by Prince Mirza Akbar Bakht of the Mughal royal family of Delhi, who enjoyed a pension from the Government, the *Bengalee* alleged that 'the League and its branches were engineered—mostly by Government pensioners or gentlemen who are compelled to solicit Government assistance in their family or pecuniary difficulties'.[13] The newspaper further charged that the League and its branches did not represent the opinions and sentiments of the 'independent section' of the Muslims.[14]

These allegations and insinuations of the Hindu press and leaders had been strongly refuted by various leading members of the League. Salimullah called them 'false and mischievous'.[15] Mazhar-ul-Haque,, a barrister of Bihar, considered them as the outcome of 'either blind prejudice or deliberate misrepresentation'.[16] He was convinced that the Bengali Hindus fully realised the importance of the League and were trying 'to kill the infant in its cradle'. He also accused the Hindu newspapers of Bengal of sowing dissensions among the Muslim leaders.[17] Muhammad Yusuf Khan of Patna condemned Surendranath Banerjea for his malicious criticism of the League and its leaders.[18]

The vendetta of the influential Hindu public opinion against the League, however, had some effect upon the policy of the League. This was to be noticeable in the proceedings of the Karachi session of the All-India Muslim League held in December 1907. Meanwhile, the

---

[11] *The Amrita Bazar Patrika* quoted in annexure XIV of enclosure No. I to Home (Public) No. 10 of 1907. *Vide* India—Public Letters, 1907, Vol. 34.

[12] Mazhar-ul-Haque's letter to the editor, the *Englishman*, 25 January, 1907.

[13] The *Bengalee*, 18 January, 1907.

[14] *Ibid.*

[15] The *Englishman Weekly Summary*, 28 March, 1907.

[16] Mazhar-ul-Haque's letter to the editor, the *Englishman*, 25 January, 1907.

[17] *Ibid.*

[18] Muhammad Yusuf Khan's letter to the editor, the *Eastern Bengal and Assam Era*, 16 March, 1907.

League came under the influence of certain elements which were less concerned with the fate of the province of Eastern Bengal and Assam— the main cause of Bengali Hindu opposition to the League.

At the inaugural meeting of the All-India Muslim League held at Dacca in December, 1906, Salimullah was offered the party secretaryship. He refused it[19] and Mohsin-ul-Mulk and Viqar-ul-Mulk were elected joint secretaries. Salimullah's decision was possibly guided by the considera- tion of his pre-occupations with the political and educational develop- ment of the Muslims of Eastern Bengal and Assam. But the subsequent election of two secretaries instead of one is significant. Mohsin-ul-Mulk and Viqar-ul-Mulk were friends, former high officials of the Hyderabad State and veteran leaders of the Aligarh movement. Mohsin-ul-Mulk was senior in age and experience, better versed in the English language, more cosmopolitan in outlook and, as the secretary of the Mahomedan Educational Conference and of the Aligarh College, enjoyed a wider prestige. Viqar-ul-Mulk was conservative in his social attitude, more religious-minded and more outspoken. He was also more active in politics, more sympathetic towards the political aspirations of the younger generation and a stronger supporter of the province of Eastern Bengal and Assam. He was possibly more acceptable to the organisers of the League than Mohsin-ul-Mulk, which may explain his election as the president of the conference that created the League. But Mohsin- ul-Mulk's greater reputation had perhaps induced the League members to appoint him as secretary of the party along with Viqar-ul-Mulk.

Mohsin-ul-Mulk did not take much interest in the activities of the League. The Aligarh College was and remained his primary concern. Consequently, Viqar-ul-Mulk was left in full control of the League's policy-making and organisational work. By March, 1907, Viqar-ul- Mulk's influence had prevailed over Mohsin-ul-Mulk, who 'yielded to the breath of every wind'.[20] It was possibly under the influence of Viqar-ul-Mulk that about this time Mohsin-ul-Mulk 'threw a certain amount of cold water on the idea of the union between Hindus and Mohammedans' at a party held in honour of G. K. Gokhale.[21]

The cordial relations between the two secretaries of the League seem, however, to have been strained in April, 1907, by the report of a sub- committee appointed by the Board of Trustees of the Aligarh College.

[19] Mazhar-ul-Haque's letter to the editor, the *Englishman,* 25 January, 1907.
[20] Hewett to Dunlop Smith, 4 November, 1907, Min. P., Corr. India, 1907, Vol. 2.
[21] Hewett to Minto, 24 February, 1907, Min. P., Corr. India, 1907, Vol. 1.

The committee which included Viqar-ul-Mulk, Muhammad Ali and another gentleman opposed a decision of Mohsin-ul-Mulk's to approve Archbold's rustication of several students.[22] Mohsin-ul-Mulk was very much upset by the incident and his interest in the activities of the College diminished. Soon afterwards he fell ill, and died in October, 1907.

The death of Mohsin-ul-Mulk left Viqar-ul-Mulk as the only secretary of the League. He was now as much interested in the affairs of the Aligarh College as he had been in that of the League and aspired to becoming secretary of the Board of Trustees of the College. This brought him in contact with government officials who had considerable influence with a number of the trustees. Hewett, the Lieutenant-Governor of the U.P., considered him 'very conservative, [and] not very fond of English ideas'.[23] Hewett also knew that Viqar-ul-Mulk's appointment as the secretary of the Aligarh College 'would certainly be most unpopular with the staff'.[24] But it would have been difficult to keep him out. Apart from the large support which he enjoyed among the trustees, to deny him the secretaryship would be to make him 'a fervent supporter of Mahommed Ali and his gang'. Hewett, therefore, thought it better to enlist him as 'an efficient engine to squash Mahommed Ali and his followers'.[25] Thus Viqar-ul-Mulk was elected secretary of the Aligarh College without any opposition from the Government side.

However, it may be conjectured that in return for the secretaryship of the Aligarh College, Viqar-ul-Mulk promised to retire as the secretary of the All-India Muslim League. The idea of making Aligarh the centre of Muslim activities in India was encountering increasing resistance from British officials including Hewett. Hewett saw 'dangers' also in the 'unlimited expansion of the Aligarh College', tending towards the possible development of 'Pan-Islamism in direct hostility to Christendom'.[26] Furthermore, the Lieutenant-Governor was apprehensive of 'the possibility of a change of feeling on the part of the Mohammedan community towards Government'.[27] Consequent upon this attitude of the Government, Viqar-ul-Mulk, soon after his election as the secretary

[22] Choudhury Khaliquzzaman, *Pathway to Pakistan*, p. 11.
[23] Hewett to Dunlop Smith, 4 November, 1907, Min. P., Corr. India, 1907, Vol. 2.
[24] *Ibid.*
[25] *Ibid.*
[26] Hewett to Minto, 3 October, 1908, Min. P., Corr. India, 1908, Vol. 2.
[27] *Ibid.*

of the Aligarh College, became less active in the work of the League
and expressed his desire to resign from its secretaryship;[28]    this however, was not to become effective until March, 1908.  One can compare
this incident with Mohsin-ul-Mulk's retirement as the secretary of
the Urdu Defence Association in 1900 under direct pressure from
A. Macdonnell, then Lieutenant Governor of the U.P.[29]

Viqar-ul-Mulk's pre-occupation with the Aligarh College and his subsequent resignation as secretary of the League had far-reaching consequences in League politics.  By the end of 1907, the League had come
under the increasing influence of men like Ali Imam and Shah Din, who
were anxious to conciliate the Hindu moderates.  Their views on Muslim
politics were more in line with the Aga Khan's than with those of
Salimullah and Viqar-ul-Mulk.  Very soon these leaders paved the way
for the Aga Khan's election as the president of the League.

The new trend in the League politics found expression in the address
of Sir Adamjee Peerbhoy, the president of the first annual session
of the All-India Muslim League held at Karachi on 29 and 30
December, 1907.  Indeed Adamjee Peerbhoy's election as the president
of the League session signified the victory of such League leaders as
despised any kind of agitation over those who had already embarked on
agitating for the safeguarding of certain Muslim interests.  Adamjee was
one of the foremost industrialists and philanthropists in India.  Many
Muslim and Government institutions had been recipients of his generous
donations, which by 1907 exceeded rupees 5,000,000.[30]  But Adamjee
had never participated in active politics, nor was he highly educated.
His presidential address at the Karachi session, written in English, was
read by his son, Muhammad Bhai.[31]  His recent knighthood was partly
a recognition of his philanthropy, which the Aga Khan drew forcefully
to the notice of the Governor of Bombay.[32]  Adamjee seems further to
have been over-effusive in his tribute to the Aga Khan for his services
towards the Muslim community.[33]    Thus Adamjee's election as

---

[28] The *Pioneer Mail,* 3 January, 1908.

[29] *Supra,* p. 6.

[30] Shah Din's speech at the Karachi session of the A.I.M.L., *vide The Civil
and Military Gazette,* 31 December, 1907.

[31] The *Times of India Mail,* 4 January, 1908.

[32] The Governor of Bombay (Lammington) to Minto 8 April, 1906, Min.
P., Corr. India, 1905, Vol. I.

[33] Presidential Address of Adamjee Peerbhoy at the Karachi session of the
A.I.M.L., *vide* Appendix E of *The Surat Congress and Conferences* published by
G. A. Natesan & Co., Madras, p. xxxii.

president of the League session appears to have been at least partly due to the influence of the Aga Khan with a section of the League leaders. Another consideration which may have favoured Adamjee's election was the prospect of financial assistance from him and his fellow merchants of Bombay for the purposes of the League.

A most significant feature of Adamjee's presidential address was its emphasis on mutual toleration between Hindus and Muslims. It 'passes my understanding', the address read, 'why the Mahomedans should in the advancement of their own interest injure those of any other people . . . It is no part of the purpose of this League to oppose the progress of other communities or to be aggressive towards them in any direction whatever.'[34]

Except for announcing a new approach towards inter-communal relations and restating strongly the League's absolute loyalty towards the Government, Adamjee's address did not throw light on any of the issues confronting the Muslims of India. As regards the burning question of Muslim representation in the councils, Adamjee confined himself to an appreciation of the Viceroy's recognition of the principle of 'class representation'. He admitted that separate representation of communities was not the ideal form of representation, but was none-theless wise in the existing situation in India.[35] As for the economic condition of the Muslims, Adamjee prescribed industrialisation as the means of their attaining 'a high position in the Empire'.[36]

The League's new policy towards other communities as propounded in the presidential address of Adamjee Peerbhoy was finally and formally incorporated in the creed of the party adopted at the Karachi session. The aim of the League was no longer to be 'to prevent the rise among the Mussalmans of India of any feeling of hostility towards other communities',[37] but rather 'to promote friendly feelings between the Mussalmans and other communities'.[38]

At Karachi, the League leaders had definitely moved away from their earlier stand of fighting the Congress and the Hindus towards one of co-operation with them. As recently as July, 1907, Viqar-ul-Mulk had expressed his apprehension that in case of British withdrawal from India 'the Mussalmans will find themselves at the mercy of an oppressive

---

[34] *Ibid.,* p. xxxvi.
[35] *Ibid.,* p. xxxv.
[36] *Ibid.,* p. xxxiv.
[37] *Supra,* p. 38.
[38] *Rules and Regulations of the All-India Muslim League, 1909,* printed by Mumtazuddin at the Institute Press, Aligarh, pp. 5–6.

Hindu majority'.[39]   About the same time he had also warned the Muslims that co-operation with the Congress in the political field was impossible because 'we and the Congressmen do not have common political objectives'.[40]

The significant change in the creed of the League seems to have been the product of four factors: first, the activities of moderates like Ali Imam and Shah Din who seem to have entered into a sort of under-standing with the Aga Khan and his supporters to bring him into the fold of the League; second, a lack of proper appreciation by a majority of the delegates at the Karachi meeting of the gravity of the Hindu-Muslim conflict in Bengal over the question of the new province; third, the absence of Salimullah[41] and most other leaders from Bengal and Eastern Bengal and Assam at the Karachi session;   and, fourth, the anxiety of certain League leaders to conciliate the Hindu moderates and particularly the Hindu press which had already menaced the League.

The new course in the League politics was further reflected in the constitution of the party which was passed at the Karachi conference. The constitution converted the League into a restricted body of a maximum of 400 members at the all-India level.[42]   These 400 members were to be elected or nominated by the different provincial Leagues, or in their absence by district or town Leagues affiliated to the All-India Muslim League.  The maximum number of members to be taken from the various provinces was fixed as follows: the United Provinces of Agra and Oudh, seventy;  Bombay (including Sind), forty;  Madras, twenty-five;   North-Western Provinces and Baluchistan, fifteen;   the Punjab, seventy;  Upper Bengal, Bihar and Orissa, seventy;  Eastern Bengal and Assam, seventy;  Berar, Central India and Ajmer, fifteen;  Burma, ten; and Muslim British subjects residing in Native States or elsewhere outside British India, together with such subjects of Native States as the central committee might exceptionally admit as members of the organisation, fifteen.[43]   In cases where the provincial quota had not been filled

---

[39] Viqar-ul-Mulk's article in the *Aligarh Institute Gazette,* 29 December, 1908, *vide* the *U.P. N.N.R.,* 1908.

[40] Quoted in *The Muslim League–Its History, Activities and Achievements* (p. 43) by Lal Bahadur.

[41] Salimullah was elected president of the All-India Mahomedan Educational Conference held at Karachi on 26, 27 and 28 December, 1907, but he had declined the offer on grounds of ill-health.

[42] *Rules and Regulations of the All-India Muslim League, op. cit.,* clause 4, p. 6.

[43] *Ibid.,* clause 5, pp. 14–15.

owing to the absence of local branches, the all-India League might itself nominate the necessary members.[44] The provincial quota, however, was to be subject to revision after each decennial census, such revisions to be based on considerations of the strength of Muslim population, their educational condition, as well as their financial position in the provinces.[45]

The qualifications for membership of the All-India Muslim League were also restrictive. Every candidate for membership was required to have four qualifications.[46] First, he must be a British—Indian Muslim subject. Second, he must not be less than twenty-five years of age. Third, he must be capable of reading and writing with facility any of the Indian languages. Fourth, his yearly income, including the income of his parents, must not be less than rupees 500 per annum. In individual cases an exception might be made with the sanction of the central committee and a candidate exempted from any of these conditions.[47]

The framers of the League constitution had, by limiting the maximum number of members of the all-India League to merely 400 and by imposing educational, financial and age qualifications on its membership, turned the League into more of a conservative upper-middle class assembly rather than into a dynamic association of the Indian Muslims. Salimullah's proposal for a Confederacy with automatic membership for all Muslim *anjumans* and associations and their members throughout India could not be further removed from the provisions of the League constitution. Furthermore, while Salimullah had proposed a subscription of ten rupees per annum the framers of the League constitution had raised the annual subscription to twenty-five rupees and had fixed an entry fee of equal amount. Indeed, the League leaders assembled at Karachi seem to have been determined to confine the party to the Muslim aristocracy and the upper-middle class, thus debarring the commoners as well as the young educated section of the community. The restrictive clauses in the League constitution may be understood when one considers the Aga Khan's earlier plan to perpetuate the Simla deputation as a counter-suggestion to Salimullah's scheme. The Aga Khan could not prevent the birth of the League in 1906, but he seems

[44]*Ibid.*, clause 7(*b*), p. 16.
[45]*Ibid.*, clause 6, p. 15.
[46]*Ibid.*, clause 3(*a*—*d*), p. 6.
[47]*Ibid.*, clause 3(*e*).

to have played some part from behind the scenes in limiting its character and scope in 1907.

The makers of the League constitution had also by a dubious stratagem declared the Aga Khan a member of the All-India Muslim League. The provisional committee of the League had consisted of fifty-six members whose names were published over the signature of Viqar-ul-Mulk.[48] But the Karachi session divided the League members into three categories. The first category consisted of those members— 'thirty three in number—of the Simla deputation of 1 October, 1906, who are alive and who have not entered the service of the Government'.[49] Clearly, this group was created to confer on the Aga Khan the automatic membership of the League. The creation of the second group, comprising 'the thirty members' of the League appointed at Dacca, was an attempt to further justify the *ex-officio* character of the members of the Simla deputation. The members of the third group were those who were nominated by the provisional Committee at the Karachi meeting.[50]

According to the constitution the members of the All-India Muslim League were to be elected for five years and were eligible for re-election.[51] After election every member was to pay an entrance fee of twenty-five rupees in addition to his annual subscription of twenty-five rupees.[52] These amounts were not refundable under any circumstances. No person elected to be a member of the All-India Muslim League was to be allowed to exercise his rights and privileges of membership until such time as he had paid his entrance fee and annual subscription.[53]

For the purpose of the All-India Muslim League the year was to commence on each first day of January and end on each thirty-first day of December.[54] At the annual meetings of the League a quorum was to be formed by not less than one-fifth of the total number of members borne on the rolls of the League.[55] But at other meetings one-eighth of the total members were to be considered sufficient for the quorum.[56]

[48]Proc. Home (Public), January–April, 1907, vol. 7587.
[49]*Rules and Regulations of the A.I.M.L.*, 1909, *op. cit.*, p. 7.
[50]*Ibid.*
[51]*Ibid.*, clause 8, p. 16.
[52]*Ibid.*, clause 10, p. 17.
[53]*Ibid.*, clause 11, p. 17.
[54]*Ibid.*, clause 14, p. 18.
[55]*Ibid.*, clause 15, p. 18.
[56]*Ibid.*

Except for the election of members of the All-India Muslim League neither votes sent in writing nor proxies were to be regarded as valid at any of the meetings of the League.[57]

The All-India Muslim League was to have a central committee consisting of not less than thirty and not more than forty members.[58] The members of the central committee as well as the office-bearers of the League were to be elected for a term of three years and were to be eligible for re-election.[59] These elections were to be held by ballot, absentee members being allowed to send their votes in writing.

The central committee was to carry out the executive functions of the League. The members of the central committee were also required to endeavour to form a provincial League in each province.[60] Other functions of the central committee were to take necessary steps for giving practical effect to resolutions passed by the central committee or the all-India League; to collect all useful information in connection with the objects of the League; to send to the members the agenda of the annual and other meetings of the League and to fix the time and place of all such meetings; to supervise the funds of the League; and to appoint the president for the annual sessions of the League.[61] In the event of three-fourths of the members of the central committee or of the All-India Muslim League complaining against any member, the central committee was, after having given the accused the opportunity of clearing himself, to take necessary disciplinary measures. Any such disciplinary action, however, was to be ratified by the All-India Muslim League.[62]

The procedures through which the central committee was to transact its business were,[63] firstly, to secure by correspondence the views and opinions of the members of the League on any matter in hand, to decide it in accordance with the majority of votes and to adopt measures for putting such decisions into effect. Secondly, to postpone temporarily for further consideration any question that might be under discussion. Thirdly, to convene at some suitable time and place the annual sessions or any other meetings of the League for the discussion of topics relating

[57]*Ibid.*, clause 16, p. 18.
[58]*Ibid.*, clause 17.
[59]*Ibid.*, clause 19(*a*), p. 19.
[60]*Ibid.*, clause 24(*a*), p. 22.
[61]*Ibid.*, clause 24(*b–f*), pp. 22–23.
[62]*Ibid.*, clause 34, p. 25.
[63]*Ibid.*, clause 23(*a–g*), pp. 20–22.

to its aims and objects. In case of a requisition from not less than two-thirds of the members of the central committee or from not less than one-third of the total members of the League the central committee was to convene an extraordinary meeting of the League for the further-ance of its objects.

The office-bearers of the League were to comprise one president, six vice-presidents, one secretary and two joint-secretaries.[64] The secretary was to be responsible for the working of his office and for its accounts.[65] He was to carry out the day to day routine work and could appoint a temporary sub-committee for any special purpose. The joint secretaries were to assist the secretary in his work and to perform their duties under his guidance.[66]

The funds of the League were to consist of all fees received from members and visitors at the annual and other meetings, and all donations, subscriptions or other contributions which the League or the central committee might from time to time receive or collect either for the promotion of the general objects of the League or for any particular purpose.[67] The funds were to be deposited in the name of the All-India Muslim League with the Bank of Bengal. But in places where the Bank of Bengal had no branch the central committee could deposit the funds with any other bank.[68] The secretary or, in his absence his *locum tenens*, could draw on such funds under his signa-ture. Every year the central committee was to appoint a finance committee consisting of three members, one president, one vice-president, one secretary and one joint secretary.[69] The finance committee was to prepare an annual budget of income and expenditure which was to be passed by the central committee. The finance com-mittee was further required to prepare a statement of the actual income and expenditure for the year, which, after audit by a firm of chartered accountants, was to be submitted to the central committee for its consideration and acceptance.[70]

The constitution of the All-India Muslim League was not to be added to, amended, or cancelled except at the annual meetings and by a

[64] *Ibid.*, clause 25, p. 23.
[65] *Ibid.*, clause 29, p. 24.
[66] *Ibid.*, clause 32, p. 24.
[67] *Ibid.*, clause 36, pp. 25–26.
[68] *Ibid.*, clause 37, p. 26.
[69] *Ibid.*, clause 38(*a*), p. 26.
[70] *Ibid.*, clause 38(*b–c*), pp. 26–27.

majority of votes of not less than two-thirds of the members present.[71] All such additions and alterations were to be duly proposed and seconded, in writing, and forwarded to the secretary not less than eight weeks before the date of the annual meeting. The central committee could make bye-laws concerning those matters which were found to be necessary for conducting the business of the League and which were not covered by the existing rules and regulations, provided that no bye-law was to be considered valid if it contravened the principle of any of the recognised rules and regulations.[72]

The constitution of the All-India Muslim League adopted at Karachi had several shortcomings which were rectified from time to time. A most important omission in the constitution was the absence of any clause regarding the allocation of membership of the central committee between the various provinces. This issue was taken up at the special general meeting of the League held at Aligarh on 18 and 19 March, 1908, when the forty seats of the central committee were distributed as follows: the United Provinces of Agra and Oudh, seven, the Punjab, seven, Bombay including Sind, four, Madras, two, N.W.F.P. and Baluchistan, one, Berar and C.P., two, West Bengal, Bihar and Orissa, seven, Eastern Bengal and Assam, seven, Burma, one, and Indian States, two.[73]

The League constitution was silent about the nature of the control of the all-India League over its provincial and other branches. It did not even indicate whether the rules and regulations of the all-India League were to be followed as a model for the constitution of the provincial Leagues. Thus the provincial Leagues had been free to frame constitutions of their own according to the needs and circumstances of the respective provinces.

The provincial Leagues, however, generally followed the principles of the rules and regulations of the All-India Muslim League, though in matters of detail there were several innovations in the constitutions of the different provincial Leagues. As regards their local membership, some provincial Leagues reduced the income qualification of members to three hundred rupees a year (including the parent's income).[74] The

---

[71]*Ibid.,* clause 39(*a*), p. 27.

[72]*Ibid.,* clause 40, p. 28.

[73]Lal Bahadur, *The Muslim League, Its History, Activities and Achievements,* p. 73 (quoted from the *Aligarh Institute Gazette,* March 18, 1908, pp. 1 and 2).

[74]The *Madras Weekly Mail,* 3 December, 1908 (report of the inaugural, meeting of the Madras Presidency League).

literacy qualification of members was accepted by every provincial
League, but the minimum age qualification varied from twenty-five
years in Burma to twenty-one in Madras.[75]   Similarly the membership
fees for different provincial Leagues also varied from rupees twenty-four
to rupees six per year.[76]

The passing of the constitution at the Karachi meeting was followed
by the election of office-bearers of the All-India Muslim League at
the Aligarh session held on 16 and 17 March, 1908, under the presidentship of Shah Din.   On the motion of Rafiuddin Ahmad, barrister,
Bombay, seconded by Viqar-ul-Mulk, the Aga Khan was elected
president of the League.[77]   The Aga Khan had not attended the two
previous meetings of the League and he did not attend the Aligarh
session.   He had, however, sent five hundred rupees as a donation to the
League fund and this was thankfully acknowledged.[78]

The Aga Khan's election as the president of the League appears to
have been mainly due to the manipulation of Shah Din, Ali Imam,
Rafiuddin Ahmad and a few other leaders of the Punjab, Bihar and the
Bombay Leagues.   But the Aga Khan's prestige with the Government
and his affluence probably attracted the average League members
anxious to secure strong and influential support for the party.   However, the Aga Khan never accepted the full responsibility of his office,
nor was his financial backing of the League sufficient to meet its
requirements.[79]

On being telegraphically informed of his election as the president of
the League the Aga Khan had wired back: 'Though I should have gladly
seen someone else as president and myself only a member, yet I feel
that modesty might be misunderstood for want of patriotism, so gladly
accept'.[80]   At the same time the Aga Khan was not prepared to let the
members of the League expect him 'to do much during the immediate
future', although he informed them that he would be 'heart and soul'
with them later.[81]   However, the Aga Khan did not attend any meeting
of the League until January, 1910.

[75] The *Pioneer Mail*, 14 January, 1909 and the *Madras Mail*, 3 December,
1908.
   [76] *Ibid.*
   [77] The *Pioneer*, 21 March, 1908.
   [78] The *Madras Weekly Mail*, 26 March, 1908.
   [79] On 23 October, 1913, Wazir Hasan told Ameer Ali: 'You cannot be
unaware of the fact that if it [the League] has starved you here, it has had to
starve itself also, in India'. *Vide* the *Comrade*, 8 November, 1913.
   [80] The *Pioneer*, 22 March, 1908.
   [81] *Ibid.*

The Aga Khan's election to the League presidency was perhaps balanced by the election of Major Syed Hasan Bilgrami, a retired member of the Indian Medical Service, as secretary, and Haji Musa Khan, *raees* of Dataoli, as joint secretary of the All-India Muslim League. Both Major Bilgrami and Musa Khan shared Viqar-ul-Mulk's political views and were elected at his instance. While accepting his somewhat forced retirement from the League secretaryship, Viqar-ul-Mulk seems to have been able to re-assert himself at the Aligarh meeting. His apparent compromise with the Aga Khan was a matter of expediency. Whenever the League president sought to act according to his own discretion Viqar-ul-Mulk was the first to raise his voice in protest. Viqar-ul-Mulk's role in the League politics, had, however, added to the anxiety of the Lieutenant-Governor of the U.P. who now sought to exert his influence with a section of the League leaders in removing the headquarters of the All-India Muslim League from Aligarh.[82]

The Aligarh meeting also elected the members of the Central Committee of the League, thus placing the party on a stronger foundation and passed several resolutions relating to the advancement of Muslim interests in general.

In a lengthy resolution moved by Rafiuddin Ahmad, seconded by Aftab Ahmad Khan, barrister, Aligarh, and supported by Yakub Hasan and Ghulam Sadiq of Madras and the Punjab respectively, the League expressed its hope that the Government would take steps to meet such demands of the Simla deputation as had not yet been conceded.[83] In particular, the resolution invited the Government's attention to four of the Muslim demands: first, 'the imperative necessity' which existed in India for the appointment of Muslim judges to each of the High Courts and Chief Courts in the country where such appointments had not already been made; second, the urgent need for giving the Muslims their proper share of employment in the public service; third, the vital importance of adequate representation of Muslims 'as a distinct community' in the various legislative councils as well as in the municipal and district boards throughout the country; fourth, the great desirability of safeguarding Muslim educational interests by securing their due representation on the senates and syndicates of the universities and on text-book committees connected with the department of public instruction.[84]

[82] *Infra*, pp. 177–178.
[83] The *Pioneer*, 21 March, 1908.
[84] *Ibid.*

In another resolution the League thanked the Viceroy for the appointment and confirmation respectively of Syed Karamat Husain and Syed
Sharfuddin—the former to the Bench of the Allahabad High Court and
the latter to that of the Calcutta High Court.

The League session also appointed a sub-committee consisting of
Viqar-ul-Mulk, Syed Hasan Bilgrami, Rafiuddin Ahmad, Fazl-i-Husain,
Yakub Hasan, Syed Nabiullah, barrister, Lucknow, and Syed Zahur
Ahmad, pleader, Lucknow, as members, to formulate and forward to the
Government of India the League's opinion on the Government's reforms
proposals that were to lead to the Government of India Act of 1909.

Furthermore, the League session, on the motion of Muhammad Shafi,
seconded by Aftab Ahmad Khan, passed a resolution on the current
question of the separation of the judiciary from the executive. The
question was an old one on which 'volumes have been written',[85] and
which had been repeatedly discussed by the Congress. In Bengal it was
a political fight in legal garb to curb the power of the executive and to
make the independent judiciary guardians of the King's subjects. The
demand was for the creation of a subordinate cadre of judicial officers
immune from the influence of the executive and responsible to the
High Court. As early as 1899, ten British gentlemen, seven of whom
had held high judicial offices in India, had memorialised the Secretary
of State on the subject.[86] The memorial was alleged to have been
based on the notes of Monomohan Ghose, a renowned criminal lawyer
of Calcutta. The Secretary of State had set in motion an investigation
into the question as demanded by the memorialists, but nothing
seemed to come out of it until questions were raised in the Parliament
in 1906.[87] Thereafter, in 1908, the Government of India decided to
experiment, subject to certain limitations, with the idea of the separation of the judiciary from the executive in a few districts of Bengal and
Eastern Bengal and Assam. The Hindu press was very critical of this
half-hearted measure.[88] The Aligarh session of the League, however,

[85] Harvey Adamson's speech at the Imperial Legislative Council, 27 March,
1908. Proc. Council of the G.G., vol. XLVI, p. 246.

[86] *Ibid.*

[87] On 24 May, 1906, while replying to a question on the separation of the
judiciary from the executive by H. Cotton, Morley stated that 'until a very recent
date the Government of India did not regard the time as opportune for pressing
this question . . . I will draw the attention of the Government of India to the
subject . . . *vide Parl. Debates, Fourth Series,* Vol. 157, C. 1415.

[88] The *Hitavarta,* 1 March, 1908; the *Bangabasi,* 4 April, 1908, and the *Bharat
Mitra,* 4 April, 1908, *vide* the *Bengal N.N.R.,* 1908.

supported the Government proposal as, perhaps, half a loaf seemed to be better than no loaf at all. Apart from the legal and political aspects, the Government proposal also opened up possibilities for the creation of new judicial posts with Muslim representation therein. Therefore, while welcoming the proposed experiment in some parts of the two Bengals, the League resolution suggested its extension to other provinces, of course, 'with due regard to local circumstances'.[89]

Towards the middle of 1908, the conditions of Indians in South Africa and more particularly in the Transvaal became one of the chief concerns of the All-India Muslim League and its branches. The Transvaal Government had, in 1885, passed an anti-Asiatic Act in order to restrict Indian immigration. The Act had also placed the Indians resident in the Transvaal under a number of disabilities. The British Government was opposed to the implementation of this Act and 'ill-treatment of the Indians was made one of the reasons' for the Boer War.[90] But when after the war the Transvaal was made a self-governing colony of the British Empire, an Act worse than the old one was brought into existence. While this Act was strongly resented by the Indians, who considered it 'degrading, humiliating and insulting', the British Government followed a policy of non-intervention in the matter.[91] As a large majority of the Indians in the Transvaal were Muslims, leading members of the League like Viqar-ul-Mulk and Rafiuddin Ahmad had expressed their abhorrence of the ill-treatment of the Indians in the Transvaal early in 1908.[92] On 29 January, 1908, at a public meeting held at Lahore under the auspices of the Punjab Provincial League, a resolution was passed strongly denouncing the Asiatic Immigration Ordinance of the Government of the Transvaal and sympathising with the Indians living in the colony in their hardships and humiliations.[93]

In April, 1908, the question of the Indians in the Transvaal was also taken up in London by Ameer Ali, who had been in communication with some leading Muslims of the colony. Writing in the *Nineteenth Century*, Ameer Ali observed that 'the pagan empire of Rome extended

[89] The *Pioneer*, 21 March, 1908.

[90] Muhammad Ali Jinnah's speech at a public meeting held at Bombay in July, 1908, *vide* the *Times of India Mail*, 11 July, 1908.

[91] *Ibid.*

[92] Letter to the Editor, the *Times of India Mail*, 8 February, 1908, by Rafiuddin Ahmad, Bombay.

[93] Quoted in an article by 'An Indian Mussalman' in the *Hindustan Review*, April, 1909, pp. 348–49.

to all its subjects the rights of citizenship, and the "provincial" was as much entitled to the full enjoyment of those privileges as the Roman-born. The Christian empire of Great Britain can not secure considerate treatment of its "provincials" in its own Colonies.'[94]   On 29 July, 1908, the matter was formally noted by the London League on receipt of a telegram from Johannesburg addressed to Ameer Ali. The telegram reported: 'Chairman Hamidia Islamic Society and priest [and] other prominent Indians [are] imprisoned. [They have been sentenced to] Hard labour [for] non-compliance [with] Asiatic Act. All Indian business in South Africa [is] closed [as a] symbol [of] mourning. [Hamidia Islamic] Society [is] fighting [for] India's honour. [The] Government offer repeal [of the] Act if we accept prohibition [of] entry [of] eminent Indians. Indians reject this.'[95]   While forwarding a copy of this telegram to the Under-Secretary of State for the Colonies, the London League protested against the humiliating treatment of 'our fellow-countrymen and co-religionists in the Transvaal which, it warned, was likely to create disaffection among our fellow-countrymen in India'.[96]

Meanwhile, on 8 July, 1908, presiding over a public meeting at Bombay, the Aga Khan made an emotional speech on the issue of the Indians in the Transvaal. The Aga Khan's deep concern for the Transvaal Indians was mainly due to the fact that a considerable number of them happened to belong to the Ismaili sect of which he was the spiritual head.   After Muhammad Ali Jinnah had spoken of the 'scandalous pieces of legislation' in South Africa, and reported on his mission to England to represent the case of the Transvaal Indians, the Aga Khan observed that the excuse given by the Imperial Government that they could not interfere in the affairs of a self-governing colony, was 'absolutely insufficient'.[97] Endorsing Jinnah's suggestion that India as a country should retaliate by enacting similar legislation against the offending colonies, the Aga Khan remarked that for years he had been conscious that 'in common fairness the Imperial Government should allow the Government of India to pass Acts penalising the citizens of

---

[94] Ameer Ali's article–'The Anomalies of Civilisation'–published in the *Nineteenth Century,* April, 1908, p. 569.

[95] Copy of the telegram to Ameer Ali enclosed with the London League's representation, dated 25 July, 1908. J. & P. 2755/1908, Vol. 881.

[96] London League's representation to the Under Secretary of State, Colonial Office, 25 July, 1908. *Ibid.*

[97] The *Times of India Mail,* 11 July, 1908.

the colonies in question when they come to India'.[98]    He further remarked that the Indians should, irrespective of their religion, 'unite in carrying on throughout this country an agitation such as had never been known in this peninsula for securing the repeal of those laws which were most insulting to the Indian peoples and their religions'.

The conditions of Indians in the Transvaal also came up at the meeting of the central committee of the All-India Muslim League held at Aligarh on 9 August, 1908.    The central committee urged the Viceroy and the Secretary of State for India to impress upon His Majesty's Government in England the necessity of intervention on behalf of the British Indians for the repeal of the Asiatic Law Amendment Act and the Immigration Registration Bill of the Government of the Transvaal.[99]    Compared with the statements of the Aga Khan and a few other Muslim leaders, particularly of Bombay, the resolution of the central committee seems to have been couched in the most moderate terms.    The same moderate tone was noticeable in a subsequent representation submitted by the London League to the Under-Secretary of State for India demanding full investigation into the grievances of Indians in the Transvaal and Natal by a Royal Commission or some other suitable body.[100]

The meeting of the League central committee held on 9 August, 1908, once again demanded the fulfilment of the claims embodied in the memorial submitted to the Viceroy by the Simla deputation in 1906.    This time the League drew the particular attention of the Government to the question of the appointment of one Muslim to the Viceroy's executive council.[101]    They also thanked the Government of India for the appointment of Abdur Rahim, a prominent member of the League, as a Judge of the Madras High Court.[102]

In two other resolutions the central committee expressed the profound anxiety of the League about the situation in Eastern Bengal and Assam. They cautioned the Government that 'any modification whatsoever in the partition of Bengal will produce an extremely harmful

[98] *Ibid.*

[99] Resolution No. 5 passed at the meeting of the Central Committee of the A.I.M.L. held on 9 August, 1908. *Vide* Proc. Home (Public), September, 1908. Proc. No. 249.

[100] London League's representation to the Under Secretary of State for India, 28 September, 1908, J. & P. 3612/1908, Vol. 889.

[101] Resolution No. 1 passed at the League Central Committee meeting held on 9 August, 1908. Proc. Home (Public), September, 1908, Proc. No. 249.

[102] Resolution No. 2. *Ibid.*

effect from one corner of India to the other'.[103]  They also, for the first time, demanded the creation of a separate High Court in Eastern Bengal and Assam.[104]

The League had taken up the Eastern Bengal and Assam issue after a lapse of more than a year and a half.  This was perhaps partly because of the re-assertion of its importance by men like Salimullah and Viqar-ul-Mulk.  But the most important reason for the League's great concern about the future of the new province was obviously the intensity of the anti-partition agitation both in India and in England.  While in India the anti-partition agitation had become a menace to the maintenance of law and order as early as December, 1907,[105] in England its impact was not seriously felt until the middle of 1908.  In June–July, 1908, heated discussion took place in both House of Parliament.  Henry Cotton, Keir Hardie, Rutherford, C. J. O'Donnell and other members of Parliament who had been actively agitating for the annulment of partition, repeatedly raised the issue in the Commons.[106]  On 30 June, 1908, in the course of a debate in the House of Lords, Curzon, Midleton and Amphthill vied with each other in disclaiming the paternity of the partition of Bengal.[107]  In the same debate Morley, who on earlier occasions had declared partition a 'settled fact',[108] observed somewhat sarcastically: 'When I consider all the circumstances under which the partition was made—it was a matter of adjusting boundaries and operations of that kind—I could never see why it should have been regarded as so sacrosanct'.[109]

The debates in Parliament had greatly encouraged the anti-partitionists. The *Bengalee* declared that 'the strongest condemnation of the partition lies in the horror with which its authorship is repudiated by those who are more or less responsible for it.  If everybody concerned is ashamed of the measure, including Lord Curzon . . . it should be withdrawn.'[110]

---

[103] Resolution No. 3. *Ibid.*

[104] Resolution No. 4. *Ibid.*

[105] By December, 1907, terrorist activities aiming at the lives of government officials had greatly increased. Attempts were made even against the life of the Lieutenant-Governor of Bengal. *Vide,* Min. P. Diary (December, 1907).

[106] Parl. Debates, Fourth Series, Vol. 191, columns 348–349;  Vol. 193, c.c. 178, 209, 215.

[107] *Ibid.,* Vol. 191, columns 510–12 and 542–46.

[108] Parl. Debates, Fourth Series, Vol. 152, column 844.

[109] Parl. Debates, Fourth Series, Vol. 191, p. 525.

[110] The *Bengalee,* 5 July, 1908.

Several other anti-partitionist newspapers wrote in the same vein.[111] The *Hitavadi* even went so far as to assert that it was 'in the air' that 'the partition will be modified and that the Bengali-speaking population will be placed under one governor'.[112]

The Parliamentary debates and the consequent Hindu jubilation had greatly alarmed the Muslims about the permanence of Eastern Bengal and Assam.[113] And it was to draw the attention of the Government towards the Muslim feelings that the central committee of the All-India Muslim League had passed the two resolutions in August, 1908.

The Muslim case on the partition of Bengal was also presented to the Under-Secretary of State for India in a representation submitted by the London League on 11 November, 1908. The representation maintained that though it was not sufficiently apprehended in England, until quite recently, the fact was that the people of Eastern Bengal, predominantly of Muslim faith, were regarded by those 'of the Western districts as a distinct people'.[114] It further noted that the partition had affected the interests of those people of the Eastern districts who as 'lawyers, merchants, traders and journalists [were] practising or carrying on business in Calcutta and in the cities of Upper and Central India,' but not that of the general people of the new province who had found 'a new stimulus for development'.[115]

The representation of the London League, however, differed slightly from the views of the central committee of the All-India Muslim League on the subject of the creation of a new High Court. The London League was perhaps better informed about the legal and technical difficulties[116] involved in the creation of a new High Court. They were, therefore, prepared 'to maintain absolutely intact the powers and privileges of the Indian High Courts'.[117] But they submitted that without affecting the original jurisdiction of the Calcutta High Court

[111] The *India* (London), 10 July, 1908; the *Advocate*, 5 July, 1908 (*vide* U.P. N.N.R.*, 1908) and the *Hitavadi*, 19 July, 1908 (*vide* the *Bengal N.N.R.*, 1908).

[112] The *Hitavadi*, 10 July, 1908. The *Bengal N.N.R.*, 1908.

[113] The *Aligarh Institute Gazette*, 15 July, 1908. The *U.P. N.N.R.*, 1908.

[114] The London League's representation to the Under Secretary of State for India, 11 November, 1908. J. & P. 4264/1908, Vol. 898.

[115] *Ibid.*

[116] The creation of a new High Court could not have been undertaken without passing an Act of Parliament which required time for preparation.

[117] The London League's representation to the Under Secretary of State for India, 11 November, 1908. J. & P. 4264/1908, Vol. 898.

in civil and criminal matters, the interest of justice and convenience of suitors from eastern districts required that there should be an Appellate Branch of the High Court at Dacca.

Despite occasional waverings and a significant change of attitude towards the non-Muslim communities, as embodied in its creed, during the first twenty-three months of its existence, the League may be said to have acted in general conformity with the policy of its founders. By adding the demands for the separation of judiciary from executive and for fair treatment of South African Indians to those claimed by the Simla deputation and the Dacca conference, the League leaders showed their growing alertness towards the furtherance of Muslim interests both within and outside India. However, during this early period the major achievements of the League were the accommodation of its internal divisions and the framing of a constitution.

## Chapter III

## THE FORMATION OF PROVINCIAL ORGANISATIONS

Even before the adoption of the constitution of the All-India Muslim League in December, 1907, several members of the provisional committee of the League had set themselves the task of organising local and even provincial branches of the party. These members appear to have been more concerned with the attainment, as soon as possible, of the different objectives which they severally and jointly held to be essential for the good of the community than with observing constitutional proprieties.

Almost immediately after the inauguration of the League at Dacca, Salimullah and Nawab Ali Choudhury had begun mobilising Muslim public opinion in Eastern Bengal and Assam in favour of the new party. Early in 1907, they visited several places in the Dacca, Chittagong and Rajshahi divisions, addressing public meetings and setting up local branches of the League. They were well received at Munshiganj,[1] Comilla,[2] Pabna[3] and other important towns. However, by the end of 1907, perhaps due to some misunderstanding arising out of the limitations imposed upon the membership of the League, the Eastern Bengal leaders seem to have lost much of their enthusiasm for the League. It was not before April, 1908, that a provisional committee of the Eastern Bengal and Assam League was formed. Later, in October, 1909, this provisional committee was replaced by a formally constituted provincial League with Salimullah as president and Raziuddin Ahmad, municipal commissioner, as secretary. Other office-bearers of the Eastern Bengal and Assam League included Nawab Abdus Subhan Choudhury, Zamindar, Bogra, Wazed Ali Khan Panni, Zamindar, Mymensingh, Seraj-ul-Islam, pleader, Comilla, Syed Hussam Haidar Choudhury, Comilla, Raziuddin Ahmad Siddiqi, Zamindar, Dacca and Choudhury Rahim Nawaz Khan as vice-presidents; Ameeruddin Ahmad, municipal commissioner as joint secretary, Moulvi Sharafatullah as auditor, and

---

[1] The *Eastern Bengal and Assam Era,* 23 January, 1909.
[2] The *Englishman Weekly Summary,* 28 March, 1909.
[3] *Ibid.*

Khawaja Abdul Aziz as treasurer.[4]    The headquarters of the Eastern Bengal and Assam Muslim League was established at Dacca.

One significant aspect of the Eastern Bengal and Assam League was that most of its office-bearers were leading members of the Provincial Mahomedan Association.  Although both the League and the Association owed their origin to the same set of leaders, no attempt was made to amalgamate them till October, 1910.  At a joint meeting of the provincial League and the Association held at Dacca on 16 October, 1910, which was attended by Aziz Mirza, the then secretary of the All-India Muslim League, it was decided to merge the latter with the former.[5]  But the following year the decision was reversed.  At the insistence of Nawab Abdus Subhan Choudhury and a few others it was resolved that both organisations should exist and that while the provincial League should concern itself with the political activities only, the Mahomadan Association should concentrate its activities in the field of education and social welfare of the Muslims of the province.[6]

The establishment of a provincial Muslim League at Bombay had been undertaken by Rafiuddin Ahmad.  Through his efforts a provisional committee of the 'Deccan Provincial Muslim League' was set up at Poona in April, 1907.[7]  Towards the end of 1907, Rafiuddin Ahmad visited different districts of the Deccan acquainting himself with the municipal and other needs of the Muslims and establishing local branches of the League.[8]  The first meeting of the Deccan provincial League was held at Poona on 13 August, 1908.[9]  The meeting was presided over by Kazi Ghiyasuddin, *sirdar* of Nasik.  It was attended by delegates from Poona, Nasik, Khandesh, Satara, Sholapur, Belgaum, Dharwar, Maha-baleswar and other districts of the Deccan.  It passed several resolutions expressing loyalty to the Government, admiring 'the wisdom and capacity' displayed by Minto in the administration of India, and demanding the safeguard of Muslim interests in the local self-governing bodies.[10]  On the motion of Sirdar Bahadur Captain

[4] *Proceedings of the Third Annual Session of the A.I.M.L.*, held at Delhi in January, 1910, p. 108.

[5] The *Pioneer Mail*, 28 October, 1910, and the *Statesman Weekly*, 20 October, 1910.

[6] The *Statesman Weekly*, 23 March, 1911.

[7] *The Times of India Mail*, 12 October, 1907.

[8] *Ibid.*

[9] The *Bombay Gazette*, 15 August, 1908.

[10] The *Bombay Gazette*, 15 August, 1908; and the *Times of India Mail*, 15 August, 1908.

Muhammad Khan, seconded by Nawab Abdul Feroz Khan, the meeting unanimously elected the Aga Khan and Rafiuddin Ahmad as president and secretary respectively of the Deccan League.[11]

By the beginning of 1909, the leaders of the Deccan League had extended their activities throughout the Bombay Presidency. District Leagues were formed in Ahmadabad,[12] Konkan,[13] and Gujrat.[14] Consequently a conference of delegates of all the branches of the Deccan League held at Poona on 13 April, 1909, redesignated their organisation as the Bombay Presidency Muslim League.[15] Poona was selected as the headquarters of this League. The office-bearers of the Bombay Presidency Muslim League comprised the Aga Khan as president, Rafiuddin Ahmad as secretary and Sir Adamjee Peerbhoy, Sir Currimbhoy Ibrahim, Ghulam Muhammad Bhurgri, barrister, the Thakore Sahab of Amod, the Nawab of Wai and Cassim Ali Jairajbhoy Peerbhoy, merchant, as vice-presidents.

The list of office-bearers of the Bombay Presidency League, though impressive, did not include any influential and active Muslim politicians of Bombay city. It appears that a section of the leaders of the Anjuman-i-Islam, Bombay, who had for several years collaborated with the Indian National Congress did not co-operate with the Bombay Presidency League at the initial stage.[16] However, within about a year most of them had joined the League, thus strengthening its hold among the Muslims of Bombay.

Unlike those of Bombay, the pro-Congress Muslim leaders of Madras had been engaged in enhancing their own position and even attempted to overtake the formation of a provincial League in the Presidency. On 20 September, 1908, presiding over a Muslim public meeting held in the Madrasa-i-Azam building, Madras, Nawab Syed Muhammad expressed his surprise that, while other provinces had 'their own political League or National Association, voicing Muslim sentiments and views' on important public questions of the day, the Madras Presidency alone lacked a recognised Muslim association.[17] He, therefore, urged his listeners not to allow further time to be lost in forming an organisation

[11] *Ibid.*
[12] *The Times of India Mail,* 13 March, 1909.
[13] *Ibid.,* 27 February, 1909.
[14] *Ibid.,* 17 April, 1909.
[15] *Ibid.*
[16] Rafiuddin Ahmad's speech at the meeting of the Bombay Presidency League held in April, 1907 (*vide The Times of India Mail,* 17 April, 1909).
[17] The *Madras Weekly Mail,* 24 September, 1908.

'modelled more or less on the lines of the All-India Muslim League'. On the conclusion of Syed Muhammad's speech, Meer Abbas Ali proposed that 'an Association named the Central Muslim Association of Southern India be formed to protect the political interests of the Moslems of this Presidency'. The resolution was seconded by Abdur Rahim Shatir. At this stage Yakub Hasan moved an amendment to the effect that the matter be referred to a representative committee. He pointed out that the notice given for holding the meeting was short and that the meeting was not sufficiently representative to take any decision on such an important question.[18] He also noted that the proposed organisation should be 'run on the same lines as the All-India Muslim League'. The amendment was seconded by Khan Bahadur Waljee Laljee Sait, merchant, and supported by Maulana Ziauddin and Muhammad Azam. On this the original proposition was withdrawn and the amendment was carried.[19]

The meeting then appointed a preliminary committee consisting of forty-three members including all the Madras members of the All-India Muslim League.[20] The committee was authorised to take steps necessary for bringing the proposed organisation into existence. They were also asked to give wide publicity to the idea, to communicate with different parts of the mofussil, and to submit the question for final discussion and settlement at a representative meeting to be held in Madras towards the end of November, 1908.[21]

The preliminary committee held a meeting on 17 October, 1908, and after protracted discussion 'decided unanimously that an organisation called "The Madras Presidency Muslim League" should be established to safeguard the political rights of the Muslims'.[22] The committee also resolved to hold a representative meeting of the Muslims of the Presidency to be presided over by Khan Bahadur Muhammad Mahmud, on 28 November, 1908, and appointed a sub-committee of five members to appeal to the Muslim public to send delegates to that meeting. The members of the sub-committee were Syed Muhammad, Ahmad Mohiuddin, Abdul Aziz Badshah Saheb, Turkish vice-Consul

---

[18]*Ibid.*

[19]*Ibid.*

[20]*Ibid.*

[21] The *Madras Weekly Mail,* 24 September and 10 December, 1909. Yakub Hasan's letter to the editor.

[22] Muhammad Mahmud's presidential address at the meeting of the Madras League held on 28 November, 1908 (*vide* the *Madras Weekly Mail,* 3 December, 1908).

Shams-ul-Ulama Moulvi Ghulam Rasool, and Maulana Amjad Ali, a leading Shia *alim*.[23]

That the preliminary committee would decide to form a provincial League had been a foregone conclusion. Syed Muhammad's participation in the Congress movement and his non-co-operation with the Simla deputation had alienated him from a large majority of the politically conscious sections of the Muslims of Madras. His initiative and anxiety for a Muslim political association on the model of the League made it clear that his differences with the League leaders had been due to his ambition as well as to differences in political conviction. Moreover, the Madras members of the All-India Muslim League, particularly the young enthusiasts Yakub Hasan and Hameed Hasan, seem to have already prepared a favourable ground for the League among a considerable section of the Muslims of Madras.

The response to the call for the formation of the Madras Presidency Muslim League was very encouraging and far in excess of the expectations of its organisers.[24] Within a few days of the launching of the project numerous letters and telegrams of support were received from various individuals all over the Presidency. The *ulama* and the merchants—the two influential sections of the Muslims of Madras—threw their full weight behind the proposal.[25] In largely attended public meetings held at Salem, Vaniyambadi, Bangalore, Trichinopoly, Udumalpet, Metapollium, Madura, Tanjore, Chidambaram, Vellore, Nellore, Guntur, Bezwada, Cocanada and other places resolutions were passed emphasising the necessity of establishing the proposed League as well as electing delegates for the purpose.[26]

The inaugural meeting of the Madras Presidency Muslim League was held at Madras on 28 November, 1908. It was attended by most of the leading Muslims of Madras city and about 150 delegates from mofussil.[27] One notable absentee in the meeting was Syed Muhammad who had been put in a delicate situation of his own making. His quest for a Muslim Association having been frustrated, Syed Muhammad had

[23] The *Madras Weekly Mail*, 12 November, 1908.

[24] Muhammad Mahmud's presidential address at the meeting of the Madras League in November, 1908. The *Madras Weekly Mail*, 3 December, 1908.

[25] An analysis of the organisers, presidents and main speakers at the various public meetings held in the interior of Madras Presidency reveal a predominant number of *Ulama* and merchants.

[26] Reports of a number of these meetings were published in the *Madras Weekly Mail*, 12, 19 and 26 November, 1908.

[27] The *Madras Weekly Mail*, 3 December, 1908.

become a party to the decision to establish the Madras Presidency League. But he seems to have been disappointed at the election of Muhammad Mahmud—a man of comparatively less political experience, as the president of the inaugural meeting of the League. Syed Muhammad's name was indirectly mentioned in connection with the publication, on the eve of the League meeting, of certain handbills alleging differences of opinion among the Muslims on the question of the formation of the Madras League.[28] Despite strong support from the Hindu press[29] the allegation had failed to deter the sympathisers of the League. In the event Syed Muhammad had perhaps thought it wise not to attend the meeting.

Nevertheless, the meeting formally resolved to form the Madras Presidency Muslim League.[30] It passed two resolutions outlining the constitution of the organisation and also decided to elect its office-bearers in a subsequent meeting to be held on 29 December, 1908. The meeting on 29 December, 1908, was attended by only those of the 159 delegates who had paid their membership fees of six rupees per head (numbering 129).[31] These members by a consensus of votes elected Ghulam Muhammad Ali Khan, the Prince of Arcot, and Muhammad Mahmud as the president and secretary respectively of the Madras Presidency League.[32] Other office-bearers elected in the meeting were Ahmad Mohiuddin and Waljee Laljee Sait vice-presidents and Rouf Ahmad Partoo, joint secretary. Later in 1910, on the resignation of Muhammad Mahmud, Yakub Hasan was elected secretary of the Madras League.

The obstacle put in the way of the foundation of the Madras Presidency League was not a phenomenon peculiar to the Muslim leaders of Madras alone. Ambition, local and personal jealousy and differences in political opinion had also delayed the establishment and proper functioning of the provincial Leagues of the Punjab, Bengal and the United Provinces of Agra and Oudh.

On the eve of the formation of the All-India Muslim League there were three broad political divisons among the Muslims of the Punjab. The Anjuman-i-Musalmani, Lahore, founded by Muharram Ali Chishti, a leading member of the Central National Mahomedan Association, had

---

[28]*Ibid.*, 10 December, 1908 (Yakub Hasan's letter to the editor).
[29]The *Indian Patriot*, 9 December (*vide* the *Madras N.N.R.*, 1908).
[30]The *Madras Weekly Mail*, 3 December, 1908.
[31]The *Madras Weekly Mail*, 31 December, 1908.
[32]*Ibid.*

been in favour of co-operating with the Punjab Congress in political matters.[33] The Muslim League brought into being by Fazl-i-Husain and a group of young men, mostly from Lahore, had not yet announced its political programme. But Fazl-i-Husain himself was ambitious and his political views had an overtone of Pan-Islamism.[34] The Anjuman-i-Islamia, the largest and most influential of the Muslim organisations in the Punjab, had taken a moderate line in politics. Its leaders, Shah Din and Shafi, though opposed to the Congress, had collaborated with the Hindus in improving the economic condition of the province.[35] They had also actively participated in the Simla Deputation in October, 1906.

Since the formation of the All-India Muslim League the leaders of the Anjuman-i-Islamia had become active in organising a provincial League in the Punjab. But the non-co-operation of Fazl-i-Husain who along with Shafi and five other Punjab leaders had been appointed members of the provisional committee of the All-India League, delayed the success of their project.

On 30 November, 1907, a meeting of the representatives of several Muslim associations from different parts of the Punjab was held at Lahore with a view to forming a provincial League. The meeting was convened by Shafi and presided over by Shah Din. It was attended by twenty-three delegates from Lahore and twenty-one delegates from mofussil associations.[36] Another thirteen delegates had telegraphed their support for the object of the meeting while regretting their inability to attend. Fazl-i-Husain did not attend this meeting or telegraph his support.

On the motion of Shaikh Abdul Qadir, barrister, Delhi, seconded by Muhammad Umar, barrister, Amritsar, and supported by Shaikh Tajuddin, pleader, Lahore, Gul Muhammad, pleader, Ferozepur, Eijaz Husain of Ambala, and Ghulam Jilani of Lyallpur, the meeting unanimously resolved to constitute itself into the "Punjab provincial branch of the All-India Muslim League".[37] The meeting also elected Shah Din and Shafi as president and secretary respectively of the provincial League. Other office-bearers elected were Shaikh Abdul Aziz,

[33] G. N. Barrier, "The Arya Samaj and the Congress Politics in the Punjab", *Journal of Asian Studies*, May, 1967, p. 373.

[34] *Supra*, p. 35.

[35] G. N. Barrier, "The Arya Samaj and the Congress Politics in the Pinjab", *op. cit.*, p. 371.

[36] *The Times of India Mail*, 7 December, 1907.

[37] *Ibid.*

editor of the *observer,* and Mahbub-ul-Alam, editor of the *Paisa Akhbar* as joint secretaries; Shaikh Ghulab Din, pleader, and Jalal Muhammad Din, barrister, as financial and assistant financial secretary respectively.[38]

The formation of the Punjab League under the chairmanship of Shah Din was welcomed by Viqar-ul-Mulk, secretary of the All-India Muslim League.[39]  At the Karachi session of the All-India Muslim League, however, the Punjab League's right to be regarded as a branch of the former was disputed by Fazl-i-Husain, who claimed an All-India Muslim League affiliation for the Muslim League formed under his initiative in 1906.[40] A decision on the matter was deferred by the All-India League till its Aligarh session in March, 1908.  At Aligarh Fazl-i-Husain was persuaded to withdraw his claim and to work in co-operation with the provincial League formed under the chairmanship of Shah Din.[41] Accordingly Fazl-i-Husain and his supporters accepted membership of the Punjab provincial League and dissolved their organisation. The differences between Shafi and Fazl-i-Husain, however, continued for several years, and until 1916, Fazl-i-Husain took only a casual interest in the activities of the provincial League.

The Punjab provincial League had not set up all its district branches[42] when in October, 1908, Shah Din resigned its presidentship to become a Judge of the Punjab Chief Court.[43]  He was succeeded by Nawab Fateh Ali Khan Qazilbash as the president of the Punjab League. Other changes in the office-bearers of the Punjab League effected in 1909, had been the inclusion of eight vice-presidents and two assistant secretaries and the abolition of the post of assistant financial secretary. The newly elected vice-presidents, Nawab Muhammad Ali Khan Qazilbash, Nawab Zulfiqar Ali Khan, Nawab Rustam Ali Khan, Malik Umar Hayat Khan Tiwana, Khan Bahadur Ahad Shah, Khawaja Yusuf Shah and Seth Adamjee Mamoonjee were drawn from the upper aristocracy of the

[38]The *Bombay Gazette, Supplement,* 7 December, 1907.

[39]Bashir Ahmad, *Mian Mohammad Shah Din,* p. 50.

[40]Azim Husain, *Fazl-i-Husain—A Political Biography,* p. 97.

[41]*Ibid.* Azim Husain's contention that the dispute between the two groups of the Punjab League was settled at the Karachi session of the All-India Muslim League is not correct. The Karachi session of the League did not transact any business except the passing of the constitution. *Vide* The *Civil and Military Gazette,* 2 January, 1908 and the *Englishman Weekly Summary,* 9 January, 1908.

[42]By June, 1909, the Punjab Muslim League had 20 district branches, all established at the initiative of Shafi, *vide* the *Times of India Mail,* 19 June, 1909.

[43]Bashir Ahmad, *Mian Mohammad Shah Din,* p. 48.

Punjab while the two assistant secretaries, Muhammad Iqbal, Ph.D., barrister, and Mirza Jalal Din, barrister, came from the middle class.[44]

The political divisions among the Muslims of Bengal on the eve of the formation of the All-India Muslim League had been on the lines of that of the Punjab. A small group of Muslims of Bengal headed by Abdul Rasool, barrister, Mujibur Rahman, editor, the *Mussalman*, Calcutta, and Abul Kasem, *aymadar*, Burdwan, had been very active in Congress politics. While recognising the need for safeguarding the special interests of the Muslim community they would not do anything that might retard the growth of nationalism in India. None of these leaders attended the inaugural meeting of the All-India Muslim League in Dacca.

A second group of Muslim politicians in Bengal whose influence was mostly concentrated among their non-Bengali co-religionists of Calcutta and its suburbs had been actively working for the advancement of Pan-Islamic interests. Its leader, Abdullah-al-Mamun Suhrawardy Ph.D., LL.D., barrister, and a renowned scholar of Arabic and Persian, had founded the Pan-Islamic Society in London, in 1905.[45] He had travelled in several Muslim countries of the Near and Middle East and had received an 'Order' of honour from the Ottoman Khalifa. He had gathered around him several enthusiastic workers at Calcutta and also secured the powerful backing of Ghulam Husain Arif, a silk magnate, and Aga Moid-ul-Islam, editor of the *Namai Muqaddas Hablul Matin*, a Persian weekly paper published from Calcutta. Abdullah Suhrawardy had attended the Dacca conference of the Muslim leaders in December, 1906, but was not included in the provisional committee of the All-India Muslim League.

The third and the major group of Muslim leaders in Bengal consisted of the colleagues and supporters of Ameer Ali and Nawab Abdul Latif. Their leaders, Ameer Husain, Nasir Husain Khan Kheyal, Shams-ul-Huda, pleader, Seraj-ul-Islam, pleader, and Abdul Hamid, editor, the *Moslem Chronicle*, had been appointed members of the provisional committee of the All-India Muslim League. At their initiative a preliminary committee of the Bengal Provincial League was established in 1908.[46] But in the process of arriving at an understanding with other groups in order to unite the Muslims of the province under the banner of the

---

[44] *Proceedings of the Third Annual Session of the A.I.M.L., op. cit.,* pp. 107–8.

[45] The *Civil and Military Gazette,* 6 April, 1911.

[46] Aziz Mirza, *Report of the All-India Muslim League,* p. 15.

League they allowed about another year to be lost without formally organising the League.

It was not until 10 January, 1909, that a decision was taken to establish a broad-based provincial League in Bengal.[47] With this end in view a representative meeting of the Muslims of West Bengal was held at 32 Ezra Street, Calcutta, under the Chairmanship of Fazle Rubbi, Dewan of the Nawab of Murshidabad. Among others Abdul Rasool, Abdullah Suhrawardy and Ghulam Husain Arif attended the meeting.[48] On the motion of Ghulam Mowla, landholder, seconded by S. M. Sharif, barrister, the meeting unanimously decided to form the Bengal Provincial Muslim League. By another resolution proposed and seconded respectively by Sultan Ahmad, barrister, and Nawab Yusuf Ali Khan, it was unanimously resolved that the representatives present at the meeting should be 'the original members' of the League.[49]

The consensus of opinion among the leaders attending the meeting was, however, short-lived. No sooner had the questions of outlining the rules and regulations and of electing office-bearers of the provincial League been raised than the anxiety of the members for positions and posts came to the surface. To Shams-ul-Huda's proposal, seconded by Irfan Ali, barrister, that there should be five vice-presidents of the League, Sultan Ahmad proposed an amendment to the effect that the number of vice-presidents be fixed at ten. The amendment was seconded by Abdullah Suhrawardy but, on second thoughts, Sultan Ahmad withdrew it. Thereupon, Abdullah Suhrawardy proposed another amendment that there should be seven vice-presidents. This was seconded by Ghulam Mowla. The amendment, having been put to the vote, was lost by one vote only.[50] On several other clauses of the constitution the meeting was divided. After long discussion and counting of votes, it was finally decided that the Bengal Provincial League should have an executive committee of twenty-five members including ten office bearers viz., one president, five vice-presidents, three secretaries and one treasurer.

The election of office-bearers was hotly contested. On Seraj-ul-Islam's motion, which was seconded by Mahmud-ul-Haque, that Jahandar Mirza, barrister, Murshidabad, be elected president of the provincial League, Gauhar Ali, barrister, proposed an amendment that Ghulam

---

[47]The *Bengalee,* 23 January, 1909.

[48]Proceedings of the Bengal Provincial League meeting held on 21 January (*vide* the *Bengalee,* 23 January, 1909).

[49]*Ibid.*

[50]*Ibid.*

Husain Arif be elected to the presidentship. The amendment, having been seconded by Mahboob Ali, was put to the vote and was lost by a big margin.[51] Of the three secretaries, Shams-ul-Huda and Naseer Husain Khan Kheyal were elected unanimously. Ghulam Husain Arif's proposal for Badruddin Hyder Choudhury, land-holder, to be one of the secretaries was lost but another proposal of his, for Mahboob Ali to be one of the secretaries, was carried. Prince Ghulam Muhammad of the former ruling family of Mysore (that of Tipu Sultan), Seraj-ul-Islam, Nawab Yusuf Ali Khan, and Ahmad Moosaji Salehji, merchant, were elected vice-presidents of the provincial League without any opposition. But Gauhar Ali's proposal for Moulvi Muhammad Yusuf to be a vice-president was defeated while S. M. Sharif's motion for Fazle Rubbi as a vice-president was carried by a majority of votes.[52]

An analysis of votes on the various clauses of the constitution as well as for the election of office-bearers of the Bengal Provincial League shows that there were two distinct groups and a few neutral members in the meeting. The two groups were led by Shams-ul-Huda and Abdullah Suhrawardy respectively. Himself a young man, Abdullah Suhrawardy had pushed Ghulam Husain Arif to the forefront. Abdul Rasool, the renowned congressman, actively supported Shams-ul-Huda and his group,[53] thus helping them to defeat Abdullah Suhrawardy's group.

Abdullah Suhrawardy and his group, however, did not take their defeat as final. On the very date of the establishment of the Bengal Provincial League they announced the formation of a provisional Committee of the 'Bengal branch of the All-India Muslim League' at a meeting held at 5 Amratola Lane, Calcutta.[54] The provisional Committee comprised one president, seven vice-presidents, three secretaries and one treasurer. As could be expected Ghulam Husain Arif was declared president and Abdullah Suhrawardy the first secretary of this Committee.

This rival Committee, styled 'Amratola Moslem League'[55] by its critics, never got off the ground. Its founders were accused of acting for self-aggrandisement.[56] Their position was seriously compromised by the publication of the text of the proceedings of the meeting held

[51] *Ibid.*
[52] *Ibid.*
[53] *Ibid.*
[54] The *Englishman*, 22 January, 1909.
[55] Letter to the editor, the *Englishman Weekly Summary*, 28 January, 1909.
[56] *Ibid.*

under the presidentship of Fazle Rubbi, in which they had taken a prominent part. Furthermore, the committee received a fatal blow by the joint statement issued by Syed Ameer Husain, and Nawab Abdul Jabbar—two of its seven vice-presidents—to the effect that they 'were not aware of any meeting of the Moslem League at 5 Amratola Lane' and 'never consented to be vice-presidents of any such League'.[57]

The attempt for a rival League having been nipped in the bud, Abdullah Suhrawardy and his supporters seem to have taken little interest in the activities of the Bengal League. But in 1911, following the King's announcement of the annulment of the partition of Bengal, Abdullah Suhrawardy initiated a new move for a change in the Muslim attitude towards the Government as well as the Hindu community.[58]

Meanwhile, in 1910, the Bengal Provincial League was reorganised with Prince Ghulam Muhammad as president and Shams-ul-Huda and Sultan Ahmad as secretary and joint secretary respectively. Other important changes in the office-bearers of the Bengal League in 1910 were the election of Abdul Rasool as treasurer and the inclusion of Mirza Shujat Ali Baig, Persian vice-consul, Shams-ul-ulama Muhammad Yusuf, Badruddin Hyder Choudhury and Syed Husain Shustry as vice-presidents.[59]

The constitution of the All-India Muslim League had provided for the creation of three separate Leagues for West Bengal, Bihar and Orissa. Thus the activities of the Bengal League had been restricted to West Bengal only. As for the other parts of the province of Bengal, Orissa had no League while Bihar had established its own League in March, 1908.

On 16 March, 1908, at a largely-attended meeting held under the presidentship of Nawab Sarfaraz Husain Khan, Ali Imam and Mazhar-ul-Haque were elected president and secretary respectively of the Bihar Provincial Muslim League.[60] The Standing Committee of the Bihar League included about one hundred representatives from various parts of Bihar.[61] Although certain prominent Muslim leaders of Bihar like Sharfuddin, Ali Imam, Hasan Imam and Mazhar-ul-Haque had been

[57] The *Bengalee,* 23 January, 1909.

[58] *Infra.,* p. 242.

[59] *Proceedings of the Third Annual General Session of the A.I.M.L., op. cit.,* p. 109.

[60] The *Pioneer Mail,* 20 March, 1908.

[61] *Ibid.*

active members of the Congress at one time or another, there seems to have been no difference of opinion among them as regards the formation of the Bihar League. However, even after the Bihar League had come into being, some of its members, particularly Hasan Imam and Mazhar-ul-Haque remained active in the Congress as well. Their common membership of the League and the Congress had created a new situation in the Muslim politics in Bihar and had facilitated the eventual understanding between the two organisations after 1912.

Like the Punjab and West Bengal, the Muslims of the United Provinces of Agra and Oudh had been divided into three main political factions. But because of the activities of Syed Ahmad Khan and other leaders of the Aligarh movement, the pan-Islamists like Mushir Husain Kidwai, barrister, and the Congressites like Nawab Sadiq Ali Khan of Lucknow, had very little influence among the Muslims of U.P. Consequently, the U.P. members of the provisional committee of the All-India Muslim League, a majority of whom had been the leading members of the Aligarh movement, encountered little factional opposition in organising the provincial League. However, partly due to the old rivalry between the leaders of Lucknow and Allahabad and partly because of the delay in setting up district Leagues all over Agra and Oudh, the provincial League of the U.P. was not formally organised till the middle of 1909.

The main burden of organising the U.P. League had been shouldered by Viqar-ul-Mulk, who had in 1907, toured various parts of the province addressing public meetings, explaining the purposes of the League and encouraging the formation of local branches.[62] Raja Naushad Ali Khan, the provisional secretary of the U.P. League,[63] Haji Riazuddin Ahmad,[64] and Muhammad Ali[65] also actively campaigned for mobilising Muslim public opinion in favour of the formation of a provincial League in U.P.

After the formation of the district Leagues, a meeting of the delegates held at Lucknow on 26 and 27 June, 1909 unanimously decided to form one provincial League instead of two for both Agra and Oudh.[66] By a consensus of opinion and after thoroughly considering

---

[62] The *Sulaimani Akhbar*, 22 January, 1907 and the *Aligarh Institute Gazette*, 14 August, 1907 (*vide* the *U.P. N.N.R.*, 1907); also the *Times of India Mail*, 21 September, 1907.

[63] The *Bombay Gazette Weekly Summary*, 26 June, 1909.

[64] Lal Bahadar, *The Muslim League, op. cit.*, p. 76.

[65] The *Israr-e-Alam*, 21 January, 1907 (*vide* the *U.P. N.N.R.*, 1907).

[66] The *Pioneer*, 30 June, 1909.

the local circumstances, the meeting also elected ten office-bearers—five each from Agra and Oudh, for the U.P. League. These office-bearers were: Abdul Majid, barrister, Allahabad, president; Raja Naushad Ali Khan, secretary; Raja Shaban Ali of Salimpur, Abdur Rouf, barrister, Allahabad, Munshi Ehtesham Ali of Kakori and Alay Nabi, pleader, Agra, vice-presidents; Syed Zahur Ahmad, pleader, Lucknow, joint secretary; Azhar Ali and Shaukat Ali assistant secretaries; and Syed Awat Ali, auditor.

Among the Muslims of various Indian provinces, those of Burma and C.P. and Berar were generally backward and lacked political consciousness. Barring the Moslem Association, Rangoon, and the Anjuman-i-Islamia, Nagpur, there seem to have had no influential Muslim associations in either of the two provinces. Consequently, the foundation of the Burma and C.P. and Berar Provincial Leagues was long delayed. In fact, the provincial Leagues of both the provinces owed their origin more to outside help than to their local leadership.

After the sessions of the All-India Mahomedan Educational Conference held in Rangoon, in December, 1909, Viqar-ul-Mulk and Aziz Mirza (later secretary of the All-India Muslim League) had stayed in Rangoon to discuss the political problems of the Muslims with the local leaders.[67] Their suggestion for the creation of a provincial League in Burma was supported by the leading members of the Moslem Association, Rangoon, who convened a public meeting on 6 January, 1910. The meeting held under the presidentship of Moulvi Ismail Khan, pleader, was well attended.[68] Both Viqar-ul-Mulk and Aziz Mirza spoke at the meeting explaining the needs and purposes of a provincial League in Burma. The meeting unanimously resolved to form the Burma Provincial Muslim League and appointed a provisional committee with Abdul Karim Abdul Shakoor Jamal and Haji Ahmad Mulla Dawood, merchants, as president and secretary respectively.[69] After a few months of organisational activities which were helped by Viqar-ul-Mulk and Aziz Mirza's tour in several important cities of the province, the provisional committee of the Burma League was re-organised. Besides Abdul Karim Abdul Shakoor Jamal as president and Ahmad Mulla Dawood as secretary, the newly-elected office-bearers of the Burma League included Ismail Khan, pleader, and Aga Mahmud, Persian vice-consul as vice-presidents; A. S. Rafiqi, barrister, as joint secretary;

[67] The *Pioneer Mail,* 14 January, 1910.
[68] *Ibid.*
[69] *Ibid.*

H. S. Mall, merchant, as treasurer; Mulla Yusuf Mulla Ismail and Y. Ghani as auditors.[70]

Towards the middle of 1910, Maulana H. M. Malek of C.P. and Berar, had been obliged to seek the help of the All-India League in organising a branch League in his province. Accordingly, Muhammad Yusuf Khan, personal assistant to the secretary of the All-India Muslim League, was deputed to C.P. and Berar.[71] Yusuf Khan made a prolonged tour of the province and succeeded in establishing a branch League in every district. At a meeting of the delegates from all the district Leagues held at Nagpur on 27 October, 1910, the Central Provinces and Berar League was formally inaugurated by Aziz Mirza.[72] Raja Muhammad Azam Shah, a scion of the old ruling family of Gondawara, was elected president and Maulana H. M. Malek was elected secretary of the C.P. and Berar League. Other office-bearers of the provincial League included sixteen vice-presidents and one joint secretary.[73]

The most important and the most effective of the branches of the All-India Muslim League during its early years was the London League established on the initiative of Ameer Ali. Since his retirement as a Judge of the Calcutta High Court, in 1904, Ameer Ali had settled in England. But his interest in the welfare of the Indian Muslims had never ceased. Through articles in learned journals and through correspondence with his former co-workers and followers, Ameer Ali had been repeatedly urging the Indian Muslims to form an all-India political association.[74] His pleadings had considerable influence with the Muslim leaders of Bengal and Eastern Bengal who had been in the vanguard of the movement that resulted in the foundation of the All-India Muslim League.[75]

Even before the constitutional structure of the All-India Muslim League was decided, Ameer Ali had taken steps to organise the Indian Muslims resident in England on a platform that would work on similar lines to that of the League in India. At a meeting held in the rooms of

---

[70] *Proceedings of the Third Annual Session of the A.I.M.L.,* p. 110.

[71] Aziz Mirza, *Report of the All-India Muslim League for 1910,* p. 15.

[72] *Ibid.,* also *The Times of India Mail,* 29 October, 1910.

[73] *Proceedings of the Annual Meeting of the A.I.M.L. held at Nagpur,* December, 1910, pp. 128–29.

[74] *Supra,* p. 33.

[75] The *Moslem Chronicle,* 25 November, 1905, whose editor Abdul Hamid was a member of the provisional committee of the A.I.M.L., had taken prominent notice of Ameer Ali's views on the necessity of a Muslim political organisation.

the Northbrook Society towards the end of 1907, a provisional committee was appointed to consider the question of a League in London
and to suggest suitable methods of carrying out its work.[76]  But a final
decision in the matter was deferred till the adoption of the rules and
regulations of the All-India Muslim League.  The All-India Muslim
League at its Aligarh session held in March, 1908, fully appreciated the
efforts of Ameer Ali and sanctioned a sum of money to help the proper
organisation of the proposed London League.[77]  Consequently, on 6
May, 1908, at a meeting of the Indian Muslims residing in London and
their sympathisers, held in the Caxton Hall, the London Branch of the
All-India Muslim League was formally inaugurated.[78]

In his presidential address at the meeting Ameer Ali enunciated the
objects of the London Branch of the All-India Muslim League as:
firstly, to promote concord and harmony 'among the different nationalities of India';  secondly, to work for the advancement of the general
interests of the Indians;  thirdly, to advance and safeguard by all constitutional means 'the special interests of the Mahomedan subjects of the
King';  and fourthly, to bring the Muslims so far as possible into touch
with the leaders of thought in England.[79]  While explaining these
objects Ameer Ali observed that though general interests of the
nationalities in India were identical, the Muslims had their own peculiar
interests which concerned only them and the government.  It was
impossible for the Muslims to merge their separate existence with that of
'any other nationality or to strive for the attainment of their ideals
under the aegis of any other organisation than their own'.[80]

Himself an eminent lawyer and jurist, Ameer Ali's main concern had
been the reform of Muslim family law in India.  He wanted the London
League to move the government for the revalidation of *Waqf-ala'l-Aulad*
(family trusts), for proper management of the existing *waqfs* and for
the legitimacy of the children of Muslim female converts.  He also
wanted the London League to take up the question of the foundation
of a mosque in London.[81]

---

[76] *Ameer Ali's Presidential Address at the Inaugural Meeting of the London
Branch of the A.I.M.L.,* India Office Tract 1113(a), p. 5.

[77] The *Aligarh Institute Gazette,* 18 March, 1908 (*vide* the *U.P. N.N.R.,*
1908).

[78] *Ameer Ali's Presidential Address at the Inaugural Meeting of the London
Branch of the A.I.M.L., op. cit.,* p. 1.

[79] *Ibid.,* p. 6.

[80] *Ibid.,* p. 7.

[81] *Ibid.,* p. 7–8.

On the conclusion of his presidential address, Ameer Ali, on behalf of the provisional committee, proposed a set of office-bearers of the London League. The proposal was seconded by M. K. Azad and unanimously carried. These office-bearers included Ameer Ali, president, Sir H. Seymour King, M.P., Sir Raymond West, Harold Cox, M.P., vice-presidents; C. A. Latif, ordinary vice-president; Abdul Ali Anik, treasurer; Ibn Ahmad, Shaikh Zahur Ahmad, and Masud-ul-Hasan, secretary, joint secretary and assistant secretary respectively; Abdul Majid, LL.D., Muhammad Iqbal, Ph.D., Dr. Ansari, M.B., and eleven others as members.[82]

The example of the British Committee of the Indian National Congress had perhaps encouraged Ameer Ali to form the London League. The two organisations, however, wholly differed in composition as well as in their method of work. While the British Committee of the Congress had been founded, managed and to some extent financed by its British members, the London League was purely an affair of the Indian Muslims, its British vice-presidents having no say in matters of policy-making and management.[83]

Although at its initiation, the London League styled itself as a branch of the All-India Muslim League, the exact nature of relationship between the two organisations was not defined at the time. From Ameer Ali's presidential address at the inaugural meeting of the London League one could realise that the London League would be more a co-ordinating than a subordinate body to the All-India League.[84] Until 1911, the two organisations collaborated closely with each other and in certain cases it was the London League that decided matters both for itself as well as for the All-India League.[85] By 1912, however, differences cropped up between the leaders of the two Leagues. The year 1912 also saw the London League styling itself 'London All-India Muslim League'. In October, 1913, there developed a crisis over the extent of the London League's independence of, or subordination to, the All-India Muslim League. Ameer Ali's insistence on the independent or semi-independent character of the London League having been objected to by Wazir Hasan,[86] the then secretary of the All-India League, the former,

---

[82] *Ibid.*, pp. 9–10.

[83] The *Pioneer Mail,* 24 June, 1910.

[84] Ameer Ali had specifically stated that the London League while co-operating with the A.I.M.L., would also strive for the welfare of the King's Muslim 'subjects in the metropolis of the British Empire'.

[85] *Infra.*, pp. 132–136.

[86] The correspondence between Ameer Ali and Wazir Hasan was published in the *Comrade,* 15 November, 1913.

together with some of his colleagues, resigned their posts.[87]   Later on, the matter was amicably settled and Ameer Ali withdrew his resignation,[88] but the London League never regained the prestige and authority it had enjoyed before the controversy.

An analysis of the political complexion of the various provincial Leagues shows that the League was not a monolithic body.  Doubtless, at the initial stage the different political groups within the League were not as distinct and clear as they were to be in 1912.  However, some of these factions were recognisable from the very beginning.  The major provincial Leagues contained three important groups—conservative, moderate and pan-Islamist.   The moderates were themselves divided into two sub-groups—pro-Congress and 'exclusive' Muslims.   Besides these groups, there were several League members—mostly young—whose political views had not yet been formulated fully.   They held liberal and progressive views and were to play an important role in the transformation of the League in December, 1912.

[87]The *Comrade*, 1 November, 1913.
[88]The *Comrade*, 10 January, 1914.

Chapter IV

## THE AGITATION FOR SEPARATE ELECTORATES

The sub-committee appointed at the Aligarh session of the All-India Muslim League held in March, 1908, to consider the Government of India's reforms proposals as adumbrated in the Home Department letter of 24 August, 1907, had forwarded its recommendations to the Government on 24 March, 1908.[1] The sub-committee had found the Government proposals too inconsiderable and asked for much more than the Muslims had been offered.

The Government of India had proposed an Imperial Advisory Council composed both of the ruling princes and the territorial magnates in British India.[2] The League sub-committee demanded the extension of the advisory council's membership to include 'influential and recognised representatives of interests in the country such as industry, commerce, [and] the learned professions'.[3] This was already a feature of the proposed advisory councils for the provinces[4] which the sub-committee had accepted as proposed. The sub-committee also demanded that the representation of the ruling chiefs in the imperial advisory council should be reduced from about a third to one-fourth of the total membership and that the Muslim membership should be determined not only on the basis of their numerical proportion but also on consideration of their political importance in the country.[5] The sub-committee objected to the proposed limitations on the powers of the members of the Imperial Advisory Council, who were to have no 'legislative recognition' or 'formal power of initiative', and were to be 'consulted individually by the Governor General, and would occasionally

---

[1] The A.I.M.L. suggestions regarding council reforms, Min. P. Correspondence Regarding Council Reforms, vol. I, part 2.

[2] Home Dept. Circular, 24 August, 1907, Proc. Home (Public), vol. 7588.

[3] The A.I.M.L. suggestions regarding council reforms, Min. P. Correspondence Regarding Council Reforms, vol. I, part 2.

[4] Home Dept. Circular, 24 August, 1907, Proc. Home (Public), vol. 7588.

[5] The A.I.M.L. suggestions regarding council reforms, Min. P. Correspondence Regarding Council Reforms, vol. I, part 2.

be called together, either in whole or in part, for the purpose of collec-
tive deliberation'.[6]     The sub-committee suggested that a member
should be able, of his own initiative, to state his views on any subject
and that he should be allowed, with proper safeguards, to put questions
to the Government and also to request the Government to communicate
his views to his colleagues on the Imperial Advisory Council. It further
suggested that the Imperial Advisory Council should meet at least
'every other year', its proceedings being made public.[7]

The League sub-committee held strong views on the method and
extent of Muslim representation in the various legislative councils.
While appreciating the Viceroy's recognition of the principle of class
representation, it regarded the number of seats allotted to the Muslims
in the Imperial Legislative Council as inadequate.  The Government
had proposed four—two separately elected and two nominated — seats
reserved for the Muslims out of a total of fifty-three seats.  The League
hoped that out of twenty official members, one Muslim might be
nominated and that one Muslim might also be nominated from among
the ruling chiefs.  But even granting that the Muslims would get a
minimum of six representatives on the Imperial Legislative Council, the
sub-committee of the League held that Muslim representation would, in
fact, be inadequate. It, therefore, demanded at least ten reserved seats—
one for each province including one each for the Central Provinces,
North-West Frontier Province and Burma—and another seat to be filled
by the Trustees of the Aligarh College.[8]   The sub-committee further
demanded that all the ten seats reserved for the Muslims were to be
elected by purely Muslim electorates and that the principle of nomination should not be applied in regard to these seats.

The League sub-committee did not oppose the provision for a majority
of official members in the Imperial Legislative Council.  However, it
asked for the reduction of the voters' qualification from income-tax
payment of Rs. 25,000 to Rs. 5,000.  It also demanded the inclusion of
educational qualifications—that graduates of not less than ten years'
standing should be eligible for voting for the members of the Imperial
Legislative Council.

The Government's proposals for provincial councils were indefinite.

---

[6] Home Dept. Circular, 24 August, 1907, Proc. Home (Public), vol. 7588.

[7] The A.I.M.L. suggestions regarding council reforms, Min. P. Correspondence Regarding Council Reforms, vol. I, part 2.

[8] The A.I.M.L. suggestions regarding council reforms, Min. P. Correspondence Regarding Council Reforms, vol. I, part 2.

The League sought to be precise in its suggestions. The Government had suggested the possibility of some reserved Muslim seats in provincial legislative councils in addition to those who would be elected in the 'ordinary manner'.[9] The League demanded a definite number of seats 'as the fixed minimum' for each province and those to be elected 'exclusively' by the Muslims of five specific categories. These were, Muslim members of municipal and district boards, fellows of local universities, graduates of five years' standing, landholders paying a land revenue of Rs. 3,000 annually and payers of income tax.[10] As for the number of Muslim members in the provincial councils, the League sub-committee proposed at least one representative from each commissioner's division.

The sub-committee asked for a definite number of Muslim representatives in the district boards and municipalities all over the country to be elected through separate Muslim electorates. It further maintained that the qualifications for electors of local self-governing bodies need not be changed and that a rental or income of ten rupees per month should be required as a qualification for a candidate for membership of a municipal board. In case of membership of a district board, however, a candidate should pay rupees one hundred per annum in either land revenue or income tax.

Before the response of the Government of India to the demands of the sub-committee was known, events in the Bombay Presidency forced the League leaders to reiterate them both in India and in England.

In July, 1908, the Government of Bombay decided to increase the number of elected representatives in municipal boards in the presidency from one-half to two-thirds. The resolution of the Bombay Government, however, did not provide for separate electorates for the Muslims as many of them had expected.[11] The leaders of the Deccan Muslim League were worried at this development. They met Sir George Clarke, the Governor of Bombay, in a deputation at Poona, on 8 September, 1908, and presented him with an address outlining the Muslim grievances regarding separate electorates and certain other matters.

The deputation was led by Rafiuddin Ahmad, secretary of the Deccan Provincial Muslim League and a member of the central committee of the All-India Muslim League. It consisted of members of the central

[9]Home Dept. Circular, 24 August, 1907, Proc. Home (Public), vol. 7588.

[10]The A.I.M.L. suggestions regarding council reforms, Min. P. Correspondence Regarding Council Reforms, vol. I, part 2.

[11]The *Khabardar*, 18 September, 1908; the *Bombay N.N.R.*, 1908.

committee of the Deccan League and delegates from its branches. They included 'scions of ancient houses, sirdars, jagirdars, members of learned professions, veterans of the King's army, captains of industry and others'.[12]

The address presented by the Deccan League deputation was similar to that of the Simla deputation in October, 1906. The main difference between the Simla and the Poona memorials was that the former was concerned with demands of Muslims from all over India, and the latter with those of the Bombay Presidency alone. The Poona memorialists, in pleading their case, drew the attention of the Governor of Bombay to the Viceroy's reply to the Simla deputation wherein he had recognised the special importance of the Muslim community and their right to separate electorates.

The Poona deputationists pointed out that as a result of the existing electoral system, no Muslim had ever been elected to such major municipalities as Poona, Surat, Ahmadnagar and Bijapur. They also complained that the attempts made by the Government in the past to secure Muslim representation through nomination was neither adequate nor had received 'the meed of popular approval'. The deputationists, therefore, urged that in all local self-governing bodies the Muslims and Hindus should be allowed to elect their own representatives separately, as was the practice in many towns of the Punjab. They further suggested that the proportion of both Hindu and Muslim representation should be fixed in accordance with 'the numerical strength, social status, local influence and special requirements' of either community.[13]

The deputationists urged that the demand for separate representation of the Muslims should not be placed on a par with those of other minorities; for unlike the Muslims, other minorities were not affected by political and historical considerations. However, they did not define or elaborate the political and historical factors which entitled the Muslims to special treatment.[14]

Other demands put forward by the deputationists included the appointment of 'a due proportion' of Muslims in the gazetted and

[12] The memorial submitted by the Deccan Provincial Muslim League to the Governor of Bombay. *Vide The Times of India Mail,* 19 September, 1908.

[13] *Ibid.*

[14] One Muslim newspaper of Bombay explained these considerations in the following words: 'The Muhammadans have long been rulers, but have now fallen from that position . . . The Parsis and for the matter of fact even Hindus, have been more fortunate in this respect. They were already subject races before . . .' *Vide* the *Khabardar,* 9 October, 1908 (*Bombay N.N.R.,* 1908).

subordinate services of the Presidency, the appointment of at least two Muslim deputy educational inspectors in each division of the Presidency, exclusively for the supervision and control of Urdu schools, the establishment of an Urdu training college, and appropriate arrangements for the teaching of Urdu as a major subject in the schools and colleges.[15]

The Governor rejected all the demands of the deputation. He observed that the actual representation of Muslims in the local self-governing bodies was 'much less unfavourable than is generally supposed'.[16] The Governor was obviously referring to the proportion of nominated Muslim members of the local bodies and ignored the fact that the deputationists were concerned with the elective and not nominated representation of the Muslims. The Governor found 'considerable practical objections' to the introduction of separate electorates in the Bombay Presidency. He was not convinced that the system of separate representation would be really advantageous to the Muslims. He was inclined to redress the deficiency in Muslim representation by nomination but overlooked the fact that with the decrease in the number of nominated seats from one-half to one-third, it would be difficult to fulfil this assurance. As regards the deputationists' objection to the system of nomination, Clarke was prepared to 'give favourable consideration to selections made by a representative Mahomedan body in each municipality'. Turning to the question of the inadequate Muslim share in the state services, the governor maintained that the deficiency was largely due to their backwardness in education. He would not concede fixing a definite number of posts in the services to be held by Muslims in proportion to their numerical strength in the Presidency because that would impair the efficiency of the administration. As for the teaching of Urdu and the place of Urdu in Muslim education, the governor thought that Urdu was not 'a vernacular language' in Bombay, and that the establishment of an Urdu college 'would not greatly improve the situation'.

The Bombay Governor's reply to the League deputation was bitterly resented by the Muslims. The *Al-Haq* termed it 'disappointing and surprising'.[17] A correspondent of the *Urdu Daily* commented—'we thought the Government had in mind some magnificent concessions for

---

[15]*Ibid.*

[16]The Bombay Governor's reply to the Deccan Provincial Muslim League's deputation on 8 September, 1908. *Vide The Times of India Mail,* 19 September, 1908.

[17]The *Al-Haq,* 26 September, 1908. *Bombay N.N.R.,* 1908.

Mahomedans but His Excellency's reply to the Muhammadan deputation . . . has disillusioned us'.[18]   The *Khabardar* observed that the
decision of the Bombay Government regarding the extension of elective
system without any consideration of communal representation, had
'painfully shattered to pieces all the bright hopes entertained by the
Muslim community throughout the Indian Empire'.[19]  The same newspaper suspected that the 'Muslims were prematurely lulled into a sense
of security by the Viceroy's public declaration [of October, 1906]
which, only a little while after, is disregarded by a provincial Government by a pronouncement of an entirely contradictory character.'[20]
An Aligarh correspondent of The *Times of India* perhaps gave the best
expression of frustration of the Muslims when he remarked that 'If this
be the reform contemplated for our own community our doom is
sealed, we are undone.'[21]

So general was the clamour against Clarke's reply to the Bombay
League deputation that the matter was soon raised in Parliament.  On
29 October, 1908, a Liberal M.P., J. D. Rees, asked the Under-Secretary
of State for India 'whether the Government of Bombay declined to
introduce the principle of communal representation of Mahomedans
upon municipal councils;  and whether if the answer be in the affirm-
ative, the rejection of this principle is consistent with its introduction
into the reforms now under consideration by the Secretary of State in
council.'[22]

The leaders of the All-India Muslim League were also very alarmed by
the Bombay Governor's reply to the Deccan League's deputation.
Viqar-ul-Mulk, one of the vice-presidents and the ex-secretary of the
League, initiated a resolution expressing the 'disappointment and
anxiety' of the Muslims of India at Clarke's speech.[23]  The meeting of
the central committee of the All-India Muslim League held on 15
November, 1908, however, deferred consideration of the matter until
the annual session scheduled for December that year.[24]

Meanwhile the anxiety of the League leaders found further expression
in the representation submitted on 11 November, 1908, by the Committee of the London League to the Under-Secretary of State for India.

[18]The *Urdu Daily,* 16 September, 1908, *ibid.*
[19]The *Khabardar,* 18 September, 1908, *ibid.*
[20]*Ibid.*
[21]*The Times of India Mail,* 3 October, 1908.
[22]Parliamentary Debates (Authorised edition) 4th series, vol. 195, cc. 476–7.
[23]*The Times of India Mail,* 21 November, 1908.
[24]*Ibid.*

Seizing the opportunity created by the King's message to the Princes and peoples of India promising reforms, the London League informed His Majesty's Government that the Muslims of India were not prepared to 'entrust their communal interests, generally speaking, to representatives of any other community'.[25] They urged the Government to ensure the separate representation of the Muslims in all the councils and representative bodies 'on an elective basis'. They also demanded that the proportion of Muslim representatives should be determined 'with a just and equitable regard not merely to their number in any particular locality but to their past traditions and their present position' as a stable element in the somewhat unstable politics of the country.[26]

The London League was not content with the submission of a memorial. Ameer Ali, the president of the London League, was convinced that in the face of severe opposition from the Congress leaders who had already taken up the matter with the Secretary of State both in private and in public,[27] mere petitioning for separate electorates was not likely to succeed. If the Congress cause was being supported by Liberal opinion in England, the League needed support from the hitherto unorganised pro-Muslims both inside and outside Parliament. Within a week of the submission of the memorial the London League held a breakfast party at the Westminster Palace Hotel which was attended by, among others, Seymour King, M.P., W. Bull, M.P., J. M. Robertson, M.P., T. Hart-Davis, M.P., and C. E. Buckland.[28]   In his address as the president of the meeting, Ameer Ali claimed that in view of the differences 'in traditions, religion, and race' the interests of Indian Muslims 'could not be identical in all respects with those of the rest of the people of India'. He stressed the necessity for 'the direct and separate representation of the Muslims in all the elective bodies in India'.[29]   Ameer Ali's speech was favourably received. Bull, Robertson

[25]Memorial submitted by the Committee of the London League to the Under Secretary of State for India, J.& P. 4264/1908, vol. 898.

[26]*Ibid.*

[27]In May, 1908, Gokhale had gone to England with a view to laying the Congress views on the proposed reforms before Morley and other prominent politicians of the day. He stayed there till the end of November and addressed several meetings.  By 18 June, it was reported in the Indian Press that 'the Government has adopted exactly what the Indian Parliamentary Committee [of the Congress] as well as Messrs. Dutt and Gokhale have suggested [on the proposed reforms]'.  (*Vide* the *Indian Mirror,* 18 June, 1908, *Bengal N.N.R.,* 1908).

[28]*The Times,* 17 December, 1908.

[29]*Ibid.*

and Hart-Davis expressed their cordial sympathy with the Indian Muslims. Raymond West, the main speaker among the guests, assured his hosts that 'the sympathy they sought would not be withheld'. He also emphasised the need for Anglo-Muslim friendship 'in all parts of the world', thereby pointing to the importance of the Indian Muslims as a part of the international world of Islam.

The apprehensions of many Muslim leaders about Morley's attitude towards separate electorates proved to be well founded. The Secretary of State's despatch of 27 November, 1908, to the Government of India adumbrating the reforms proposals made no provision for separate Muslim representation.[30] Contrary to his earlier despatch of 17 May, 1907, wherein he had approved of a system of separate electorates for Muslims,[31] Morley now suggested a new arrangement for their representation — joint electoral colleges with reservation of certain seats. He explained the scheme as follows:

> 'Let it be supposed that the total population of the province is 20 millions, of whom 15 million are Hindus and 5 million Muhammedans and the number of members to be elected 12. Then . . . nine Hindus should be elected to three Muhammedans . . . divide the province into three electoral areas, in each of which three Hindus and one Muhammedan are to be returned. Then, in each of these areas, constitute an Electoral College, consisting of, let us say, a hundred members. In order to preserve the proportion between two religions, 75 of these should be Hindus and 25 Muhammedans . . . That body would be called upon to elect three representatives for the Hindus and one for the Muhammedans.'[32]

Although the Viceroy had publicly committed himself in favour of separate electorates, the Secretary of State's proposal regarding Muslim

[30] Despatch from the Secretary of State to the Government of India, 27 November, 1908. Public Despatches to India, vol. XXIX.

[31] Paragraph 27 of the Secretary of State's despatch dated 17 May, 1907, read: '. . . I entirely accept the principle stated by your Excellency in paragraph 52, and insisted upon by the members of the representative deputation of Muhammadans received by you in October, 1906, that the Muhammadan community is entitled to a special representation on the Governor-General's and Local Legislative Councils commensurate with its numbers and political and historical importance . . . ' Public Despatches to India, vol. XXVIII.

[32] Despatch from the Secretary of State to the Government of India, 27 November, 1908. Public Despatches to India, vol. XXIX.

representation did not evoke any immediate objection from him.[33]   By 17 December, 1908, Minto had 'not had time to go into the scheme of mixed electoral colleges'.[34]   He was 'really delighted' with the Secretary of State's despatch[35] and had been busy in enlisting the support of all possible leaders of Indian opinion[36] which could 'alone secure the success of the reforms' adumbrated in the same despatch.[37]

The reaction of the Indian Muslims towards the scheme of electoral colleges was extremely adverse. The *Observer* characterised the scheme as a 'flagrant violation' of an agreed principle and a 'weak concession to agitators' which betrayed the hope of the 'loyal and less demonstrative classes of the people'.[38]   The *Paisa Akhbar* commented that the scheme could not be 'considered just by Muhammadans'.[39]   The *Vakil* remarked that Morley's despatch had 'deeply grieved and disappointed' the Muslims.[40]   It also pointed out that the Muslims were 'not satisfied even with the proposal made by Lord Minto's Government for safe-guarding their rights and have requested the Government through the All-India Moslem League to increase the proposed number of their representatives'. Since the Secretary of State had refused their demands, the *Vakil* urged the Muslims to devise means to safeguard their rights. It further advised them to follow the Biblical saying—'knock and it shall be opened unto you'.

[33] In an attempt to justify his baseless theory of 'the Minto-Moslem alliance', and to show that Minto had encouraged the Muslims against Morley's scheme, M. N. Das, in *India under Morley and Minto* (pp. 232–3) has unjustly commented that Minto had 'immediately opposed' the scheme of electoral colleges.   In support of this allegation Das has quoted from Minto's letter to Morley, dated 31 December, 1908.   But he has conveniently overlooked the fact that Minto's objections were raised at least ten days after the serious Muslim protest against the scheme was made public.   Minto himself told Morley on 31 December, 1908, that 'the Mahommedans are already in arms' about the electoral college scheme. *Vide* Minto to Morley, 31 December, 1908, Mor. P., vol. 18.

[34] Minto to Morley, 17 December, 1908. *Ibid.*

[35] *Ibid.*

[36] In response to Minto's appeal for strengthening the Government's hands by supporting the reforms proposals (*vide Proc. Council of the G.G.*, vol. XLVII, pp. 87–88) a deputation headed by the Maharaja of Durbhanga met him on 24 December, 1908, and pledged their full support behind the Government's move. *Vide* the *Bengalee,* 25 December, 1908.

[37] Minto to Morley, 17 December, 1908, Mor. P., vol. 18.

[38] The *Observer,* 23 December, 1908.   Extracts quoted in the *Civil and Military Gazette,* 27 December, 1908.

[39] The *Paisa Akhbar,* 21 December, 1908, the *Punjab N.N.R.,* 1908.

[40] The *Vakil,* 25 December, 1908, *ibid.*

The official reaction of the All-India Muslim League towards the
electoral college scheme was not made known till the Amritsar session of
30 and 31 December, 1908. But meanwhile, Ameer Ali, the president
of the London League and the president-elect for the Amritsar session,
who had stayed behind in London,[41] probably because he suspected
what Morley's despatch would contain, publicly expressed his dissatisfaction with the electoral colleges scheme on 24 December, 1908.
He pointed out that since under the proposed system the majority of
voters in an overwhelming number of cases would be non-Muslim, they
could easily elect a Muslim of their own choice even if he did not command any following among his co-religionists.[42] He asserted that no
scheme could be regarded as satisfactory unless it provided 'for a
Mahomedan electorate distinct and separate, for the Mahomedan
representatives'.[43]

The Amritsar session of the All-India Muslim League, December,
1908, was attended by a large number of League members and visitors
from many parts of the country. The proceedings of the session were
marked by a lively enthusiasm. On the second day of the conference
about two thousand people subscribed to the funds of the League.[44]
There was a remarkable unanimity of views among various speakers who
proposed, seconded and supported the fourteen resolutions that were
adopted at the session. These resolutions included the demand for
fixing a definite Muslim share in the public service on the basis of the
'numerical strength and importance' of the community;[45]  a protest
against 'the mischievous endeavour' on the part of the Congress to re-
open the ' "settled fact" ' of the partition of Bengal;[46] the demand for
the appointment of a commission 'to enquire into the number, general

---

[41] Ali Imam in his presidential address at the Amritsar session made it known
that 'unforeseen circumstances have deprived this gathering' of the presence of
Ameer Ali. (*Vide* Ali Imam's address, p. 1). But as early as 20 November, 1908,
*India,* the official organ of the British Committee of the Congress, had noted that
Ameer Ali had decided not to go to Amritsar. The same issue of the paper had
also adversely criticised Ameer Ali for his advocacy for separate electorates.

[42] The *Englishman,* Calcutta, January 13, 1909 *vide* despatch of the London
Correspondent, dated London, 24 December, 1908. (The same report was also
published in *The Times,* 26 December, 1908).

[43] *Ibid.*

[44] The *Times of India Mail,* 2 January, 1909.

[45] Resolution No. 9 adopted at the Amritsar session of the A.I.M.L. Proc.
Home (Public), Enclosure No. 28 of the Government of India's despatch, dated
22 July, 1909, vol. 8151.

[46] Resolution No. 14 passed at the Amritsar session of the A.I.M.L., *ibid.*

purposes and manner of administration' of Muslim *waqfs* designed mainly for the public benefit,[47] and the enactment of some measures to validate the Muslim law of *Waqf-ala'l-Aulad* (family endowments).[48] But in spite of the League members' genuine interest in these topics, the proposed reforms of the Government of India and the despatch of the Secretary of State became the main theme of the Amritsar session. Of the fourteen resolutions passed at Amritsar, seven were directly or indirectly concerned with the Secretary of State's despatch of 27 November, 1908.

In the absence of the Aga Khan and Syed Hasan Bilgrami, the president and secretary respectively of the All-India Muslim League, both of whom were abroad for several months,[49] the task of conducting the deliberations as well as formulating the policy and programme of the League at Amritsar devolved on Syed Ali Imam[50] who presided over the session in the absence of Ameer Ali. Ali Imam addressed the session twice on 30 December, once in the morning and again in the afternoon. In his first address Ali Imam observed that from the truly social point of view, Hindus and Muslims are 'as far apart today as they were a thousand years ago'.[51] He believed that the two communities had 'nothing in common in their traditional, religious, social and political conceptions'.[52] He was convinced that 'under the cloak of nationalism' only 'Hindu nationalism' was being preached in India. The 'sectarian cry of "Bande Mataram" as the national cry, the sectarian worship of Shivaji as the national hero and the sectarian *Rakhibandhan* as a national observance' had filled his heart with 'despair and disappointment'.[53] Himself a former Congressman, Ali Imam urged his co-religionists to hold themselves aloof from the Congress. Drawing the attention of his audience to Syed Ahmed Khan's address

---

[47]Resolution No. 10, *ibid.*

[48]Resolution No. 11, *ibid.* The question of *Waqf-ala'l-Aulad* has been explained in Chapter VI, pp. 173–174.

[49]The Aga Khan had spent most of the year in Europe and Africa. He telegraphed regretting his inability to attend the Amritsar session 'owing to illness'. (*Vide* the *Times of India Mail,* 1 January, 1909). Syed Hasan Bilgrami had been engaged in an active campaign against Morley's scheme in London in collaboration with the London League.

[50]Muhammad Ali to Dunlop Smith, 7 January, 1909. Min. P. Correspondence, India, 1909, vol. I.

[51]*Speech of Syed Ali Imam, Bar.-at-law, President, Amritsar Session of the A.I.M.L.,* 1908, p. 3.

[52]*Ibid.,* p. 4.

[53]*Ibid.,* p. 17.

at Lucknow in 1888, Ali Imam declared that the Syed's arguments against Muslims joining the Congress still held good.[54] He was, however, in favour of League-Congress co-operation on 'many questions of practical politics'. These questions of common interest included the separation of the judicial from the administrative functions of members of the Indian civil service, the repeal of 'degrading colonial ordinances', the extension of primary education, the adoption of measures of sanitation, discontinuance of official interference in matters of local self-government, the grant of commissions in the army to Indians, an equitable adjustment of 'Home charges', and establishment of village unions for the disposal of petty civil and criminal cases.[55] Ali Imam spoke eloquently of the blessings of British rule in India and offered the loyal co-operation of the League with the Government.[56]

As the presidential address mainly touched upon general themes, Ali Imam reserved his specific comments on Morley's despatch for the afternoon session. Nevertheless, taking short but incisive notice of it, he observed that the despatch had overlooked 'the principle that representation to minorities must have its origin in a denominational basis from the very start to finish, from the first voting unit to the elected representative'.[57]

Ali Imam's speech in the afternoon session dealt exclusively with the reforms proposals. His confident remarks on the proposals were that broadly the offer of a share in government made to Indians at that stage of development was not inadequate, though only advisory in character. The mere fact of 'complete withholding of administrative control from people', should not, he argued, be allowed to prevent due acknowledgement of the concession granted to the Indians to have 'their voice heard, if not necessarily acted upon, in the administration of the country'.[58] But his soft-speaking ended there. 'I do not for a moment ask it [the League] to accept the machinery that the Despatch of the Secretary of State seems to favour for the representation of minorities. No, and emphatically not so.'[59] The scheme of electoral colleges proposed by the Secretary of State was unacceptable to the Muslims both because of the inadequate number of seats assigned to

[54] *Ibid.*, p. 19.

[55] *Ibid.*, pp. 19–20.

[56] *Ibid.*, pp. 6–9 and 15 and 16.

[57] *Ibid.*, p. 27.

[58] Syed Ali Imam's speech at the Amritsar session of the A.I.M.L., Proc. Home (Public), February, 1909. Proc. No. 245, vol. 8151.

[59] *Ibid.*

them in the councils as well as of the unsatisfactory character of the system suggested for such representation. It underestimated the proportion of Muslim representation at one to three Hindus, in total disregard of 'the social, traditional and religious considerations attaching to the Indian Mahomedans'. Mere counting of heads of the two communities was 'dangerous and misleading', it further failed to recognise the service of the Muslim community to the Empire and the importance of their Pan-Islamic relations. The tendency of Morley's despatch to rely on numerical strength in estimating the significance of the Muslim community was 'not only in the highest degree prejudicial' to Muslim interest but 'exceedingly impolitic and flagrantly unfair to the Viceregal utterances [of October, 1906]'. Paragraph 12 of Morley's despatch of November, 1908, which described the method of electing Muslim representatives to the councils was contradictory to the basic principle enunciated by Morley in paragraph 9 of the same despatch. In paragraph 9 the Secretary of State had maintained that 'no system of representation should be satisfactory if it did not provide for the presence in the councils of sufficient representation of communities so important as are the Mahomedans and the landowners'. But paragraph 12 of the despatch had suggested such a method which could not secure any Muslim 'representatives' at all. It would be a system that would result 'in returning to the councils mandatories of the majorities who are "members" of our community no doubt, but certainly not "representatives" of our people', for to be members of a community was not necessarily to be its representatives.[60] The Secretary of State had evidently disregarded the Muslim demands as well as the commitments of the Viceroy presumably because 'our more enterprising Hindu countrymen have successfully secured a hearing in England'.[61]

Ali Imam delivered this second speech whilst presenting a set of three resolutions for adoption by the League. The first of these expressed thanks to the Secretary of State and the Viceroy 'for the broad and general policy foreshadowed in the Despatch dealing with the Reform scheme'.[62] The second and the third pointed out the inadequacy of the proposed Muslim representation and absolute unworkability of the method of representation suggested. The resolutions added that the Viceregal pronouncements of 1 October, 1906, should be confirmed by

[60]*Ibid.*
[61]*Ibid.*
[62]Resolution No. 1 adopted at the Amritsar session of the A.I.M.L., Proc. Home (Public), vol. 8151.

the Secretary of State and that the method of representation envisaged 'should be materially altered to suit their requirements', or else it would mark 'the first breakdown of that implicit faith which Musalmans have so long placed in the care and solicitude of the Government'.[63]

Of the three resolutions proposed by Ali Imam the League leaders were unanimous in favour of the second and the third. As regards the first resolution, there were strong differences of opinion. Muhammad Shafi, Shaikh Abdul Qadir, barrister, Delhi, and Gul Muhammad, pleader, Ferozepur, were prepared to thank Minto for his acceptance of the principle of separate electorates but they would not thank Morley because his electoral colleges scheme was considered to have been detrimental to the interests of the Muslims.[64] Khawaja Ahad Shah, proprietor of the *Observer,* even proposed to suspend the resolution of thanks altogether till such time 'when the scheme was modified in accordance with Mohammadan wishes'.[65] Viqar-ul-Mulk, Salimullah, Nawab Ali Choudhury, Rafiuddin Ahmad, Aftab Ahmad Khan and Muhammad Ali, on the other hand, found 'nothing improper in conveying thanks [both to Minto and Morley] for what was acceptable to them and pressing their views' on points where the Muslims felt aggrieved.[66] Eventually, however, the resolution was passed *nem con.*[67]

It is significant to note here that the resolution thanking the Viceroy and the Secretary of State was in itself a compromise. The League leaders were wholly and unanimously opposed to the scheme of electorates as propounded in the Secretary of State's despatch. They were also strongly of the opinion that although the Viceroy had favoured separate electorates in principle, he had not recommended an adequate number of seats for the Muslims in the various councils.[68] Consequently, in the meeting of the subjects committee a section of the delegates had objected to passing even a general vote of thanks to the Secretary of State and the Viceroy. It was after a good deal of persuasion by certain leaders and after some modifications that the subjects committee had agreed to the draft resolution presented at the

[63] Resolution Nos. 2 and 3, *ibid.*

[64] *Proc. of the Annual Meeting of the A.I.M.L. held at Amritsar on 30 and 31 December, 1908,* pp. 10—11 and 25.

[65] *Ibid.,* p. 26.

[66] *Ibid.,* pp. 12—26.

[67] *Ibid.,* p. 27.

[68] *Ibid.,* pp. 11 and 13.

open meeting.[69]   As Muhammad Ali put it in a private letter:

we [himself and a few others] wished to be more generous and emphatic in the resolution of thanks to H. E. and Lord Morley, but our Punjab friends could not curb their antipathies in their relations with their Hindu fellow-countrymen to approve of a more generous recognition of the wise and great reforms . . . There was even some churlishness . . . because Lord Morley had failed signally to provide proper and effective safeguards against the majority nominating its own ticket holders for the minority.'[70]

At the Amritsar session the most vigorous and eloquent exposition of the League case for separate electorates *vis-à-vis* the scheme of electoral colleges was given by Muhammad Ali.  Muhammad Ali contended that Morley had ignored the most potent fact that in India the cleavage between various political interests was denominational and not territorial.[71]   Hindus and Muslims stood for 'a different outlook on life, different mode of living, different temperament and necessarily different politics'.[72]   The Muslims asked for freedom against monopolists. They were not afraid of competition.  But how could there be free competition 'between constituencies for representation?  Would Ulster be satisfied with the doctrine of free competition if the members for Ulster were to be elected by free competition with the majority of Catholic Ireland?  Would England be satisfied with an arbitration court at the Hague in which her representatives were chosen by means of free competition by the larger populations of other European countries?'[73]

Muhammad Ali thought that under the electoral college scheme the lips and the tongue would be Muslims but the voice would be that of the Brahmin.  He passionately appealed to the Secretary of State to protect the Muslims who formed 'the greater Ulster' in India by providing them with separate electorates.[74]

The Amritsar session appointed a twenty-two member sub-committee to draft a memorial to be submitted to the Viceroy at the earliest

---

[69]Muhammad Ali to Dunlop Smith, 7 January, 1909. Min. P. Corr. India, 1909, vol. I.

[70]*Ibid.*

[71]*Proc. of the Annual Meeting of the A.I.M.L. held at Amritsar on 30 and 31 December, 1908*, p. 18.

[72]*Ibid.*, p. 19.

[73]*Ibid.*, p. 22.

[74]*Ibid.*, p. 21.

convenience of the latter.[75]  The committee was given the final say in
the determination of the wording of the memorial which was to be based
on the three resolutions referred to above.  The members of the sub-
committee were chosen by name but representing various provinces—
six from the U.P. (including two from Oudh), five from the Punjab,
three from Bihar, two from Eastern Bengal and Assam, one each from
West Bengal, Bombay, Madras, Burma, the North-West Frontier Province, and one from a native state.  The chairman of the committee
was to be the president of this session at Amritsar, i.e. Ali Imam, who
was to have his secretary, Mazhar-ul-Haque, also from Bihar, and to hold
sittings of the committee at a place convenient to himself with the
condition that not less than four members should form the quorum.[76]
Evidently, the sub-committee was formed without any regard for the
number of Muslims in various provinces.  Another significant feature of
this committee was that by limiting the quorum to four only and by
authorising the president to hold its meeting in the place of his convenience instead of at the office of the League, Ali Imam had been
vested with wide powers in determining the details of the proposed
memorial.

The League session also resolved upon sending some representatives
of the League to wait on Morley.[77]

The League's anxiety for separate electorates in all elective bodies was
further embodied in a resolution that reiterated the demands contained
in the address of the deputation of the Deccan League that waited upon
the governor of Bombay.  The All-India Muslim League regretted the
reply of the governor of Bombay 'to the reasonable requests' of the
Muslims of Bombay Presidency and characterised it as 'due to a serious
misconception' regarding the Muslim demands.[78]

Referring to the intention of the Government to appoint Indians to
the Executive Council of the Viceroy and the governors of Bombay and
Madras and in the event of formation of such councils in other provinces, the League urged upon the Government 'the claims of Indian
Mahomedans' and trusted that their interests would be duly considered
in making such appointments.[79]

[75] Resolution No. 6 passed at the Amritsar session of the A.M.I.L., Proc.
Home (Public), vol. 8151.

[76] Resolution No. 6 of the Amritsar session of the A.I.M.L., Proc. Home
(Public), vol. 8151.

[77] *Ibid.*

[78] Resolution No. 7 of the Amritsar session of the A.I.M.L., Proc. Home
(Public), vol. 8151.

[79] Resolution No. 5, *ibid.*

Almost simultaneously with the All-India Muslim League's session, the London League had delivered its views on the electoral colleges scheme. The resolutions of the London League, considered in some quarters as the opinion of those entitled to speak for Mahomedans in this country,[80] differed from the Amritsar resolutions only in their greater precision and point.

The resolutions of the London League were first published (in London) on 1 January, 1909.[81] *The Times* published them on 4 January along with a report of an interview with Ibn Ahmad and Major Syed Hasan Bilgrami, the secretaries respectively of the London League and of the All-India Muslim League. Both Ibn Ahmad and Bilgrami vehemently opposed the scheme of joint electoral colleges. They asserted that 'if the electoral college [scheme] was retained in its present form, the non-Moslem majority would absolutely control the elections, and would send to the colleges only such Mahomedans as would subscribe to its political doctrines'.[82] Bilgrami gave a hypothetical example in order to justify the apprehensions of the Muslims. He assumed that in a particular constituency there were five hundred voters of which one-fifth were Muslims and that the entire Muslim votes (i.e. 100) were cast in favour of a Muslim candidate. The four hundred non-Muslim voters could cast one hundred and five votes to another Muslim of their choice and could divide the remaining two hundred and ninety-five votes among four Hindu candidates, thus electing all the five members according to their will. There would thus be a Muslim member in the college representing the wishes of the Hindu majority and not those of the Muslims.[83]

*The Times'* report of Bilgrami's views sparked off a heated debate in the British press. A large number of letters both supporting the Muslim demands and opposing them continued to be published in *The Times* and other newspapers and journals[84] for several months. Ameer Ali and members of the London League fully endorsed Bilgrami's contention. They were soon supported by a powerful section of the Tory and Liberal M.P.s and by a few retired Indian civilians. The opposition to

[80] The *Englishman*, Calcutta, 21 January, 1909. Report from its London correspondent dated 1 January, 1909.

[81] The *Englishman*, 21 January, 1909.

[82] *The Times*, 4 January, 1909.

[83] *Ibid.*

[84] Among other newspapers and journals the *Manchester Guardian*, the *Empire Review*, and the *Imperial and Asiatic Quarterly Review*, took prominent part in this controversy.

Bilgrami's views, on the other hand, came from Lord Macdonnell, former Lieutenant Governor of the U.P. and a member of the Secretary of State's reforms sub-committee, who was supported by Romesh Dutt, Lajpat Rai, the members of the British Committee of the Indian National Congress, and a number of retired Anglo-Indians.

Within two days of the publication of Bilgrami's interview, Lord Macdonnell rose up in defence of the proposed electoral colleges. He wrote not as the prime author of the scheme[85] but as 'one who thinks he understands the scheme and highly approves of it'.[86] He thought that the scheme had secured to the Muslims a 'minimum representation' both in the electoral colleges and in the Legislative Councils which would be proportionate to their numbers in the population of a particular province'. It did not preclude the electors from 'giving to the minority at a particular election a larger representation than the minimum' to which they were entitled. Macdonnell also believed that although ordinarily the Hindus would elect a Hindu and the Muslims a Muslim, there would be exceptions to the rule. The exceptions, however, would not be of the kind that Bilgrami had suggested. 'There 105 votes out of the Hindu total of 400 are given to a Mahomedan not favoured by his co-religionists, leaving 295 votes for the remaining Hindu candidates. But obviously if these 295 votes are divided equally between the four Hindu candidates, the Mahomedan candidate having 100 votes will head the poll; while if the 295 votes are unequally divided, the Mahomedan candidate must certainly stand third on the list of four vacancies'. Therefore, in Macdonnell's opinion any conspiracy on the part of Hindu voters as foreseen by the League leaders, would result in doubling the Muslim representation at the expense of the Hindu. Here Macdonnell seems to have misinterpreted the scheme deliberately. As regards the Muslim demand for larger representation on the grounds of their traditions and political importance, Macdonnell observed that such ideas were impractical and opposed to 'democratic principles'.

The opinion of Macdonnell drew the attention it deserved. The following day *The Times* published two letters—one from Romesh Dutt, supporting the electoral colleges scheme and another from Captain Murray, M.P. (Liberal) accusing Macdonnell of misleading the public.

---

[85] The scheme of electoral colleges was proposed by Lord Macdonnell and adopted by the Secretary of State's special committee dealing with the reforms proposals. Mor. P., vol. 34.

[86] Lord Macdonnell's letter to *The Times,* 6 January, 1909.

Murray challenged Macdonnell's contention that any conspiracy by Hindu voters would result in the doubling of Muslim representation. He rightly noted that even if two Muslims stood among the first five to be elected, it would be 'necessary under the scheme as it now stands' to eliminate the second Mahomedan in favour of a Hindu.[87]

Romesh Dutt, like Macdonnell, was not prepared to accept any basis for the representation of various 'races and creeds in India' other than their numerical proportion in the population of the country. He argued that the scheme of electoral colleges had been conceived with the very object of safeguarding the interests of the Muslims and other minorities and that the scheme would provide the Muslims with a larger representation than any property qualification could have secured to them.[88]

Romesh Dutt's arguments failed to convince his critics that he had really answered Bilgrami's point. Crosthwaite, formerly Lieutenant-Governor of the U.P., agreed with Murray and Bilgrami that under the proposed system the Hindus could easily elect a Muslim candidate of their own choice in the face of an overwhelming majority of Muslim voters in favour of another candidate.[89] Crosthwaite warned the Government that the electoral colleges scheme 'will put in power the Hindus and in all probability the professional classes, mainly, if not entirely, lawyers'. Pointing to the recent riots on the occasion of *Bakr 'Id* reported from Titagarh, near Calcutta, he asserted that after the Hindus are put in power, they 'will not fail to make the Mahomedans feel this [power]'.[90]

By 12 January Bilgrami joined the attack on Lord Macdonnell. He was violently incensed against Macdonnell and also directed some of his overflowing anger against the Hindu community whose cause Macdonnell was apparently taking up again. Bilgrami referred to Macdonnell's role during the Persian-Nagri character dispute in the U.P. which had caused the Muslims 'great pain' and reminded him of his opposition to the partition of Bengal which had further strengthened his reputation as anti-Muslim.[91] The League secretary ridiculed Macdonnell's idea of introducing democratic principles in India as impractical. He declared that 'the Mahomedans of India as a whole and

[87]Captain Murray's letter to *The Times,* 7 January, 1909.
[88]Romesh Dutt's letter to *The Times,* 7 January, 1909.
[89]Crosthwaite's letter to *The Times,* 9 January, 1909.
[90]*Ibid.*
[91]Syed Hasan Bilgrami's letter of 7 January, 1909 to *The Times.* This letter was published on 12 January, 1909.

as represented by the All-India Muslim League' were firmly decided in favour of communal representation as the only way of securing to them their legitimate rights.    He claimed that the Muslim demands for separate electorates and weightage were accepted by Minto in October 1906.[92]

The controversy in the British press over the electoral colleges scheme and the exposition of Macdonnell's specious arguments in favour of it greatly facilitated the League's campaign for separate electorates.    The League demands were taken up by *The Times*,[93] and the Parliamentary opposition[94] and even a section of the Liberal M.P.s supported them.[95]    It was rumoured that if the Secretary of State should turn down the League's demands, Ameer Ali would 'move Lansdowne[96] to throw out the Bill [of Indian Reforms]'.[97]    These developments had a tremendous effect on Morley who was compelled to seek Minto's advice on how effectively to answer the League's objections to the scheme of electoral colleges.[98]    Minto replied that since he considered the Muslim objections to be 'perfectly sound' and since there was 'bitter Mohammadan opposition' to the scheme in India, the only safe course lay in not considering the scheme as final but merely as tentative suggestions from the Secretary of State.[99]    Thus by about the middle of January, 1909, the agitation of the League had been effective in persuading the Secretary of State to treat the proposed electoral colleges as a mere suggestion which was liable to be modified or abandoned in favour of some other scheme acceptable to the Muslim leaders.

The London League, however, persisted in its campaign against the scheme of electoral colleges until February, 1909, when Morley

[92] *Ibid.*

[93] *The Times,* 29 December, 1908, etc.  Morley was particularly worried about *The Times'* advocacy of the League's demands.  *Vide* Morley to Minto, 13 January, 1909, Mor. P., vol. 4.

[94] Morley to Minto, 7 January, 1909, Mor. P., vol. 4.

[95] Rees, Murray and a few other Liberal M.Ps. consistently supported the League demands.

[96] Lansdowne, the leader of the opposition in the Lords and a former Viceroy of India, was known to have been sympathetic towards the Muslim demands for separate electorates and weightage.

[97] In a private discussion with Ameer Ali (probably on 21 January, 1909) Morley remarked to the former '. . . I was told you were going to move Lansdowne to throw out the Bill'.  'The Memoirs of Rt. Hon. Syed Ameer Ali', *Islamic Culture,* July, 1932, p. 38.

[98] Morley to Minto, 7 January, 1909 (telegram), Mor. P., vol. 4.

[99] Minto to Morley, 8 January, 1909 (telegram), *ibid.*

publicly announced its abandonment. A long letter from Ameer Ali was published in *The Times* on 14 January, 1909. The Muslims, it said, were not against the proposed reforms; they demanded nothing more than that 'their representations on the councils and other representative bodies should be real and not illusory, substantial and not nominal'.[100]

Ameer Ali emphasised the inapplicability of the British type of Parliamentary Government to India. He laid stress on the fact that the rank and file of the Hindus and Muslims were 'still widely divided in habits, customs and traditions of race and religion'. The Hindus were eager to preserve and extend their position and the Muslims were equally desirous of having their share in the administration of the country. Under the existing conditions and in the present stage of feelings among the general body of Hindus and Muslims, a system of popular electorates as recommended by Morley would 'lead to constant friction, heartburnings and complaints'.

Ameer Ali believed that a mixed electorate was also unworkable on economic grounds. The Hindus and Muslims often greatly differed in 'material circumstances'. The Hindus had monopolised the vocations of *Sowcar, Mahajan* and *Buniah*. In the legal and other professions and in the state service there were striking disparities between the two communities. In the event, Ameer Ali was confident that without a modification in the proposed franchise qualifications, the number of voters among the less affluent Muslims would be so limited as to make Muslim representation practically of little value. Ameer Ali, therefore, wanted a wider franchise for the Muslims.

Ameer Ali thought that the census figures for the different communities in India had been juggled with so that the ratio between the Muslims and Hindus appeared larger than it actually was. The census report had shown every non-Muslim other than the followers of well recognised religions (Christianity, Buddhism etc.) as a Hindu, even though the very touch of a vast number of them was regarded as defilement by 'the real Hindus'. As Ameer Ali saw the reform proposals, the *Chandals, Chamars, Mushairs, Bhangis* and other untouchables would derive no benefit from them. But their inclusion in the Hindu category would certainly put the Muslims in a disadvantageous position.

Ameer Ali held that 'the importance of a nation' could not be judged on numerical considerations alone. He argued that, whatever might be Morley's view regarding the historical and political importance of the

[100] Ameer Ali's letter to *The Times,* 14 January, 1909.

Muslims, their 'loyalty is an asset to the Empire which I venture to submit ought not to be lightly put aside'.[101]

Ameer Ali's communication to *The Times* was well-timed. It hastened Morley's decision to grant the London League's request to wait upon him in a deputation. On the very day of the publication of Ameer Ali's letter, Morley telegraphically asked Minto if he had 'any objection' to his receiving a deputation from the London League.[102] The following day Minto wired his agreement.[103]

Before, however, Morley actually received the deputation, he met Ameer Ali privately. Although Ameer Ali was doubtful of a welcome at the India Office, he agreed to see Morley on the latter's initiative.[104] The meeting did not change Morley's estimate of Ameer Ali, whom he considered to be 'a vain creature, with a certain gift of length'.[105] Ameer Ali, on the other hand, came out of the interview with a feeling that he had been able to discuss the Muslim demands 'from every point of view'.[106] Morley had also taken from him the numerous telegrams and letters which the League chief had received from India, promising to study 'the Muslim side of the question' as contained in them. Ameer Ali was also able to allay Morley's fears of a Muslim move through Lansdowne to throw out the reforms bill, assuring him that 'my people wish to participate on equal terms in the constitutional changes; if their right to equal participation is accepted, they will not oppose them'.[107]

On 27 January, 1909, Morley received a deputation[108] from the London League, who first stated that the Muslim League in India had authorised the London League to speak on its behalf.[109] Syed Hasan Bilgrami, the Secretary of the All-India Muslim League and a member of the deputation, asserted that neither were the Muslim demands for separate electorates and weightage in representation new, nor would

[101]*Ibid.*

[102]Morley to Minto, 14 January, 1909 (telegram), Mor. P., vol. 4.

[103]Minto to Morley, 15 January, 1909 (telegram), *ibid.*

[104]Memoirs of the Rt. Hon. Syed Ameer Ali, op. cit., p. 38.

[105]Morley to Minto, 28 January, 1909, Mor. P., vol. 4.

[106]Memoirs of the Rt. Hon. Syed Ameer Ali, op. cit., p. 38.

[107]*Ibid.*

[108]The members of the deputation included Ameer Ali, Syed Hasan Bilgrami, Ibn Ahmad, C. A. Latif, A. S. M. Anik, Zahur Ahmad, Masud-ul-Hasan Siddiqi, Dr. Abdul Majid and Dr. M. A. Ansari. *Vide The Times,* 28 January, 1909.

[109]Ameer Ali's introductory speech as leader of the League deputation to the Secretary of State, 27 January, 1909. The *Englishman,* 16 February, 1909.

they be a complete innovation in India.[110]   Already in India there were
a number of municipalities where separate registers were being maintained for Hindu and Muslim voters.  Again, the number of representatives in many local self-governing bodies were already being determined
by various considerations, including population ratio.  These practices
were based on executive authority and the League now wished them to
be statutorily recognised and extended uniformly throughout the
country.

The lengthy memorial[111] submitted by the League deputation did
not go much beyond Ameer Ali's earlier statements to *The Times*.  It
did, however, express dissatisfaction with the scheme propounded in
the Government of India's despatch of 1 October, 1908, as giving too
few seats to Muslims.  It was not clear to the memorialists that in the
Viceroy's scheme the Muslims would be given 'a definite proportion of
seats'.[112]   To them it was a proposal for supplementing the deficiency
in Muslim elections 'in the ordinary manner'.  The deputationists
believed that Minto had made this provision on the assumption that
few Muslims were likely to be elected in general constituencies.  They
did not believe this assumption to be justified.

The Indian Muslims, the memorialists claimed, did not want the
double vote provided in the Government of India's scheme.  They asked
for separate electorates—pure and simple.  Separate electorates were
needed at every stage of the elective process 'from the Rural Boards
upwards to the Viceregal Legislative Councils'.

Ignoring franchise qualifications for local self-governing bodies, the
League memorandum submitted its suggestions for voters' qualifications
in the viceregal and provincial legislative councils.  The Muslim electorate for provincial legislative councils should consist of members of the
local self-governing bodies, persons eligible for such bodies, graduates of
a certain standing and landholders possessing a certain property qualification to be determined by the Government.  The Muslim electorate
for the Viceroy's Legislative Council was to be formed from the
members of the provincial councils, other persons eligible for such
membership, fellows of universities, and the delegates from various
provincial Muslim electoral colleges.[113]

[110]Syed Hasan Bilgrami's speech, *ibid.*
[111]The memorial extended over 12 quarto pages.
[112]The memorial from the London branch of the A.I.M.L. to the Secretary of
State for India. Proc. Home (Public), No. 247, February, 1909, vol. 8150.
[113]*Ibid.*

Morley's reply was designed to satisfy the deputationists only partially. He intended to remain non-committal. It was impossible 'to blurt out the full length to which we are, or may be, ready to go in the Moslem direction'.[114] He had to take care that 'in picking up the Mussalman, we don't drop our Hindu parcels'.[115] But if Minto, in 1906, had appreciated the political importance of the Muslims in the Indian context[116] alone, Morley now referred to their international importance in unmistakable terms. The Secretary of State was well aware that 'any injustice, any suspicion that we are capable of being unjust to Mahomedans in India would certainly have a very severe and injurious reaction in Constantinople'.[117] He assured the deputationists that 'the aim of the Government and yours is identical—that there shall be (to quote Mr. Ameer Ali's words) "adequate, real and genuine Mahomedan representation" '. The electoral college scheme was 'merely a suggestion thrown out for the Government of India, not a direction of the Medes and Persian stamp'. He was not sure, though he did not commit himself to this, that there might not be a separate electoral college for the Muslims. Moreover, he thought that 'an exclusively Mahomedan electorate sending their votes to an exclusively Mahomedan electoral college for the purpose of choosing a representative to sit in the provincial council', was 'not outside' his despatch.[118]

On the question of mixed electorates Morley had said as much as he could. It was out of his 'power to be over explicit about the electoral college' until he had heard the proposals of the Government of India.[119] He had made it 'plain enough to anybody accustomed to read between the lines of ministerial statements that the mixed electoral college is practically dead'.[120]

Morley's forecast regarding the probability of a separate Muslim electoral college was received by the deputationists with murmurs of approval.[121] But the League leaders 'moved uneasily in their seats' when Morley declared population strength to be the main basis for the

[114] Morley to Minto, 28 January, 1909, Mor. P., vol. 4.
[115] *Ibid.*
[116] Minto's reply to the Simla deputation, *supra,* p. 25.
[117] Morley's reply to the London League deputation, *The Times,* 28 January, 1909.
[118] *Ibid.*
[119] Morley to Minto, 28 January, 1909. Mor. P., vol. 4.
[120] *Ibid.*
[121] The *Englishman,* 16 February, 1909.

apportionment of legislative seats.[122]    The Secretary of State recognised the 'very sharp antagonism' that existed between the Hindus and
Muslims on many matters and was prepared to take note of the 'real
social forces' and 'the needs and aspirations of the communities concerned' in determining the extent of representation.  But these factors
could only be considered as modifying influences, while the numerical
proportion of a community was to form the foundation of any representative system.[123]

As regards the demand of the deputationists for a Muslim member of
the Viceroy's Executive Council, Morley was firm.  He was adamant
against any suggestion for a second Indian or Muslim member on the
Viceroy's Executive Council.  The proposed appointment of an Indian
was intended only to demonstrate the absence of any disability on the
part of the natives to hold the very highest offices.  The Secretary of
State could not and would not entertain the deputation's proposal.[124]

Morley felt that although he had conceded all 'bar the second native
member' he had not satisfied the deputationists.  'The end of my
eloquence, so I am informed, was that the honest Moslems went away
decidedly dissatisfied', observed Morley in a private letter to Minto.[125]
Morley's information was correct.  The deputationists had received the
Secretary of State's reply with mixed feelings.  The League leaders were
reluctant to declare their reaction openly, but *The Times* in a leader on
28 January, 1909, noted the Muslim dissatisfaction, particularly with
Morley's insistence on proportional representation.[126]   *The Times'*
leader revealed the conflicting reactions of the deputationists.   Ibn
Ahmad, the young secretary of the London League, now wrote to *The
Times* to support its observations:—'You correctly interpret Mahomedan
feeling when you say, with regard to the remarks of the Secretary of
State for India on the subject of proportional representation, that if
this be the final decision of the Government, it must, we are afraid,
cause grave disappointment to the Mahomedans.'[127]  Ibn Ahmad had
signed the letter as secretary of the All-India Muslim League, deliberately or otherwise. The day the letter was published in *The Times,* Syed
Hasan Bilgrami, the real secretary of the All-India Muslim League, wrote

[122]*Ibid.*
[123]Morley's reply to the London League deputation, *The Times,* 28 January,
1909.
[124]*Ibid.*
[125]Morley to Minto, 28 January, 1909, Mor. P., vol. 4.
[126]*The Times,* 28 January, 1909.
[127]*The Times,* 1 February, 1909.

to *The Times* disowning responsibility for Ibn Ahmad's statement.[128] He pointed out that Ibn Ahmad had no authority to issue any statement in the name of the All-India Muslim League, and that to the best of his knowledge, the statement had not been authorised even by the London branch of the League.[129]

It was Ameer Ali's intervention which prevented further public controversy on the matter. The meeting of the London League held on 3 February, 1909, over which Ameer Ali presided, unanimously passed a resolution confirming itself to points of agreement rather than of difference with the Secretary of State. The resolution recorded 'the acknowledgement of the All-India Moslem League for the courtesy' with which Morley had received the deputation, and expressed satisfaction at what they considered to be 'his Lordship's acceptance of the principle of separate electorates' for the Muslims.[130] It also noted the proviso laid down by Morley 'subjecting representation on numerical considerations to modifying influences', which they trusted would be applied by the Government of India and local governments 'liberally and adequately to meet Mahomedan demands'.[131] Significantly, the resolution was circulated under the joint signatures of Bilgrami and Ibn Ahmad.[132]

There was no immediate response from the All-India Muslim League to Morley's reply to the London League. Back in India, the All-India Muslim League was lagging behind its London branch in its agitation against the electoral colleges. The reforms sub-committee of the League appointed at Amritsar failed to justify its existence. Ali Imam, the chairman of the sub-committee, had seen Minto in connection with the proposed deputations of the League to the Viceroy and the Secretary of State,[133] but nothing was heard about them after the interview. Minto was opposed to receiving any League deputation himself and he did not want any such deputation from India to meet the Secretary of State.[134] Ali Imam seemed satisfied with the outcome of the interview

---

[128] *The Times,* 3 February, 1909.

[129] *Ibid.*

[130] *The Times,* 5 February, 1909.

[131] *Ibid.*

[132] *Ibid.*

[133] Dunlop Smith wrote to Muhammad Ali that Minto would discuss the question of League deputation with Ali Imam on 13 January, 1909. *Vide* D. Smith to M. Ali, 12 January, 1909. Min. P. Corr. India, 1909, vol. I.

[134] Viceroy to Secretary of State, 15 January, 1909 (tel.), Mor. P., vol. 19.

and, as later events suggested, he was persuaded by the Viceroy not to press the question of deputations any further.[135]

One week after the London League's deputation to Morley, Ali Imam, in his capacity as the chairman of the All-India Muslim League sub-committee, addressed a letter to the Viceroy in which he noted 'with a great sense of relief that portion of Lord Morley's speech in reply to the [League] deputation that dealt with the class representation as it affected the Musalmans of India'.[136] He believed that the pronouncement of the Secretary of State that the electoral colleges scheme was a mere suggestion and that there was a possibility of the election being held in two stages with 'exclusive Mahomedan electoral colleges', was read by the Indian Muslims 'with much thankfulness'. But although there was a striking similarity between Ali Imam's objections to the electoral colleges and those put forward by the London League deputation, when it came to the question of suggesting an alternative, Ali Imam differed from the deputationists. Ali Imam thought that while 'the denominational element must be carried down to the very base, the first voting unit, and that it must necessarily be carried up to the secondary agency, the electoral colleges', it was not necessary that the representative who would be elected to the councils should also belong to the religious community concerned. This altogether new and somewhat inconsistent plea was made on the ground that 'the religious faith of the man who sits in council is not of any consequence to his constituents but that his political creed is'. Ali Imam held that this plan might enable the Muslim electorate to elect a non-Muslim candidate and a non-Muslim electorate to return a Muslim candidate, thus avoiding political isolation between the various communities.[137] His evident concern to keep open the door to Hindu-Muslim co-operation in the elective bodies led him to declare that the principle of (mixed-cum-separate) electorates adumbrated in the Government of India's despatch of 1 October, 1908, had provided the means for securing sufficient Muslim representation in the councils.[138] However, as for the appointment of a

[135] After the interview Ali Imam put aside the question of the deputations without referring the matter to the A.I.M.L. Instead, he submitted a memorandum to the Viceroy which supported the Government of India's scheme of Muslim electorates and was later used by Minto against the League demand for separate electorates.

[136] Syed Ali Imam, chairman, special sub-committee of the A.I.M.L., dated 4 February, 1909, Proc. Home (Public), No. 245. February, 1909, vol. 8150.

[137] These observations in the letter were clearly contrary to the spirit and the contents of the Amritsar resolutions on reforms proposals.

[138] Syed Ali Imam's letter to the Viceroy, 4 February, 1909, Proc. Home (Public), vol. 8150.

Muslim member to the Viceroy's Executive Council, Ali Imam insisted on the League demand. He observed that the difficulties of Indianising one-third of the Executive Council, which Morley had pointed out in his reply to the League deputation in London, could easily be met by adding a seventh member.

Other League leaders did not realise the political significance of Ali Imam's letter until later when the Government of India cited him as being against exclusive separate electorates.[139] However, as soon as the contents of the letter were made public, the Deccan and the Punjab Provincial Leagues lost no time in asserting that nothing less than Muslim representatives elected by separate Muslim electorates would satisfy the Muslims.[140] Ali Imam was later charged with 'betrayal of Mahomedan interests' by the *Observer*[141] of Lahore, while the *Mihir-o-Sudhakar*, whose proprietor was a member of the League sub-committee, claimed that Ali Imam had drawn up the letter to the Viceroy in collaboration with Mazhar-ul-Haque only and that 'none of the other members of the committee' even saw the draft.[142]

Ali Imam's letter was not forwarded to the Secretary of State till May, 1909. Meanwhile, the Aga Khan, the president of the All-India Muslim League, appeared on the scene in London, meeting Morley on 14 February, 1909. Morley was then anxious 'to soften Mahometan alienation from our plans'.[143] He reassured the Aga Khan on the fulfilment of the League demands for separate electorates and weightage. However, he remained adamant against a Muslim member as such on the Viceroy's council. The Aga Khan as an individual, 'not as president of the League', did not support the proposed appointment of a native member, but since a Hindu was going to be appointed he insisted on a Muslim or at least for a guarantee that 'five years hence, when the Hindu retires, a Mahometan shall be put in'. Morley could not bind his successor, but a Muslim, he said, might get 'extra consideration' when the time came and if there was a qualified Muslim to fill the post.

The Aga Khan was satisfied with his interview with Morley. He never divulged what passed between himself and the Secretary of State, but *The Times* of 15 February, 1909, published a lengthy statement by the

[139] *Infra*, p. 130.

[140] Resolutions of the Deccan League, 13 February, 1909, quoted in *The Indian Mahomedans and the Government* issued by the London Branch of the A.I.M.L., p. 34. Also resolutions of the Punjab League, *ibid.*, pp. 42–43.

[141] The *Observer's* comment quoted in the *Times of India Mail*, 1 May, 1909.

[142] The *Mihir-o-Sudhakar*, 11 June, 1909. The *Bengal N.N.R.*, 1909.

[143] Morley to Minto, 18 February, 1909, Mor. P., vol. 4.

League president. The statement, described by Morley as the Aga Khan's views, 'before his interview with me',[144] emphasised the differences between Hindus and Muslims. 'An Act of Parliament', the Aga Khan asserted, 'can not weld into one, by general machinery, two nationalities so distinct as the Hindus and the Mahomedans.'[145] He was confident that if either of the communities secured excessive political power or was in a position to impose its will on the other, it would 'always not only be liable but compelled by religious and social circumstances to exert that authority'. The Aga Khan endorsed Ali Imam's statement at the Amritsar session of the League, and the speeches and writings of Ameer Ali in London on the subject of the proposed reforms and wished the Secretary of State to take full note of them. As regards the Indian member on the Viceroy's council, the Aga Khan had a new suggestion. If the Government was unwilling to Indianise one-third of the Viceroy's council, they could appoint one Muslim and one Hindu as advisors without any portfolio but with the same rank, status and emoluments as the executive councillors.[146]

On 23 February, 1909, the London League arranged a luncheon meeting at the Westminster Palace Hotel. The attendance included a considerable number of public men and members of Parliament. In his speech as the president of the meeting, Ameer Ali strongly reiterated the League demands. He observed that 'it was only by recognizing the differences between the two nations and their equal importance as factors in the administration of the country', that the impending reforms could be made successful.[147]

The same evening Morley, in his speech on the second reading of the Indian Councils Bill in the House of Commons, was categorical in his acceptance of the two Muslim demands. He did not think that the scheme of electoral colleges was 'a bad plan', but since the Muslims had protested against it and the Government of India also 'doubted whether our plan would work', the Secretary of State had 'abandoned it'.[148] He knew that the Muslims demanded three things. 'I had the pleasure of receiving a deputation from them and I know very well what is in their minds. They demand the election of their own representatives to these councils in all the stages' by themselves. They also wanted a number of seats in excess of their numerical strength. 'Those two

[144] *Ibid.*
[145] *The Times,* 15 February, 1909.
[146] *Ibid.*
[147] *The Times,* 24 February, 1909.
[148] Parliamentary Debates (Lords), Fifth Series, vol. I, column 125.

demands we are quite ready and intend to meet in full.'[149]  But he could not meet their demand for the appointment of a Muslim as well as a Hindu to the Viceroy's Council.[150]  Morley, in general, urged their Lordships not to forget that the difference between Islam and Hinduism was not a mere difference of articles of religious faith. It was 'a difference in life, in tradition, in history, in all the social things as well as articles of belief that constitute a community'.[151]

The suggestion that Morley had 'unexpectedly' and 'suddenly' changed his views on the question of separate electorates in order to absolve himself from the charge of having 'had a hatred of Islam'[152] is far-fetched. Morley had an open mind on the subject. On 27 May, 1907, he had 'entirely' accepted the principle of separate electorates.[153] Later on he temporarily adopted the brain-child of Lord Macdonnell. But he had no special love for the electoral college scheme and he had simply recommended it for the consideration of the Government of India.  The vigorous agitation of the League, especially its London branch, and the support it drew from the Parliamentary circles and the press, coupled with the Government of India's endorsement of the League's objections, influenced Morley finally to drop the scheme.

The Secretary of State's unequivocal declaration in favour of separate Muslim electorates and weightage in Muslim representation marked the end of the League's campaign against the electoral colleges. Morley's announcement was greeted by the London League with 'grateful acknowledgement'.[154]  The Muslim press in India also congratulated Morley on the occasion.[155]

With Morley's declaration in the Parliament the realisation of the League demands seemed virtually assured. Nevertheless, the League found itself soon involved in another agitation to keep the Government of India up to the mark in its detailed implementation of the revised proposals.

[149]*Ibid.*

[150]*Ibid.*, columns 125–126.

[151]*Ibid.*, column 126.

[152]Stanley Wolpert, *Morley and India, 1906–1910*, pp. 194–195.

[153]Despatch from the Secretary of State to the Government of India, 27 May, 1907, (paragraph 27). Despatches to India, vol. XXVIII.

[154]*The Times*, 5 March, 1909.

[155]The *Al-Bashir*, 8 March, 1909. The *U.P. N.N.R.*, 1909.

## Chapter V

## THE AGITATION AGAINST MINTO'S ELECTORAL SCHEME

The Indian Councils Bill, 1909, did not reflect in full the solemn assurances that Morley had given in connection with the representation of the Muslims. The Bill, which was based on the Government of India's despatch of October, 1908, reserved a few seats for the Muslims in the Imperial and Provincial Legislative Councils in addition to their participation in the mixed electorates. The reserved seats were fewer than the numerical strength of the Muslims justified and were to be filled partly by separate electorates and partly by nomination. But Morley had promised the Muslims seats in excess of their numerical proportion, to be filled exclusively by separate electorates.[1] The implementation of Morley's pledge was rendered all the more difficult by the Bill's fixing the maximum number of representatives in the various councils and leaving the final determination of the method and proportion of representation of different classes to the Government of India. The Indian Councils Bill, therefore, aroused misgivings among League leaders and occasioned a fresh agitation which continued till the finalisation of the rules and regulations under the Government of India Act, 1909.

The new phase of the League movement opened when the discrepancy between the pledges of Morley and the Indian Councils Bill was revealed in a speech of Buchanan, the Under Secretary of State for India, in the House of Commons on 1 April, 1909, while moving the second reading of the Bill. Buchanan stated that in consequence of the abandonment of the electoral colleges scheme, Muslim representation would be obtained 'in different ways in different provinces'.[2] He could not give the House full particulars 'as to the various policies in the various provinces' at this stage. But he was informed by the Government of India that in the United Provinces, of the four seats reserved for Muslims two would be elected by the Muslims and two nominated by the Lieutenant-Governor; in Eastern Bengal the two seats reserved

---

[1] *Supra,* Chapter IV, pp. 113–114.
[2] Buchanan's speech in the House of Commons, Parliamentary Debates–Commons, 1909, vol. III, c. 501.

for the Muslims would be filled by the nominees of 'certain Mahomadan representatives of the province'; and, in Madras, the two seats reserved for the Muslims would be filled by Government nomination.[3]  While giving these particulars Buchanan, however, made it a point to announce that the Muslims had 'a special and overwhelming claim' upon the Government.  Their claim was based on 'the solemn promises, given by those who are entitled to speak for us, that they would get adequate representation to the amount and of a kind that they want . . . From that promise we can not go back, and we will not go back'.[4]

Ameer Ali was heartened by Buchanan's general reiteration of earlier pledges but the details of Muslim representation supplied by the Under Secretary of State were plainly unsatisfactory.[5]  Ameer Ali gave his comments on Buchanan's speech in a meeting of the London League held on 2 April, 1909, at the Caxton Hall.  The meeting was presided over by A. Duchesne[6] and attended by several M.P.s.  Ameer Ali was critical of the mode of Muslim representation and its extent in various provinces as revealed by Buchanan.  He referred to the overwhelming Muslim demand for elections as against nominations.  He claimed that unless the Muslim representatives were chosen by themselves instead of by the Government, their independence would be questioned, and it would be asserted that they were voicing the opinions of the Government by whom they had been nominated.  Ameer Ali also objected to the 'utterly inadequate' provision of only two reserved seats for Muslims in Eastern Bengal and Assam.  He hoped that the detailed statement that Buchanan had made 'did not represent the final view of the Government of India or the local Governments'.[7]  Duchesne warned the Government that to refuse the reasonable demands of the Muslims 'would be to sow the seeds of mistrust which would one day bring a bitter harvest'.[8]

While the developments in London had gone ahead, the League leaders in India were still hesitant about the next move.  Ali Imam, the chairman of the special sub-committee, had moved away from the

---

[3] *Ibid.,* cc. 501–502.

[4] *Ibid.,* c. 500.

[5] Ameer Ali's speech at the meeting of the London League on 2 April, 1909. *The Times,* 3 April, 1909.

[6] Duchesne had been editor of the *Englishman*–a daily newspaper published from Calcutta for several years.

[7] *The Times,* 3 April, 1909.

[8] *Ibid.*

official policy as enunciated in the All-India Muslim League memorandum of March, 1908, and the Amritsar resolutions of December, 1908,
having already committed himself to the Government of India's scheme
without any reservation.[9]   By April 1909, he had joined hands with
Gokhale in an attempt to provide Hindu-Muslim joint support for the
Viceroy's scheme.   The Bihar Provincial Conference (though Bihar was
still a part of the province of Bengal) held on 10 April, 1909, adopted a
resolution proposed by Deep Narain and seconded by Ali Imam that
'while it is necessary in the best interests of the country that all communities should continue as at present to participate without distinction
of race or creed in election by general electorates, it is nevertheless
essential in present circumstances to secure full and adequate representation for so important a minority as the Mahomedans are by special
Mahomedan electorates.   In the opinion of this conference similar
treatment should if necessary be accorded to the Hindus where they
are in a minority.'[10]   The resolution was attributed to the 'good
influence' of Gokhale who along with another 'moderate' leader, Khare,
was present at the conference and who complimented the people of
Bihar on 'the happy way' in which Hindus and Muslims had 'settled
the question of separate Mahomedan electoral colleges'.[11]   The Bihar
resolution was along the lines of the Government of India's scheme of
October, 1908, except for the suggestion for separate Hindu electorates.

Ali Imam's 'amicable settlement'[12] with the Hindu moderates in
Bihar was severely criticised by some League leaders and Muslim newspapers.   Ehtisham Ali, a member of the All-India Muslim League
Council, questioned Ali Imam's authority to enter into a compromise
with Gokhale without consulting the League.[13]   He asserted that Ali
Imam's views as expressed at the Bihar Conference were his personal
views and that they carried no weight in the League.[14]   The *Observer*
of Lahore considered Ali Imam's performance at the Bihar Conference
a 'betrayal of Mahomedan interests' and declared that any Muslim
who opposed the demand for exclusive separate electorates for the
Muslims voiced 'no views but his own and is a traitor to the national

---

[9]*Supra*, Chapter IV, p. 111.
[10]Quoted in Ali Imam's press statement on 2 May, 1909.   The *Pioneer*,
5 May, 1909.
[11]The *Pioneer*, 12 April, 1909.
[12]The *Indian Spectator*, 17 April, 1909.
[13]Ehtisham Ali's letter to the *Pioneer*, 13 May, 1909.
[14]*Ibid.*

cause'.[15]   The *Mihir-o-Sudhakar* of Calcutta, while condemning the
conduct of Ali Imam, observed that his activities should 'teach Musalmans the folly of selecting for their leadership a man who was once an
adherent of the Congress'.[16]

Two days after the Bihar Conference, Ali Imam presided over a meeting of the central committee of the All-India Muslim League, held at
Aligarh, in which he failed to get his Bihar Conference resolution
accepted.   The central committee, however, was still seized with
Morley's announcement of 23 February, 1909, and took no notice of
the subsequent developments in London.   In a resolution, the
committee declared their readiness to participate 'in the general elections', provided all the Muslim seats due on account of their numerical
strength and half of those due to their political importance were filled
by exclusively separate electorates.[17]   This resolution, though vaguely
worded, was a repudiation of Ali Imam's claim for the League's support
for the Government of India's scheme,[18] as expressed in his letter to
the Viceroy in February that year.   Thus Ali Imam seemed to have
deviated from his unqualified support for the Government of India's
proposals.

The central committee of the League displayed a mixed reaction to
the appointment of a 'native' executive councillor, S. P. Sinha. The
latter was profusely congratulated but regrets were expressed that the
Secretary of State could not agree to the appointment of a Muslim on
the same council.[19]

The committee also recorded their 'deepest sense of regret at the
hostility displayed by certain sections of the non-Muslim population
of the country against Mahomedan claims regarding reforms', and
looked upon them as 'impolitic, short-sighted, and calculated to injure
the best interests of India and Indians generally'.[20]   The reference was

[15] The *Observer*, quoted in the *Times of India Mail*, 1 May, 1909.

[16] The *Mihir-o-Sudhakar*, 11 June, 1909. The *Bengal N.N.R.*, 1909.

[17] Resolution No. 2 adopted at the meeting of the League Central Committee
on 12 April. The *Pioneer*, 15 April, 1909.

[18] The separate Muslim representation provided in the Government of India's
scheme of October, 1908, was less than proportionate to the numerical strength
of the Muslims;   it did not provide any seat for the Muslims on grounds of their
'political importance'.

[19] Resolution No. 3 passed at the League Central Committee meeting on
12 April. The *Pioneer*, 15 April, 1909.

[20] *Ibid.*

to the hostile Hindu agitation against the principle of separate electorates and Morley's acceptance of that principle.[21]

Shortly after the League central committee's meeting at Aligarh, Ali Imam observed that he wanted the Government of India's scheme to be modified in accordance with the Aligarh resolution.[22] The Government of India's scheme had provided for five seats for the Muslims in the Viceroy's Legislative Council. Ali Imam now thought that if the council consisted of sixty members, including twenty-eight non-officials (as was proposed in the scheme), then the League would claim a total of ten reserved seats for the Muslims, six on the basis of their numerical strength and four on the basis of their political importance. Of these ten members, the League wanted eight to be elected on the basis of separate electorates and two to be surrendered to general electorates in lieu of Muslim participation in them.

The League central committee's conciliatory attitude towards the principle of general electorates, provided the number of Muslim representatives to be separately elected was substantially increased (by sixty per cent over the Government of India's scheme), had however, little effect on the London League and a large number of provincial and district Leagues which had already started another round of agitation for exclusively separate electorates.[23] The London League had succeeded in securing the active support of a considerable number of M.P.s during the discussion of the Indian Councils Bill at the committee stage. On 19 April, 1909, Earl Percy pointed out that the Bill was not consistent with the Secretary of State's pledge to the Muslims regarding the unqualified acceptance of their demands for separate electorates and representation in excess of their numerical strength.[24] Hobhouse,

---

[21]Morley's reply to the League deputation in January, 1909, had created anger among the Hindu leaders and associations, who violently opposed the League demands and started an agitation against separate electorates. Rashbehari Ghose, S. P. Sinha, Surendranath Banerjea, Sarada Charan Mitter and other Hindu leaders of Bengal headed the agitation (*vide The Times,* 23 and 24 February, 1909). After Morley's formal announcement regarding separate electorates in the Parliament the anti-separate electorate campaign by the Hindus spread all over India. The U.P. Association (*vide* the *Times of India Mail,* 13 March, 1909), the British Indian Association (*vide* the *Times of India Mail,* 3 April, 1909), and several other organisations and almost all Hindu newspapers joined the campaign.

[22]Ali Imam's statement to the press, 2 May, 1909, published in the *Pioneer,* 5 May, 1909.

[23]The *Times of India Mail,* 8 May, 1909.

[24]Parliamentary Debates (official reports) Commons, 1909, vol. III, cc. 1307–8.

who was officiating for Buchanan, confirmed the intention of the Government to abide by the pledges.[25]   But he could not give detailed information and only read the Viceroy's telegram of 12 April, 1909, to the Secretary of State on the matter.  The telegram read:–'The method proposed simply that in general electorates such as municipalities and district boards, and members of Provincial Councils, all sects and classes including Mohammedans, will vote together.  By this means some, but not sufficient, representation will be provided for Mohammedans.  In addition, a certain number of seats will be reserved for Mohammedans and none but Mohammedans will have a voice in filling these.  They may be filled in various ways, by election pure and simple, by election by associations, by electoral colleges, or by nomination, as circumstances of each province require . . .'

Earl Percy was not satisfied with this reply.  He again pointed out that since those numbers were allocated by the Government of India 'long before the Mahometan [*sic*] came to put their views' which were accepted by Morley, he would like to know if the Government intended to increase the number of Muslim representatives from the figures supplied by Buchanan on 1 April.  Hobhouse found it difficult to reply positively.  However, he asserted that he was authorised by the Secretary of State to make it clear that 'he stands by his declaration, and that he does not abate it in any way whatever'.[26]

Hobhouse's reply further confused the question of Muslim representation.  The League leaders, both in England and in India, were indignant at the inconsistency between the pledges given by the highest authorities on Indian affairs and the method adopted for their implementation.  The India Office was 'inundated with protest telegrams from India, and Ameer Ali and the Moslem League here [London] thundered'.[27]  No one inside the India Office pointed out that 'those pledges [of the Secretary of State and the Under Secretary] were absolutely irreconcilable with the Government of India's policy'[28] as described in their despatches and telegrams.  Until 28 April, 1909, the India Office 'took no particular notice' of the widespread Muslim opposition to the Indian Councils Bill.  It was thought that like most people they 'were asking for more'.

[25]*Ibid.*, c. 1311.

[26]*Ibid.*, c. 1312.

[27]Hirtzel, private secretary to the Secretary of State, to Dunlop Smith, private secretary to the Viceroy, 30 April, 1909, Min. P. Corr. England and Abroad, 1908–10.

[28]*Ibid.*

By the last week of April, the Parliamentary opposition, having been 'thoroughly well coached in the Mahomedan cause', brought the question of Muslim representation to a head. On 26 April, 1909, the Earl of Ronaldshay moved the following amendment to the Indian Councils Bill: '. . . the ratio of Mussalman and Hindu representation on all representative bodies, from the rural boards upwards to the Viceregal Council [must] be fixed by executive authority, and . . . in every case in which any seat on a representative body thus assigned to the Mahomedan community is to be filled by election, the necessary electorate [must] be composed exclusively of Mahomedans'.[29] Hobhouse, in reply, remarked that there had been a misunderstanding of the Viceroy's telegram of 12 April, 1909. The details of Muslim representation were still being worked out by the Government of India and the Viceroy's telegram to the Secretary of State did not close discussion.[30] He assured the House that both the Government of India and the Government at home would make efforts to remove any obstacle that might 'be found to lie within our power to the carrying out of the pledges which had been given before this House'.[31] On being interrupted by J. D. Rees, a Liberal M.P. who had supported the Muslim demands, Hobhouse again asserted that 'where elections were found possible they shall be carried on the basis of separate representation of the Mahomedan community'.[32] Ronaldshay was satisfied with Hobhouse's categorical assurances regarding the implementation of the pledges and withdrew his motion.[33]

Meanwhile, in India the agitation for separate electorates, which had received a fresh momentum from the reading of the Viceroy's telegram in the Commons, continued unabated. It was thought that the Government had surrendered the cause of the Muslims to the pressures exerted by the Hindu leaders and particularly by Gokhale.[34] Consequently, the movement for separate electorates reached its high water mark in India in April and May, 1909. A large number of public meetings were held in various parts of the country reiterating the Muslim demands and protesting against any going back from the promises given to the Muslims. The reports of the public meetings held at Lucknow,

[29] Parliamentary Debates (official reports) Commons, 1909, vol. IV, c. 33.
[30] *Ibid.*, c. 51.
[31] *Ibid.*
[32] *Ibid.*
[33] *Ibid.*, c. 60.
[34] *The Times*, 22 April, 1909. Also the *Englishman*, 21 April, 1909.

Allahabad, Fyzabad, Cawnpore, Meerut, Shahranpur, Bhandra, Rai-Bareilly, Mirzapur, Muradabad, Lahore, Sialkot, Nagpur, Jabbalpur, Basti, Gorakhpur, Madras, Muzaffarnagar, Murshidabad, Muzaffarpore, Sherpur, Dacca, Mymensingh, Tangail, Bakerganj and several other places were forwarded to the Government of India either directly or through the provincial government concerned.[35]  Some of these meetings were attended by thousands of Muslims. For the first time in the history of Indian Muslims, vast attendances by a variety of people were reported at a large number of meetings. In Lucknow and Dacca Muslim shops were closed on the day of the meetings.[36]  This was really indicative of the depth of Muslim feeling in favour of separate electorates.

The organisers and speakers at these meetings included landholders, *taluqdars,* zamindars, *raises,* pleaders, mukhtars, *pirs, ulama, peshimams, mujtahids,* titled aristocrats, government pensioners, honorary magistrates, medical practitioners, college, school and *madrasa* teachers, journalists, newspaper proprietors, businessmen, members of the vice-regal and provincial councils, and members of the district boards and municipalities.[37]  An analysis of the vocations of the participants of these meetings showed that practically almost every section of the Muslim population, English-educated or *madrasa*-educated, Shia *mujtahid* or Sunni *moulvi,* industrialist or shop-keeper, landlord or tenant, attended these meetings. This shows how the League demands for separate electorates and weightage were being generally regarded as demands of the Muslim community.

Perhaps the general Muslim support behind the League demands was due more to the peculiar characteristics of the Muslim society rather than any organisational skill of the All-India Muslim League. As

[35] For reports of most of these meetings see enclosures to the Government of India's despatch of July 22, 1909. Proc. Home (Public), vol. 8151. However, a large number of meetings held in Calcutta (*vide The Times,* 2 April, 1909), Pabna (*vide* the *Englishman Weekly Summary,* 22 April, 1909), Monghyr (*vide* the *Pioneer,* 7 April, 1909), Poona (*vide* the *Pioneer Mail,* 23 April, 1909), Broach (the *Times of India Mail,* 10 April, 1909), etc. were not reported to the Government officially.

[36] Confidential report from the Commissioner of Lucknow, 5 May, 1909, enclosure no. 176 to the Government of India's despatch of July, 1909, and letter from the Government of Eastern Bengal and Assam, 10 May, 1909, enclosed with the Government of India's despatch, July, 1909. Proc. Home (Public), vol. 8151.

[37] An analysis of the reports of the proceedings of various meetings forwarded to different provincial governments referred to above disclosed these professional groupings.

Lancelot Hare, the Lieutenant-Governor of Eastern Bengal and Assam, had rightly pointed out on an earlier occasion, unless the Muslim leaders were opposed by the *moulvi,* they could always carry the masses with them.[38]  Similar views were expressed by a League leader of Lucknow when asked by an official how they could organise the masses of the people including the Shias and the Sunnis on the same platform in spite of their religious differences.  These views were:—'We have no organisation to speak of, though the Muslim League is doing its best, but with us a man has only to stand forth and shout "Allah Akhbar" [*sic*] and every one will follow.'[39]  Whether the unity of the Muslims when called in the name of religion and religious interests was of such a unique nature (as claimed by the League leader) or not, in this instance at least the influence of Islam seemed to have been the main reason for the overwhelming Muslim support for the League demands.  The demands for separate and adequate representation of the Muslims easily captured the imagination of the *ulama.*  Some of them took a leading part in the movement itself.  As Shibli Nomani pointed out, the importance of the occasion demanded that the *ulama* should throw in their lot with the rank and file of the community.[40]

The agitation for separate electorates, while producing an unprecedented political unity among the general body of Muslims, also created a division among the Muslim members of the Indian National Congress.  A small section of the Congress Muslims including Nawab Sadiq Ali Khan,[41] Abbas Tyabji,[42] and Mushir Husain Kidwai[43] wanted joint electorates.  Other leading Muslim members of the Congress like Ibrahim Rahimtullah, Qazi Kabiruddin, Muhammad Ali Jinnah and Mazhar-ul-Haque, openly associated themselves with the League movement.  Among this latter group only Muhammad Ali Jinnah had some reservations at the beginning.  He was prepared to accept joint electorates provided one-third of the elected seats were assigned to the Muslims.[44]  He thought that in such a situation the Muslims would be

[38] Hare to Dunlop Smith, 1 September, 1906. Min. P. Corr., 1906, vol. 2.

[39] Ehtisham Ali to the Commissioner of Lucknow.  Enclosure No. 176 to the Government of India's despatch of 22 July, 1909. Proc. Home (Public), vol. 8151.

[40] Shibli Nomani's speech at a public meeting at Lucknow.  Enclosure No. 176. *Ibid.*

[41] Ram Gopal, *Indian Muslims—A Political History,* p. 104.

[42] B. B. Majumdar, *Indian Political Associations and Reform of Legislature (1818—1917),* p. 247.

[43] The *Indian Spectator,* 17 April. 1909.

[44] Jinnah's letter to the *Times of India Mail,* 20 February, 1909.

able to safeguard their interests against the majority community and at the same time avenues would be left open to both the communities to co-operate with each other which could 'in course of time nationalize them'.[45] Ultimately, however, he conformed to the League's standpoint.[46]

The overwhelming Muslim support behind the League movement was further evident from the considerable number of representations and reports submitted to the Government by various non-League associations. It is noteworthy that the Anjuman-i-Islam of Bombay, which had always supported the Congress in politics and whose former president, Badruddin Tyabji, had presided over the Indian National Congress session in 1888, was one of the non-League Muslim organisations to support the League demands for separate electorates and weightage.[47] Similarly, the All-India Shia Conference[48] and the Central National Mahomedan Association,[49] who had no love for the League as a political party also joined the League agitation. The Anjuman-i-Musalman-i-Bangala, a rival body to the Bengal Provincial Muslim League, also fully associated itself with the struggle for separate electorates.[50] The Provincial Mahomedan Association of Eastern Bengal and Assam and its branches popularised the League demands in the new province and took a prominent part in the campaign.[51] It appears from the records of the Government of India (Home, Public) and newspaper reports that as many as thirty-three non-League associations supported the League demands for separate and effective Muslim representation. Of them eighteen came from Eastern Bengal and Assam, seven from the United Provinces, four from Bengal, two from

[45] *Ibid.*

[46] Jinnah's speech in the Bombay Muslim public meeting. The *Times of India Mail,* 14 August, 1909.

[47] The representation submitted to the Government of Bombay by the Anjuman-i-Islam, Bombay (*vide* the *Times of India Mail,* 27 February, 1909).

[48] Telegram from Ali Gazanfar, secretary, All-India Shia Conference, 22 June, 1909. Enclosure no. 201 to the Government of India's despatch, 22 July, 1909, Proc. Home (Public), vol. 8151.

[49] *The Times,* 4 May, 1909.

[50] Letter from Jahandar Mirza, president Anjuman-i-Musalman-i-Bangala, 12 June, 1909. Enclosure no. 192 to the Government of India's despatch July, 1909. Proc. Home (Public), vol. 8151.

[51] Letter from the Government of Eastern Bengal and Assam, 10 May, 1909, forwarding proceedings of the public meeting held at Dacca under the auspices of the Provincial Mahomedan Association. Enclosure no. 182 to the Government of India's despatch July, 1909. Proc. Home (Public), vol. 8151.

Bombay, and one each from North-West Frontier Province and Burma.[52] Besides these non-League bodies, the Provincial Leagues of Bombay,[53] Madras,[54] the Punjab,[55] Bengal,[56] Eastern Bengal and Assam,[57] and the U.P.,[58] as well as several district Leagues[59] emphatically supported the demands for separate electorates and weightage in Muslim representation.

Simultaneously with the representations from various organisations, prominent Muslim leaders like Raja Muhammad Ali Muhammad Khan of Mahmudabad, Nawab Salimullah, Nawab Viqar-ul-Mulk, Muhammad Shafi and others, addressed individual communications to the Viceroy urging him to satisfy the Muslim claims. The Raja of Mahmudabad's memorandum asking for eight separately elected and one nominated seat for the Muslims in the Imperial Council, with the provision for a further elected seat for the Muslims of C.P., in the event of the formation of a legislative council in that province, was endorsed by a large number of Muslims. Within a few days of the submitting of the memorandum, one hundred and thirty-three telegrams were addressed to the Government of India in its support.[60]

In a series of 'private' and 'confidential' letters to the private secretary of the Viceroy, Muhammad Shafi, in his individual capacity, argued in favour of separate electorates and weightage.[61] Like many other League leaders Shafi had thought that Morley was not favourably disposed towards their claims and that his pledges were not sincere. Shafi

---

[52] See enclosures to the Government of India's despatch of 22 July, 1909, *ibid*; and the *Times of India Mail,* 6 February, 27 February, and 4 May, 1909;

[53] Telegram from Moulvi Rafiuddin, secretary Bombay Presidency League, 23 April, 1909. Enclosure no. 137 to the Government of India's despatch, 22 July, 1909. Proc. Home (Public), vol. 8151.

[54] Letter from Syed Muhammad Mahmud, secretary, Madras League, 29 April, 1909. Enclosure no. 163, *ibid.*

[55] Telegram from Muhammad Shafi, secretary, the Punjab League, 25 April, 1909. Enclosure no. 138, *ibid.*

[56] The *Englishman Weekly Summary,* 26 August, 1909.

[57] *Ibid.,* 29 April, 1909.

[58] *Ibid.,* 6 September, 1909.

[59] Telegrams and letters for and on behalf of the district Leagues of Barabanki, Hardoi, Gonda, Muzaffarpore, Shahjahanpur, and Sandila. Enclosure nos. 126, 140, 151, 190, 203, and 67 respectively to the Government of India's despatch of 22 July, 1909. Proc. Home (Public), vol. 8151.

[60] Enclosures to the Government of India's despatch, 22 July, 1908, Proc. Home (Public), vol. 8151.

[61] Muhammad Shafi to Dunlop Smith, 8, 10, 13, and 18 January; 30 April and 18 June, 1909. Min. P. Corr. India, 1909, vol. I.

was all praise for 'Minto's statesmanship, strength of purpose, tact, strong sense of fairness and justice',[62] but he never failed to protest against the Government of India's scheme. On 30 April, 1909, he warned Dunlop Smith that the 'non-fulfilment of the pledge of separate and adequate representation will not only cause deep disappointment' among the Muslims but would also be taken 'as a sign of weakness on the part of Government' before Hindu agitation against the League demands.[63]

Shafi was, however, careful enough not to prejudice the Viceroy's mind against the League. He drew a favourable picture of Muslim politics, observing that while the interests of the Muslims were 'in a line with those of their rulers', they were 'separate from and often antagonistic to those of the majority' community.[64] He conjectured that the educated Indians could be divided into three broad classes, namely, the Indian nationalists, Hindu nationalists, and the followers of the Anglo-Muhammadan school. In his opinion the Hindu nationalists consisted of moderates and extremists, while the Indian nationalists included a large number of persons belonging to miscellaneous communities and 'a very small number of Mahomedans capable, so to speak, of being counted on the fingers of the two hands'. Shafi considered himself to be a follower of the Anglo-Muhammadan school, which he thought also included the members of the All-India Muslim League. Shafi's eulogy of Minto had apparently pleased Dunlop Smith and he had promised Shafi to convey some of his letters to the Viceroy.[65] Dunlop Smith's reply to Shafi, however, did not indicate Minto's reactions to the latter's advocacy of the Muslim case and did not commit itself to Shafi's line of argument. On the other hand, the 'outburst on the part of the Mahommedans' took him 'very much by surprise'.[66] It is interesting to note that although the Viceroy did not take Shafi into his confidence, one modern writer has purposely referred to Shafi's correspondence with Dunlop Smith as evidence of the alleged 'Minto-Moslem alliance'.[67]

Shafi's reference to the members of the All-India Muslim League as loyal to the British Raj needed no confirmation. But his claim that Anglo-Muslim interests were identical was an over-statement of the

---

[62] Muhammad Shafi to Dunlop Smith, 8 January, 1909, *ibid.*
[63] Muhammad Shafi to Dunlop Smith, 30 April, 1909, *ibid.*
[64] Muhammad Shafi to Dunlop Smith, 18 June, 1909, *ibid.*
[65] Dunlop Smith to Shafi, 2 May, 1909, *ibid.*
[66] *Ibid.*
[67] M. N. Das, *India under Morley and Minto*, p. 234.

Muslim feelings of loyalty to the Raj. The struggle for separate electorates had greatly influenced the political outlook of the Indian Muslims. In the beginning they had asked for separate electorates as a favour or as a concession. With the passage of time and with the spread of agitation among various sections of the Muslims, many began to object to 'the use of the word concession; it was the right of the Mahomedans they asked for'.[68]

This gradual but unmistakable change in the concept of Muslim loyalty was noted by Raja Naushad Ali Khan in his prepared speech delivered at a public meeting held at Lucknow on 27 April, 1909. The Raja thought that 'there is a danger that the action of Government [in not fulfilling the Muslim demands] may excite the younger Muhammadans and this might lead to deeds such as to make one's hair stand on end'.[69]   A similar apprehension was expressed by Abdul Majid in a speech at Allahabad.[70]   Even the sober Musa Khan, the officiating secretary of the All-India Muslim League, felt that if the Government did not dispel the idea among the younger generation of Muslims that it had reneged from its pledges to the Musalmans because of the Hindu agitation against them, 'the result will be rather unfortunate'.[71]

The anxiety of the Muslims of India at the vacillating attitude of the Government towards the League demands was also noticeable in the contemporary newspapers and journals all over India. The native newspaper reports from different provinces showed a remarkable unanimity among the Muslim journals. The *Aligarh Institute Gazette*,[72] the *Riyaz-ul-Akhbar*,[73] the *Al-Bashir*,[74] the *Indian Daily Telegraph*,[75] the *Zulqarnain*,[76] and the *Rohilkhand Gazette*[77] from the United

---

[68] Speech by a leading member of the Anjuman-i-Musalman-i-Bangala at a public meeting held at Murshidabad. The *Pioneer Mail*, 30 April, 1909.

[69] Quoted in the confidential report of the Commissioner of Lucknow. Enclosure No. 176 to the Government of India's despatch, July, 1909. Proc. Home (Public), vol. 8151.

[70] The *Abhyudaya*, 19 February, 1909. The *U.P. N.N.R.*, 1909.

[71] Haji Musa Khan's article in the *Aligarh Institute Gazette*, 28 April, 1909, *ibid.*

[72] The *Aligarh Institute Gazette*, 10 February, 24 March, etc., 1909, *ibid.*

[73] The *Riyaz-ul-Akhbar*, 8 April, 24 April, 1909, *ibid.*

[74] The *Al-Bashir*, 26 January, 2 February, etc., 1909, *ibid.*

[75] The *Indian Daily Telegraph*, 22 April, etc., 1909, *ibid.*

[76] The *Zulqarnain*, 28 April, etc., 1909, *ibid.*

[77] The *Rohilkhand Gazette*, 8 April, etc., 1909, *ibid.*

Provinces; the *Observer*,[78] the *Paisa Akhbar*,[79] the *Vakil*,[80] and the *Watan*[81] from the Punjab; the *Mihir-o-Sudhakar*,[82] the *Soltan*,[83] and the *Darus-Saltanat*[84] from Bengal; the *Mukhbir-e-Dakhan*[85] and the *Jaridah-e-Rozgar*[86] from Madras; and the *Akhbar-e-Islam*,[87] the *Muslim Herald*[88] and the *Political Bhomiyo*[89] from Bombay, all remained occupied with the agitation for several months. The editorials, the signed articles, the letters to the editors and the reports of speeches of the Muslim leaders published in the columns of these newspapers and journals closely followed the various stages of development of the movement. It was mainly through the columns of these journals and a few Anglo-Indian newspapers[90] that several additional arguments[91] were put forward to strengthen the League demands.

[78] The *Observer*, 2 April, etc., 1909. The *Punjab N.N.R.*, 1909.

[79] The *Paisa Akhbar*, 12 March, 12 May, etc., 1909, *ibid.*

[80] The *Vakil*, 2 June, etc., 1909, *ibid.*

[81] The *Watan*, 12 March, etc., 1909, *ibid.*

[82] The *Mihir-o-Sudhakar*, 12 March, etc., 1909. The *Bengal N.N.R.*, 1909.

[83] The *Soltan*, 12 February, etc., 1909, *ibid.*

[84] The *Darus Sultanat*, 12 March, 13 April, etc., 1909, *ibid.*

[85] The *Mukhbir-e-Dakhan*, 12 May, etc., 1909. The *Madras N.N.R.*, 1909.

[86] The *Jaridah-e-Rozgar*, 20 March, etc., 1909, *ibid.*

[87] The *Akhbar-e-Islam*, 2 March, 1909. The *Bombay N.N.R.*, 1909.

[88] The *Muslim Herald*, 25 February, etc., 1909, *ibid.*

[89] The *Political Bhomiyo*, 25 June, etc., 1909, *ibid.*

[90] A majority of the Anglo-Indian newspapers supported the Muslim demands but a few like the *Indian Daily News*, the *Empire*, the *Capital*, etc., strongly opposed them.

[91] Most of the common arguments in favour of separate electorates were advanced by Ameer Ali, Syed Hasan Bilgrami, the Aga Khan and Ali Imam. *Supra*, Chapter IV, pp. 91, 97, 99, 101, 105, etc. Some of the additional arguments put forward by various newspapers and journals as well as other Muslim leaders were: Firstly, Muslims had had little advantage from the local self-governing bodies which generally elected non-Muslims as their members (*vide* Rafiuddin Ahmad's article in the *Times of India Mail*, 15 May, 1909). Secondly, Muslim members of the Imperial Council elected through mixed electorates had failed to serve the interests of the community for fear of offending the Hindu voters (*vide* Rafiuddin Ahmad's speech at Poona, the *Pioneer Mail*, 23 April, 1909). Thirdly, the Hindu predominance in the councils would enable them to prohibit cow slaughter and prevent the Muslims from performing their religious obligations by legislative enactments (*vide* the *Mihir-o-Sudhakar*, 22 January, 1909, the *Bengal N.N.R.*; also the *Agra Akhbar*, 14 January, 1909, the *U.P. N.N.R.*, 1909). Fourthly, if the Hindus and their mandatories were allowed to form a majority in the councils they would legislate for the liquidation of the Muslim majority province of Eastern Bengal and Assam and would also replace Urdu by their own language (*vide* the *Mihir-o-Sudhakar*, 22 January, 1909, the *Bengal N.N.R.*, 1909, and the

But whatever might have been the depth of Muslim feelings regarding the League demands, they appeared to have had little immediate effect either in the Government House or in the India Office. The Viceroy adhered to his own scheme of Muslim representation (as adumbrated in the Government of India's despatch of October, 1908,) and the Secretary of State did not press him to re-open the issue.

Meanwhile, by the end of April, 1909, the Secretary of State was greatly disturbed by other circumstances relating to the Muslim agitation. The discomfiture of Hobhouse in the House of Commons on 26 April, 1909, had awakened the India Office to the gravity of the situation. As the private secretary to the Secretary of State admitted, Ronaldshay's Amendment had made them 'look rather foolish' and left no other alternative for Hobhouse 'but to re-affirm the pledges and explain away (as far as possible) everything that had been said contrary to them'.[92]  It was now realized that Charles Elliot, the member of the India Council who had been dealing with the Muslim question, had 'failed' to keep the India Office 'straight' and that Morley's pledges in accepting the Muslim demands had gone much beyond the recommendations of the Viceroy.  The confusion at the India Office was also partly due to 'the ambiguous use of the words "separate electorates" ', for, as Hirtzel saw it, 'the Government of India were using them in one sense, and the Mahomedans in another, whereas we treated both as identical'. The mistake was pointed out, in the first instance, by Morison, who had replaced Charles Elliot as member of council with special responsibility for Muslim questions.  Morison had further 'revealed the fact' that the Muslims had all along considered 'the Government of India's scheme worse than the electoral colleges, but had not troubled to say so because they had assumed that when electoral colleges went *a fortiori,* the Government of India's scheme had gone also: consequently, they were *bouleversés* when Buchanan made his statement'.[93]

Morison's view of the Muslim case seems to have unnerved Morley. He could neither dispute it nor reconcile it with his assurances to the Muslims. Almost in desperation he telegraphed the Viceroy to ascertain: '(1) Whether we can reasonably maintain, in face of Mahomedan denial,

---

*Watan,* 12 March, 1909, the *Punjab N.N.R.,* 1909). Fifthly, separate electorates were nothing new. This was already in operation in Cyprus, Ceylon, Bohemia and some other countries (*vide* the *Soltan,* 21 May and the *Mihir-o-Sudhakar,* 23 April, 1909, the *Bengal N.N.R.,* 1909).

[92]Hirtzel to Dunlop Smith, 30 April, 1909.  Min. P. Corr. England and Abroad, 1908–10.

[93]*Ibid.*

that their [Government of India's] present proposal fulfils our pledges; (2) if not, whether they can be fulfilled by anything short of separate electorate in all stages for all elected Mahomedans'.[94]  The Viceroy was further advised to acquaint himself fully with the 'views of authoritative Mahomedans' by receiving a deputation or by any other means. Morley was afraid for the Indian Councils Bill when it came before the House of Lords.  The opposition had already taken up the question of Muslim representation 'with some cleverness and much pertinacity' and Morley knew that 'an astute logician would have been able to make merry over our sophisms and subterfuges'.[95]  The thing was 'horribly difficult to manage'.[96]

Minto did not share Morley's anxiety.  Contrary to his earlier expressions on the subject,[97] the Viceroy now thought 'very little' of the 'Mahomedan storm'.[98]  He was confident that his telegrams of 26 March and 12 April, 1909, to which Buchanan and Hobhouse had referred in the Commons, were 'perfectly sound and violate no pledges'.[99]  However, on an examination of the texts of the Muslim representations in the Home Department, the Viceroy was able to state his position more clearly.  He had found a passage in Ali Imam's letter of 4 February, 1909, in which the League leader had expressed the satisfaction of the Muslim community with the Government of India's despatch of 1 October, 1908.  While quoting the particular passage in a telegram to the Secretary of State on 2 May, 1909, the Viceroy claimed that 'these views were shared by the Deccan Moslem League, Bombay and [that] Madras Presidency Moslem League also intimated general approval'.[100]  He further asserted that he had received no representations from the Muslims taking exception to any essential features of the Government of India's despatch.  The Government of India had intended that 'Mahomedans should have by means of separate electorates, a number of seats closely approaching that to which their numerical proportion in the population would entitle them, and that over and

[94]Secretary of State to the Viceroy, 27 April, 1909 (telegram), Mor. P., vol. 35.

[95]Morley to Minto 28 April, 1909. Mor. P., vol. 4.

[96]*Ibid.*

[97]During the controversy over the electoral colleges Minto had supported the League's viewpoints on grounds of bitter Muslim opposition towards Morley's scheme. *Vide* Minto to Morley, 31 December, 1908, Mor. P., vol. 18.

[98]Minto to Morley, 29 April, 1909, Mor. P., vol. 20.

[99]*Ibid.*

[100]The Viceroy to the Secretary of State, 2 May, 1909, Mor. P., vol. 20.

above this they would obtain some seats in mixed electorates such as district boards, municipalities, universities, presidency corporations and as landholders'. Minto thought that the misunderstanding arising out of Hobhouse's statement was more complicated. 'I do not understand', observed the Viceroy, 'any Muhammadan here to claim the concession suggested by Hobhouse, namely, that wherever elections are found possible they should be conducted on the basis of separate representation of the Muhammadan community. If interpreted literally that would involve having separate Muhammadan electorates within the various electorates proposed, such as presidency corporations, district boards and municipalities . . . This is manifestly impracticable and has never been suggested.'[101]

Minto's interpretation of Hobhouse's speech was absolutely correct. Precisely this was the demand of the Simla deputation and of the League and it was accepted unreservedly by Minto, in October, 1906. Why the Viceroy was misrepresenting the Muslim demand is not far to seek. Two factors appear to have been responsible for the inconsistency in Minto's attitude. First, by 1909, Minto realised the practical implications of introducing separate electorates in all the elective bodies, including the councils, which had not been clear to him in 1906. Secondly, the violent Hindu agitation against separate electorates had possibly convinced him of the danger involved in annoying the most powerful of the Indian communities.

Morley, on 4 May, 1909, put the Viceroy's telegram to good use. In reply to a question from Curzon, Morley quoted extensively from Minto's telegram and claimed that Muslims were contented and grateful to the Government of India for its despatch of 1 October, 1908. As for the confusion created by the Government's statements, he admitted that it was 'easy to discover inconsistencies in a matter so intricate, complicated and difficult as this adjustment of Mahomedan representation'.[102] However, the Secretary of State assured the Lords that the Government of India's latest proposals, when fully worked out, would fulfil the pledges given to the Muslims.[103]

Minto's telegram of 2 May, 1909, as read by Morley in the House of Lords and later published as a Command paper,[104] greatly incensed the Muslim leaders both in India and in England. They considered it to be

[101]*Ibid.*
[102]Parl Debates, Lords, vol. I. c. 757.
[103]*Ibid.*, c. 758.
[104]Cd. 4652. Issued on 10 May, 1909.

a 'bolt from the blue'.[105]  On 6 May, 1909, the Committee of the London League expressed 'extreme regret and disappointment' at the views of the Viceroy and considered them to be 'absolutely at variance with the repeated assurances' given to the Muslims that their demands for separate electorates in all stages and in excess of their numerical strength would be definitely fulfilled.[106]  The London League found it difficult to reconcile the proposed arrangements (of separate-cum-mixed electorates-cum-nomination) with the unambiguous promises made by Minto on 1 October, 1906, by Morley on 23 February, 1909 and by Hobhouse on 26 April, 1909.[107]  They apprehended that 'the inconsistent and unsatisfactory manner' in which the question of Muslim representation had been dealt with would leave behind 'a rankling sense of injustice' in the minds of Muslims and earnestly hoped that the Viceroy's telegram would not be regarded as final.[108]

The latest views of the Government of India were so disturbing to the London League that throughout May and June, 1909, they campaigned vigorously against them.  At its meeting of 12 May, the Committee of the London League considered the significance of the official publication of the Viceroy's telegram of 2 May, 1909.  They took 'respectful but strong exception' to the Government's publishing 'an isolated passage' from Ali Imam's letter of 4 February.[109]  Such publication was considered to be 'likely to confuse the issues and to create a wrong impression on the public mind'.  The Committee of the London League claimed that the views expressed in that particular passage were self-contradictory and that the 'assurance' which elicited those views was 'not identical with the proposals now put forward' by the Government of India.  Moreover, Ali Imam's views 'must be read in conjunction with other portions of the document, and with recognition of the situation as it then existed'.[110]  Elsewhere in that letter Ali Imam strongly objected to mixed electorates and had demanded separate Muslim electorates from the first voting unit to the last.

[105]The *Observer*, 8 May, 1909, the *Punjab N.N.R.*, 1909.

[106]Resolution No. 1 adopted at the meeting of the London League on 6 May, 1909.  *The Indian Mahomedans and the Government*, published by the London League, pp. 51–52.

[107]Resolution Nos. 2 and 3, *ibid*.

[108]Resolution No. 4, *ibid.*, p. 52.

[109]Resolution No. 1 adopted by the London League on 12 May, *The Indian Mahomedans and the Government, op. cit.*, p. 53.

[110]Resolution No. 2, *ibid.*, pp. 53–54.

The Committee of the London League also disputed the Viceroy's contention that the Deccan and the Madras Leagues had approved of the Government of India's scheme. The Committee asserted that both these Leagues *inter alia* had definitely opposed mixed electorates in any form.

The resolutions adopted by the Deccan and the Madras Leagues confirmed the claim of the London League. As Muhammad Mahmud, secretary of the Madras Presidency Muslim League, had pointed out in his letter to the chief secretary to the Government of Madras on 5 February, 1909, the resolution adopted by the Madras Presidency Muslim League on 19 December, 1908, had expressed its satisfaction 'not with the entire scheme of Indian reforms', as expounded in the Government of India's despatch, but only with 'the recognition that was accorded in the reform proposals to the principle of class representation'.[111] The secretary of the Madras League had further noted that unless the scheme of joint electorates was so modified as to provide the Muslims with the opportunity 'to elect its own representatives through its own denominational electorates, these in their turn being brought into existence by the united action of Mahomedan electors themselves, the Mussalman community will not obtain that protection of its interests which the scheme itself seeks to give to the representation of all important interests'.[112] Similarly, the Deccan Muslim League had on a number of occasions unequivocally demanded separate electorates. Rafiuddin Ahmad, the energetic secretary of the Deccan League, was one of the earliest and most persistent supporters of separate electorates. The resolutions of the Deccan League conveyed to the Viceroy through Rafiuddin[113] did not create any confusion in any quarter. As early as 5 January, 1909, Risley, secretary of the Government of India's reforms committee, had brought it to the notice of the Viceroy that the Muslims of Bombay were demanding separate representation in all the elective bodies.[114] In the presence of these pronounced views of

[111] Muhammad Mahmud, secretary, Madras Presidency Muslim League, to the chief secretary, Govt. of Madras, 5 February, 1909. Proc. Home (Public), vol. 8150.

[112] *Ibid.*

[113] Rafiuddin Ahmad to the private secretary to the Viceroy, (telegram) 15 February, 1909. Proc. Home (Public), February, 1909. Also Rafiuddin to the private secretary to the Viceroy, 23 April, 1909. Enclosure No. 137 to the Government of India's despatch, 22 July, 1909, Proc. Home (Public), vol. 8151.

[114] Risley's note of 5 January, 1909. Min. P., Correspondence of 1909 Regarding Council Reforms.

the Deccan League, it was really difficult for the London League to reconcile the Viceroy's interpretation of the stand taken by the Deccan League.

Further, to counteract the purport of the Viceroy's telegram the London League forwarded the full text of Ali Imam's letter of 4 February to the Under Secretary and the Secretary of State.[115] The India Office was reluctant to comment officially on the controversy. Hirtzel found Ali Imam's communication to be 'a very involved letter' and thought that 'when the Mahomedans asked for separate representation *in all stages* they proposed to graft this in some way on to the electoral colleges'.[116]

The matter was taken up by the president of the London League on 20 May, 1909. In a long letter to *The Times* Ameer Ali argued that the Viceroy, by partial quotation of Ali Imam's letter to him, had managed to misrepresent its general drift.[117] Ameer Ali considered it inequitable for the Government of India 'to pin the general body of the Mahomedans down to an isolated passage from a long and somewhat discursive letter, and to meet all their demands, solemnly conceded not once but repeatedly, with a summary *non-possumus*'.[118] He cited several Muslim associations and public meetings as well as individual Muslim leaders like the Raja of Mahmudabad, the Raja of Jahangirabad, Nawab Salimullah and the Nawab of Murshidabad, who had strongly opposed mixed electorates and demanded separate electorates as the only means of securing proper Muslim representation. He feared that those representations had not reached Minto.[119]

Ameer Ali's apprehensions that Muslim representations had not reached the Viceroy appear to have been unfounded. The Home Department of the Government of India did possess most of these documents. Of two hundred and seven Muslim representations forwarded by the Government of India to the Secretary of State on 22 July, 1909,[120] at least one-fourth were definitely received in the Home Department before the Viceroy's telegram[121] of 2 May, which

---

[115] Secretary, London League, to the Private Secretary to the Secretary of State, 12 May, 1909. Mor. P., vol. 35.

[116] Note by Hirtzel on the London League's letter dated 13 May, 1909, *ibid.*

[117] *The Times,* 20 May, 1909.

[118] *Ibid.*

[119] *Ibid.*

[120] Enclosures to the Government of India's despatch, 22 July, 1909. Proc. Home (Public), vol. 8151.

[121] Enclosure Nos. 114, 149, 142, 182, 109, 137, 138, 163, 146, 147, etc., etc., *ibid.*

claimed that not a single Muslim representation demanding separate electorates was ever received by the Government. The inconsistency between the records of the Home Department and the Viceroy's telegram was probably due to the Viceroy not being properly briefed by his officials. The confusion in the Home Department was no less than that in the India Office.

Ameer Ali went on to argue that Minto's telegram had violated the pledges of the Government and had created a new situation. It had proposed two methods of electorates for the Muslims—one separate and the other mixed. Ameer Ali believed that the introduction of these methods would result in splitting the Muslim representatives into two camps. Those elected through joint electorates being 'mandatories of the majority', would not join others elected by separate electorates.[122] Furthermore, if separate electorates were practicable 'as *ex concesso* they are' for the specially elected Muslim seats, why would it be difficult to extend them to all the seats which the Muslims could rightfully claim?[123]

On 29 May, 1909, the London League reinforced its views with a sixty-page pamphlet which gave a chronological account of the Muslim case. The pamphlet styled 'The Indian Mahomedans and the Government'[124] accused the Government of India of conflicting statements and claimed that 'the Indian Mahomedans have been taken to the verge of the Land of Promise but have not been given possession'.[125]

The London League's views were fully shared by the All-India Muslim League. On 21 May, 1909, the Aga Khan endorsed in full the London League's resolutions of 6 May, 1909.[126] On 23 May, 1909, the 'extraordinary general meeting' of the All-India Muslim League held at Lucknow under the presidentship of Viqar-ul-Mulk expressed similar opinions.[127] The meeting recorded their confidence in the Aga Khan and Ameer Ali as 'the trusted representatives of the All-India Muslim League'.[128] The first resolution of the meeting expressing 'great alarm and dismay upon any intention of Government to limit separate

[122] *The Times,* 20 May, 1909.
[123] *Ibid.*
[124] *The Indian Mahomedans and the Government,* published by the London branch of the A.I.M.L., *op. cit.,* p. 1.
[125] *Ibid.,* p. 2.
[126] *The Times,* 21 May, 1909.
[127] The *Times of India Mail,* 29 May, 1909; also enclosure No. 191 of the Government of India's despatch, 22 July, 1909. Proc. Home (Public), vol. 8151.
[128] The *Times of India Mail,* 29 May, 1909.

Muhammadan representation' to a few seats as indicated in the Viceroy's telegram of 2 May, and demanding 'separate electorate composed entirely of Muhammadan electors' for all the seats to be assigned to the Muslims both on the basis of numerical strength and political importance, was moved by Ali Imam. The choice of the mover was significant since Ali Imam was being portrayed by Minto as a supporter of his scheme. Ali Imam also appeared to be conscious of the gravity of the situation. In moving the resolution he made no reference to his short-lived acclaim for Minto's proposals. On the other hand, he fully associated himself with the disappointment and indignation of the rank and file of the League members. He described the Muslims of India as a 'dynamic force' and 'trembled to pronounce the effects' of any departure by the Government from its pledges towards them. Muhammad Shafi, in seconding the resolution, was even more emphatic in his warning, remarking that 'a breach of faith in an oriental country was a most dangerous thing'. The resolution was carried, supported by Haji Musa Khan, acting secretary of the All-India Muslim League, Abdul Raoof of Allahabad, Nawab Naseer Husain Khan Kheyal of Calcutta, Raja Naushad Ali Khan of Lucknow, Muhammad Abdul Aziz of Peshawar and Ali Mahdi of Dacca.[129]

The bitter tone of the speakers and the clear and emphatic character of the Lucknow resolutions were intended to oblige the Government of India to accept the League demands in their entirety. The Viceroy, however, was not in a mood to take note of such 'cantakerousness' [sic].[130] He continued to tell the Secretary of State that Ali Imam was the 'president of the All-India Muslim League', and that the Aga Khan who had joined hands with Ameer Ali was rather 'a better authority on *"café chantants"*' than on Indian reforms.[131] The Viceroy had been plainly annoyed with Ameer Ali, the Raja of Mahmudabad[132] and other League leaders who were agitating against the Government of India's scheme. He thought that the Government of India 'having accepted the principle of distinct Mahomedan representation ought to be trusted to work it out'.[133] At this stage Minto did not like to 'risk Hindu dissatisfaction' by increasing the proportion of Muslim representatives as demanded by the League.[134]

[129] The *Pioneer,* 26 May, 1909.
[130] Minto to Morley, 27 May, 1909, Mor. P., vol. 20.
[131] *Ibid.*
[132] Minto to Morley, 10 June and 17 June, 1909, Mor. P., vol. 20.
[133] Minto to Morley, 10 June, 1909, Mor. P., vol. 20.
[134] Minto to Morley, 23 June, 1909, *ibid.*

The rigid attitude of the Viceroy was not shared by his colleagues. The Reforms Committee of the Governor-General's Council was averse to ignoring Muslim claims. Adamson, the Home member, informed the Viceroy on 19 June, 1909, that the 'members were not inclined to agree that the pledges had been fulfilled, though they admitted that they were capable of more than one construction'.[135] This committee was prepared to give 'some further concessions to the Muslims', but considered it impossible to grant them entirely separate electorates as this would require lengthy and troublesome reference to the Provincial Governments. The members of the committee suggested summoning some leading Muslims to a meeting at Simla in order that the proposals of the Government of India might be fully explained to them. After initial opposition,[136] Adamson pointed out the advantage of being able 'to say to the Secretary of State that we had consulted representative Mahomedans which would be something gained even if we negatived their requests', and suggested that Ali Imam, Salimullah, the Raja of Mahmudabad, Abdul Majid of Allahabad, Muhammad Shafi of Lahore and Ibrahim Rahimtullah of Bombay be invited to a conference with the Councils Committee at Simla.

Although Minto was opposed to any discussion with the Muslim leaders, it was now difficult to avoid it.[137] It would certainly become known that the possibility of a consultation had been discussed and negatived at the Viceroy's instruction, and the opportunity for serious mischief would not be lost. The Viceroy accepted the suggestion but he made it clear that in the coming consultation the committee 'must be absolutely firm' in their determination not to go beyond the increase in the Muslim representation which 'the committee now thinks possible'.

The meeting between the Muslim leaders arbitrarily chosen by the Government of India and the Viceroy's reforms committee was held on 26 June, 1909. Among those proposed by Adamson, the Raja of Mahmudabad was not invited,[138] his opposition to the Government of India's scheme being too well known. The revised list included two new names—Abdul Aziz of Peshawar and Rafiuddin Ahmad of Bombay, from the second of whom there was no response. Apparently the

---

[135] Adamson to Dunlop Smith, 19 June, 1909. Min. P. Corr. India, 1909, vol. 1.

[136] Adamson was opposed to the suggestion personally, *ibid.*

[137] Minto to Adamson, 20 June, 1909, *ibid.*

[138] Min. P., Correspondence of 1909 Regarding Council Reform, p. 104.

telegram had not reached him in time.[139] Another absentee through illness was Salimullah.[140] The discussion was dominated by Adamson and Ali Imam. Adamson made it clear that since reform proposals were concerned only with the Viceregal and Provincial Councils, the question of Muslim representation in the district boards and municipalities could not be discussed at the meeting.[141] He indicated that the Government might increase the number of Muslim seats in the Viceregal Council from five to six. Ali Imam pointed out that the Muslims of Bengal were prepared to 'run the risk of political association' with the Hindus provided that ten seats were reserved for Muslims to be filled in by separate electorates.[142] Ali Imam himself believed that the Muslims of other parts of the country were likely to participate in the mixed electorates only if two more seats—one filled by separate electorates and the other by nomination (from N.W.F.P. and Baluchistan) were granted to them.[143] The latter was immediately contradicted by Abdul Majid who, insisting that the Muslims would not be satisfied without completely separate electorates, also claimed that the Muslim leaders assembled at Simla had, in their individual capacity, no right to bind the community.[144] Abdul Majid was supported by Abdul Aziz and Muhammad Shafi who argued that 'any departure' from the expressed views of the All-India Muslim League would necessitate a reference back to it. Even Ibrahim Rahimtullah, who did not belong to the League at that time, remarked that if some Muslim seats were left to a mixed electorate 'it would be by no means certain that they would fall to the Muhammadans'. It was finally decided that the leaders should 'consult with the League' before intimating their views to the Government.[145]

The purpose of the meeting at Simla was lost through the divisions among the Muslims present, even though only one had supported the Government's compromise proposals. This development caused uneasiness in Minto, who had a long talk with Ali Imam, Abdul Majid and Ibrahim Rahimtullah on 28 June, 1909. In a letter to Morley, Minto asserted that he had found Ali Imam to be 'strongly against "separate

---

[139]The telegram was sent to Rafiuddin's Bombay address but since his usual residence was at Poona it is possible that the telegram did not reach him in time.  ·

[140]Min. P., Correspondence of 1909 Regarding Council Reform, p. 105.

[141]Proceedings of the meeting between the Governor-General's Council Reform Committee and the Muslim leaders at Simla, *ibid.*, p. 109.

[142]*Ibid.*, p. 113.

[143]*Ibid.*, pp. 113–114.

[144]*Ibid.*, p. 115.

[145]*Ibid.*, p. 116.

electorates" alone—the others supporting him'.[146]   He had also gathered that the three Muslim leaders would direct their community in India to accept the Government's scheme, that they would do likewise with their London branch and that they would publicly support the Government's proposals.[147]   In the absence of any record of the discussion that took place between Minto and the Muslim leaders, one would be inclined to accept Minto's account.   Later events revealed that Minto had exaggerated the support of the Muslim leaders for the Government's proposals.   Abdul Majid and Ibrahim Rahimtullah had some reservations.   Moreover, Minto himself had doubts on how far he had been able to convince the Muslim leaders.   Within hours of the interview Minto asked Lord Kitchener to give 'Ali Imam a pat on the back' when he saw him the following day.[148]   Only Ali Imam seems to have responded to the Viceroy's influence.

Ali Imam's role was bewildering.   Ali Imam had been a member of the Simla deputation in October, 1906, which had asked for separate electorates pure and simple.   Never having dissociated himself either from the memorial submitted by the Simla deputation or from the representation put forward by the All-India Muslim League in March, 1908, reiterating the Simla deputation's claim for exclusively Muslim electorates, he had, moreover, as president of the Amritsar session of the All-India Muslim League in December, 1908, himself moved the resolution repeating once again the demand for separate electorates.   It was only after his private interview with Minto in January, 1909, that Ali Imam seemed to have deviated from his own concept of separate electorates and thus from the hitherto accepted policy of the League.   His support for the Government of India's scheme, as expressed in his letter of 4 February, 1909, however, did not last and on 23 May, 1909, he spoke very strongly against it.   On that occasion he also expressed his full confidence in Ameer Ali.   When summoned by the Government on 26 June, 1909, Ali Imam again changed his tone.   Two days later he was said to have promised Minto to publicly support the Government's proposal.   This vacillating role of Ali Imam was perhaps to some extent due to his lack of conviction in the cause he stood for but mainly due to motives of self-interest.   His support of the Government's scheme in February, 1909, was possibly the result of Minto's persuasion coupled with a vague hint of some office.   When in May, 1909, once again he

---

[146]Minto to Morley, 1 July, 1909, Mor. P., vol. 21.
[147]*Ibid.*
[148]Minto to Kitchener, 28 June, 1909. Min. P. Corr. India, 1909, vol. 1.

shifted ground, Minto possibly thought it expedient to make him a definite offer. This assumption becomes more intelligible in the light of Minto's letter of 29 May, 1909, to Baker, the Lieutenant-Governor of Bengal. Minto, worried about 'acute Mahomedan dissatisfaction' with his scheme, had felt that part of it was 'due to Mahomedan soreness at Sinha's appointment' to his council and that 'some similar recognition of Mahomedan ability might go far to lull the storm'.[149] He had, therefore, suggested the appointment of Ali Imam as a member of the Lieutenant-Governor's council, confident that the result of this appointment 'would be excellent'.[150] Thus it appears that when Ali Imam met the Viceroy on 28 June, 1909, he had already before him the prospect of a highly-coveted office.

Immediately after the talks at Simla, Ali Imam made a desperate bid to carry the All-India Muslim League along with the Government of India's proposal. He was assisted by Abdul Aziz of Peshawar who accompanied him to Aligarh and Lucknow,[151] where they persuaded Viqar-ul-Mulk, Musa Khan and others to convene, at a very short notice,[152] an extraordinary general meeting of the All-India Muslim League at Lucknow on 10 and 11 July, 1909.

On 10 July, 1909, only nineteen members were present at Lucknow—less than a quorum. The same day, as urgent messages were being sent to the League members in the neighbourhood of Lucknow, the members present met informally at the house of Raja Naushad Ali Khan. This informal meeting was a stormy one. Several members were strongly opposed to its being held.[153] Some of them were determined that the League in India should have 'no initiative of its own' without prior consultation with the London branch.[154] Questioning Musa Khan's authority to convene the meeting, they asked the officiating secretary whether the central committee of the League under rule 23 clause (d) had decided to hold the meeting and whether he had sent the agenda of

[149]Minto to Baker, 29 May, 1909, Min. P. Corr. India, 1909, vol. 1.

[150]*Ibid.*

[151]Musa Khan, officiating secretary, A.I.M.L., to the private secretary to the Viceroy, 15 July, 1909. Enclosed with Minto to Morley, 22 July, 1909, Mor. P., vol. 21.

[152]The notice for the meeting was sent by 'post and wire' and was published in the Press towards 'the end of the first week' of July, 1909. *Vide* Muhammad Rahmatullah's letter to the *Pioneer,* 30 July, 1909.

[153]*Ibid.*

[154]Ali Imam to Dunlop Smith, 14 July, 1909. Min. P. Corr. India, 1909, vol. 2.

the meeting to the members of the League.[155]   Musa Khan conceded the irregularities and pointed out that the meeting was convened at the instance of Ali Imam supported by Viqar-ul-Mulk.[156]   At this stage Viqar-ul-Mulk declared that since a sufficient number of members was not present, it was not desirable to hold the meeting.   However, Ali Imam and his supporters insisted that the meeting should be held and that the question of violating the constitutional provisions etc. should be considered at the meeting itself.

By 11 July, 1909, twenty-six League members had reached Lucknow. They formed themselves into a subjects committee with Nawab Ali Choudhury of Eastern Bengal as chairman.   As soon as the chairman had taken his seat, Wazir Hasan of Lucknow proposed that the consideration of 'the present situation should be deferred'.[157]   Ali Imam opposed this motion.  He then read a set of six resolutions conforming to the Government of India's compromise proposals and proposed they be adopted by the formal meeting to be held in the afternoon. On the other hand, Wazir Hasan's proposal was supported by four members from Allahabad including Abdul Majid and the chairman of the subjects committee.[158]   These members pointed out that besides the technical objections against the meeting, Ali Imam's proposed resolutions were contrary to the hitherto accepted policy of the League and to its former resolutions. A majority of the members present, however, voted in favour of the meeting being held in the afternoon.

When the members assembled at the Qaisarbagh Baradari, the venue of the formal meeting, Mazhar-ul-Haque of Bihar proposed Viqar-ul-Mulk to the chair.  But before the proposal could be seconded, Nawab Ali Choudhury accompanied by Abdur Rouf and Sheikh Abdul Raoof of Allahabad and Abdul Majid staged a walk-out.[159]   The gathering was then left with twenty-one members present—four short of a quorum.  Thereupon Viqar-ul-Mulk refused to accept the chair. The supporters of Ali Imam were still adamant that the meeting should be held and proposed first Raja Naushad Ali Khan and then Nasim Ahmad

[155]Muhammad Rahmatullah's letter to the *Pioneer,* 30 July, 1909.

[156]*Ibid.*

[157]Report of the A.I.M.L.'s abortive meeting at Lucknow enclosed with Ali Imam to Dunlop Smith, 14 July, 1909. Min. P. Corr. India, 1909, vol. 2.

[158]Muhammad Rahmatullah's letter to the *Pioneer,* 30 July, 1909.

[159]Report of the A.I.M.L.'s abortive meeting at Lucknow enclosed with Ali Imam to Dunlop Smith, 14 July, 1909, Min. P. Corr. India, 1909, vol. 2.

as chairman.[160]   Both of them declined in the absence of a quorum
and the meeting was dissolved.

Ali Imam's failure to carry his resolutions at Lucknow saved the All-
India Muslim League from a serious crisis.  Evidently Ali Imam was
fully aware of the fact that a majority of the League members would
not accept the Government's compromise.  He had taken care to see
that, despite constitutional provisions, the agenda of the hurriedly,
unconstitutionally convened meeting was not circulated to the members.  He had also mustered his strength at Lucknow while an overwhelmingly large number of the opponents of the Viceroy's scheme was
ignorant of the inside story of the Government of India's intervention
in the matter.  The Provincial Leagues of Bombay, Madras and Bengal,
which repeatedly asked for exclusively separate electorates, were wholly
absent from Lucknow.  The other two Provincial Leagues, Eastern
Bengal and Assam and the Punjab, which were known to be supporters
of exclusively separate electorates, were represented at Lucknow by
one and two members respectively.  In the event, it fell mainly on the
members of the Bihar and the U.P. League to decide the fate of the
proposed meeting.  The Bihar members supported Ali Imam, the
president of the Bihar Provincial League.  The members from the
U.P., on the other hand, were divided amongst themselves.  While all
the members from Allahabad strongly opposed the meeting and the
Government's proposals, a majority of the members from Lucknow
were in favour of it.  The Aligarh members followed a middle course,
favouring a formal discussion of the Government's compromise offer
but refusing to commit themselves to the same.

Ali Imam's unsuccessful attempt to modify the League demands for
separate electorates produced sharp reactions among Muslim leaders of
various provinces.  While many Provincial Leagues and individual members of the League reaffirmed the earlier resolutions of the All-India
Muslim League as opposed to those suggested by Ali Imam at Lucknow,
the Bihar leader continued to be a target of attack from Muslim newspapers on the grounds of his complicity with Gokhale.[161]  The council
of the Madras Presidency League telegraphed the Viceroy that they
wanted eleven Muslim seats—ten separately elected and one nominated—
on the Imperial Council.[162]  They also emphasised that any Muslim
member who was not elected by 'a purely Musalman agency be not

[160]Muhammad Rahmatullah to the *Pioneer*, 31 July, 1909.
[161]The *Mihir-o-Sudhakar*, 22 July, 1909, the *Bengal N.N.R.*, 1909.
[162]The *Times of India Mail*, 24 July, 1909.

recognised as a Musalman representative'.[163]   The Punjab Provincial
League 'emphatically' dissented from the modifications suggested by
Ali Imam and reiterated its demand for absolutely separate electorates.[164]    The U.P.,[165] Eastern Bengal and Assam[166] and the
Bombay[167] Leagues also reaffirmed their demands for completely
separate electorates. Ali Imam, however, was able to get the resolutions
he had intended to propose at Lucknow adopted at a meeting of the
Bihar Provincial League[168] and thus establish himself as a leader of a
section of the All-India Muslim League.

Although Minto's intervention had succeeded in dividing the League
leaders in India, Ameer Ali and other League leaders in London were
engaged in a ceaseless campaign against the Government's scheme. At
the annual meeting of the London League held on 24 June, under the
chairmanship of the Aga Khan, Ameer Ali complained of attempts
being made by the authorities 'to minimize the unanimity of the Indian
Musalmans in respect to the reforms'.[169]   The Aga Khan solemnly
warned the Government that the reform scheme would fail if Muslim
claims were ignored.[170]

The Aga Khan's continuous presence in London from June onwards
greatly helped the London League's struggle for exclusively separate
electorates. The Aga Khan used his extensive contact among the English
ruling classes to further the League demands. *The Times* strongly
supported him.[171]    Moreover, as it appears from a letter from the
private secretary to the Prince of Wales to Minto, written at a later
date, even the Prince of Wales had favoured the Aga Khan's view of the
Muslim case.[172]   The Aga Khan and Ameer Ali also utilised the murder

[163] *Ibid.*

[164] The *Times of India Mail*, 28 August, 1909.

[165] The *Englishman Weekly Summary*, 9 September, 1909.

[166] *Ibid.*, 26 August, 1909.

[167] The *Pioneer Mail*, 22 October, 1909.

[168] *Ibid.*, 20 August, 1909.

[169] *The Times*, 25 June, 1909.

[170] *Ibid.*

[171] *Ibid.*, 26 June, 1909.

[172] *a)* '. . . But don't you think it was well that Morley gave in to him [the Aga
Khan] about the Mahomedan representation . . .' private secretary to the Prince
of Wales to Minto, 8 February, 1910, Min. P. Corr. England and Abroad, 1908–10.

*b)* The Prince of Wales himself told Minto 'to clear up any misunderstanding,
that existed in the mind of the Aga Khan regarding the Muslim representation.
*Vide* the Prince of Wales to Viceroy, 14 October, 1909, *ibid.*

of Curzon Wyllie and Lalcaca by a Hindu extremist, Madanlal, in London to remind the Government of the advantage of Muslim loyalty.[173.]

Despite widespread support for the Muslim demands both in India and in London, the Viceroy was adamant on his own proposals. The Government of India's despatch containing the draft rules and regulations to be framed under the India Act of 1909 were despatched to the Secretary of State on 22 July, 1909. The numbers of Muslim representatives to be elected by separate electorates in Eastern Bengal and Assam and Bengal were increased by two and one respectively.[174] In the Viceregal Council one additional Muslim seat to be separately elected was given.[175] At the same time, provisions for Muslim representation through nomination and mixed electorates made in the despatch of 1 October, 1908, were left undisturbed. The Viceroy was 'very decidedly of opinion that we should permit no more haggling and should make known the despatch and the regulations at once'.[176] The Secretary of State, agreeing with him, told Morison, whom he considered to be 'a too vehement partisan of the Mahometans', that 'the time had now come not to argue but to decide', and that only small amendments could be grafted on to the Government of India's despatch.[177]

By August, 1909, both Morley and Minto were extremely sensitive about mentioning 'pledges' to the Muslims. Although both the Secretary of State and the Viceroy, as well as other responsible ministers and officials, had earlier freely used the term,[178] Morley was now inclined to 'rebel against the word "pledge"'.[179] Morley told Minto: 'We declared our view and our intentions at a certain stage. But we did this independently and not in return for any "consideration" to be given to us by the M[uslims] as the price of our intention. This is

[173] *The Times,* 6 July, 1909.

[174] Government of India's despatch, 22 July, 1909. Proc. Home (Public), vol. 8151.

[175] *Ibid.*

[176] Minto to Morley, 22 July, 1909, Mor. P., vol. 21.

[177] Morley to Minto, 29 July, 1909, *ibid.*

[178] *a)* On 21 January, 1909, Minto told Lansdowne that the electoral colleges were 'contrary to pledges I had given to the Mahommedans . . .', Minto to Lansdowne, 21 January, 1909, Min. P. Corr. England and Abroad, 1908–10.

*b)* As late as 27 April, 1909, Morley asked Minto whether the Government of India's latest proposals fulfilled 'our pledges' to the Muslims, *vide* the Secretary of State to the Viceroy, 27 April, 1909, Mor. P., vol. 4.

[179] Morley to Minto, 6 August, 1909, Mor. P., vol. 4.

assuredly not a "pledge" in the ordinary sense, where a Minister induces electors to vote for him, or members of Parliament to support his measures in the House of Commons, by promising that if they will, he will do so and so.'[180] Minto absolutely agreed with Morley's interpretation of the word. 'I entirely object to being saddled with "pledges", I deny that I ever gave one', remarked the Viceroy.[181]

However, not all the members of the India Council were prepared to accept Morley's interpretation of 'pledge'. Morison was 'pertinacious up to the eleventh hour about his M[uslim] friends',[182] insisting that the Government had given 'pledges' to the Muslims and proposed a number of amendments to increase Muslim representation on various councils on these grounds.[183] Morison's amendments were strongly opposed by Gupta who thought that the Muslims had already been given more than their rightful share.[184] The members of the India Council were equally divided on the question of Muslim representation and the proposals of the Government of India were carried only by the casting vote of the Secretary of State.[185]

Even after the adoption of the Government of India's proposals by the Secretary of State in Council, Morley himself showed considerable nervousness about them.[186] He was very uneasy at the London League's and the Aga Khan's pressure.

Meanwhile, Ali Imam, accompanied by Abdul Aziz of Peshawar, had sailed for England. It was hoped that his presence in London at the time of the publication of the rules and regulations of the Government of India Act would neutralise the storm predicted by Ameer Ali and the Aga Khan. Apparently Ali Imam went privately and on his own initiative and expense.[187] Circumstantial evidence, however, shows that Ali Imam's trip was either directly arranged by the Government House or was inspired by the Viceroy. The mail ship that carried Ali Imam and Abdul Aziz also carried a letter from the Viceroy's private

[180] *Ibid.*

[181] Minto to Morley, 26 August, 1909, Mor. P., vol. 17.

[182] Morley to Minto, 20 August, 1909, Mor. P., vol. 4.

[183] Note by T. Morison upon pledges given to the Muslims, Mor. P., vol. 35.

[184] Note by Gupta on Muslim representation, *ibid.*

[185] Morley to Minto, 26 August, 1909, Mor. P., vol. 4.

[186] Adamson to Dunlop Smith, 24 September, 1909. Min. P. Corr. England and Abroad, 1908–10.

[187] It was reported in the *Times of India Mail,* 28 August, 1909, that Ali Imam and Abdul Aziz were 'not deputised and authorised by the All-India Muslim League to represent its views on the reform scheme'.

secretary to the private secretary of the Secretary of State saying that 'the Viceroy thinks it would be useful if the Secretary of State were to see him [Ali Imam]', and also introducing Ali Imam as the leader of the moderate Muslims as regards the question of separate electorates, and as 'a coming man'.[188]   According to Dunlop Smith, Ali Imam and Abdul Aziz were 'going home to confer with Ameer Ali on the knotty subject of Moslem representation'.[189]   Morley was highly encouraged by the news of Ali Imam's visit and hoped that Ali Imam would support him 'against Ameer Ali'.[190]  The Secretary of State arranged to see Ali Imam immediately after the latter's arrival.[191]   He told Minto 'Amere Ali is suffering anguish lest the new visitor should find his way to me, before he, Amere Ali, has had a chance of getting at him, and giving him his bearings!!  This pious design will probably be frustrated.'[192]   Morley was so pleased at the news that he suggested Ali Imam for membership of the India Council even before the latter had arrived in London.[193]  But Ali Imam had already been tipped for the post of 'Standing Counsel' in the Government of Bengal[194] and, as later events suggested, for the Viceroy's executive council as well.

'Ali Imam's mission' to London, however, was unsuccessful.[195]   He could not persuade Ameer Ali that 'Our [Government's] figures (as they were apparently communicated to A. Imam at Simla) give the M[uslim]s the promised share of representation, and in the proper way'.[196]   Ameer Ali adhered to his demands and had some parliamentary support behind him.[197]   These factors increased Morley's nervousness about Muslim dissatisfaction.  He feared that Ameer Ali would stir up another agitation 'comparable with the partition agitation', that *The Times* would charge him with breach of faith with the Muslims, and that Ameer Ali's parliamentary friends would create a difficult situation in England.

[188]Dunlop Smith to Hirtzel, 11 August, 1909, Min. P. Corr. England and Abroad, 1908–10.

[189]*Ibid.*

[190]Adamson to Minto, 1 September, 1909, *ibid.*

[191]*Ibid.*

[192]Morley to Minto, 26 August, 1909, Mor. P., vol. 4.

[193]*Ibid.*

[194]Minto to Morley, 14 September, 1909, Mor. P., vol. 22.

[195]Adamson to Dunlop Smith, 24 September, 1909, Min. P. Corr. England and Abroad, 1908–10.

[196]Morley to Minto, 17 September, 1909, Mor. P., vol. 4.

[197]Adamson to Dunlop Smith, 24 September, 1909 and 28 October, 1909, Min. P. Corr. England and Abroad, 1908–10.

The unequivocal support of the All-India Muslim League of the stand taken by Ameer Ali and the Aga Khan further confirmed Morley's apprehensions of a renewed Muslim agitation. The central committee of the All-India Muslim League at its meeting held on 12 September, 1909, had strongly reiterated its persistent demands for exclusive Muslim electorates at all stages and a number of seats in excess of their numerical strength.[198] The meeting was presided over by Sarfaraz Husain Khan,[199] vice-president of the Bihar Provincial Muslim League, and the resolution affirming the views of the Aga Khan was moved by Mazhar-ul-Haque, secretary of the Bihar League.[200] Indeed the All-India Muslim League appears to have taken full care in bringing the Bihar leaders back to their original stand—thus isolating Ali Imam. Following the lead given by the central committee of the All-India League, the provincial Leagues of Bombay,[201] Madras,[202] and the Punjab[203] again reaffirmed the views of the London League and showed restlessness at what the Bombay League termed 'Gokhale's and Ali Imam's suggested compromise'.[204]

The widespread support in India and the powerful Parliamentary and public support in London behind Ameer Ali and the Aga Khan forced the Secretary of State to reopen the issue of Muslim representation two months after the acceptance of the rules and regulations of the Government of India Act by the India Council. Despite very strong and repeated objections from the Government of India and Minto himself,[205] despite also the continuous persuasion by Adamson,[206] who had been on leave at home, Morley decided to resort to personal negotiations with the Muslim leaders and some of their British

---

[198] Resolutions of the All-India Muslim League meeting held on 12 September, 1909. Proc. Home (Public), vol. 8152.

[199] The *Pioneer Mail*, 17 September, 1909.

[200] Resolutions of the A.I.M.L. meeting held on 12 September, 1909. Proc. Home (Public), vol. 8152.

[201] The *Pioneer Mail*, 22 October, 1909.

[202] The *Pioneer Mail*, 29 October, 1909.

[203] *Ibid.*

[204] The *Pioneer Mail*, 22 October, 1909.

[205] *a)* From the Viceroy to the Secretary of State, 24 October, 1909; also
*b)* From the Viceroy to the Secretary of State, 3 November, 1909, Mor. P., vol. 35.

[206] Adamson to Dunlop Smith, 24 September and 28 October, 1909; Adamson to Minto, 1 September, 1909, Min. P. Corr. England and Abroad, 1908–10.

supporters. Having endeavoured 'to "placate" Ameer Ali'[207] with no success, his next target was Chirol who was completely 'in the hands of Ameer Ali and the Aga Khan'.[208] Morley invited Chirol to a luncheon together with Adamson, hoping that 'the friendly meal will do good and at all events keep *The Times* from being over ferocious' when the regulations were published.[209] Morison had already been persuaded to accept the regulations. At the prompting of Morley, he now 'worked hard upon the Aga Khan, and induced him to part company with Ameer Ali'.[210] When Morley personally talked to the League president, he was rather surprised to find him 'in a thoroughly rational humour', and favouring a compromise which was an increase in the number of Muslim representatives to be separately elected in the Imperial Legislative Council from six to eight. The Aga Khan also undertook to persuade the Muslims of India to accept the compromise.[211] Ameer Ali's reaction to the compromise proposal was not favourable[212] but he appears to have agreed not to oppose them publicly.

The Aga Khan appealed to the Indian Muslims to accept the rules and regulations framed under the Government of India Act, 1909. He spoke of them as fulfilling the pledges made to the Muslims. Ameer Ali, on the other hand, told a representative of Reuter that certain features of the regulations concerning Muslim representation 'give rise to misgiving'. However, he admitted that they represented a distinct advance on the Government of India's first proposals and hoped that the Muslims of India would give them 'a fair and not unsympathetic trial'. The reaction of the central committee of the All-India Muslim League was closer to that of Ameer Ali than to that of the Aga Khan. The central committee considered the provision for separate electorates in the Government of India Act, 1909, as 'to a great extent redeeming the pledges publicly given' by Minto and Morley, and further noted that 'the reforms now promulgated' were 'a distinct advance on the proposals originally made'.[213] They drew the attention of the Government to the fact that the right of representation by election in the

---

[207] Morley to Minto, 26 August, 1909, Mor. P., vol. 4.

[208] Morley to Minto, 7 October, 1909, *ibid.*

[209] *Ibid.*

[210] Morley to Minto, 29 October, 1909, *ibid.*

[211] Adamson to Dunlop Smith, 28 October, 1909, Min. P. Corr. England and Abroad, 1908–10.

[212] The *Empire,* 16 December, 1909.

[213] Resolution No. 1, adopted at the meeting of the Central Committee of the A.I.M.L. held on 28 November, 1909, the *Pioneer Mail,* 3 December, 1909.

Viceroy's Council was not conceded to the Punjab and hoped that they would take an early opportunity of redressing this just grievance. They also trusted that the claims of the Central Provinces and Burma for representation in the Viceroy's Council would be considered by the central and provincial governments concerned.

Thus the League accepted the reforms with reservations, for after nearly two years' struggle they had not gained all the seats under a system of separate representation which they had demanded. None the less, it was an achievement of which any political party could feel proud, especially when the comparative backwardness of the Indian Muslims in education, economic status and political training is taken into account. The League was particularly fortunate in its formative phase in having Ameer Ali as the president of its London branch. Ameer Ali was a man of outstanding ability and zeal. His tactful but firm handling of the agitation, coupled with the support he drew within and outside Parliament, were the most important contributory factors to the success of the League movement. Often Ameer Ali and the London League took the lead and the All-India Muslim League responded, but the laurels were won by the combined and sustained efforts of both.

It has been suggested that the 'Muslim leadership' was 'unable to grasp the significance of what it was demanding' and that it was divided when it came to defining separate electorates.[214] If Muslim leadership is a synonym for the League leadership then these observations have no basis. The League leaders considered the Indian Muslims as a distinct political entity and asked for representation on that basis. It is, there-fore, plain that they were perfectly conscious of the significance of their demand. The division in the League leadership was also more apparent than real. Only Ali Imam, and perhaps Abdul Aziz, seem to have persisted in supporting the Viceroy's scheme, which gave a different version of separate electorates from that of the League. Ali Imam's isolation was almost completed when the leaders of the Bihar League, the only branch of the All-India Muslim League to have endorsed his support for the Government's scheme, closed their ranks in demanding exclusively separate electorates. Furthermore, Ali Imam's difference with the League's demand for separate electorates was neither spon-taneous, nor steady, nor due to his lack of understanding of its significance. As has already been noted, it was fostered and sustained by the Viceroy. The circumstances of Ali Imam's visit to London in September, 1909, which was spoken of as a 'mission' by the Home

---

[214] S. R. Wasti, *Lord Minto and the Indian Nationalist Movement,* p. 190.

Member of the Government of India,[215] clearly exposed Ali Imam as an agent of the Viceroy rather than a leader of the League.

It has been further claimed that in the controversy over separate electorates 'Minto's view prevailed over all others'.[216] Nothing could be further from the truth. A comparison between the Muslim representation recommended in the Government of India's despatches of March, 1907 and October, 1908, and that provided in the Government of India's Regulation of 1909 will convince any careful observer that Minto had largely yielded to the League agitation, an agitation that had compelled the Government of India to raise the Muslim representation by more than thirty-eight per cent in the provincial councils and one hundred per cent in the Viceroy's Council.[217]

Minto not only compromised in matters of detail but also in matters of principle. The Government of India had originally proposed to reserve a few seats for the Muslims in each of the councils to be filled partly by separate electorates and partly by nomination.[218] The provision for reservation of seats, however, was made in order to supplement those seats which the Muslims would secure through election 'in the ordinary manner', i.e. mixed electorates.[219] Eventually Minto was persuaded to increase substantially the number of reserved seats so as to make their proportion closely approaching to the numerical strength of the Muslims. It was also admitted that while the reserved seats would provide the primary representation of the Muslims, they would be supplemented by seats won in the mixed electorates.[220] Furthermore, the Government of India agreed to allow all the reserved seats to be filled by separate electorates thus abandoning the provision

[215] Adamson to Dunlop Smith, 24 September, 1909, Min. P. Corr. England and Abroad, 1908–10.

[216] S. R. Wasti, *Lord Minto and the Indian Nationalist Movement*, p. 190.

[217] The Government of India's despatch of March, 1907, recommended only four seats to be reserved for the Muslims—two to be elected separately and two to be filled by nomination—in the Viceroy's Legislative Council. The Government of India Act, 1909, provided them with eight seats—six of them to be elected separately and two to be filled by nomination from the Punjab where reforms were not introduced. Similarly, the despatch of October, 1908, recommended thirteen reserved seats for the Muslims in the provincial councils but ultimately they were given eighteen seats—all to be filled by separate electorates.

[218] The Government of India's despatch 27 March, 1907. Proc. Home (Public), vol. 7587.

[219] *Ibid.*

[220] Viceroy's telegram of 2 May, 1909, to the Secretary of State, Mor. P., vol. 35.

for nomination in regard to portions of them. The League leaders, however, were not satisfied with the new arrangements. They did not want the Muslims to supplement the reserved seats by participating in mixed electorates. They insisted on all the seats due to the Muslims both on account of their numerical strength as well as their political importance to be filled by separate electorates pure and simple. In the event, the Secretary of State was compelled to affect a compromise with the League by increasing the number of seats reserved for the Muslims in the Viceroy's Legislative Council. This raised the number of reserved seats, i.e. the seats to be filled by separate electorates in the Viceroy's Council, beyond the numerical proportion of the Muslims while keeping the door open for their participation in the mixed electorates. Minto's opposition to this compromise was overruled by Morley.

Minto was never tired of reminding Morley that there would be 'serious trouble over the excess of representation granted to the Muslims' and that he could not see 'that they [the Muslims] are in the least entitled to the number of seats now allotted to them'.[221] On 30 December, 1909, after the results of the elections to the provincial councils held under the Morley-Minto reforms were known, Minto once again told Morley that the excessive representation of the Muslims had 'given good cause for Hindu grumbling which I wish we had avoided'.[222] Morley, on his part, was no less emphatic in his denunciation of Minto's contribution to the dilemma. On 6 December, 1909, Morley had written to Minto: 'I respectfully remind you once more that it was your speech about their extra claims that first started the Mahometan hare. I am convinced that my decision was best.'[223]

It is evident that neither Minto nor Morley liked the ultimate form and extent of Muslim representation as provided by the Government of India's Regulations of 1909. These had been the outcome of the agitation of the League which was aided by several important factors. First, there was the Viceroy's lack of caution. His unqualified agreement with the Simla deputation's demand for separate electorates in October, 1906, proved too difficult to be explained away or to be reconciled with the Government of India's scheme. Secondly, the initial failure of the India Office to differentiate between the Viceroy's proposals and the League demands led the Secretary of State to commit His Majesty's

[221]Minto to Morley, Nov. 11, 1909, Mor. P., vol. 22; Minto to Morley, Jan. 6, 1910, Mor. P., vol. 23.
[222]Minto to Morley, 30 December, 1909, Mor. P., vol. 22.
[223]Morley to Minto, 6 December, 1909, Mor. P., vol. 4.

Government in favour of the League's cause in such unequivocal terms that any departure from that would have been rightly interpreted as a serious breach of faith. It was very late in the day that the Government of India and the India Office discovered that they had been talking at cross purposes over the separate electorates issue. Thirdly, Morley's genuine concern to leave no loopholes in the reform measure and his fear of opposition from the dominantly Conservative House of Lords on grounds of breach of pledge with, or dissatisfaction of, the Muslims (which was likely to be supported by powerful public opinion in Britain) convinced Morley of the necessity of a compromise with the League. Soon after the finalisation of the rules and regulations under the reform scheme Morley asserted 'I am very sure of one thing, and this is that, if we had not satisfied the Mahometans, we should have had opinion here, which is now with us—dead against us. Nothing has been sacrificed for their sake that is of real importance.'[224] Morley's conscience was clear. Of late, he had fully realised that both the Government of India and the India Office had muddled the question of separate electorates. He admitted that the inconsistency between the Government's statements was due to the fact that the matter was 'horribly difficult to manage'.[225]

The allegation so persistently repeated of 'divide and rule' policy by the Government[226] in connection with the granting of separate electorates for the Muslims has no foundation. The Government of India's original scheme was distinctly aimed at guaranteeing the minimum representation of the Muslims as past experience had shown that their representation in the Imperial Council was far less than their numerical proportion justified.[227] The scheme was the same as that provided for the representation of the landholding class and was based on the principle of representation by 'classes and interests' recognised in the Act of 1892[228] as well as on the principle of separate Muslim electorates introduced in some municipalities during the Viceroyalty of

[224] Morley to Minto, 18 November, 1909, Mor. P., vol. 4.

[225] Morley to Minto, 28 April, 1909, *ibid.*

[226] a) N. S. Bose, *Indian National Movement,* p. 48.

　　b) Sachin Sen, *The Birth of Pakistan,* p. 59.

　　c) R. C. Majumdar, *History of the Freedom Movement in India,* vol. II, p. 258.

[227] The Government of India's despatch 1 October, 1908. Proc. Home (Public), vol. 7874.

[228] *Ibid.*

Ripon.[229]   It had the support of Gokhale, the leader of the Congress 'moderates', and fully conformed to his own scheme privately submitted to Morley in September, 1908.[230]   One can reasonably conclude that Gokhale and other moderate leaders like Khare, S. Sinha and Raja Deep Narain, who had supported separate electorates,[231] would never have done so had they had any doubt about the Government's motive behind it.

Moreover, the question of dividing the Muslims from Hindus did not arise at all, for division was already there.  It was precisely because of this that eminently realistic politicians like Gokhale supported separate electorates.  Gokhale observed that the union of all communities 'is no doubt the goal towards which we have to strive, but it cannot be denied that it does not exist in the country today and it is no use proceeding as though it existed when in reality it does not'.[232]   The Government of India in fact relentlessly resisted the demand for completely separate electorates which was ultimately accepted in the League-Congress pact at Lucknow in 1916, when such extremist Hindu leaders as Tilak found no objection to the principle.  It was on the basis of the Lucknow pact that the Government finally conceded the League demand while condemning the principle in severest terms.[233]   Thus 'separate electorates were the consequence, and not the cause, of the separation between Mussalmans and their numerous Hindu brethren'.[234]

In fulfilling the Muslim demands, both Minto and Morley were anxious to avoid offending the Hindus.  Both disliked the prominent leaders of the movement for exclusively separate electorates.  To the Viceroy and the Secretary of State, Ameer Ali was 'a windbag'[235] the Aga Khan —an expert on *'café chantantes'*,[236] and Bilgrami a 'stupid'.[237]   Minto

---

[229]In 1882 for the first time separate electorates were introduced in some municipalities in the Punjab and Burma.

[230]Gokhale's letter to Risley, published in the *Englishman,* 15 January, 1909.

[231]S. Sinha presided over the Bihar Provincial Conference in April, 1909, and strongly supported separate electorates.  Gokhale, Khare and Deep Narain took prominent parts in the same conference. *Vide* the *Pioneer,* 12 April, 1909.

[232]Gokhale's speech in the Viceroy's Council, 29 March, 1909. Proc. Council of the G.G. of India, vol. XLVI, p. 211.

[233]*Report on Indian Constitutional Problems,* p. 112.

[234]Muhammad Ali's Presidential address at the Congress session in 1923, *vide* A. Iqbal, *Select Writings and Speeches of Maulana Muhammad Ali,* vol. II, p. 116.

[235]Morley to Minto, 20 July, 1909, Mor. P., vol. 4.

[236]Minto to Morley, 27 May, 1909, *ibid.,* vol. 20.

[237]Minto to Morley, 29 April, 1909, *ibid.*

also disliked the Raja of Mahmudabad[238]—another leading figure in the agitation.   On the other hand, both Minto and Morley had better opinions regarding Gokhale and maintained closer contact with him.[239] Among other Hindu leaders the Maharaja of Darbhanga and Rashbehari Ghose, the president of the Congress in 1908, enjoyed the confidence of Minto and gave valuable support to his policy.   On the eve of the publication of the reform despatches in December, 1908, Minto reached an understanding with Rashbehari Ghose by which the latter was expected to 'assist' the Viceroy 'by confirming his own position in Congress and so being able to direct that body in conformity with ideas as to which he and I might agree'.[240]   The Maharaja of Darbhanga played an important rôle in keeping the Government informed about the inner developments in the Congress.[241]   On Minto's initiative the Maharaja had also organised a Hindu-Muslim joint deputation supporting the reform despatches of the Viceroy and the Secretary of State in December, 1908.[242]

Far from dividing the Hindus and Muslims on political issues, Minto sought to strengthen secular politics by encouraging and even initiating the establishment of an all-India non-communal political party, i.e. the Imperial League, with the Maharaja of Burdwan, the Maharaja Prodyut Kumar Tagore, Nawab Salimullah and the Raja of Bobbili as leaders.[243] Minto rejoiced over every demonstration of joint action by moderate leaders of Hindu and Muslim communities.   In March, 1907, after meeting a group of Hindu and Muslim leaders he told Morley 'of all wonderful things that have happened since I was in India, this to my mind is most wonderful'.[244]   His joy after receiving the Hindu-Muslim deputation on 24 December, 1908, was even greater.  The same day he wrote to Morley 'It [the deputation] is the most remarkable event of my time here . . . all classes were represented and all shades of political opinion.'[245]   At times Minto even anticipated the gradual eradication

[238] Minto to Morley, 17 June, 1909, *ibid*.

[239] M. N. Das, *India under Morley and Minto*, pp. 80, 82, and 91.

[240] Minto to Morley, 17 December, 1908, Mor. P., vol. 18.

[241] M. N. Das, *India under Morley and Minto*, p. 94.

[242] The *Bengalee*, 25 December, 1908.

[243] Arthur Lawley to Minto, 8 April and 15 June, 1909;  Minto to Lawley, 7 May and 28 June, 1909.  Min. P. Corr. India, 1909, vol. 1.  Also Prodyut Kumar Tagore to Dunlop Smith, 25 August, 1908;  Dunlop Smith to Harold Stuart, 4 September, 1908.  Min. P. Corr. India, 1908, vol. 2.  And Maharaja of Burdwan to Pinhey, 12 February, 1910. Min. P. Corr. India, 1910, vol. 1.

[244] Minto to Morley, 19 March, 1907, Mor. P., vol. 11.

[245] Minto to Morley, 24 December, 1908, Mor. P., vol. 18.

of 'castes and religious differences'.[246] His stubborn resistance to the League demand for exclusively separate electorates seems to have been greatly influenced by this hope of eventual political unity between the Hindus and Muslims or at least between the moderates of the two communities.

All available evidence suggests that Minto's policy was guided by the consideration of loyalty and co-operation of individuals or groups of politicians rather than by their religious affiliations. If there was any divide and rule policy it was in uniting the moderates among Hindu and Muslim leaders as against the extremists among their respective co-religionists.[247] While the Government of India's dealings with the moderates of both the communities were sympathetic, their firm attitude towards men like B. G. Tilak and Lala Lajput Rai on the one hand,[248] and Muhammad Ali[249] and Hasrat Mohani[250] on the other, left no doubt that they despised the Hindu and Muslim extremists alike.

[246] Minto to Morley, 5 June, 1907, Mor. P., vol. 12.

[247] Bepin Chandra Pal, *Nationality and Empire,* p. 385.

[248] Lajpat Rai and B. G. Tilak were sentenced to imprisonment and deportation respectively on charges of seditious activities.

[249] Muhammad Ali's activities were closely watched by the officials from 1907. *Vide* Secretary to Government of the U.P., to Secretary to the Government of India, Education Dept., 13 September, 1913. Proc. Dept. of Education, vol. 9196.

[250] In August, 1908, Hasrat Mohani was sentenced to two years' rigorous imprisonment and a fine of Rs. 500 on charge of having written a seditious article. *Vide* the *Times of India Mail,* 8 August, 1908.

## Chapter VI

## THE ELABORATION OF A PARTY PLATFORM

The struggle for separate electorates having ended, the All-India Muslim League took no steps to take advantage of its success. Officially, the League was a silent spectator of the elections held in December—January, 1909—10, under the Morley—Minto reforms. There were many reasons for this inaction. The very restricted and complicated franchise[1] prescribed under the Government of India Act, 1909, as well as the short notice for elections,[2] were great obstacles for any election campaign on an all-India basis. Moreover, the League itself was not organisationally equal to the task. The League was like the Indian National Congress, more of a platform than a political party in the true sense of the term. The lack of proper organisation, the unsatisfactory conditions prevailing in the central office mainly due to the absence of the president and secretary of the League for the whole of 1909, the shortage of full-time workers, the want of any official organ and, more particularly, the absence of any constitutional provision for co-ordination and cohesion between the all-India League and its provincial branches rendered it impossible for the League to participate in the election on a party basis.

Despite the League's passive role as an organisation, individual League members contested most of the constituencies and did very well in them. League members captured all the Muslim seats in the provincial Legislative Councils of Eastern Bengal and Assam,[3] Bengal,[4] the United Provinces,[5] Bombay,[6] and Madras.[7]

---

[1] Electoral colleges or groups were formed by delegates of different categories in different localities. The qualifications prescribed for voters varied from province to province and even within a particular province.

[2] The rules and regulations under the Government of India Act, 1909, were published towards the middle of November, 1909. The provincial elections were held within a month of the publication of these rules.

[3] Muslim members of the Eastern Bengal and Assam Provincial Council elected by separate electorates were: Muhammad Hemayetuddin Ahmad, pleader, Barisal; Hussam Haider Choudhury, Zamindar, Comilla; Abdul Majid, pleader, Sylhet and Yakunuddin Ahmad, pleader, Dinajpur.

Apart from their success in the exclusively Muslim electorates, the League members captured a number of general seats in the provincial councils. In Bombay Fazulbhoy Currimbhoy Ibrahim was elected by the Mill-Owner's Association without any opposition.[8]  Ghulam Muhammad Bhurgri and Syed Allahando Shah were elected by the jagirdars of Sind and by the district local boards of Sind respectively, their Hindu opponents having withdrawn from the contest.[9]  However, since a majority of jagirdars and a considerable number of members of the local bodies in Sind were Muslims, the uncontested election of two League members from these general constituencies was of no special significance. The election of another League leader, Sirdar Narsinghji Iswarsinghji Thakur of Amod against his Hindu rival was due to the fact that as a *taluqdar* he obtained the undivided support of the *taluqdars* who constituted the majority of *sardars* of Gujrat.[10]

In other provinces the competition for general seats was very keen. Muhammad Habibullah, chairman, Vellore municipality, was elected to the Madras Council by a minority of votes. Habibullah's five opponents polled one hundred and fifteen votes altogether, whereas he polled fifty-six votes only.[11]  Khawaja Muhammad Yusuf and Choudhury Muhammad Ismail Khan secured their election to the Eastern Bengal and Assam Council mainly because of the boycott of their opponents by the Hindu voters.[12]  Nawab Sarfaraz Husain Khan and Syed Zahiruddin were elected to the Bengal provincial council by the district municipal commissioners and the district boards of Patna division

---

[4] Muslim members of the Bengal Legislative Council elected through separate electorates were: Doctor Abdullah-al-Mamun Suhrawardy, Ghulam Husain Arif, Wasi Ahmad, pleader, Patna, and Syed Fakhruddin of Patna.

[5] Muslim members of the United Provinces' Council elected through Muslim electorates were: Abdul Majid, barrister, Allahabad; Aftab Ahmad Khan, barrister, Aligarh; Asghar Ali, pleader, Bareilly and Muhammad Nasim, advocate, Lucknow.

[6] The following members of the Bombay Legislative Council were elected by separate Muslim electorates: Ibrahim Rahimtullah, Bombay; Syed Ali-al-Edros, landholder, Bharoch; Rafiuddin Ahmad, barrister, Poona; and Abdul Husain Adamjee Peerbhoy, merchant, Bombay.

[7] Abdul Quddus Badshah Sahib and Syed Murtaza Sahib were elected to the Madras Legislative Council by the Muslim electorates for the presidency of Madras.

[8] The *Bengalee,* 3 December, 1909.

[9] The *Times of India Mail,* 18 December, 1909.

[10] Secretary, Bombay Government Legal Department, to Home Secretary, Government of India, 6 June, 1910. Public and Judicial Department, vol. 42.

[11] The *Madras Weekly Mail,* 23 December, 1909.

[12] The *Pioneer Mail,* 14 January, 1910.

respectively, after severe contests.[13]   In the Punjab both Muhammad
Shafi and Fazl-i-Husain lost to Rai Bahadur Shadi Lal in the contest for
the university seat.[14]   All three municipal seats in the Punjab, however,
were captured by League members.  Khawaja Ahad Shah, representative
of the cis-Sutlej group of municipalities, had a tie at first with Rai
Bahadur Srikrishen Das.[15]   Adamjee Mamoonjee and Yusuf Shah were
elected by the western and central groups of municipalities respectively,
defeating their rivals Harichand and Ramsaran Das by one vote each.
Similarly, in the United Provinces, Syed Ali Nabi was elected by the
Agra municipal boards, beating Lala Fakirchand by one vote only.
Tasadduq Rasul Khan, the Raja of Jahangirabad, too, was elected to
the United Provinces' Council from the Fyzabad general constituency
by a meagre margin.

The results of the elections to the Viceroy's Legislative Council were
also favourable to members of the League.  Of the eleven Muslim
members of the Viceroy's Council—nine elected and two nominated—
nine were members of the League.  Allah Bakhsh Khan Talpur, the
representative of the jagirdars and zamindars of Sind in the Viceregal
Council, was not a member of the League at the time of election. But
soon afterwards he joined the League.  The only other non-League
Muslim member of the Viceroy's Legislative Council was Muhammad
Ali Jinnah who did not join the League until 1913.  Jinnah was a
prominent member of the Indian National Congress.  He successfully
challenged Rafiuddin Ahmad, the Bombay League secretary and a
member of the Provincial Legislative Council, in the exclusively Muslim
constituency for the Bombay Presidency.  His success was as much due
to the lack of cohesion among the members of the Bombay League as
it was to the extremely limited number of electors, namely eight. The
electorate for the Bombay Presidency Muslim seat consisted only of the
non-official Muslim members of the Bombay Council.[16]   This extraordinary arrangement was the result of the Bombay Governor's persistent opposition to separate Muslim electorates.  This electorate was
approved by Minto only as a sop to Clarke's wounded feelings.[17]   The
Muslim electorates for the Imperial Legislative Council in the United
Provinces, Madras, Bengal and Eastern Bengal were several times larger

[13] The *Pioneer Mail*, 17 December, 1909.
[14] The *Bengalee*, 17 December, 1909.
[15] The *Madras Weekly Mail*, 23 December, 1909.
[16] The *Times of India Mail*, 8 January, 1910.
[17] Minto to Morley, 27 October, 1909, Mor. P., vol. 22.

than that for Bombay. In all these constituencies the candidates were members of the League. The Raja of Mahmudabad and Ahmad Mohiuddin were returned by the Muslim electorates of the U.P. and Madras respectively, without much opposition.[18] The Bengal and Eastern Bengal and Assam Muslim seats for the Imperial Legislative Council were, however, keenly contested. Mazhar-ul-Haque was elected from Bengal with a minority of votes. Mazhar-ul-Haque received one hundred and twenty-one votes while his rivals, Nawab Abdul Jabbar, Mirza Shujaat Ali Baig, Sahebzada Bakhtiyar Shah, Nazmul Huda and Seraj-ul-Islam together polled two hundred and ten votes.[19] The Eastern Bengal and Assam seat was won by Shams-ul-Huda who defeated his rival Nawab Ali Choudhury.[20]

League members also improved upon the reserved quota of Muslim seats in the Viceroy's Legislative Council by winning three general seats. One of these seats went to Syed Muhammad who enjoyed membership of the League and the Congress simultaneously. The other League members elected by mixed electorates were Abdul Majid of Allahabad and Abdul Karim Abu Ahmad Ghaznavi of Mymensingh. Abdul Majid was returned with a majority of two votes,[21] while Ghaznavi's success was a question of mere luck. Ghaznavi had a tie with Raja Sitanath Roy and was elected on subsequent drawing of lots.[22]

Although the results of the elections in the central and provincial councils were favourable to the League and the Muslims in general, the trend of voting justified the original suspicion of the Muslim leaders that without separate electorates their community would not be able to secure adequate representation. The success of the Muslim candidates in the mixed constituencies was marginal and in certain cases accidental, i.e. either due to the cancellation of certain Hindu votes or by the drawing of lots in the event of a tie.[23] Moreover, the Muslim candidates were in several cases supported by the non-Indian voters and they also

---

[18] The *Pioneer Mail*, 17 December, 1909 and 7 January, 1910.

[19] The *Bengalee*, 17 December, 1909.

[20] The *Bengalee*, 21 December, 1909.

[21] The *Pioneer*, 14 January, 1910.

[22] The *Englishman Weekly Summary*, 5 January, 1910.

[23] Officiating Chief Secretary to the Government of the Punjab to the Home Secretary, Government of India, 21 July, 1910; Chief Secretary to the Government of Eastern Bengal and Assam to the Home Secretary, Government of India, 31 January, 1910, and Chief Secretary, Government of the U.P. to the Home Secretary, Government of India, 25 April, 1910. Public and Judicial Department, vol. 42.

Table showing Muslim representation in the various Councils
in 1909–10.†

| Council | Total number of elected seats provided in the Morley–Minto Reforms | Separate Muslim seats | Muslim representation obtained through mixed electorates | Total number of Muslim seats (elected) |
|---|---|---|---|---|
| The Viceroy's Legislative Council | 28 | 6+2=8* | 3 | 11$^X$ |
| The Bombay Presidency Legislative Council | 21 | 4 | 4 | 8 |
| The Madras Presidency Legislative Council | 20 | 2 | 1 | 3 |
| The Bengal Provincial Legislative Council | 26 | 4 | 2 | 6 |
| The U.P. Legislative Council | 21 | 4 | 2 | 6 |
| The Eastern Bengal and Assam Legislative Council | 19 | 4 | 2 | 6 |
| The Council of the Lieutenant Governor of the Punjab | Reforms not introduced | | 3 | 3 |

† Except Muhammad Ali Jinnah all other Muslim members of the various councils were members of the League.

* Of the eight reserved seats five were elected by the Muslim electors of Bombay, Madras, the U.P., Bengal and Eastern Bengal and Assam; one was elected by the jagirdars and zamindars of Sind and two others were nominated from the Punjab where reforms were not introduced.

$^X$ This included two nominated members from the Punjab.

took advantage of the divisions in the Hindu ranks.[24]   The League
leaders could hardly rely on such 'unusual phenomenon' occurring in
future,[25] (in the subsequent election the Muslims had little success in
the mixed electorates).   Furthermore, despite the provision for separate
electorates, the Muslims failed to secure proportional representation in
Eastern Bengal and Assam.   There were about eighteen million Muslims
and eleven and a half million Hindus in this new province, but the number of Muslim representatives in the provincial council was only eight—
four separately elected, two jointly elected and two nominated by the
Government—as against ten Hindus—seven elected and three nominated.[26]   Even in the Punjab, another Muslim majority province, but
for the division of the Hindu votes in the marginal seats and for the
cancellation of certain ballot papers belonging to Hindu voters, Muslims
would not have received proportionate representation in the election.
And in the subsequent election not a single Muslim was elected to the
Punjab Provincial Council.

The results of the elections were carefully analysed by the League
leaders in the third annual session of the All-India Muslim League held
at Delhi on 29 and 30 January, 1910.   Hakim Ajmal Khan, chairman of the reception committee of the League session cautioned the
delegates against 'premature elation' at the success of Muslim candidates
in certain general constituencies.[27]   He held that these successes were
'purely accidental' and due to various unusual circumstances.   He
thought that the impression prevalent in some quarters that the Muslims
had gained excessive representation in the Viceroy's Council was mis-
taken.   He further remarked that those Muslims who had been sent up
by the joint electorates could not be regarded as representatives of
Muslims alone;   they were the joint representatives of all classes and
creeds.   He claimed that the resentment of the Hindus at the success of
the Muslim candidates in some mixed electorates was unfair.   If the
Hindus had accepted the Muslim demand for exclusively separate
electorates at all levels of representation they could have easily avoided
the existing situation.   Ajmal Khan vigorously pleaded for the introduction of the principle of separate electorates in the Punjab and also
for the extension of the same principle in the municipalities, district
boards and universities all over India.

[24] *Ibid.*
[25] *Proceedings of the Third Annual Session of the A.I.M.L.,* held at Delhi on
29 and 30 January, 1910, p. 9.
[26] The *Englishman,* 2 January, 1910.
[27] *Proceedings of the Third Annual Session, op. cit.,* p. 9.

The president of the League session Ghulam Muhammad Ali, the Prince of Arcot, also interpreted the success of a few Muslims in the general seats as due only to sheer chance, 'the Hindus generally voting only for the candidates of their own persuasion'.[28]   He declared emphatically that separate representation was the only way to prevent undesirable conflict between Hindus and Muslims. The Prince of Arcot was also inclined to support the demand for separate electorates put forward by the Parsees and the native Christians. He regretted the fact that separate electorates were not conceded to the Muslims of the Punjab and that his co-religionists in the North-West Frontier Province, Baluchistan and Central Province were denied the right of electing their representatives in the Central Council.[29]

The Prince of Arcot almost echoed the voice of Ajmal Khan in pressing for the formation of separate electorates in all municipal, *taluq* and district boards. He urged opponents of the measure not to belittle the opinions and sentiments of the Muslims by insisting that they give up their demand for separate representation in local bodies. He thought that a liberal-minded recognition of the differences that existed among various Indian communities, and a general desire to give each its due share of influence and benefit was essential for the advancement of the common motherland.[30]

The Delhi session held in January, 1910, was a landmark in the history of the All-India Muslim League. The earlier sessions had been held in conjunction with those of the All-India Mahomedan Educational Conference where educational matters received prior attention.[31] Moreover, these sessions had been mainly occupied with a few subjects of immediate concern to the League. The Delhi session was the first annual conference of the League to be held separately from the Educational Conference. Another outstanding feature of this session was that the delegates present showed a keen interest in the League as an association by devoting considerable time to discussing organisational matters as well as the programme of the League.[32] This third annual conference of the League was also the first to be attended by its

---

[28] *Ibid.*, p. 32.

[29] *Ibid.*, pp. 30–31.

[30] *Ibid.*, p. 32.

[31] In the earlier conferences the first two or three days were devoted to the business of the Educational Conference and the affairs of the League were discussed after the formal session of the Educational Conference was over.

[32] The *Times of India Mail*, 12 February, 1910.

president—the Aga Khan. The attendance at the session—about three hundred delegates and four thousand visitors[33]—marked a distinct advance in the growth of the League. Because of these special features of this session, Hakim Ajmal Khan observed that 'it was in the fitness of things that a body which took its birth at the city of Jahangir (Jahangirabad or Dacca) should have completed the stage of its infancy in the city of Shahjahan (Shahjahanabad or Delhi)'.[34]

The third annual session of the League had been scheduled to meet in December, 1909. The date was changed to January, 1910, to suit the convenience of the president-elect, Ameer Ali.[35] However, as in 1908, Ameer Ali was again unable to preside over the League session. Owing to his recent appointment to the Judicial Committee of the Privy Council—the first Indian to hold the position—Ameer Ali was unable to leave England for India.[36] However, this time Ameer Ali sent his written address to be read before the conference.[37] The address was followed with keen interest by the audience and most of the suggestions put forward by Ameer Ali were ultimately incorporated in the programme of the All-India Muslim League.

Ameer Ali characterised the Muslim attitude throughout the controversy arising from the reform proposals of the Government as singularly sober and moderate. The Muslims were solely concerned with safeguarding their rights and interests and bore no ill-will or antagonism towards any other community. He hoped that the two great communities whom the reforms mainly affected would decide to work together for the good of their common country. Despite differences of 'religion, customs, habits of life and ideals' Hindus and Muslims were bound to live together.[38] Even the fulfilment of the 'dream of self-government' for India depended on the co-operation of the two communities.

Ameer Ali had used the word 'dream' in relation to self-government not with any thought of disparagement but because he felt that 'for many years to come British rule in India is a vital necessity'.[39] He

[33] *Proceedings of the Third Annual Session, op. cit.,* p. 1.

[34] *Ibid.,* p. 3.

[35] Ameer Ali's address read at the Delhi session. *Ibid.,* p. 37.

[36] *The Times,* 5 January, 1910.

[37] According to *The Times,* 5 January, 1910, Ameer Ali's address was to be read by the Raja of Mahmudabad, but it was actually read by Mia Muhammad Shafi: *vide Proceedings of the Third Annual Session, op. cit.,* p. 37.

[38] Ameer Ali's address read at the Delhi session. *Ibid.,* p. 39.

[39] *Ibid.,* p. 40.

firmly believed that if Britain were to loosen her hold over India before
the diverse races and creeds and nationalities had thoroughly learnt the
value of a spirit of compromise and toleration in the management of
public affairs, it would mean 'a relapse into the anarchy of a hundred
and fifty years ago, a fierce religious and racial struggle and a collapse
of the fabric so laboriously built up within the last half century'.[40]
Moreover, to the Muslims of India, the permanence of British rule was a
matter of great importance.   The sympathies and interests of the
Muslims extended beyond the boundaries of India.   These interests
would be greatly hampered if British influence were weakened in the
council chambers of the civilised world.   It was, he maintained, therefore
essential that they should associate themselves with the maintenance of
law and order and loyally co-operate with the Government in promoting
the country's welfare.[41]

Loyal co-operation with the Government, however, should not
connote subservience to the executive.   Ameer Ali never desired that
the Muslims should cease to urge their claims to share in the benefits of
British rule or that they should not protest against the unfair treatment
of their fellow-countrymen in any part of the Empire.  Himself a privy
councillor, Ameer Ali never concealed his dissatisfaction with 'the
rigidity displayed by so many high-placed officials towards the Mussulman claims' in connection with the reforms proposals.  He proclaimed
that the Muslims should never hesitate to express their views strongly
but always constitutionally.

The dominant theme in Ameer Ali's address was his earnest appeal to
the Muslims of India for self-regeneration.  He regretted the fact that
while other communities had been busy in gaining political training the
Muslims sedulously refused to occupy themselves with the question of
communal organisation or the consideration of communal interests.  Of
late when they awoke to the pressing needs of the day they found the
field captured by more alert rivals.  Well-considered plans and sustained
efforts were needed for regaining the ground lost.  Ameer Ali was disturbed to note that the Muslims still lacked the solidarity and determination for the purpose.  He considered it an unhappy sign of political
activity that at the time of the elections several Muslim candidates
should emerge from their solitude and engage in hot contests for a
limited number of seats.  In the greater interests of the community
these unhealthy contests based mostly on personal rivalries rather than

---

[40]*Ibid.*
[41]*Ibid.*, pp. 40–41.

differences of principle or policy should be avoided, which object could be achieved by means of a 'system of moderation', established by the All-India Muslim League and other Muslim organisations all over India.[42] An 'advisory committee' consisting of influential leaders of particular areas should take upon themselves the task of bringing about compromise between rival candidates. Ameer Ali knew that the task of the advisory committee would be difficult, but it was worthy of a trial. This system of moderation proposed by Ameer Ali would not 'interfere with the legitimate ambitions of any politician but by endeavouring to remove frictions and personal rivalries, assure to each candidate a successful issue and to the community some degree of credit'.[43]

Ameer Ali thought that the League should no longer be content with 'merely passing resolutions' and should endeavour to create a real, abiding and intelligent interest amongst the Muslims in their own welfare.[44]

Ameer Ali was greatly concerned with the impoverishment of Muslim families. He suggested a five point programme to arrest further impoverishment.[45] In the first place, the Muslims must be taught thrift, which was a part of their religion. Secondly, they must learn the value of co-operation and self-help. Thirdly, they must move the Legislature for the re-establishment of Courts of Arbitration which existed in the early part of the nineteenth century for the settlement of family disputes. Fourthly, they should obtain from the Legislature a validating act that would give statutory recognition to *Waqf-ala'l-Aulad*. Lastly, they should form 'Co-operative Associations' whose primary duty should be to save Muslim families, as far as possible, from disruption, and when necessary to 'buy in' Muslim estates.[46]

As regards the poorer sections of the Muslims, Ameer Ali advised them to take to trade, commerce, handicrafts and industry. He asked them to emulate their prophet's example in recognising the dignity of labour. He urged the Muslim leaders to make arrangements for scientific and technical education of their youths by establishing specialised institutions and charitable foundations. He observed that deserving students could also be helped by co-operative associations, formed not on charitable but on strictly business lines.[47]

[42]*Ibid.,* p. 44.
[43]*Ibid.,* pp. 44–45.
[44]*Ibid.,* p. 46.
[45]*Ibid.,* pp. 47–49.
[46]*Ibid.,* p. 49.
[47]*Ibid.,* p. 50.

Ameer Ali's address concluded with a plea for the formation of four departments or sections of the Committee of the All-India Muslim League.[48]    Each of these sections was to be charged with special duties and special functions, namely, the economic, the political, the educational and the sociological.    Ameer Ali thought that the provincial Leagues, which had a very vital role in the formulation of the programme of the League as well as in its implementation, should also be divided into four sections.[49]

Addressing the session as the president of the All-India Muslim League, the Aga Khan fully endorsed Ameer Ali's proposals for dividing the work of the League, along with his other suggestions relating to its programme.[50]    The Aga Khan, however, sounded a new note by emphasising the need for an *entente cordiale* between Hindus and Muslims.  He strongly advocated the absolute necessity for co-operation between the two communities both on grounds of the development of mutual interests as well as in the interests of the Government of India.[51] He asked the two communities to reduce their religious differences 'to the minor position' as had been done in America and Western Europe.[52] He argued that the granting of separate electorates for the Muslims had removed the greatest obstacle between Hindu-Muslim co-operation and that the Muslims were now in a position to collaborate with their Hindu brethren in all nation-building activities.

The Aga Khan described the functions of the Muslim representatives of various councils as of a three-fold character.  Firstly, they must co-operate with other Indians 'by working for the spread of education, for the establishment of free and universal primary education, for the promotion of commerce and industry, for the improvement of agriculture by the establishment of co-operative credit and distribution societies and for the development of all the natural resources of the country'.[53]    Secondly, they should collaborate with the representatives of the Hindus and all other communities in securing for them all those advantages that serve their peculiar needs and help their social welfare.[54]    Thirdly, they must watch and promote social measures for the

[48]*Ibid.*, pp. 51–52.
[49]*Ibid.*, p. 53.
[50]The Aga Khan's speech at the Delhi session of the A.I.M.L.  *Ibid.*, pp. 19 and 25.
[51]*Ibid.*, p. 24.
[52]*Ibid.*, p. 18.
[53]*Ibid.*, p. 17.
[54]*Ibid.*, p. 18.

exclusive benefit of the Muslims with the co-operation of Hindu and other members.

The Aga Khan even suggested what he called 'a comprehensive programme' to be jointly worked out by Hindu and Muslim leaders both in and outside the Councils. He wanted them to give priority to primary education for the masses. They should see that it was not only free and universal, but substantially practical to be of use to agriculturists and labourers. They should endeavour to introduce special courses for scientific and technical education and improve the teaching machinery. Arrangements should also be made for co-operative societies to help train students abroad thus making them useful citizens.

In the economic sphere, the Aga Khan advised the Hindu and Muslim leaders to establish co-operative societies under the aegis of the Government to foster local industries, to relieve agricultural indebtedness and to ameliorate the lot of the peasantry and encourage artisans. In the political field, they should immediately start working together on the problem of Indians in South Africa. The South African government should be made, by a ban on all indentured labour from India, to realise its injustice and cruelty to Indians. Hindus and Muslims should also co-operate with each other in preaching loyalty to the Government. They 'must send earnest missionaries, from organisations and vigilance committees and from pulpits and platforms, from mosques and temples, orders must emanate for the prevention of political crime'.

Although the Aga Khan agreed with Ameer Ali about the League's programme, he differed with the latter as to how it should be materialised. The Aga Khan exhorted the Muslims to work out the programme in co-operation with the Hindus, whereas Ameer Ali wanted them to implement it through their own efforts while co-operating with the Hindus only in matters of common interests.

The emphasis on Hindu-Muslim co-operation in the Aga Khan's speech was also absent in the presidential address of the Prince of Arcot. On the contrary, the Prince of Arcot's insistence on the extension of separate electorates to the local self-governing bodies, his earnest appeal for making Urdu the common language for the whole of India,[55] and his reference to the 'renewed agitation of the Bengalees' for the repeal of the partition of Bengal as causing uneasiness among the Muslims[56] showed his deep concern for exclusively Muslim interests. Similarly, none of the delegates who spoke on various resolutions

[55] *Ibid.*, p. 35.
[56] *Proceedings of the Third Annual Session of the A.I.M.L., op. cit.*, p. 36.

adopted at the League session expressed any interest in the Aga Khan's suggestion for united action by Hindus and Muslims. Thus, it seems that the Aga Khan's plea for inter-communal co-operation was out of tune with the existing trend in League politics.

The Aga Khan's emphasis on joint action by Hindus and Muslims, despite other League leaders' reluctance to respond to his call, is understandable from his insistence that such action was to be based only on 'active loyalty'.[57]    The Aga Khan thought that the division between Hindus and Muslims would weaken British rule in India.[58]    He therefore appealed to his co-religionists for absolute loyalty to the Government and urged that their 'relations with the Hindus and all other Indian communities who share that loyalty must frankly be most cordial'.[59]    The Aga Khan was aiming for co-operation not with the entire Hindu community, but with its pronouncedly loyal or politically moderate section.    This line of approach was distinctly in conformity with the policy of Minto and appears to have been inspired by some of the high officials.    Before the Delhi session the Aga Khan had been approached by Hewett, the Lieutenant-Governor of the U.P., in connection with the removal of the All-India Muslim League office from Aligarh.[60]    Only three days after the Delhi session Hewett observed that the policy adopted by the Aga Khan was 'such as Government can sympathise with'.[61]

The resolutions adopted at the Delhi session did not indicate any difference of opinion among the members of the League.    All the resolutions were carried *nem con,* this perhaps being due to their character, for the League leaders seem only to have selected those questions on which the politically conscious section of the community held strong opinions.

Of the eleven resolutions passed at the Delhi session, three were moved on 29 January and eight on 30 January, 1910.  The first resolution which concerned the Government of India Act, 1909, was proposed by Fazulbhoy Currimbhoy, member, Bombay Legislative Council, in his capacity as the temporary president of the session, the Prince of Arcot being absent for a while.[62]    The resolution appreciated the 'beneficial scheme of reform' embodied in the Act and offered 'on behalf of Indian

[57]*Ibid.,* p. 17.

[58]*Ibid.,* p. 24.

[59]*Ibid.*

[60]Hewett to Minto, 3 February, 1910, Min. P. Corr. India, 1910, vol. I.

[61]*Ibid.*

[62]*Proceedings of the Third Annual Session, op. cit.,* p. 55.

Mussulmans' their co-operation with the Government for the success of the scheme.[63]  Muhammad Shafi and Nawab Ali Choudhury, members, respectively, of the Punjab and Eastern Bengal and Assam Legislative Councils and Syed Wazir Hasan and Masudui Hasan, pleaders of Lucknow and Muradabad respectively, supported the resolution. Both Shafi and Nawab Ali Choudhury pointed out the grievances of the Muslims of their respective provinces with regard to the Act.  Shafi thought that the denial of separate electorates to the Muslims of the Punjab was not only 'in the highest degree prejudicial to Punjabi Mussulmans' but also 'exceedingly impolitic'.[64]  Nawab Ali Choudhury held that the provision for four separately elected Muslim seats in Eastern Bengal and Assam Legislative Council was quite inadequate. He argued that although the Muslims of Eastern Bengal and Assam formed about two-thirds of the population of the province their representation in the council through separate electorates was less than one-fifth of the total non-official members.[65]  He further noted that since most of the voters of the local self-governing bodies in the new province were either tenants of Hindu zamindars or indebted to them for loans, they could not but vote for Hindu candidates in a mixed electorate.  Nawab Ali Choudhury was convinced that so far as the Muslims of Eastern Bengal and Assam were concerned the pledges given by Morley and Minto had not been fulfilled.[66]

The second resolution of the session was also moved by Fazulbhoy Currimbhoy. The resolution expressed the abhorrence of the League for the terrorist movement prevalent in parts of India and condemned emphatically 'the dastardly outrages' recently committed at Allahabad, Nasik and Calcutta.[67]  The resolution also appealed to all patriotic citizens to co-operate with the authorities in uprooting the anarchists from the country.[68]  While moving the resolution, Fazulbhoy Currimbhoy referred to the unsuccessful attempt on the life of the Viceroy and his wife at Ahmedabad and of the murders of A. M. T. Jackson, Collector of Nasik and Shams-ul-Alam, inspector, criminal investigation department, Calcutta, as the symptoms of dangerous disease in the politics of the country.[69]  He also mentioned the murder

[63] *Ibid.*
[64] *Ibid.*, p. 56.
[65] *Ibid.*, p. 57.
[66] *Ibid.*
[67] *Ibid.*, p. 59.
[68] *Ibid.*
[69] *Ibid.*, pp. 60–61.

of Curzon Wyllie in London, of which he was a spectator, as horrible and urged the League to adopt some practical means of checking the growth of terrorist activities among Indians.   Aftab Ahmad Khan, barrister and member of the U.P. Legislative Council, in seconding the resolution stressed the necessity of proper guidance for youths. At the same time he advised European officers to treat educated Indians with greater courtesy, for it was the educated people who could best appreciate the advantages of British rule.

The third and the last resolution of 29 January, 1910, was proposed, seconded and supported respectively by Muhammad Shafi, Yakub Hasan (of Madras) and Mahbub-ul-Alam, editor, the *Paisa Akhbar* of Lahore.   The resolution considered the number of Muslims employed in the various branches of the public service as 'absolutely inadequate' and urged the Government to give the Muslim community that share in the public service to which it was 'entitled by reason of its importance and numerical strength'.   This claim for a greater share for the Muslims in the services had repeatedly been pressed by the League. The Government had not taken any practical measure in this respect. On the other hand, some of the high officials had remarked that the paucity of Muslims in the Government services was due to their backwardness in education or in other words lack of qualified candidates amongst them.[70]   The League leaders refused to accept this viewpoint and alleged that even qualified people were ignored by the authorities. The point was made clear by Shafi who observed that the Muslims did not expect the Government to show undue favour to them by lowering the standard of qualification for public service. What they wanted was that whenever qualified Muslims were available they should be employed in preference to other candidates till their due proportion according to their importance and population was secured.[71]   Shafi thought that adequate Muslim representation in the services was essential for the proper 'adjustment of the political balance' between various communities.[72]

30 January, 1910, was a busy day for the League Conference. The League had two sittings in the course of the day and the second sitting continued till late in the evening. The morning session was mostly devoted to the consideration and adoption of the report submitted by

---

[70]This was the view of the Governor of Bombay. *Supra*, p. 89.

[71]*Proceedings of the Third Annual Session of the A.I.M.L., op. cit.*, pp. 65–66.

[72]*Ibid.,* p. 66.

the sub-committee of the All-India Muslim League for the revision of the party's rules and regulations. The sub-committee had been appointed at the Amritsar session of the League in December, 1908.[73] The main recommendations of the sub-committee adopted in the constitution were an increase in the number of members of the All-India League from four hundred to eight hundred; the abrogation of the income qualification of the members and the reduction of the age limit from twenty-five to twenty-one; the cancellation of the provision for entrance fee of the members; the reduction of the membership subscription from twenty-five rupees to twenty rupees; and the provision for the payment of the membership fee in four equal instalments.[74] The revised constitution also increased the number of vice-presidents of the League from six to twenty and changed the name of the executive body of the League from committee to council.[75] All these amendments were aimed at liberalising the League and bringing it into closer touch with the educated section of the Muslim community.

However, the most important defects in the revised rules and regulations of the League were the absence of any rules relating first, to affiliations of provincial and district Leagues; secondly, to the central League's control and supervision over them; and lastly, to division of functions between the central League and its branches. Without such provisions, it was difficult for the different organs to pursue a co-ordinated programme of activities. Moreover, lack of provisions for control and supervision of the activities of the provincial Leagues rendered it impossible for the All-India Muslim League to decide whether or not a particular provincial branch was sufficiently representative of the Muslims of the province.[76]

Having passed the amended constitution, the session took up the question of electing new office-bearers of the League. The task was accomplished with complete unanimity amongst the delegates.[77] The Aga Khan was re-elected president. Aziz Mirza, formerly judicial secretary, the Nizam's Government, Hyderabad, was elected secretary and Haji Musa Khan, the acting secretary, and Syed Wazir Hasan, pleader of Lucknow, were elected joint secretaries. The newly-elected vice-presidents were: the Prince of Arcot from Madras, Currimbhoy Ibrahim

---

[73]*Foreword by Aziz Mirza to the 'Rules and Regulations of the A.I.M.L.',* Allahabad, 1910.

[74]*Rules and Regulations of the A.I.M.L., 1910,* pp. 2 and 3.

[75]*Ibid.,* pp. 4, 5 and 7.

[76]*Ibid.*

[77]The *Statesman Weekly,* 3 February, 1910.

and Fazulbhoy Currimbhoy from Bombay, H. M. Malek from C.P., Abdul Karim Jamal from Burma, Salimullah and Nawab Ali Choudhury from Eastern Bengal and Assam, Prince Jahandar Mirza and Syed Ali Imam from Bengal, Fateh Ali Khan Qazilbash, Zulfiqar Ali Khan and Muhammad Shafi from the Punjab, and Viqar-ul-Mulk, the Raja of Jahangirabad and Abdul Majid from the U.P.[78]

The next item of business of the conference was the financial requirements of the League. The Prince of Arcot and the Aga Khan appealed to its members for financial assistance. A lump sum of eight thousand six hundred rupees was collected on the spot and annual subscriptions amounting to sixteen hundred rupees were promised.[79]    On the previous day the Aga Khan had declared a permanent annual grant of four thousand rupees to the All-India League and fifteen hundred rupees to the London League.[80]    These promises, when they materialised, were supposed to be sufficient for the immediate needs of the League.

The afternoon meeting of 30 January was mainly occupied with the passing of a number of resolutions. Rafiuddin Ahmad, secretary, Bombay Presidency League and member of the Bombay Legislative Council, moved that in view of the Viceroy's promise to the Simla deputation in 1906, and also as a 'necessary corollary' to the application of the principle of separate electorates in the Imperial and Provincial Councils, 'the speedy extension' of the principle of communal representation to all self-governing bodies was essential.[81]   The proposition was seconded by Nawab Ali Choudhury who declared that adequate and effective representation of Muslims could never be secured without an extension of the system of separate electorates to the lowest rung of the elective ladder and that the absence of this method had resulted in the neglect of Muslim interests in the local bodies.[82]   He sought to strengthen his contentions by quoting from the recommendations of the Royal Commission upon Decentralisation.  The Commission had entirely agreed with the principle of class representation (in the local bodies) as laid down in the Government of India's resolution of 1882. They had thought 'it essential that the system adopted in each [rural] board should be such as to provide for the due representation of

[78] *Ibid.*

[79] *Proceedings of the Third Annual Session of the A.I.M.L., op. cit.,* p. 55.

[80] *Ibid.*

[81] *Ibid.,* pp. 71–72.

[82] *Ibid.,* pp. 72–73.

different communities, creeds and interests'.[83]  They had further remarked that 'A class system of representation which exists in Rangoon
and in some of the Punjab municipalities, seems to have worked fairly
satisfactorily'.[84]  Drawing the attention of the Government to these
weighty remarks of the commissioners, Nawab Ali Choudhury asserted
that if the principle of denominational representation had been found
working satisfactorily in the Punjab, there was no reason why the same
principle when applied to other provinces should not work equally well.
Nawab Ali Choudhury was followed by Shaikh Abdul Qadir, barrister,
who supported the resolution.  Before, however, the resolution was put
to the vote Syed Raza Ali, pleader, Muradabad, supported by
Muhammad Yakub, pleader of the same place, proposed certain verbal
alterations in the motion.[85]  The alterations were accepted by the
proposer and the resolution as amended was passed unanimously.[86]

The next resolution was proposed by Aziz Mirza, the newly-elected
League secretary.  It demanded that in view of the disintegration of
Muslim families 'consequent on the misrepresentation of the Mohamedan
Law of family *waqf* and the disastrous effects resulting therefrom to
the well-being of the community' the Legislature should enact some
measure to validate *waqfs* in favour of the executor's family and
descendants with necessary safeguards that might be considered
expedient against the perpetration of fraud.[87]  The resolution was
seconded by Zahur Ahmad, pleader, Lucknow.  After a forceful speech
by Shibli Nomani in support of the motion,[88] it was carried
unanimously.[89]

The doctrine of *Waqf-ala'l-Aulad* (family trusts) had started from the
days of Muhammad, the prophet of Islam, who sanctioned and himself
created such *waqfs*.  During Muslim rule innumerable *waqfs* of this kind
had existed all over India.  It was only in 1887 that Justice Farran of
the Bombay High Court suggested that a *waqf* under which income of
the property was reserved for the benefit of the founder's life, and after

---

[83] Nawab Ali Choudhury quoted these remarks from section 789 of the
Decentralisation Commission's report.

[84] The speaker quoted it from section 850 of the Report of the Royal Commission Upon Decentralisation.

[85] The *Statesman*, 3 February, 1910.

[86] *Proceedings of the Third Annual Session of the A.I.M.L.*, op. cit., p. 75.

[87] *Ibid.*, p. 82.

[88] The *Statesman*, 3 February, 1910.

[89] *Proceedings of the Third Annual Session of the A.I.M.L.*, op. cit., p. 84.

[90] Ameer Ali's article in the *Nineteenth Century*, October, 1905, p. 618.

him for that of his descendants in perpetuity, was not valid.[91]    In 1888, Ameer Ali, then a Judge of the Calcutta High Court, gave his verdict in favour of *Waqf-ala'l-Aulad* but the Full Bench of the High Court declared it invalid.  In 1889, for the first time the Judicial Committee of the Privy Council decided that to create a valid *waqf* there must be a substantial dedication and not an 'illusory' one of property to charitable uses.[92]  At that time they did not define whether or not a gift to charity which was only to take effect after the failure of all the grantor's descendants, would be illusory.  In 1894, in another case they reaffirmed their former decision and further laid down that a provision for the poor after the total extinction of the family would be illusory.[93] This decision wrecked a large number of old *waqfs* and thus ruined their beneficiaries.[94]

The Privy Council's decision on *Waqf-ala'l-Aulad* had been opposed by various Muslim leaders, including Ameer Ali, Muhammad Yusuf and Shibli Nomani.[95]  In May, 1908, Ameer Ali had declared the validation of this kind of *waqf* as one of the main items in the London League's programme.[96]   The All-India League had taken up the matter at its Amritsar session in December, 1908.  Its Delhi resolution on the subject was thus a repetition of an old and popular Muslim demand.

In another resolution, the League urged upon the Government the necessity of 'instituting a thorough enquiry into and the preparation of the statement of the number, general purposes, and manner of administration of Mahomedan endowments designed mainly for the public benefits'.[97]   The resolution was proposed by Muhammad Yakub, pleader, Muradabad, and seconded by Ghulam Sadiq, member, the Punjab Legislative Council, both of whom alleged that the *waqf* estates were maladministered and their funds misapplied.  The mismanagement of *waqfs* had been a long-standing grievance of the Muslims.  The matter had been brought to the notice of the Government as early as 1885, by Ameer Ali, then secretary of the Central

[91]*Proceedings of the Annual Meeting of the A.I.M.L.,* held at Nagpur, December, 1910, p. 63.
   [92]*Ibid.,* pp. 63–64.
   [93]*Ibid.,* p. 64.
   [94]*Ibid.*
   [95]Muhammad Ali Jinnah's speech at the Imperial Legislative Council, 17 March, 1911. *Vide Proc. Indian Legislative Council,* vol. XLIX, p. 480.
   [96]*Supra,* p. 82.
   [97]*Proceedings of the Third Annual Session of the A.I.M.L., op. cit.,* p. 80.

National Mahomedan Association.[98]  The Government of Bengal had responded by appointing a Commission to enquire into the question. But the views represented on that Commission were so divergent that the Government of India found it impossible to grapple with the matter.[99]  Since then the question had been repeatedly raised by various Muslim leaders but without any effect.

The next resolution adopted by the League session deplored the attempts made by some Hindu leaders to deprecate the importance of Urdu as 'the principal vernacular of India' and affirmed that the preservation and advancement of Urdu language and literature were essential for the general progress of the country.[100]  In moving the resolution, Shaikh Abdul Qadir, barrister, claimed Urdu to be the only language which was understood by the educated classes all over India and which was read and spoken both by Hindus and Muslims. To him the search for another language looked like 'the digging of a well for drinking water when the Ganges flowed nearby'.[101]  He warned the opponents of Urdu that any attempt to damage the importance of this language would be suicidal to the best interests of India. The resolution was seconded by Qazi Kabiruddin, barrister, Bombay and supported by Mahbub-ul-Alam, editor, the *Paisa Akhbar*.

One of the most important resolutions passed at the Delhi session emphasised the desirability of raising the Mahomedan Anglo-Oriental College, Aligarh, to the status of a Muslim University.[102]  The resolution was proposed by Aftab Ahmad Khan and seconded by Qazi Kabiruddin. The establishment of a Muslim university at Aligarh had been the concern of a considerable section of Muslim educationalists and politicians for several years. Syed Ahmed Khan, founder of the Aligarh College, himself dreamt of upgrading the institution into a separate University.[103]  Later on the matter was taken up by the All-India Mahomedan Educational Conference and since 1898 it had formed the most important demand of the Educational Conference.[104]  This claim was also

[98] Ameer Ali's speech at the meeting of the Society of Arts (London), on 13 December, 1906. The *Bengalee,* 11 January, 1907.

[99] *Ibid.*

[100] *Proceedings of the Third Annual Session of the A.I.M.L., op. cit.,* p. 77.

[101] *Ibid.*

[102] *Ibid.,* p. 80.

[103] The *Indian Review,* May 1916, vol. XVII, p. 333.

[104] Almost every annual session of the Educational Conference since 1898 passed resolutions supporting the Muslim University scheme. Resolution Nos. 3, 4 and 5, 7, 7, 1, 10, 5 and 7 passed at the 12th, 13th, 14th, 15th, 16th, 17th, 19th

included in the address submitted by the Simla deputation in 1906. However, it was not before December, 1909, when on the motion of Aziz Mirza, seconded by Aftab Ahmad Khan, the Educational Conference proposed to create 'a national fund' for the foundation of the Muslim University,[105] that any practical step had been taken in this regard. By 1910, the question of the Muslim University was no longer an educational issue. The president of the Delhi session of the League declared that it was 'as intimately connected with the fortunes of the political movement in the community as with its educational or social advancement'.[106] He therefore suggested that the question 'should be taken up and handled' jointly by the League and the Educational Conference.[107]

The need for a Muslim University at Aligarh was also stressed by the Aga Khan. He considered the establishment of such an institution as 'pre-eminent amongst' the nation building activities of the League.[108] The Aga Khan also threw light on the scheme of the proposed university and indicated the courses of studies he wanted such an institution to adopt. He thought that the efforts of the Muslims of India 'ought to be bent to the task of making Aligarh a Moslem Oxford—an educational centre and intellectual capital to which all Moslems should turn for light and guidance'.[109] Thus from early 1910, the question of the foundation of the Muslim University at Aligarh became one of the chief concerns of the League leaders all over India.

The condition of the Indians in South Africa formed the subject of another important resolution of the League session. The lengthy resolution proposed by Muhammad Ali and seconded by Zahur Ahmad expressed the League's admiration of 'the intense patriotism, courage and self-sacrifice of the Indians in the Transvaal' in their heroic suffering of persecution in the interest of India and appealed to Muslims to help the cause of Indians in the colonies 'with funds and in other ways'.[110] The League also urged upon the Government the necessity of prohibiting the recruitment of indentured Indian labour for South African

and 20th sessions of the Conference respectively approved of the scheme of the Muslim University. (M. S. Jain, *The Aligarh Movement*, p. 77).

[105] Proc. Home (Education), vol. 8432. Proc. for March, 1910, No. 21; also the *Pioneer Mail*, January 7, 1910.

[106] *Proceedings of the Third Annual Session of the A.I.M.L., op. cit.*, p. 34.

[107] *Ibid.*, pp. 34–35.

[108] *Ibid.*, p. 23.

[109] *Ibid.*,

[110] *Ibid.*, p. 78.

Union 'as a measure of retaliation' so long as any South African Colony adhered to their existing discriminatory and harsh policy towards the Indians and hoped that the Imperial and the Indian Governments would take further measures necessary for the obliteration of racial discrimination within the Empire.[111]

In 1908, the League had repeatedly drawn the attention of the Government towards the ill-treatment of Indians in the Transvaal. The Delhi resolution, however, showed the growing concern and the hardening attitude of the average League members at the failure of the South African Government to secure justice to the Indians. Besides passing the resolution, the League also announced a donation of one thousand rupees to the Transvaal Indians. The individual League members also responded to the call for financial aid to the Indians in South Africa by promising a sum of rupees two thousand on the spot.[112]

The formal session of the All-India Muslim League came to a close on the evening of 30 January, 1910, after having passed two resolutions highly appreciating the services of the Aga Khan and Ameer Ali towards the Muslim cause and expressing the continued confidence of the League in both of them.[113] However, since the original session was fixed for three days and the whole business of the session had to be rushed through in two days in order to facilitate the Aga Khan's other commitments, certain matters had been left over to be considered informally on the following day. The informal meeting was presided over by Fazulbhoy Currimbhoy. The report of the acting secretary, Musa Khan, reviewing the activities of the League and its branches during the year 1909 was considered at this meeting. The meeting also discussed the educational problems of the Muslims when Viqar-ul-Mulk and Aftab Ahmad Khan appealed to the members of the League to strive their best for the foundation of the Muslim University at Aligarh.

One significant step with far-reaching consequences taken by the All-India Muslim League during the Delhi session was the decision for transferring the central office of the organisation from Aligarh to Lucknow. This was done mainly at the insistence of the Aga Khan and despite serious opposition from Viqar-ul-Mulk, Aftab Ahmad Khan and a few others.[114] The Aga Khan's move for the removal of the League office from Aligarh was the result of a request by Hewett, Lieutenant-

---

[111] *Ibid.*

[112] *Ibid.*, p. 79.

[113] *Ibid.*, p. 85.

[114] Hewett to Minto, 3 February, 1910. Min. P. Corr. India, 1910, vol. I.

Governor of the U.P., to the same effect.[115] Hewett had been seriously concerned with the possible change in the Muslim League's attitude towards the Government.[116]    The growing political importance of Aligarh as the headquarters of the All-India Muslim League had greatly added to his anxiety.  Consequently, in 1908, he had approached some League leaders 'with the suggestion that the headquarters of the League should be removed from Aligarh to elsewhere'.[117]

For about two years the League leaders took no action on Hewett's suggestion.  Meanwhile, in 1909, Hewett himself was involved in a dispute between Archbold and Viqar-ul-Mulk, principal and secretary respectively of the Aligarh College over the management of the college affairs.[118]    Hewett's intervention in favour of Archbold was strongly resented by the trustees of the College and by a section of the League leaders.  Finally, due to public pressure led by some members of the League,[119] both Hewett and Archbold had to concede the demands of the trustees.  This incident seems to have upset Hewett.  The agitation showed the way the wind was blowing.  Viqar-ul-Mulk and the younger generation of the League politicians, particularly from Aligarh, could not be trusted by the Government.  Hewett 'felt frightened lest the lawyer-party, mainly consisting of young and irresponsible persons, would attain a predominant position in the League and that they might at some time coalesce with the advanced Hindu politicians against the Government on one or more questions'.[120]  Therefore, he renewed his attempt to have the League office removed from Aligarh and this time got hold of the Aga Khan who managed to carry out his desire amidst strong opposition.

The removal of the League office to Lucknow, however, was not a permanent arrangement.  'That would not be fair to other provinces'—

[115]*Ibid.*

[116]*Supra*, p. 49.

[117]Hewett to Dunlop Smith, 3 October, 1909.  Min. P. Corr. India, 1909, vol. 2.

[118]The dispute centred round the question of jurisdiction of the secretary of the college over its internal administration.  As a protest against Viqar-ul-Mulk's interference in the day to day administration of the college, Archbold had tendered his resignation but despite Hewett's support he was eventually compelled to accept the secretary's authority.

[119]R. Gopal, *Indian Muslims: A Political History*, pp. 118–19; and the Times *of India Mail*, 10 July, 1909.

[120]Hewett to Minto, 3 February, 1910.  Min. P. Corr. India, 1910, vol. 1.

admitted the Aga Khan.[121]   Moreover, the shifting of the League's headquarters from Aligarh was not solely due to the behind-the-scene intervention of Hewett, as had been suggested by one writer.[122]   A section of the Muslim public had never liked Aligarh being the head office of the League.  They claimed that 'the political League and the College can not go together'.[123]   From the point of view of communication, too, Aligarh was not regarded as ideally suited for the central office of an all-India political party.[124]   But the most important factor in the controversy was the fact that Aligarh had always been regarded as the temporary seat of the All-India Muslim League.  As early as December, 1906, it was decided that the headquarters of the League should be established at a provincial capital.[125]   Thus, although the circumstances of the Aga Khan's suggestion were strongly resented by a section of the League leaders, the proposal itself could not have been turned down in consistency with the earlier decision of the founders of the League.

Immediately after the Delhi session the Aga Khan visited Lucknow in connection with League activities.  There he attempted, with some temporary success, to reconcile the Lucknow and Allahabad factions of the U.P. League between which jealousies had existed.  He also persuaded the U.P. League to transfer its office from Lucknow to Allahabad on the understanding that if the central office of the All-India League were removed from Lucknow during his presidentship of the organisation, he would do his best for the provincial League office to be re-transferred to Lucknow.[126]   As a further move towards the reorganisation of the U.P. League, the Aga Khan arranged the resignation of its secretary Naushad Ali Khan.  This resulted in the election of Ibn Ahmad, barrister, Allahabad, formerly secretary of the London League, as secretary of the Provincial League of the United Provinces.

[121]The *Times of India Mail*, 5 February, 1910.  Possibly the Aga Khan was thinking of rotating the League office between various provincial capitals.

[122]M. N. Das, *India under Morley and Minto*, p. 181.  Das further suggests that 'under the eyes of the Lucknow Government' the League was expected to 'remain loyal and faithful'.  But the facts show that Hewett's main interest in getting the League office removed from Aligarh had been his anxiety to get rid of the Aligarh politicians, particularly of the younger generation rather than to watch the League activities.

[123]Mushir Husain Kidwai's letter to the editor of the *Advocate*, 20 August, 1908.  The *U.P. N.N.R.*, 1908.

[124]The *Indian Daily Telegraph*, quoted in the *Statesman Weekly*, 3 February, 1910.

[125]Rafiuddin Ahmad's interview with the *Englishman*, 4 January, 1907.

[126]The *Times of India Mail*, 5 February, 1910.

While in Lucknow the Aga Khan visited the *Darul uloom* of the *Nadwat-ul-ulama* and was cordially received by the *ulama, moulvies* and Muslim notables of the city. He assured the *Nadwa* of his support in their movement for spreading Islamic culture and learning all over India and stressed the need for co-operation among the different sects of Islam in matters common to all Muslims.[127] The Aga Khan's sympathy with the *Nadwat-ul-ulama* was largely helpful in securing their understanding of the programme of the League.

The Aga Khan had several interviews with the Lieutenant-Governor of the United Provinces in Lucknow.[128] He was able to convince Hewett of the *bona fides* of the League. The Aga Khan told Hewett that he wanted the League to be 'a conservative institution, designed to further the Mahomedan cause, and also to strengthen the hands of Government, but with no animosity towards the Hindus'. He wished it to act 'in co-operation with the Government, and in loyal association with it; to be cordial without being servile'. Hewett fully appreciated the Aga Khan's intentions. He had no doubt that 'a number of good men' had been joining the League and that its stability would be greatly increased. From the Aga Khan's talk, Hewett understood that the League wanted the Government to recognize it as the authority to which matters connected with the affairs of the Muslims should be referred. Hitherto the practice of the Government had been to refer such questions to all important Muslim organisations. However, personally, Hewett saw no reason why the Government should refuse to recognize the League 'as an authoritative body representing Mahomedan public opinion, though it can not agree that it is the only authority that is entitled to be consulted in matters affecting the Mahomedan community'.

The Aga Khan's anxiety to convince the Government of the loyalty of the League and of himself was apparently unnecessary, for there had hardly been any occasion to raise any doubt about it. But the Aga Khan appears to have been aware of Minto's annoyance with him for the part he had played in the agitation against the Viceroy's scheme of Muslim electorates. Already in October, 1909, writing in connection with Morley's compromise with the League, the Prince of Wales had reminded Minto about the loyalty of the Muslims and of the Aga Khan. Minto was told: 'No doubt you will see the Aga Khan and will be able to clear up any misunderstanding which may exist in his mind; you

---

[127] The *Statesman Weekly,* 10 February, 1910.
[128] Hewett to Minto, 3 February, 1910. Min. P. Corr. India, 1910, vol. I.

could not possibly find a more loyal man in the whole of India and one who wishes to do all he can to help the Government in their difficulties.'[129]   On 8 February, 1910, the Aga Khan's case was taken up by Arthur Bigge, private secretary to the Prince of Wales. Bigge hoped that Minto had 'forgiven him [the Aga Khan]'.[130]   He attempted to interpret the Aga Khan's activities in connection with the movement for separate electorates as more against Morley than Minto and asked the latter whether or not he thought it 'well that Morley gave in to him [the Aga Khan] about the Mahomedan representation'.[131]

Before, however, Bigge's letter had reached Minto, the Aga Khan himself called on the Viceroy at Calcutta. His explanation of the 'line he hoped the League would follow' seemed to Minto to be 'thoroughly sound'. Minto hoped that 'the Aga Khan's visit will have done a great deal of good'.[132]   Minto was so much pleased with the League leader that although the Aga Khan said nothing as to the Government recognising the authority of the League, he was prepared to accept it 'as a very representative Mahomedan body'—though not the only one to which the Government should refer for an opinion on any question of importance.[133]

Thus the Aga Khan's eagerness for co-operation with the Government and his personal charm coupled with the very weighty attestation of his integrity from royal quarters and high officials entirely changed Minto's estimation of him. The Aga Khan was no longer considered 'thoroughly discredited—so much so that many people think he will never return [to India] again'.[134]   Minto now thought it to be a great pleasure 'to have the chance of seeing him [the Aga Khan]' and looked to his assistance and support.[135]

In February, 1910, a meeting of the provincial secretaries of the League was held in Delhi under the chairmanship of the Aga Khan. The meeting was attended by Rafiuddin Ahmad, Yakub Hasan, Abdul Majid and Muhammad Shafi representing respectively, the Bombay,

---

[129] The Prince of Wales to the Viceroy, 14 October, 1909. Min. P. Corr., England and Abroad, 1908—10.

[130] Arthur Bigge, private secretary to the Prince of Wales, to Minto, 8 February, 1910. *Ibid.*

[131] *Ibid.*

[132] Minto to Hewett, 15 February, 1910. Min. P. Corr. India, 1910, vol. 1.

[133] *Ibid.*

[134] Minto to Moberly Bell, 27 November, 1909. Min. P. Corr. England and Abroad, 1908—10.

[135] Minto to Hewett, 15 February, 1910. Min. P. Corr. India, 1910, vol. 1.

Madras, the U.P. and the Punjab Leagues.[136] Aziz Mirza, the secretary and Musa Khan, joint secretary of the All-India League, also attended the meeting. This meeting, being the first of its kind, provided an opportunity for the central and provincial League leaders to exchange views, thus strengthening the inter-provincial understanding for mutual benefit. The proceedings of the meeting were not published. But the *Times of India* understood that the meeting had discussed 'many important points concerning the moral and material progress' of the Muslims and that it had enjoined upon the secretaries to carry out the League's programme of communal welfare into practice.[137]

On 14 February, 1910, Aziz Mirza formally took charge of his duties as secretary of the All-India Muslim League.[138] Until Aziz Mirza's election the League had not been fortunate in its choice for the post of the secretary. Among the previous secretaries, both Mohsin-ul-Mulk and Viqar-ul-Mulk were too old to shoulder the arduous task of the assignment. Moreover, both of them had been mostly occupied with the Aligarh College and could not devote much of their time to the activities of the League. Major Syed Hasan Bilgrami possessed the requisite qualities for the secretaryship of the League. He was middle-aged and of active habits. His command over the English language, his experience as a retired major in the Indian Medical Service, his amiability and his family background (his brothers Syed Husain and Syed Ali Bilgrami were well-known politician, administrator and scholars) had made him the choice to succeed Viqar-ul-Mulk. But he spent most of the time of his secretaryship in England. Musa Khan, who acted as secretary in the absence of Bilgrami, despite his sincere devotion to the League was handicapped by his lack of knowledge of the English language.[139] Aziz Mirza was eminently suited for his office. As a former student of the Aligarh College and a former official of the Nizam's Government he had watched developments in Muslim politics with interest. Since his retirement from Hyderabad he had settled in Aligarh and actively participated in the affairs of the College and of the Muslim League. He was in his fifties and full of enthusiasm for the League. He was also a scholar and held moderate views in politics.[140]

[136] The *Times of India Mail*, 19 February, 1910.
[137] *Ibid.*
[138] *Report of the A.I.M.L. for 1910*, published at the Indian Daily Telegraph Press, Lucknow, p. 2.
[139] Muhammad Ali to Dunlop Smith, 7 January, 1909. Min. P. Corr. India, 1909, vol. I.
[140] Hewett to Minto, 3 February, 1910. Min. P. Corr. India, 1910, vol. I.

Soon after the assumption of his duties, Aziz Mirza opened the central office of the League in a '*bungalow*' on the Lalbagh Road, at Lucknow.[141]   Thereafter, he devoted himself to being a full-time honorary worker of the League.  During the first year of his secretary-ship, Aziz Mirza travelled more than twenty-thousand miles covering most of the important cities in the U.P., Bombay, Madras, Burma, Eastern Bengal and Assam, Bengal and C.P.[142]   He was on tour for four months in 1910.  Most of the remaining period of the year he spent in Lucknow carrying out the doubly-increased correspondence and routine work of the League.  One of his most outstanding contri-butions to the League was a number of brochures written and published by him in Urdu and English.[143]  These publications, while explaining the aims, objects and policy of the League, also sought to popularise the party's programme in some detail and attracted wide public atten-tion.[144]

Unlike in 1909, in 1910 the League leaders did not concentrate their energies on any particular issue.  The questions of the Indians in South Africa, the introduction of separate electorates in local bodies, the adequate share of Muslims in the services, the extension of educational facilities for Muslim students and other matters raised at the Delhi session received the attention of the League during the first ten months of 1910.  Most of these issues were represented to the Government through memorials and by passing resolutions at the committee and the public meetings.  Some of the questions were also brought to the notice of the authorities by the Muslim members of the different councils, either in their speeches or in the form of interpellations.

Like the previous year, 1910 also saw the London League in the fore-front of League activities.  Early in January, 1910, the Committee of the London League directed their secretary, Zahur Ahmad, to submit a representation to the Under-Secretary for the Colonies regarding the treatment of the Indians who as passive resisters were undergoing or had undergone imprisonment in the Transvaal.[145]  They considered the pressure exerted on the prisoners by ignoring or over-riding their religious scruples and requirements as unfair and as an attempt on the

---

[141] The *Civil and Military Gazette*, 3 March, 1910.
[142] *Report of the A.I.M.L. for 1910*, pp. 14, 15 and 18–22.
[143] *Ibid.*
[144] *Ibid.*, pp. 17–19. One of these brochures '*A talk on Muslim politics*' drew hostile criticism from some Hindu newspapers for the views expressed in it. (*Vide Leader*, 15 September, 1910. The *U.P. N.N.R.* - 1910.
[145] *The Times*, 15 January, 1910.

part of the authorities to break down their passive resistance. The London League appealed to the British Government to prevail upon the Government of the Transvaal to provide the prisoners with facilities for observing the fast of the *Ramzan* and to supply them with food according to the requirements of their religion. They cautioned the Government that already attempts were being made by the enemies of British rule in India to utilize the intense feeling of indignation among all classes against the policy of the South African Government to foment disaffection.[146]

In his reply to the London League's representation, Francis Hopwood, the permanent Under-Secretary for the Colonies, referred to an earlier statement of the Earl of Crewe, the Secretary of State for Colonial Affairs, on the subject.[147]  On 16 November, 1909, the Earl of Crewe had observed in the House of Lords that His Majesty's Government realized 'the force of appeals made to them and have not failed to endeavour to bring about as favourable a settlement as is possible, having regard to the views of the responsible Government and Parliament of the Colony'.[148]  Regarding the particular question of the diet to the prisoners, Hopwood replied that necessary directions for providing suitable food had already been issued by the Government of the Transvaal and that the Secretary of State had no reason to believe that those orders were not being observed. As for the facilities for observing the fast of *Ramzan* in prison, Hopwood had nothing definite to say except that the Colonial Office was still in correspondence with the Transvaal on this question.[149]

Within a few days of the submission of their representation on the Indians in South Africa, the London League addressed another memorandum, this time to the Permanent Under-Secretary of State for India demanding the introduction of separate Muslim electorates in the district boards, local boards and municipalities.[150]  Assuming that the report of the Royal Commission upon Decentralisation was being considered by the Secretary of State, the London League argued its case with several quotations from the recommendations of the Commission as well as from the observations of Minto and Morley on the question.

[146]*Ibid.*

[147]*The Civil and Military Gazette,* 5 February, 1910.

[148]*Ibid.,* 25 February, 1910.

[149]*Ibid.*

[150]Proc. U.P. Local Self-Government Department, June, 1911, vol. 8659, No. 336.

They submitted that the extension of the principle of separate electorates to the local bodies was essential to give cohesion and symmetry to the electoral scheme adumbrated in the Government of India Act, 1909, more especially as the personnel of the Councils would be dependent in large measure upon the composition of the district and municipal boards which would return a considerable proportion of the elective members of the Councils. They reminded the Government that not only the Viceroy and the Secretary of State were committed to the introduction of separate representation of the Muslims in the local bodies but that the Decentralisation Commission had definitely pronounced its verdict in favour of this principle. They also pointed out that while none of the three hundred and seven witnesses examined by the commission raised any objection to the system on the basis of experience of its working in those municipalities of the Punjab and Burma where it had already been in operation, several witnesses had testified that it had worked most satisfactorily. In the event, the London League urged that the separate electorates should be introduced in all the local bodies in accordance with the plan suggested by the deputation to Morley in January, 1909.

The India Office reply to the memorandum was evasive, merely inviting the attention of the League to its previous correspondence on the subject with them.[151] On 24 March, 1909, in reply to a representation from Ibn Ahmad, the then secretary of the London League, the India Office had asked him to take up the question of Muslim representation in the local bodies with the various local Governments and the Government of India. The India Office now repeated this suggestion, telling the London League to direct, if necessary, the Indian branches of the League to contact the local Governments and the Government of India, who had been considering the whole subject of the recommendations of the Decentralisation Commission.[152]

The question of separate representation of Muslims in the local bodies had been considered to be of paramount importance by the All-India Muslim League. On 7 March, 1910, the matter was taken up by Aziz Mirza in a letter to the Secretary to the Home Department, Government of India.[153] In reply he was informed that the Government had not

[151] R. Ritchie to the secretary, A.I.M.L., London Branch, 17 February, 1910. *Ibid.,* Proc. No. 33(c).
[152] *Ibid.*
[153] Aziz Mirza to the secretary, Home Department, Government of India, 7 March, 1910. Proc. U.P. Local Self-Government, June, 1911, vol. 8659, No. 33(d).

yet formulated its views on the recommendations of the Decentralisation Commission and that the question of separate electorates had been under their consideration.[154] The League leaders, not fully satisfied with this answer, continued to press the different local Governments to accept their demand. Prominent League leaders like Rafiuddin Ahmad and Allahando Yusuf Shah of Bombay[155] and Aftab Ahmad Khan of the U.P.[156] repeatedly voiced this demand in their respective provincial councils. As in 1909, several non-League Muslim organisations like the Anjuman-i-Musalman-i-Bangala[157] and most of the Muslim newspapers strongly supported this demand.[158]

Besides the question of separate electorates, Aziz Mirza also represented the League demands for adequate Muslim share in the state services, investigation into the management of the *waqf* estates and the demand for the validation of *Waqf-ala'l-Aulad* to the Government of India. The replies of the Government to these representations were non-committal, vague and even negative. In reply to the claim for the appointment of more Muslims in the government services, the League secretary was told that the Governor-General-in-Council desired that the Muslims, 'like every other community should enjoy the share of government patronage to which the number and importance of their community and their educational and other qualifications entitle them' and that the Government had 'no information to show that the local Governments and Administrations do not share this desire'.[159] This was a denial that the Muslims had any reason to be dissatisfied about their proportion in the state services. The Government of India's reply, however, did not end there. It further suggested that if the League had reason to think that in any province the Muslims did not receive due consideration over appointments they should represent their grievances to the local Government who, the Government of India had no doubt, would accord careful and sympathetic consideration to any such grievances.[160]

[154]*Report of the A.I.M.L. for 1910*, p. 7.

[155]Proceedings of the Legislative Council of the Governor of Bombay, 1910, vol. XLVIII, pp. 143–145.

[156]Proceedings of the Legislative Council: United Provinces, 1910, p. 51.

[157]Petition from honorary secretary, Anjuman-i-Musalman-i-Bangala. Proceedings of the Government of Bengal for the month of April, 1910, vol. 8419.

[158]The *Al Bashir*, 8 February, 1910; the *Naiyar-e-Azam*, 5 February, 1910; *Al-Fasih*, 3 May, 1910, the *Mukhbir-e-Alam*, 15 August, 1910, etc., etc. The *U.P. N.N.R.*, 1910.

[159]Quoted in the *Report of the All-India Muslim League for 1910*, p. 6.
[160]*Ibid.*

In view of the several representations submitted by the League and other Muslim organisations, the Government of India could not have been unaware of the Muslim grievances on this score. The reply of the Government, therefore, only strengthened the determination of the League leaders to continue their agitation for adequate Muslim representation in the various services. On 25 June, 1910, Rafiuddin Ahmad complained in the Bombay Legislative Council that notwithstanding the availability of qualified Muslims 'a tendency is unfortunately perceptible to reject them on the ground of relatively superior qualifications having to be given precedence'.[161] Rafiuddin Ahmad, Ibrahim Rahimtullah and other League leaders sought to establish this contention by referring to the very small number of Muslim employees in various branches of the Bombay Government.[162]

The Government of India's reply to the question of enquiring into the management of *waqfs* was more unfavourable to the League. The Government rejected the demand on the grounds that any definite action could not be taken unless the League established its contention that the *waqfs* were mismanaged and that there was a consensus of Muslim opinion in favour of reform.[163] The two conditions were difficult for the League to satisfy. No Indian political party could ever claim to undertake successfully the stupendous task of surveying the management of *waqf* estates all over India. This was all the more difficult because a considerable number of such *waqfs* were known only to the endowers and their trustees. On the other hand, the Government through the agency of their district officers could obtain the necessary information within a short time. The next condition of proving the consensus of the Muslims in the matter was almost impossible for the League to meet. The League leaders were puzzled by the attitude underlying such a condition. This was thought to have questioned the League's *bona fides* to speak for and on behalf of the Muslims, which the Government had never done before.[164]

Undaunted by this discouraging reply, the League secretary pointed out that the unanimity of the Muslim public on the *waqf* question could be gathered from the fact that a dissentient voice had never arisen against the League's contention. He further asserted that even the interested

---

[161] Proceedings of the Legislative Council of the Governor of Bombay, 1910, vol. XLVIII, p. 154.

[162] *Ibid.*, pp. 130, 139, 143–146.

[163] *Report of the A.I.M.L. for 1910*, p. 8.

[164] *Ibid.*

parties who had been 'fattening' on the proceeds of these *waqfs* did not dare protest against the demand for investigation. The League secretary contended that the maladministration of *waqfs* had become 'a perfect scandal'. Citing the instance of Rangoon where Muslim *waqfs* were reported to be worth more than one crore of rupees, Aziz Mirza remarked that if the *waqf* estates were properly administered and their revenues spent on communal welfare the Muslims would no longer remain a backward community. The League, therefore, asked its branches to collect data regarding *waqfs* in their respective provinces. In response, the Bengal Provincial League appointed a committee to enquire into the management of certain large *waqfs*,[165] while the League leaders in other provinces persisted in the demand for government investigation into the matter. On 18 April, 1910, when Aftab Ahmad Khan raised the question in the U.P. Legislative Council the provincial Government followed in the footsteps of the Government of India in placing on the Muslims the onus of establishing the allegation against the *waqfs* before undertaking any measures on the issue.[166] As a partial redress of the problem, Ibrahim Rahimtullah intended to move a bill for the registration of charities in the Bombay Legislative Council. In June, 1910, he sounded the Governor of Bombay on the matter[167] and on being encouraged by the latter he took up the preparation of the bill, finally giving notice of the same in January, 1911.[168]

The Government's reply to the demand for the validation of *Waqf-ala'l-Aulad* was of a different nature, simply referring the League to the Government's answer to Muhammad Ali Jinnah's interpellation on the question in the Imperial Council on 25 February, 1910.[169] On that occasion the Government had admitted that although they were aware of objections entertained by the Muslims to the decisions of the Judicial Committee of the Privy Council on *Waqf-ala'l-Aulad*,[170] they were not at that moment prepared to legislate with the express object

---

[165] The Bengal League, however, does not appear to have achieved any success in the matter. The *Mussalman*, 9 September, 1910, regretted that the League sub-committee failed to submit its findings on the alleged mismanagement of Haji Mohsin's Syedpur Trust Estate. *Vide* the *Bengal N.N.R.*, 1910.

[166] Proceedings of the Legislative Council, U.P., 1910, p. 124.

[167] Proceedings of the Council of the Governor of Bombay, 1911, vol. XLIX, p. 65.

[168] Government of Bombay: Legal Department Proceedings, 1911, vol. 8837, p. 15.

[169] *Report of the A.I.M.L. for 1910*, p. 9.

[170] Proc. Council of the G.G., vol. XLVIII, p. 185.

of 'upsetting judicial decisions to which objection is taken'.[171] However, they were ready to consider 'any specific proposals for legislation directed to the object of securing family settlements of a limited nature, provided that such proposals are generally approved' by the Muslims. The League leaders considered it a good gesture of the Government and requested Muhammad Ali Jinnah to undertake the preparation and submission of a bill on the subject.[172] Jinnah gladly accepted the request, for he had already been working on the matter. He prepared a draft bill on the validation of *Waqf-ala'l-Aulad* in consultation with Ameer Ali in England. By about the same time, however, Shams-ul-Huda, another member of the Imperial Council and secretary, Bengal Provincial League, circulated a draft bill on the same subject among the leading Muslims of India,[173] but since his version was of a limited nature and it took him some time to improve upon it he was overtaken by Jinnah in the presentation of the bill before the Council in 1911.

While knocking at the door of the Government for the preservation and advancement of the political and economic interests of the Muslims, the League also worked for the educational and cultural progress of the community. The League leaders continuously preached of the urgent need for the Muslims to take to English education in larger numbers and took several steps to facilitate the growth of education and science among them. By March, 1910, two funds for granting scholarships to deserving students for higher studies abroad were created in the names of the Aga Khan and Ameer Ali.[174] The Aga Khan, Fazulbhoy Currimbhoy, Fazulbhoy Muhammadbhoy Chinoy, Muhammad Ali and Qazi Kabiruddin were the moving spirits behind these foundations. While the Aga Khan himself initiated the Ameer Ali scholarship fund with a personal donation of ten thousand rupees, the Aga Khan fund was jointly sponsored by Fazulbhoy Currimbhoy and Qazi Kabiruddin with donations of ten thousand rupees and one thousand rupees respectively.[175] Within a few months several thousands of rupees were contributed to these funds by people from various parts of the country.[176]

---

[171]*Ibid.*

[172]*Report of the A.I.M.L. for 1910*, pp. 9–10.

[173]The *Pioneer Mail*, 16 December, 1910.

[174]The *Statesman*, 10 February, 1910 and the *Times of India Mail*, 26 March, 1910.

[175]*Ibid.*

[176]The *Times of India Mail*, 9 April, 1910.

Of the other measures adopted by the League leaders for the spread of education among the Muslims, the most remarkable was the decision to establish a technical school at Aligarh. This institution was expected to remove one of the chief causes of Muslim backwardness in technical education. The appeal for subscription for the establishment of the school launched by the Aga Khan, the Raja of Mahmudabad, Viqar-ul-Mulk and nine other distinguished leaders,[177] evoked favourable response, but the project took several years to materialise. Towards the middle of 1910, the League leaders also took certain preliminary steps for the collection of funds for the proposed Muslim University at Aligarh.[178]

The importance attached by the League to the diffusion of higher education among the Muslims was further evidenced by the demand advanced by some of its leaders for a special educational tax on the community. The annual meeting of the Bombay Presidency League held under the presidentship of the Aga Khan adopted a resolution proposed by Ghulam Muhammad Bhurgri and seconded by Allahando Yusuf Shah asking the Government to make special enactment for an educational cess at the rate of a quarter of an anna in the rupee, on assessment from the jagirdars and zamindars of Sind to be spent on the secondary and higher education of the Sindhi Muslims.[179] Similarly, the provincial League of Eastern Bengal and Assam urged upon the Government 'the absolute necessity of an educational tax' to be levied on the Muslims of the province for the encouragement and support of education amongst them.[180] The Eastern Bengal and Assam League also endorsed the public appeal for donations sponsored by Salimullah and Nawab Ali Choudhury for the establishment of a residential hall for the Muslim students at Dacca.[181]

The promotion of Urdu language and literature was an important object in the League's programme of educational and cultural development. The League leaders were alarmed about the future of Urdu by the agitation in favour of Hindi by an influential section of the Congress leaders including Madan Mohan Malaviya, the president of the Congress

[177] The *Aligarh Institute Gazette*, 26 October, 1910. The *U.P. N.N.R.*, 1910.
[178] The *Times of India Mail*, 21 May, 1910.
[179] The *Civil and Military Gazette*, 22 March, 1910.
[180] The *Pioneer Mail*, 28 October, 1910.
[181] *Ibid.*

and particularly of the Hindu Sabhas of the Punjab and the U.P.[182] They were determined to maintain the position occupied by Urdu in the Punjab, the U.P. and Bihar, and at the same time work for the enhancement of its status in the provinces of Bombay, Madras and Bengal. Aziz Mirza directed the provincial Leagues to be on the look out and see that in the ensuing census Urdu-speaking people were returned as speaking that language alone.[183]   In a speech at the Urdu Conference at Badaun, in the U.P., the League secretary appealed to the educated Muslims to strive for the development of the Urdu language.  The Badaun Urdu Conference gave a new impetus to the campaign for the promotion of Urdu by demanding its introduction in the Allahabad University examinations.[184]   The Bombay Presidency Urdu Conference held under the presidency of the Nawab of Wai and opened by the Aga Khan also demanded the recognition of Urdu in the B.A. and M.A. examinations.[185]

In carrying into effect its programme for the regeneration of the Muslims, the League had been severely handicapped by the absence of any influential Muslim daily newspaper. There was not a single Muslim daily newspaper in English in the whole of India. One or two vernacular dailies enjoying limited circulation could hardly cope with the demand on their space. The League leaders were fully conscious of this weakness in their movement, but lack of funds prevented them from taking any positive step in this respect. Attempts were, however, made to remedy partially this shortcoming by patronising a few existing journals and by establishing others in various important cities and towns.  In March, 1910, the Bombay League had decided to establish a weekly organ to be published in several languages.[186]   The first issue of the journal—the *Moslem*—published from Poona, the headquarters of the provincial League, saw the light of day in July, 1910.[187]  By that time the *Muslim Review*—the monthly journal of the U.P. League issued from Allahabad was a few months old. On 16 October, 1910, the Eastern Bengal and Assam League decided to revive two vernacular weeklies—the *Mihir-o-Sudhakar* and the *Soltan*—as a single amalgamated weekly under the

[182] Indirect references to the activities of these Hindu leaders and organisations were made by the mover, seconder and supporters of the A.I.M.L. resolution on Urdu at the Delhi session in January, 1910.

[183] *Report of the A.I.M.L. for 1910*, pp. 10—11.

[184] The *Advocate*, 7 April, 1910. The *U.P. N.N.R.,* 1910.

[185] The *Times of India Mail*, 26 March, 1910.

[186] The *Times of India Mail*, 19 March, 1910.

[187] The *Times of India Mail*, 23 July, 1910.

title of the *Mihir-o-Sudhakar*.[188]   In November, 1910, the council of
the All-India Muslim League passed a resolution to take under its control the *Al-Rafio,* a periodical published at Rangoon.[189]

However beneficial the increasing activities of the League had been
in the sphere of Muslim welfare, some of its demands caused serious
misgivings among the Hindus.   Since early 1909 the violent Hindu
agitation against the movement for separate electorates had been widening the gulf between the two communities.  The partial recognition of
separate electorates in the Government of India Act of 1909, which
was followed by Gokhale's acquiescence in the anti-separate electorates
campaign by the Congress leaders,[190] resulted in the ascendancy of
Hindu communalists as an influence upon the formation of Congress
policy on this matter.  Malaviya's presidential address at the Congress
session held at Lahore in December, 1909, greatly exacerbated the ill-
feeling between large numbers of Hindus and Muslims.[191]   By March,
1910, the bitterness between the two communities reached a new peak
in the Punjab with the Hindu boycott of Muslim traders.[192]   The
Hindus openly refused 'to trade with Mahomedans until Mahomedans
rally to the national cause'.[193]   The boycott even extended to the
liberal professions and caused the Muslims heavy losses, the Hindus
being generally wealthier.[194]

On 16 April, 1910, the grievances of the Punjab Muslims against
the Hindus were taken up by the London League.  At a special meeting
of the Committee of the London League, Zahur Ahmad, the secretary
was asked to submit a memorandum to the permanent Under-Secretary
of State for India demanding prompt amelioration of the condition
created by the Hindu boycott of the Muslims in the Punjab.[195]   The

[188]The *Pioneer Mail,* 28 October, 1910.

[189]*Ibid.,* 4 November, 1910.

[190]Although in his speech at the Imperial Council in March, 1909, Gokhale
had strongly supported the Government of India's scheme of Muslim electorates,
he did not oppose the violent condemnation of the measure at the Lahore session
of the Congress in December, 1909.  This change in Gokhale's attitude was
possibly due to the fact that the number of separately elected seats sanctioned in
the regulations under the Government of India Act, 1909, was much greater than
those proposed in the Government of India's despatch of October, 1908.

[191]Malaviya's attack on separate electorates became the subject of strong
support and denunciation by the Hindu and Muslim press respectively.

[192]*The Times,* 28 March, 1910.

[193]*Ibid.*

[194]*Ibid.*

[195]J. & P., 1166/1910, vol. 992.

London League, while deploring the situation in the Punjab, was not surprised at the bad turn of events. Some nine months ago, in July, 1909, they had been constrained to draw the attention of the Secretary of State to the 'domineering and aggressive attitudes' assumed by certain sections of the Hindus towards the Muslims in different parts of India.[196] The London League had then complained that the Hindus, 'not content with attempting to dictate [to] the Government the policy it should pursue', had been resorting to 'overt and in many cases unlawful pressure' upon the Muslims to 'reduce them to subservience to their own political programme by a system of organised boycott in every direction'.[197] Recalling these warnings, the London League now asserted that their worst apprehensions had come to be true in the case of the Punjab. They held that in the existing social and economic conditions of India, boycott was a 'formidable instrument of terrorism' and that in the Punjab where there were hardy and martially-spirited elements in the population there was 'much greater danger of reprisals being provoked than in some other parts of India'.[198] Referring to the statements of some Hindu leaders, especially of Pratul Chatterjee, as president of the Punjab Hindu Conference, which had accentuated the differences between the Hindus and Muslims, the London League claimed that 'the Government cannot view with indifference the proscription of a community on the ground that it is loyal to the British connexions'.

The Committee of the London League repeated their earlier appeal that the Government should take such measures as might be considered expedient 'to ensure the Mahomedans quiet enjoyment of their rights and privileges' without 'molestation or interference by any section'. They suggested that in order to check further deterioration in the situation in the Punjab, the law against criminal intimidation should be put in force and should be strengthened if required. They also proposed that in localities where feelings between Hindus and Muslims were liable to run high, conciliation boards should be formed under the auspices of the divisional and district authorities. They believed that the development of arbitration systems for the settlement of both international and industrial disputes had been one of the most remarkable features of the progress of mankind and that in India there were important instances of the value of conciliation committees in preventing social strife.

[196] J. & P., 2711/909, vol. 948.
[197] *Ibid.*
[198] J. & P., 1166/1910, vol. 992.

The memorandum of the London League failed to elicit any positive reply from the India Office, which would not go beyond a formal acknowledgement.   The official attitude towards the matter, however, was made clear in a note by Risley, secretary of the Judicial and Public department and a former Home Secretary of the Government of India.   Admitting the truth of the Hindu boycott of the Muslims in the Punjab, he noted that some months ago 'the Hindu majority of the Bar Library at Lahore turned out on the re-election of the committee, all the Mahomedan members', and that even the Punjab Government had faced difficulty in securing the election of a Muslim to the Syndicate of the University.[199]   He thought that the 'enmity between Hindus and Mahomedans is no new thing in the Punjab' and that it was not surprising that it should have been accentuated by the speeches of leading Muslims in connection with the council reforms and the rejoinder of the Hindu press.   He was satisfied that the local Government were well aware of the state of things and had been endeavouring to bring about more amicable relations between the two communities.

As regards the particular suggestion for the creation of conciliation boards, Risley noted that it would be 'highly impolitic to recognise officially the existence of strained relations between the two communities and to create special machinery for improving those relations'.   He considered the matter as one for the exercise of personal influence and 'not for the intervention of a formal Board which might prove very embarrassing if the disturbances occurred and had to be suppressed'.   This ostrich-like policy of non-recognition of the very grave differences between Hindus and Muslims while knowing and privately admitting them to be true, seems, in retrospect, to have been one of the blunders of British statesmanship in India.   If Morley and Minto had had the courage to accept the serious nature of the differences between the two communities, thereby applying themselves to a conscientious and practical solution of the same, the course of British Indian history might have been different.[200]

In the absence of any attempt at conciliation between Hindus and Muslims either by the Government or by the leaders of the two com-

---

[199]Note by Risley on the London League's memorandum on 16 April, 1910. *Ibid.*

[200]Even the Congress leaders believed that the formation of conciliation committees would have prevented communal riots which had greatly aggravated the Hindu-Muslim tension in different parts of India, *vide—Report of the Twenty-Fifth I.N.C.,* pp. 95–97.

munities, the relations between them continued to deteriorate in various parts of the country throughout the later part of 1910. With the approach of the time for the census the Hindu and Muslim leaders came out with conflicting demands regarding the position of the Urdu and Hindi languages as well as the status of the depressed classes.[201] The Muslims of the U.P. strongly resented the provision for separate entries of Hindi-speaking people in the census forms and asserted that Urdu was the only language in the province.[202] The All-India Muslim League did not take official notice of this controversy. But their demand for the classification of the depressed classes as different from the Hindus raised a storm of protest from the latter.[203] Individual League leaders had always declared that the depressed classes were a separate community and that they should not be included in the Hindu category. This view had also found place in the memorial of the Simla deputation in October, 1906. But it was not until October, 1910, when under instructions from the Council of the All-India Muslim League, Aziz Mirza submitted a representation to the Government that the separate enumeration of the depressed classes became an issue between the Hindus and Muslims.

The League demand regarding the depressed classes was claimed to have been as much in the interest of the depressed classes themselves as it was in the interests of the Muslims. The League secretary observed that if 'these so-called untouchables' who had 'no religious or ethnic affinity' with the Hindus were considered as a separate entity then the Government would have certainly enquired into their wretched conditions and done something to ameliorate them.[204] He thought that the depressed classes had been deprived of the benefits of various development activities of the Government and that they could not take advantage even of the primary schools where the high-caste teachers were afraid of being polluted by their touch. He appealed to the Government to give the untouchables opportunities to assert their rights and privileges as a community and to see that they were no longer

[201] Writing to the Secretary of State on 1 December, 1910, the Viceroy, Hardinge, reported '. . . I hear that in Northern India Mahommedan feeling has never been so intense as it now is . . .' Hardinge to Crewe, H.P., vol. 117.

[202] The *Naiyar-e-Azam*, 12 November, 1910; the *Sahifa*, 12 November, 1910; the *Jadu*, 15 November, 1910, etc., etc. The *U.P. N.N.R.*, 1910.

[203] The *Tohfa-i-Hind*, 25 November, 1910; the *Abhyudaya*, 1 December, 1910, etc. *Ibid.*

[204] *Report of the A.I.M.L. for 1910*, p. 11.

regarded as helots. The League secretary also made it clear that the inclusion of the depressed classes under the Hindu category was detrimental to the interests of the Muslims as it gave 'a fictitious numerical importance' to the Hindus to which they were not entitled. He further noted that in case the Government found it impracticable to show the depressed classes separately from the Hindus, measures should be taken to enumerate them at least in such a way that their exact numbers might be easily found out in the census returns.

The Government was inclined to consider favourably the League memorandum. The reply by the census commissioner, while pointing out the practical difficulties in separately enumerating the depressed classes told the League secretary that the Government had been considering the feasibility of preparing an estimate of the number of persons who, though classed as Hindus, could not properly be so regarded. Aziz Mirza was thus led to think that, undeterred by the Hindu agitation against his memorandum, the census commissioner would take measures to implement his alternative suggestion. Finally, however, the gravity of the Hindu agitation compelled the Government to revise their opinion in the matter.[205]

Between December, 1909, and November, 1910, the All-India Muslim League had established itself firmly as the sole all-India Muslim organisation. Its authority as the mouthpiece of the Muslims was now recognised by the Government and by the Indian National Congress. During this period the League liberalised its constitution, set up several branch organisations, and formulated a wider programme for itself. By now the League was fully prepared to undertake the more ambitious task of the politico-cultural regeneration of the Muslims of India.

[205] In reply to a question from S. Sinha, Butler, Education Member, Government of India, said that the Government had no intention of altering the procedure hitherto adopted for the enumeration of the depressed classes and that they simply wanted to add some explanatory notes to the census returns so that those interested could have some idea about the total strength of these people. Proc. Council of the G.G. of India, vol. XLIX, p. 77.

## Chapter VII

## RE-ORIENTATIONS

Between December, 1910 and August, 1911, the membership and objectives of the League entered a state of flux. The growing number of young professional men in the ranks of the League helped to produce re-orientations in the League's relation with the Hindu community and in important matters of policy. During this period the ground work was laid for the transformation of the nature and purposes of the League which became apparent in December, 1912.

As has been seen, in January, 1910, the Aga Khan had appealed for an *entente cordiale* between Hindus and Muslims, particularly the loyalists among them.[1] The olive branch was spurned by the Hindu press[2] and the Congress turned a deaf ear to the offer. By October– November, 1910, however, in view of the grave deterioration in Hindu– Muslim relations, Wedderburn, president of the Indian National Congress, 1910, in consultation with Pherozeshah Mehta, a former Congress president, raised the matter with the Aga Khan.[3] The opportunity was seized by the Aga Khan, whose concern for reconciliation between the two communities seems to have been increased many-fold by King George V's desire to make Hindu–Muslim amity the cornerstone of the policy of his Government.[4] The move was also supported by Ameer Ali, dissatisfied as he had been with the Government's rejection of his suggestion for the creation of conciliation boards. It was then decided to hold a meeting of the leading members of the League and the Congress, either before or after the annual sessions of the respective organisations. Consequently, the Aga Khan suggested that Allahabad, the venue of the Congress session, should also be the site for the conference of the All-India Muslim League. He even promised to subscribe upwards of five thousand rupees towards the cost of the session if it was held at Allahabad.[5]

[1] *Supra*, p. 166.
[2] The *Advocate*, 3 February, 1910, and the *Leader*, 3 February, 1910. The *U.P. N.N.R.*, 1910.
[3] The *India*, 25 November, 1910 and the *Pioneer Mail*, 9 December, 1910.
[4] The *Zamindar*, 1 January, 1911. The *Punjab N.N.R.*, 1911.
[5] The *Times of India Mail*, 8 October, 1910.

But earlier the League had accepted an invitation to hold its annual meeting at Nagpur and accordingly preliminary arrangements had already been made there.[6] Even then, the council of the League was willing to shift the meeting to Allahabad.[7] However, at the insistence of the Muslim leaders of Nagpur, it was finally decided not to change the venue of the meeting. In the event, the council of the League advanced the date of the session by two days—from 30 December, 1910 to 28 December, 1910—so as to enable the League leaders to attend the conciliation meeting at Allahabad immediately after the conclusion of the session.[8]

The Nagpur session of the All-India Muslim League started at 9 a.m. on 28 December, 1910. It was largely attended by delegates and observers from C.P., Bombay, U.P., Madras, Bengal and Eastern Bengal and Assam.[9] This session had several remarkable characteristics. In the first place, it marked the ascendancy of the younger members in the leadership of the League. Among the young activists, Muhammad Ali, Wazir Hasan, Yakub Hasan, Muhammad Yakub (pleader, Muradabad), Syed Zahur Ahmad (pleader, Lucknow), Sheikh Zahur Ahmad, (barrister, Allahabad and formerly secretary of the London League) and A. H. M. Anwar (barrister, Khandwa), played significant parts in the conference. The president of the session, Syed Nabiullah, barrister, himself belonged to this younger group. Secondly, prominent Congress members like Qazi Kabiruddin and Ibrahim Rahimtullah who had recently joined the League took active parts in the session. Their active interest in the affairs of the League had paved the way for the eventual success of the League in enlisting almost all Congress Muslims in its fold. Thirdly, the Nagpur conference relegated political questions to a secondary position and laid stress on questions of Muslim self-improvement in socio-economic life. Fourthly, the Nagpur session introduced a new element in League politics by adopting the demand for free and compulsory primary education in India, despite strong opposition from at least one of its prominent leaders. This appears to have been the first time that the League followed the principle of decision by a majority of votes instead of unanimity among the members. Fifthly, the Nagpur meeting's demands for free and compulsory primary education, for the curtailment of military and civil expenditure,

---

[6] The *Statesman Weekly,* 22 September, 1910.
[7] The *Pioneer Mail,* 4 November, 1910.
[8] The *Pioneer,* 12 January, 1911.
[9] *Ibid.*

for the appointment of Indians in the commissioned ranks of the Army, as well as its opposition to the reduction of the age-limits for the Indian Civil Service examinations, clearly showed that the League leaders had been rapidly expanding their interests beyond questions concerning the Muslims exclusively to those concerning other Indians generally.

The Nagpur session was opened with an address from H. M. Malek, chairman of the reception committee, who made a plea for Hindu-Muslim co-operation. Malek was, however, convinced that while co-operation between the two communities was a necessity, there could be no unity between them in the immediate future, for the enormous majority of the Indians were still 'at the stage where the whole process of differentiation still remains to be begun'.[10] He strongly advocated separate Muslim representation in the district boards and municipalities and remarked that 'short of it our doom will be more or less sealed and all the privileges of the extension of Local Self-Government will be a sealed book to the Mussulmans'.[11] He was equally emphatic in his appeal for the development of the Urdu language, which he considered to be pre-eminently fitted to serve the cause of eventual unity among the Indians.

Malek's speech was followed by the formal election of the president of the session, Syed Nabiullah. Nawab Ghulam Ahmad of Madras, in a brief speech recounting the services of Nabiullah to the Muslim community, proposed his election to the presidential chair. The proposal was seconded by Asghar Husain, barrister of C.P., and carried with acclamation.[12]

Nabiullah's presidential address breathed a deep sense of loyalty to the Government, a tolerant spirit towards the other communities and a lively solicitude for the progress of the Muslims of India. He expressed the gratitude of the Muslims towards Minto and Morley for their practical recognition of the hardships and claims of the community.[13] He vehemently repudiated the allegation that the Government was trying to play off one community against the other, maintaining that if such a sordid game were ever tried, it would inevitably end in disaster. The real interests of the rulers and the ruled lay in the peaceful and ordered development of the country which could only be secured by

[10] The *Pioneer*, 2 January, 1911.
[11] *Ibid.*
[12] *Proceedings of the Annual Meeting of the A.I.M.L. held at Nagpur on 28 and 29 December, 1910,* by Aziz Mirza, Allahabad, 1911, p. 17.
[13] *Ibid.*, pp. 19–20.

co-operation between the Government and the leaders of the people, without distinction of race and creed.[14]

Nabiullah sincerely hoped that the ensuing conference of the Hindu and Muslim leaders would result in a satisfactory settlement of all outstanding differences between the two communities. He suggested that Hindu and Muslim leaders, particularly the legislators belonging to the two communities, should meet together from time to time. Such meetings would render great service to the country, by removing misunderstandings and by promoting an atmosphere of mutual forbearance, tolerance and goodwill.[15]

Nabiullah was grieved to point out that certain events and incidents of recent years had offended the Muslims and caused many of them to search their hearts.[16] He would not discuss all such events but only referred to the cult of Shivaji. He admitted that men like Shivaji, Clive, and Dalhousie, could not be judged by the usual standard of morality applied to ordinary human beings. But did not the Shivaji celebrations 'suggest the revolt of Hinduism against Islam and by implication against foreign domination?' The apotheosis of Shivaji gave a foretaste 'of what the poor Mohamedans have to expect under Hindu hegemony'.[17]

Nabiullah's apprehensions regarding the attitude of the Hindu extremists towards the Muslims had been shared by many League leaders. But Nabiullah greatly differed from some of his fellow-workers in his diagnosis of the socio-economic problems of the Muslims. He observed that the demand for greater employment of the Muslims in the state services should not be over-emphasised as the subject affected only the educated classes—an infinitesimal part of the population.[18] The League leaders and workers should think more and more of how to ameliorate the condition of the poorer sections of the Muslims who formed the bulk of the community. This would require reforms in social customs, extension of primary and technical education, and development of agriculture, trade and industry. Nabiullah believed that the improvement of the economic conditions of the Muslims, as well as other Indians, was closely linked with the development of agriculture. He gave a gloomy picture of the agriculturists, a vast number of whom had been continually hovering on the border of destitution and starvation.[19]

[14]*Ibid.*, p. 29.
[15]*Ibid.*, p. 28.
[16]*Ibid.*, p. 26.
[17]*Ibid.*
[18]*Ibid.*, p. 29.
[19]*Ibid.*, p. 30.

Nabiullah put forward a three-fold measure which, by removing the obstacles to the development of agriculture, would greatly improve the condition of the agriculturists. First, the state demand on land revenue, which varied from province to province and was excessive in certain provinces, should be reconsidered. Second, since the short period of the land revenue settlement (after fifteen, twenty or thirty years), as prevalent in most of the provinces, had tended to discourage investment of capital in land, it should be extended to sixty years in all major provinces, and to a minimum term of forty years in less economically developed tracts. Third, in view of the heavy debts of the cultivators to 'the wily money-lenders', the co-operative credit societies should be multiplied and central banks established to finance them.[20]

Nabiullah was greatly concerned with the extension of education all over India and urged the Government to reform the educational policy with special emphasis on technical, industrial and scientific education. He thought that money required for the improvement of education and agriculture could be made available through retrenchment in the civil and military expenditure, as well as by curtailment of railway allocation.[21] He was firmly convinced that a reduction in military expenditure, which had increased by eight or nine crores in the course of nine or ten years, was essential in the interest of the development of the country. In case this was not found feasible, then at least a portion of India's military expenditure should be borne by the British Government, for India had been maintaining forces in excess of her own requirements and partly for imperial purposes.

Nabiullah drew the attention of the Government towards the 'deep concern and alarm' of the Muslims of India regarding the recent British note to Persia on the question of policing the trade-routes in Southern Persia. He feared that there was 'something amiss in latter-day British diplomacy', otherwise Muslim states like Persia and Turkey would not have looked more and more to Germany for assistance and advice. He believed that England's hold on the Muslim world would be increased if Turkish and Persian loans could be successfully placed on the London market, instead of in Paris and Berlin.

At the conclusion of his speech Nabiullah himself moved the first three resolutions of the session, which were passed unanimously. The resolutions gave expression to the profound sorrow of the Muslim community at the lamented death of King Edward VII, tendered the loyal

[20]*Ibid.,* p. 31.
[21]*Proceedings of the Annual Meeting of the A.I.M.L. held at Nagpur, op. cit.,* p. 33.

and respectful homage of the Muslims of India to King George V, and thanked the Government for the elevation of Syed Ali Imam to the Imperial Executive Council.[22]

The second sitting of the League session, held on the afternoon of 28 December, 1910, devoted itself to the consideration of four resolutions, all of which were adopted *nem con.* The first two resolutions, proposed respectively by Mirza Shujaat Ali Baig, Persian consul-general, Calcutta, and Shams-ul-Huda, member, Imperial Legislative Council, deeply appreciated the services of Lords Minto and Morley to the cause of Indian progress.[23] The third resolution, proposed by Rafiuddin Ahmad and seconded by Syed Tufail Ahmad, pleader, Fatehpur, strongly reiterated the demand for the extension of separate and adequate Muslim representation in the local self-governing bodies.[24] The fourth resolution proposed by Qazi Kabiruddin, barrister, Bombay, and seconded by Syed Zahur Ahmad, pleader, Lucknow, reiterated the firm conviction of the League that their Lordships of the Privy Council had erred in deciding that *Waqf-ala'l-Aulad* was not valid under the Muslim law and strongly urged upon the Government the desirability and urgency of legislative enactment declaring the validity of such *waqfs.*[25] In proposing the resolution, Qazi Kabiruddin made a lengthy and well-reasoned speech. He pointed out that *Waqf-ala'l-Aulad* was a time-honoured and religiously sanctioned right of the Muslims which was still recognised in Indian states like Hyderabad, Bhopal, Bahawalpur, Rampur, as well as in Muslim countries outside India.[26] He earnestly hoped that the Government would support the Bill for the validation of such *waqfs,* which was shortly going to be introduced into the Supreme Council.

On the second day of the session, Syed Nabiullah, barrister, Raja Naushad Ali Khan, *taluqdar,* Lucknow, Rafiuddin Ahmad and Hakim Ajmal Khan were elected to the vacant posts of vice-presidents of the All-India Muslim League.[27] The same day, in the course of two sittings, the League adopted altogether nine resolutions. Of them three reiterated the demands for the institution of a thorough inquiry into the purposes and the manner of administration of *waqf* estates; for

[22]*Ibid.,* pp. 52–53.
[23]*Ibid.,* pp. 54–56.
[24]*Ibid.,* pp. 57–59.
[25]*Ibid.,* p. 59.
[26]*Ibid.,* p. 64.
[27]*Ibid.,* p. 96.

more employment of Muslims in the government services; and for the prohibition of Indian indentured labourers for the South African Union so long as any South African Colony adhered to the existing discriminatory policy against them.[28]

Of the six other resolutions, the one relating to the Urdu language was a stronger version of the League's Delhi resolution on the same subject. The resolution deplored the persistent attempts that were being made by a section of the Hindu leaders to set up Hindi and Punjabi as the vernaculars of the U.P. and the Punjab respectively. Declaring Urdu *'the lingua franca'* of India and the only vehicle of progress and unity in northern India, the resolution also appealed to the Government to discountenance all endeavours to displace Urdu.[29] In proposing the resolution, Shaikh Zahur Ahmad, barrister, Allahabad, observed that few questions had created more ill-feeling between Hindus and Muslims than the controversy over Urdu and Hindi. He claimed that ever since the days of Emperor Shahjahan, Urdu had been to all intents and purposes the *lingua franca* of India. He ridiculed Hindi as 'Urdu degraded and vulgarised' and remarked that those who sought to resuscitate Sanskritic Nagri in the name of Hindi were only trying to bring an Egyptian mummy to life by constant puffs of human breath. He further declared that Punjabi had no better claim than Hindi to be called a language by itself.[30]

The resolution was seconded by Muhammad Yakub, pleader, Muradabad, who warned the protagonists of Hindi that their efforts to substitute other languages for Urdu would be disastrous.[31] In supporting the motion, Rafiuddin Ahmad recalled that twenty-five years earlier Urdu had been the medium of instruction in the Bombay presidency, but now Gujrati and Marathi had usurped its place and it had been relegated to the place of a second language, and that only in a few schools. He strongly criticised the recent statement of the Director of Public Instruction, Bombay, to the effect that Urdu should be excluded from public schools and Muslims be left to learn it at home as they did their theology.[32] The resolution was also supported by Muhammad Ali, who was grieved to observe that the Hindus were objecting to the use of Urdu on grounds of its alleged foreign origin. He asserted that Urdu had not been imported from Arabia, Persia, or Afghanistan; it had grown

[28]*Ibid.,* pp. 84–85, 96–97, 101–102.
[29]*Ibid.,* p. 76.
[30]*Ibid.,* pp. 77–79.
[31]*Ibid.,* p. 80.
[32]*Ibid.*

up in the Indian camp and in the market place. Muhammad Ali noted that the Muslim leaders were going to Allahabad in the sincere hope of establishing better relations with the Hindu community; they regarded the question of Urdu as the touchstone of Hindu sincerity. In a land where important elements of nationality like races, creeds, customs, traditions and even modes of thought and action were different, 'the one thing that was common was the *lingua franca* of Urdu'.[33] Ibrahim Rahimtullah, and Ishaque Ali, pleader, Lucknow, also spoke in the same vein in supporting the resolution.[34]

The vigour of the speakers, including young and old leaders of the League, on the position of Urdu showed the increasing concern of the Muslims at the movement for the propagation of Hindi spearheaded by some prominent leaders of the Congress. The League leaders seem to have been greatly alarmed by the recent activities of the promoters of Hindi who had just concluded the 'Common Script Conference'[35] and the Conference of the 'All-India Suddhi Sabha' at the Congress *pandal* at Allahabad.[36]

Of the remaining resolutions passed at the session, the one urging the Government to provide for a Muslim representative to be elected by the Muslims of C.P. and Berar for the Imperial Council was the repetition of an earlier demand made by the League Council in November, 1909.[37] The subjects of the four other resolutions, however, were completely new. These resolutions reflected the influence of the younger and liberal members of the League over their old and conservative colleagues.

The most important of these resolutions concerned the expansion of primary education. It declared that the All-India Muslim League 'is of opinion that the time has arrived when a beginning, however modest, [should] be made in the direction of making primary education free and gradually compulsory throughout the country, and for this reason respectfully suggests that experiment be made in selected areas'.[38]

[33] *Ibid.*, p. 81.

[34] *Ibid.*, p. 82.

[35] The Common Script Conference demanded the adoption of Devanagri as the script for all the Indian languages including Urdu. *Vide* the *Madras Weekly Mail*, 5 January, 1911.

[36] The All-India Suddhi Sabha aimed at the conversion or reconversion of Muslims and other non-Hindus into the fold of Hinduism. *Ibid.*

[37] *Supra*, p. 149.

[38] *Proceedings of the Annual Meeting of the A.I.M.L. held at Nagpur, op. cit.,* p. 86.

In moving the resolution, Fazulbhoy Currimbhoy made a prolix speech. He lamented the fact that three out of every four Indians grew up without primary education and that despite the recommendations of the Education Commission of 1882, the Government had not taken adequate measures for the expansion of primary education.[39] He urged with cogency and force the importance of education for the masses of all creeds and races in India. He had little doubt that the deplorable socio-economic conditions of the masses had been due mainly to illiteracy and ignorance. The plea that the lack of funds was an obstacle to free primary education was incomprehensible to him. He thought that there were many sources of revenue which could be tapped without causing hardships to the taxpayers. A judicious saving in the overgrown and evergrowing charges for the military and civil services could be utilised towards the cost of education. Fazulbhoy Currimbhoy was convinced that making primary education free would not be enough unless it was made compulsory as well. As for compulsion, he did not ask for any revolutionary policy. He wanted compulsion to take place gradually.[40]

The resolution was seconded by Shaikh Zahur Ahmad in a forceful speech.[41] It was supported by Ibrahim Rahimtullah and Haji Yusuf Haji Ismail, merchant, Bombay,[42] both of whom stressed the justice of the demand. Citing the example of Baroda, which had already made primary education free and compulsory, Ibrahim Rahimtullah further asserted that the measure would not entail much financial difficulty for the Government of India. Rahimtullah was glad to see many members of the Bombay Corporation present at the League session and hoped that they would support him in his endeavours to make education free within the limits of Bombay city.[43]

The resolution, however, was opposed by Shams-ul-Huda, who believed that reforms should not be forced but should be the result of gradual evolution. Shams-ul-Huda feared that in launching this scheme the League would be rousing an enthusiasm that would retard progress'.[44] He had no experience of Bombay, but he knew that this demand would not be supported in Bengal. He had no doubt that the system of free

[39] *Ibid.*
[40] *Ibid.*, p. 89.
[41] *Ibid.*, p. 93.
[42] *Ibid.*, pp. 93–94.
[43] *Ibid.*, p. 93.
[44] The *Bombay Gazette,* 31 December, 1910.

and compulsory primary education, if introduced by the Government, would injure the interests of the poor cultivators by compelling them to send their children to school and thus deprive them of their labour. He pointed out that when this system was started in England and Japan forty-three and twenty-eight per cent of the children of school-going age of these respective countries had already been in school, whereas in India only one point nine per cent of children were under instructions.[45]   Shams-ul-Huda further contended that the example of Baroda was not relevant to British India. The ruler of Baroda, being a native of the state, could easily convince his subjects of the urgent need for education, but in British India the good intentions of the foreign Government were liable to be misinterpreted and misrepresented.[46]

Shams-ul-Huda's views were challenged by Muhammad Ali, who argued that hypothetical difficulties and conjectured evils should not stand in the way of the introduction of free and compulsory primary education. Muhammad Ali held that convenient school hours and holidays, as well as generous exceptions for the children of the agriculturists and the poor, could easily be introduced along with the system of compulsory primary education.[47]   He deprecated Shams-ul-Huda's contentions regarding the inapplicability of the analogy of Baroda and noted that the Government of British India was foreign only 'if it alienated the sympathies of the best of its subjects'. He felt sure that the Government could make its good intentions perfectly clear by explaining the urgency of primary education among the masses and by supporting Hindu and Muslim leaders on this question.

When put to the vote the resolution was carried with only one dissentient.

Despite the overwhelming support behind the resolution, the question of free and compulsory primary education remained highly controversial among the League leaders.[48]   The halting and somewhat clumsy

[45] *Proceedings of the Annual Meeting of the A.I.M.L. held at Nagpur, op. cit.,* p. 94.

[46] *Ibid.,* pp. 94–95.

[47] *Ibid.,* pp. 95–96.

[48] *(a)* The annual meeting of the Bombay Presidency League held on 24 and 25 July, 1911, opposed the principle of compulsion in primary education. *Vide* the *Times of India Mail,* 29 July, 1911.

*(b)* Muhammad Shafi strongly opposed the provision for compulsory primary education in a memorandum submitted to the Government of the Punjab on 18 June, 1911. *Vide* J. & P. 4776/1911, vol. 1071.

nature of the resolution, as well as the mover's admission that he thought the proposition could have been 'more pointed and attractive', showed the indecisive mood of the League members as regards the precise nature of the demand. As it stood, the All-India Muslim League could not produce a comprehensive programme on the question until several months later and even then it was not agreed unanimously.[49]

In another resolution relating to the educational problems of Indians as a whole, the League protested against the recent regulations of the Council of Legal Education in England making the possession of a degree and the submission of a character certificate conditions for the admission of Indian students to the Inns of Court.[50]

The resolution also urged the council of Legal Education to admit all Indian students who had passed the Intermediate or F.A. examination of an Indian university on condition that they must secure their degree before being called to the Bar.

The other two significant resolutions of the League session demanded the appointment of 'the younger sons of the Ruling Chiefs and the scions of other noble houses' to the higher posts in the army and deplored the recent reduction by one year of the age-limit in the competitive examination for the Indian Civil Service, with a corresponding increase in the period of probation in England.[51] As regards the Civil Service, it was pointed out that the age limit had been raised from twenty-one to twenty-three after considerable agitation and great deliberation and that to lower it again would be against the best interests of the country. The two resolutions were in line with the policy of the Indian National Congress and indicated the League's willingness to cooperate with the Congress in such matters.

Indeed, the proceedings of the Nagpur session made it clear that, barring the questions of the introduction of separate electorates and the position of Urdu, there was hardly any matter of immediate public importance on which the League leaders were not in substantial agreement with their counterparts in the Congress. The differences on these two issues, however, proved formidable. The Congress had already demonstrated its position on the Urdu-Hindi controversy by allowing the Common Script (Devanagri) and the Suddhi Conferences to hold

[49]Memorandum submitted by Aziz Mirza to the Government of India on 5 October, 1911. *Vide* J. & P. 4924/1911, vol. 1071.

[50]*Proceedings of the Annual Meeting of the A.I.M.L. held at Nagpur, op. cit.,* p. 104.

[51]*Ibid.,* p. 103.

their meetings in its *pandal*.   On 28 December, 1910, the Congress
session passed two resolutions—one mildly opposing the introduction of
separate electorates in the Supreme and Provincial Legislative Councils[52] and the other strongly objecting to the demand for the extension
of the same principle to the local bodies.[53]   The Congress leaders also
made it a point to see that the resolution opposing separate electorates
in the local bodies was moved and seconded by two Muslims—
Muhammad Ali Jinnah and Mazhar-ul-Haque.[54]  Although both Jinnah
and Mazhar-ul-Haque had pointedly and emphatically declared that in
opposing separate electorates for the local boards and municipalities
they spoke for none but themselves and that their individual opinions
should not be confused with those of the Muslim community or any
section of it,[55] the very fact that they were themselves elected to the
Supreme Legislative Council by separate Muslim electorates added
weight to the Congress case against the League demand.

While the Congress leaders were evidently jubilant in being able to
exhibit the differences of opinion among the Muslim leaders on this vital
question, Nabiullah, in winding up the proceedings of the Nagpur session,
charged Jinnah and Mazhar-ul-Haque with inconsistency in their views.[56]
He thought it paradoxical of the two Muslim leaders who had been
elected by exclusively Muslim electorates and were still supporting the
principle of separate Muslim representation for the Legislative Councils
to have objected to the extension of the same principle to the local
bodies.  Nabiullah left no doubt in the minds of his audience that the
League would not compromise on this issue.[57]   In the event, the
League leaders—forty of them—left for Allahabad on the night of 29
December, 1910, with serious misgivings.

On 31 December, 1910, the conference between the Muslim and
Hindu leaders started at Raja Hotel (Allahabad) instead of at the Mayo
Hall as originally arranged.[58]   William Wedderburn, who was elected

[52] *Report of the Twenty-fifth I.N.C. held at Allahabad on 27–30 December,*
1910, pp. 84–93.

[53] *Ibid.*, pp. 93–95.

[54] Both Jinnah and Mazhar-ul-Haque admitted that they had had no intention
of speaking on this occasion, but that they responded to the special requests from
prominent Congress leaders, including  Surendranath  Banerjea. *Ibid.*, pp. 93–94.

[55] *Ibid.*

[56] *Proceedings of the Annual Meeting of the A.I.M.L. held at Nagpur, op. cit.,*
pp. 106–7.

[57] *Ibid.*, p. 107.

[58] The *Pioneer*, 4 January, 1910.

president of the meeting, made a short speech emphasising the urgent need of rapprochement between the two communities. He urged the leaders present to condone his 'rashness in intervening in so delicate a matter' and thanked the Aga Khan for abridging the proceedings at Nagpur in order to attend the conference with so many of his colleagues.[59] He was not very optimistic about the outcome of the conference but considered it an augury of good for the future that prominent Indian leaders should meet together to seek a solution to the problem of Hindu-Muslim relations. He observed that even if the leaders failed to reach definite conclusions they could greatly contribute towards the reconciliation of the two communities in three ways. In the first place, they could freely and frankly exchange views on the more important questions that divided the two communities. Secondly, they could locate grounds for joint action by the Hindus and Muslims, and if possible arrange such joint action. Thirdly, they could detect the questions on which the two communities differed and ensure that controversies and pursuits of different interests should be conducted without unnecessary bitterness and with reasonable regard for the legitimate interests of both parties. Wedderburn, however, was not oblivious of the difficulties confronting the leaders. He, therefore, suggested that in case they failed to arrive at a decision on any question, they might agree to appoint a small committee of influential leaders from both sides and refer to it such matters as appeared capable of adjustment by friendly consultation. Following Wedderburn, the Aga Khan and Sarada Charan Mitra addressed the conference, stressing the necessity of approaching the questions under consideration in a spirit of conciliation, forbearance and goodwill. At this stage Wedderburn retired from the meeting, leaving the chair to be taken by the Aga Khan.

The discussion at the conference centred round a memorandum of business, drawn up by Ameer Ali in London, to which certain additions were made by the Muslim leaders in India. Ameer Ali's proposals were,[60] first, the establishment of a conciliation board as suggested earlier by the London League to the Secretary of State for India. Second, the submission of a joint representation to the Government for the re-establishment of the 'courts of Arbitration'. Third, combined

[59] *Ibid.*
[60] The *India,* 6 January, 1911. Ameer Ali's memorandum was dated, London, 18 November, 1910. *Vide* the *Observer,* 18 November, 1910, the *Punjab N.N.R.,* 1910.

efforts to discourage litigation and to reduce its cost. Fourth, the abolition by each side of the practice of boycott against the other. Fifth, the liquidation by each side of 'rings' formed in government offices and departments of state to keep out or to oust members of the other community. Sixth, stoppage of endeavours to proscribe the language of either community. Seventh, the recognition of the right of separate and adequate representation of the Muslims in the local self-governing bodies. Eighth, joint efforts to promote the economic development of Hindus and Muslims by discouraging high rates of interest and, if possible, to limit them. Ninth, discouragement of forced sales of mortgaged properties. Tenth, recognition by each side of the religious institutions of the other, for example, *debutter* and *waqf,* and an agreement between the two sides not to buy or sell such properties. Other questions included in the memorandum of business were national education, provocative propaganda by the Arya Samaj, an understanding regarding cow-killing and the playing of music before mosques, as well as the demand that since the Muslims were 'bound to be in a minority in any case, no question should be urged which the Muslims, as represented by the Muslim League, may look upon as detrimental to their communal interests'.[61]

Since the detailed proceedings of the Allahabad Conference were never published, it is open for any one to guess the reactions of the Hindu leaders to the questions mentioned in the agenda. So far as the League leaders were concerned, the adoption of the agenda including the claim for the recognition of the League as *the* representative of the Muslim community was in itself a gain of considerable significance. By acceding to the inclusion of this particular demand of the League leaders in the agenda, as well as by giving them *defacto* approbation as the representative of the Muslim community, the Congress had weakened the position of its Muslim members and thus virtually impaired its claim to speak for all communities and interests in India. Another remarkable feature of the agenda was that of its fourteen points at least half a dozen were constantly mentioned in all subsequent discussions on Hindu-Muslim reconciliation.[62]

The Allahabad Conference failed to come up to the modest expectations of its convenors. This first meeting of prominent Hindu and

[61] The *Times of India Mail,* 7 January, 1911.
[62] Jinnah's fourteen points drawn up in 1929 and a list of disputed topics between the Hindus and Muslims prepared by Jawharlal Nehru in 1938 included several points raised at Allahabad in 1910.

Muslim leaders from almost all over India could not even produce lists of subjects on which the two communities had identical and different interests. As a last resort, and as if to save the face of the convenors, the conference appointed a committee to consider and make recommendations on several questions raised in the meeting.[63]   The committee consisted of two secretaries, Nabiullah and Gangaprasad Varma, and seven Muslims and eight Hindus.   The eighth Hindu, Gokhale, was appointed at the special insistence of the Aga Khan.   The League members of the committee were Aziz Mirza, Abdul Majid, Shams-ul-Huda, Rafiuddin Ahmad, Muhammad Shafi, Syed Muhammad and Ibrahim Rahimtullah.    The  Congress  members  included  the  Maharaja  of Durbhanga, Sarada Charan Mitra, Surendranath Banerjea, Madan Mohan Malaviya, Lala Munshi Ram, Lala Harkishen Lal and Harchand Rai Vishindas.[64]   A most notable characteristic of the committee was that a majority of the members from both the League and the Congress were extremists on communal questions.   The ommission of Gokhale's name from the list submitted by the Hindu leaders and the exclusion of Jinnah and Mazhar-ul-Haque from the Muslim group indicated the dominance of the extremists among their respective communal groups.

The failure of the Allahabad Conference had been a foregone conclusion.   One of its convenors, Wedderburn, had no authority either from the Congress or from the Hindu community to organise any such meeting.   It was only because the Aga Khan had accepted the responsibility of bringing the League leaders to the conference, and 'no one on the Hindu side could undertake to issue corresponding invitations', that Wedderburn had taken it upon himself to invite the Hindu leaders to attend the conciliation talks.[65]   The Hindu leaders having had no initiative in the matter, a considerable section of their co-religionists did not appreciate the Aga Khan-Wedderburn move.   On the eve of the Allahabad conference the extreme communalists among the Hindus had interpreted the eagerness of Ameer Ali and the Aga Khan for reconciliation with the Hindus as being motivated by the purpose of 'making Congress Hindus ratify the principle of communal representation'.[66] Some of them had taken strong objection to the agenda of the meeting as drawn up by Ameer Ali.   *Hitavadi*, a pro-Congress daily newspaper, even seized this opportunity to remind the Muslims that it might be

[63] The *Pioneer*, 4 January, 1911.
[64] *Ibid.*
[65] *Ibid.* Wedderburn's speech at the Allahabad Conference.
[66] The *Punjabee*, 31 December, 1910. The *Punjab N.N.R.*, 1910.

possible to live in water by displeasing the crocodile, but 'it is not possible for the Muhammadans to live in this country by giving pain to the Hindus'.[67]    Lal Chand, a leading member of the Punjab Hindu Sabha, went to the extent of challenging the representative character of the Hindu leaders who were to attend the meeting at Allahabad. He had further stated that unless and until an all-India Hindu association was formed, no Hindu leader could speak in the name of his community with the same authority as the League leaders could speak on behalf of the Muslims.[68]    This agitation by the extreme Hindu communalists, as well as the contradictory stand of the League and the Congress on important questions like the electorates and the national language, had left little ground for negotiation by the leaders of the two parties assembled at Allahabad.

Soon after the conclusion of the Allahabad conference, a section of the Hindu press asserted that the leaders attending the meeting had no right to speak on behalf of their community and that the Hindu members of the conciliation committee did not represent the Hindus truly. The *Tribune*, Lahore, noted that the Hindu members of the conciliation committee should have included at least one representative each from the Punjab and the Bihar Hindu Sabhas and one more from the Arya Samaj.[69]   The *Hitavadi*, Calcutta, commented that because of the lack of authority of the Hindu members to enter into any deal with their Muslim counterparts in the conciliation committee, the decision of the said committee would not be binding on Hindus.[70]   This assertion of lack of confidence in the Hindu members and thus in the conciliation committee itself shattered the hope of reconciliation between the two communities.   The death-knell of the Aga Khan-Wedderburn move was, however, rung by one of the members of the conciliation committee— Madan Mohan Malaviya.

On 24 January, 1911, less than a month after the Allahabad conference, Madan Mohan Malaviya, while moving a resolution in the Supreme Legislative Council for the appointment of a committee to consider and report what changes should be made in the regulations promulgated under the Government of India Act, 1909, so as to remove the alleged inequality in the treatment of the various sections of the population in regard to some of the disqualifications and restrictions placed on the

[67]The *Hitavadi*, 28 December, 1910. The *Bengal N.N.R.*, 1910.
[68]The *Statesman Weekly*, 15 December, 1910.
[69]The *Tribune*, 11 January, 1911. The *Punjab N.N.R.*, 1911.
[70]The *Hitavadi*, 5 January, 1911. The *Bengal N.N.R.*, 1911.

choice of candidates on the councils, and also to ensure the non-official majority in the provincial councils,[71] complained that the Muslims had been over-represented in the various councils.[72] Reiterating some of the old arguments advanced by the Congress against the demand for separate Muslim electorates, Malaviya disputed the political importance of the Muslims and asserted that in the case of the former being adamant about separate representation and the Government being reluctant to disturb the system, the Muslims should not be permitted to participate in the mixed electorates.[73] This speech fell like a bomb-shell in the council, provoking an angry debate in which Muslim members including Syed Muhammad and Mazhar-ul-Haque vehemently criticised it.[74] The most severe comments on Malaviya's speech came from Abdul Majid who blamed Malaviya for exacerbating ill feeling between the Hindus and Muslims at a time when efforts were being made for reconciliation between them.[75] Claiming the provision for separate electorates as a settled fact, Abdul Majid also pointed out that even the Hindu leaders who had attended the Allahabad conference did not include the subject in the list of controversial issues between the two communities.[76] Shams-ul-Huda, Omar Hayat Khan and the Raja of Mahmudabad also spoke in similar terms and deeply regretted Malaviya's motives in moving the resolution.[77] The tirade against Malaviya's resolution was so overwhelming that he was ultimately obliged to withdraw it.[78] But the damage done by Malaviya's speech was beyond any immediate repair. Once again the Muslim League was convinced that a powerful section of the Congress leaders were determined to destroy separate electorates and that no rapprochement between the Hindus and Muslims was possible unless and until the Congress had changed its attitude towards separate Muslim electorates.[79]

During the first nine months of 1911, the leaders of the All-India Muslim League and their provincial branches focused most of their attention upon the collection of funds for raising the Aligarh College into a Muslim University. At the Delhi session of the League in

[71] Proc. Council of the G.G., vol. 49, p. 133.
[72] *Ibid.,* pp. 133–134.
[73] *Ibid.,* p. 135.
[74] *Ibid.,* pp. 148–150.
[75] *Ibid.,* p. 138.
[76] *Ibid.,* p. 139.
[77] *Ibid.,* pp. 143–146.
[78] *Ibid.,* p. 155.
[79] Aziz Mirza, *Report of the All-India Muslim League for 1911,* p. 10.

January, 1910, it had been unanimously decided to establish a Muslim University at Aligarh.[80]   The question, however, was not mentioned in the agenda of the Nagpur session of the League in December, 1910. Instead, the Aga Khan had given notice of a resolution to be moved at the All-India Mahomedan Educational Conference which had been meeting at Nagpur simultaneously with the League, proposing the creation of a national fund for founding the Muslim University during the King's visit to India towards the end of 1911.[81]

The Aga Khan's move to approach the Muslims of India for funds for the Muslim University project from the platform of the Educational Conference appears to have been a matter of strategy. Since the Muslim University was to be based on the Aligarh College, the co-operation and assistance of the trustees and members of the teaching staff of the same college was a pre-condition for the success of the University scheme. This co-operation would have been difficult to obtain if the call for funds had been launched from the platform of a political party like the League. Furthermore, by initiating the project as a question of Muslim educational development rather than of their general political progress, the Aga Khan seems to have hoped for active support from the Government and individual government officials, as well as from the chiefs of the native states who would have never associated themselves with any scheme undertaken by a political party.

Despite the Aga Khan's caution regarding the non-political character of the Muslim University movement, the fact remained that it was initiated, controlled and conducted by the League leaders both at the all-India and provincial levels. The 'Committee for the Foundation of a Mahomedan University' formed at Aligarh on 10 January, 1911,[82] could be termed as an adjunct of the All-India Muslim League. Besides the Aga Khan and Viqar-ul-Mulk, who were appointed president and secretary respectively, sixteen of the twenty-one vice-presidents and three of the four joint secretaries of the university foundation committee were either members of the executive committee or of the council of the All-India Muslim League. The five vice-presidents of the committee who were not members of the League included J. H. Towle, Principal, Aligarh College, Shaikh Sadiq Ali, Wazir, Khairpur State, Prince Obaidullah Khan of Bhopal, Rahim Baksh, president of the Council of Regency, Bahawalpur State, and Salimullah Khan, a

[80] *Supra*, p. 175.
[81] The *Pioneer Mail*, 6 January, 1911.
[82] The *Pioneer Mail*, 27 January, 1911.

retired government official of Berar.[83] The only non-Leaguer joint secretary of the committee was Shaukat Ali, elder brother of Muhammad Ali and an opium collector of the Government of U.P.; who had decided to devote his long leave from the service to the cause of the Muslim University. The members of the foundation committee consisted of all members of the All-India Muslim League as well as of all members of important Muslim socio-cultural organisations, *Anjumans*, educational institutions and prominent individual Muslims.[84]

The provincial branches of the Muslim University foundation committee were also dominated by the members of the League. Except in Bihar, where Hasan Imam[85] had recently become more active in the Congress, and in Baluchistan, where a non-politician Muslim leader headed the provincial committee, the presidents of the provincial branches of the Muslim University committees were also presidents of the respective provincial Leagues. Similarly, except in Baluchistan, where no branch of the League had yet been established, the secretaries of the provincial committees of the Muslim University were also secretaries of the respective provincial branches of the League.

The campaign for the collection of funds for the proposed University was opened by the Aga Khan at Calcutta in January, 1911.[86] In a press interview on 23 January, 1911, the Aga Khan explained the aims and objects of the University. He thought that the educational requirements of the Muslims were very great and in some respects peculiar. The University at Aligarh would satisfy the wants of the Muslims most effectively. The special features of the University would be the introduction of the residential system for students from all over India, the creation of a Muslim environment and the encouragement of Muslim culture and learning.[87] The political influence of the University would be 'most salutary on the public life' of the Muslims of India. It would break the isolation of Muslim students in big cities and improve their outlook on life socially, 'maturing their views on the things that matter, thus making them better citizens of the Empire'. If the Muslim University became an accomplished fact it would 'produce educational missionaries' who would work for the establishment of a Muslim College on the model of the Aligarh College at each provincial headquarters. The

---

[83]*Ibid.*

[84]*Ibid.*, and the *Times of India Mail*, 25 February, 1911.

[85]The *Times of India Mail*, 3 June, 1911.

[86]A. Mirza, *Report of the All-India Muslim League for 1911*, p. 6.

[87]The *Englishman Weekly Summary*, 26 January, 1911.

Muslim University, however, would be a non-sectarian and non-communal institution; non-Muslims would be welcomed to study there and religious education would not form a compulsory part of their studies.

The Aga Khan, Aziz Mirza, Shaukat Ali and a small band of earnest workers from Aligarh stayed in Calcutta for more than a week in connection with the collection of funds for the Muslim University. Their task was greatly facilitated by the support received from the leaders of the Bengal Provincial League,[88] the Mahomedan Literary Society,[89] the Central National Mahomedan Association,[90] as well as from the Muslim merchants[91] of the city. By 29 January, 1911, Calcutta's contribution to the University fund rose to more than fifty thousand rupees.[92]

Early in February, 1911, the Aga Khan and his party visited Allahabad, Lucknow, Cawnpore and Rampur. In all these places they were enthusiastically received and their appeals for funds evoked generous response. On 7 February, 1911, the Muslims of Lucknow gave a tremendous demonstration of goodwill and support for the University movement by announcing a donation of rupees 317,000 partly in cash and partly in pledges.[93] The earnest and eloquent speech of the Raja of Mahmudabad, who had announced his own and the Raja of Jahangirabad's donations of rupees 100,000 each, and the exhortation of highly respected *ulama* like Maulana Abdul Bari, Shah Sulaiman of Phulwarisharif and Mujtahid Syed Muhammad Husain, had roused the fervour of the Muslims of Lucknow to such an extent that the provincial branch of the University committee expected to collect another sum of 200,000 from Oudh.[94]

By the middle of February, 1911, the leading members of the university committee had formed themselves into several 'deputations' to visit

[88] Sultan Ahmad, barrister, joint secretary of the Bengal Provincial League, was appointed secretary of the Calcutta Committee of the Muslim University Fund Collection Committee. *Ibid.*

[89] Nawab Abdur Rahman, secretary, Mahomedan Literary Society, actively supported the Muslim University project and personally contributed one thousand rupees for the scheme. *Ibid.*

[90] Prince Ghulam Muhammad, president, C.N.M.A., assisted the Aga Khan's campaign for collection of funds for the University. *Ibid* and *Englishman Weekly Summary*, February, 1911.

[91] The *Pioneer Mail*, 3 February, 1911.

[92] *Ibid.*

[93] The *Pioneer Mail*, 10 February, 1911.

[94] *Ibid.*

various provinces. Of these deputations the one to the Punjab was the most impressive. It included, among others, the Aga Khan, the Raja of Mahmudabad, Viqar-ul-Mulk, Aziz Mirza, Syed Nabiullah, Aftab Ahmad Khan, Rafiuddin Ahmad, Shaukat Ali, Maulana Shibli Nomani, Shah Sulaiman of Phulwarisharif, and Dr. Syed Ali Bilgrami.[95] The deputation received a warm reception at Lahore when the carriage carrying the Aga Khan and a few others was drawn by the students of the local colleges through a gaily decorated route and triumphal arches.[96] At a public meeting held on 25 February, 1911, which was attended by several thousand people, the Muslims of Lahore declared a total subscription of rupees 250,000, partly collected and partly pledged.[97] Most of the subscribers at the meeting were middle class people: lawyers, journalists, teachers, petty landholders, merchants etc. But the enthusiasm of the poorer section of the community was reflected by the donations paid in cash by the gardeners and butchers of Lahore.[98] Another remarkable feature of the meeting was the announcement made by the religious leaders, including the *Ahmadis,* that they would contribute towards the university fund.[99] One of the religious leaders, Pir Jamat Ali Shah, announced that he had already collected rupees 4,000 from his followers, who came mostly from the cultivating class.

From Lahore the Aga Khan, Aziz Mirza and Shaukat Ali left for Bombay, while another deputation consisting of the Raja of Mahmudabad, Aftab Ahmad Khan, Dr. Syed Ali Bilgrami and Dr. Muhammad Waris, started for Karachi.[100] At Karachi, through the exhortations of Sadiq Ali, Mir Ayub Khan, secretary, Sind National Mahomedan Association, and prominent businessmen like Haji Abdullah Haroon and G. G. Chagla, a total of about rupees 126,400 were collected in cash.[101] Considering the comparative prosperity of the Muslim merchants in Bombay, the total donation both paid and promised by the Muslims of the city fell short of the expectations of the leaders. Bombay announced only three hundred and sixty thousand rupees, including Kasim Ali Jairajbhoy's contribution of one hundred and

[95] The *Madras Weekly Mail,* 2 March, 1911.

[96] The *Civil and Military Gazette,* 26 February, 1911.

[97] *Ibid.,* 28 February, 1911.

[98] The *Statesman Weekly,* 2 March, 1911.

[99] *Ibid.,* and the *Civil and Military Gazette,* 28 February, 1911.

[100] The *Pioneer Mail,* 24 March, 1911.

[101] *Ibid.*

twenty-five thousand rupees. However, the Aga Khan's personal promise for a sum of one hundred and twenty-five thousand rupees was expected to raise the share of Bombay to five hundred thousand.[102]

Towards the middle of March, 1911, the Aga Khan left for England promising to finalise the drafting of a Royal Charter for the proposed Muslim University with the help of parliamentary lawyers.[103] It was understood that the draft of the charter would be presented to the King-Emperor by a small deputation consisting of the Aga Khan, Ameer Ali, the Nawab of Rampur and the Begum of Bhopal,[104] after George V's coronation in London.

In the absence of the Aga Khan the primary responsibility for the university movement in India was shared by the Raja of Mahmudabad, Viqar-ul-Mulk, Aziz Mirza, Aftab Ahmad Khan and Shaukat Ali. The Raja of Mahmudabad, Viqar-ul-Mulk and Aftab Ahmad Khan toured Muradabad, Lakshmipur, Shahjahanpur, Etawah, Bulandshar and other important cities in the U.P.[105] Under their guidance the district and local branches of the university committee in U.P. were able to mobilise widespread support for their cause. In certain areas the members of the local committees resorted to door to door begging and met with considerable success in the collection of funds.[106]

Throughout the months of March, April, May and June, 1911, Aziz Mirza, Aftab Ahmad Khan, Shaukat Ali and a few others continued to campaign for the proposed Muslim University in various parts of India. Aftab Ahmad Khan's deputation to the North-West Frontier and Baluchistan enlisted the support of several influential *sardars* and of the Khan of Kalat for the University project.[107] Aziz Mirza's deputation to Rangoon was equally successful. In the course of a nearly two months stay in Rangoon, Aziz Mirza and his colleagues, Amir Mustafa Khan and Muhammad Yusuf Khan (both members of the League) were able to raise rupees 222,500 and annas 12, including cash and promises of payments.[107] This collection consisted of donations ranging from rupees 100,000, by Sulaiman Adamji to two annas in individual cases.[108]

On his way to Rangoon, Aziz Mirza had attended a meeting of the

[102] The *Statesman Weekly,* 16 March, 1911.

[103] The *Madras Weekly Mail,* 16 March, 1911.

[104] *Ibid.*

[105] The *Pioneer Mail,* 17 March, 7 April, 14 April, 2 June and 29 September, 1911.

[106] *Ibid.,* 24 February, 1911.

[107] The *Times of India Mail,* 22 April, 1911.

[108] The *Rangoon Gazette,* 8 May, 1911.

Eastern Bengal and Assam Provincial League held at Dacca.[109] At the same meeting a provincial committee for the collection of funds for the Muslim University project was formed with Salimullah as its president.[110] Salimullah had already been appointed one of the vice-presidents of the foundation committee of the Muslim University. But he seems to have had some reservations about the project in the beginning.[111] This had been partly because of his lack of confidence in, or rather rivalry with, the Aga Khan and partly due to his conviction that the Muslims of Eastern Bengal and Assam should concentrate their resources towards the development of educational facilities within their own province. The active interest of some Muslim leaders from outside the province in the establishment of a Muslim hostel at Dacca[112] and the prospect of a Muslim University with powers of affiliation with Muslim schools and colleges all over India[113] had finally brought him round to the view of his colleagues from other provinces.

However, the work for the Muslim University project in Eastern Bengal and Assam had not started till Aziz Mirza's visit to the provincial capital. During subsequent months and particularly in July and August, 1911, when Shaukat Ali and Nawab Ali Choudhury toured the province addressing public meetings at Mymensingh, Comilla, Noakhali, Chittagong, Pabna, Rangpur, Dinajpur, and Faridpur, the university movement was vigorously pushed through the various districts of the new province.[114] East Bengal and Assam's contribution both paid and promised had been a modest sum of about 150,000 rupees.[115]

The task of organising the Muslim University movement in the Madras Presidency had been left primarily with the local Muslim leaders. However, in April-May, 1911, Shaukat Ali made a prolonged stay in Madras, visiting important cities like Vellore, Cochin, Bangalore and Mysore.[116] In most of these places he was accompanied by Yakub

[109] The *Rangoon Gazette*, 24 April and 8 May, 1911.

[110] The *Statesman Weekly*, 17 March, 1911.

[111] Butler to Hardinge, 4 April, 1911, H.P., vol. 81.

[112] Two donations of rupees fifteen thousand each were made by two anonymous Muslim leaders, possibly the Aga Khan and the Raja of Mahmudabad, towards the establishment of the Muslim hostel at Dacca. *Ibid.*

[113] Aziz Mirza had repeatedly asserted that the Muslim educational institutions all over India would be affiliated to the proposed Muslim University. *Vide* the *Rangoon Gazette*, 17 April, 1911.

[114] The *Times of India Mail*, 15 July and 12 August, 1911.

[115] The *Times of India Mail*, 12 August, 1911.

[116] The *Madras Weekly Mail*, 20 April, 27 April and 4 and 11 May, 1911.

Hasan and a few other prominent Muslims, mostly members of the League. The total subscription from Madras, including promises of subsequent payments, amounted to about 100,000 rupees.[117]

In May, 1911, Aziz Mirza had written and published a pamphlet explaining the various aspects of the Muslim University movement and appealing for further contributions.[118]    This pamphlet had been regarded as attractive and persuasive.[119]    It was distributed all over India and was well received.

Aziz Mirza admitted that the university movement 'overshadowed all our [the League's] activities during the year 1911'.[120]    He had no regrets for his and his colleagues' neglect of the affairs of the League. He argued that 'substantial work done in one direction amply compensates for neglect in another, specially when the success of the university movement has been so great'.[121]    That the university campaign had been a success is beyond doubt. The first three months of the operation brought donations and promises of donations to nearly 2,500,000 rupees.[122]    After about another eight months the total amount had risen to Rs. 3,076,403–3–10, including Rs. 1,711,529–6–9½ actually collected.[123]    Despite the wide gap between the promised and the paid-up donations, which was caused partly by the uncertainty of the Government's decision on the question of a charter for the university, the amount already collected fell only about 288,470 rupees short of the requisite amount declared in the first instance.[124]

The success of the Muslim University campaign, however, should not be considered merely from the viewpoint of funds. The active and almost unanimous[125] support of the Muslim intelligentsia, middle classes, and influential *ulama* towards the university movement had

[117]The total subscription from Madras was not announced till the end of 1911. The sum of nearly one hundred thousand rupees has been estimated on the basis of reports published in the *Madras Weekly Mail* from April to August, 1911.

[118]The *Pioneer Mail*, 5 May, 1911.

[119]*Ibid.*

[120]A. Mirza, *Report of the All-India Muslim League for 1911*, p. 6.

[121]*Ibid.*, p. 11.

[122]*Ibid.*, p. 6.

[123]The *Times of India Mail*, 9 December, 1911.

[124]The Aga Khan had estimated that Rs 2,000,000 would be adequate to make a modest beginning towards the foundation of the University. *Vide* the *Pioneer Mail*, 6 January, 1911. Later on, however, the amount required was stated to be rupees 2,500,000. *Vide* the *Pioneer Mail*, 2 June, 1911.

[125]We have not come across any opposition from any section or group of Muslims to the University project.

far-reaching consequences for the politico-cultural development of the Muslims of the sub-continent. The speeches and writings of the advocates of the university scheme, recalling the traditions of the Muslim Universities of Baghdad, Cordova and Nishapur in glowing terms and emphasising the solidarity of the Muslims of India as a distinct cultural unit, had a great impact on their listeners and readers. The 'political enthusiasm' created by the movement was the subject of a special note by the Education Member of the Government of India.[126]

Indeed, the leaders of the university project, though tactful enough not to identify the movement with politics, never disguised its political importance. The Prince of Arcot looked upon Aligarh as 'the modern seat of Mussulman power, in place of old Imperial Delhi'.[127] Shaukat Ali saw the foundation of the university at Aligarh as a means for the 'revival of the true spirit of Islam' and proudly announced that in every province of India he had observed a remarkable unanimity of sentiments among the Muslims 'regarding 'the vital questions of the day'.[128] The proposed University was also freely spoken of as a machine for welding the Muslims 'into a homogeneous whole' and for producing good citizens.[129]

The All-India Muslim League derived large benefit from the university movement. By asserting the separate cultural entity of the Muslims the movement had popularised and strengthened the League's concept of special and exclusive Muslim interests. Moreover, the visit to the important centres of Muslim population from Quetta to Cochin and from Peshawar to Chittagong and Rangoon by university deputations consisting mostly of the League leaders had extended the prestige and influence of the League over a wide area. While on tour with the university deputations some League leaders had also campaigned for the League, thus recruiting new members for the organisation. The substantial increase (about 23 per cent) in the number of the members of the All-India Muslim League between June, 1910 and June, 1911,[130]

---

[126] Butler to Hardinge, 4 April, 1911. H.P., vol. 81.

[127] The *Madras Weekly Mail*, 4 May, 1911.

[128] The *Madras Weekly Mail*, 4 May and 27 April, 1911.

[129] Fateh Ali Khan Qazilbash's speech at a public meeting held at Lahore on 25 April. *Vide* the *Civil and Military Gazette*, 28 February, 1911.

[130] The increase of about twenty-three per cent in the membership of the A.I.M.L. has been calculated on the basis of the list of the League members published in 1910 and 1911. *Vide The Proceedings of the Delhi Session and the Nagpur Session of the League.*

was due partly to the wide contacts of the League leaders in the course of the university movement.

The newly elected members of the All-India Muslim League swung the class balance of the membership in favour of the professional classes, consisting of lawyers, merchants and journalists. In June, 1910, the professional classes formed about forty-four per cent of the total membership of the League as against about forty-six per cent formed by the landed interests, comprising zamindars, jagirdars, *taluqdars, raees* and a few lawyer-cum-landholders and honorary magistrates-cum-landholders.[131] In June, 1911, however, the professional classes held about forty-seven per cent of the membership of the League as against the landed classes' forty-three per cent.[132] By the last few months of 1911, the professional classes had made further gains in the membership of the All-India Muslim League and had thus prepared the ground for significant changes in the policy of the League.

Although the changing social complexion of League membership had little immediate effect on the top leadership of the party (consisting mostly of big landholders and barristers) by the middle of 1911, a clash between the interests of the different classes within the League became perceptible. The League Council's attitude towards Gokhale's Elementary Education Bill, 1911, showed that while the interests of the Muslims as a community had been the chief concern of the party it was also mindful of safeguarding the interests of the different classes among them. Agreeing 'in the main' with the provisions of Gokhale's Bill and insisting that necessary arrangements be made for the religious education of the Muslim students imparted by Muslim teachers under the supervision of Muslim inspectors; for the introduction of Urdu as the medium of instruction (except in parts of Eastern Bengal, Burma and Madras); as well as for equal representation of Muslim and Hindu members in the managing committees of the schools, the League Council demanded that since 'the clerkly and commercial classes' would be the principal beneficiary of the Act, care should be taken that 'only those

---

[131] An exact estimate of the professions of the League members is difficult, as in certain cases the published lists do not indicate the professions and in certain other cases members having more than one profession, e.g. landholder-lawyers and landholder-honorary magistrates have been listed under one class only.

[132] This percentage has been calculated on the basis of the lists of the League members published with the proceedings of the Delhi and the Nagpur Sessions of the League and partly from the knowledge acquired from various newspapers regarding the professions of prominent League leaders.

people are taxed who benefit directly from the scheme'.[133]    The
Council noted that taxing the immediate beneficiaries of the measure
would protect the interests of the landowning and agricultural classes.
As a further safeguard to the interests of the agricultural classes and
other lower income groups, particularly in the rural areas, the League
Council suggested that 'if a standard for levying fees is to be fixed, it
should be as high as rupees 25 *per mensem* instead of rupees 10 as mentioned in the Bill'.[134]

The League's approach to Gokhale's bill, however, was not guided
entirely by communal or class considerations.  The most stubborn
opponents of the bill among the League leaders included men like Shafi
and Rafiuddin who came from the professional class.  Again, the arguments against the bill had been based primarily on financial and other
practical considerations.[135]

The All-India Muslim League's support for the principle of compulsory
primary education as contained in Gokhale's Bill was strongly opposed
by Ameer Ali and the London League.[136]  This was the first time that
Ameer Ali publicly criticised a decision of the all-India League as
impracticable and contrary to the public interests.  Ameer Ali's difference with the Indian League is more significant when one remembers
that for about three years the League's policy on important matters,
e.g. separate representation, conciliation boards and Hindu-Muslim
rapprochement had been mostly guided by him.  Ameer Ali seems to
have sensed the winds of change in the policies of the all-India League
and took the first opportunity to warn it against any hasty decisions.

Ameer Ali himself remained in the vanguard of the movement for
advancing the special interests of the Indian Muslims.   He was
indefatigable on the questions of the extension of separate electorates
in the local bodies and the preservation of the Muslim interests in
Eastern Bengal and Assam.  Besides formal representations by the
London League, Ameer Ali had, on several occasions, brought these
matters privately to the notice of the India Office.[137]    Under his
direction on 8 May, 1911, the Committee of the London League once
again submitted a memorandum to the Secretary of State demanding a

[133] Memorandum submitted by Aziz Mirza to the Government of India, dated
5 October, 1911. J. & P. 4924/1911, vol. 1071.
[134] *Ibid.*
[135] Muhammad Shafi's memorandum to the Government of the Punjab,
dated 18 June, 1911. J. & P. 4776/1911, vol. 1071.
[136] The *Times of India Mail,* 22 July, 1911.
[137] Morley to Minto, 25 March, 1909. Mor. P., vol. 4.

superior court for Eastern Bengal and Assam. The memorandum drew the Secretary of State's attention to the serious congestion of business at the Calcutta High Court, where no less than six thousand special appeals and two thousand regular appeals, some filed in 1908, were pending.[138] The memorandum held that no portion of the vast area under the jurisdiction of the Calcutta High Court suffered more from the congestion of files than the distant districts of Eastern Bengal and Assam where, owing to the number and immensity of the waterways, facilities for travel were less rapid and convenient than in Bengal proper. The judicial concentration in Calcutta involved loss of time, money and energy for the litigants of Eastern Bengal and Assam. It was anomalous that the province standing fourth in population and sixth in area among the Indian provinces should be denied a court of superior jurisdiction when such courts existed, not only in all the other major provinces, but even in portions of them. A Chartered High Court would be 'most acceptable to the people, and would best accord with the dignity and greatness of the new province'.[139] But having regard to the difficulty His Majesty's Government might face in finding time for passing a bill through the current session of Parliament, the memorandum noted that Eastern Bengal and Assam might be content if in the first instance a chief court was constituted in the province.[140]

On 9 May, 1911, the London League's representation was received by M. C. Seton, secretary of the Judicial and Public Committee at the India Office. Seton thought that the London League's views concerning the contentment of Eastern Bengal and Assam with a chief court was 'a rash conjecture'.[141] However, the following day he referred the representation for the opinion of the Legal Adviser who considered the arguments set forth in the representation as 'very weighty' and 'sound'.[142] The Legal Adviser strongly supported the demand for the foundation of a chief court in the new province. But already on 9 May, 1911, Montagu's suggestions for an act enlarging the bench of the Calcutta High Court, and empowering His Majesty's Government by Letters Patent to establish a High Court in any province in India,[143] had been

---

[138] Representation from the Committee of the London League, 8 May, 1911. Question of High Court for Eastern Bengal, J. & P. 1656/1911, vol. 1066/11.

[139] *Ibid.*

[140] *Ibid.*

[141] Seton's note on the London League's representation, *ibid.*

[142] The Legal Adviser's note on the London League's representation, *ibid.*

[143] Montagu's note, *ibid.*

accepted by the India Council and the Secretary of State.[144]  In due course the Indian High Court Bill was presented before Parliament in July, 1911.

In view of the changed circumstances, the Committee of the London League, on 21 July, 1911, submitted another representation modifying their former proposals.[145]  While expressing their gratitude for the bill which would give the Government requisite authority to create a High Court in any province in India, the Committee of the London League urged that when the bill was passed the Government should apply its provision in establishing a High Court in Eastern Bengal and Assam. Hardly could the London League imagine that even before their second representation was drawn up, a decision for the liquidation of the very province in whose interest they were memorialising His Majesty's Government would have been secretly taken by the Government of India in utter disregard of repeated public pledges by the Viceroys and Secretaries of State—thus shattering the confidence of the Muslims in the British Raj and forcing them to reconsider their political objectives.

[144] J. & P. 864/1911 (Question of High Court for Eastern Bengal), vol. 1066/11.

[145] London League's representation to the Under Secretary of State for India, London, 21 July, 1911.  Question of High Court for Eastern Bengal, J. & P. 2647/1911, vol. 1066/11.

## Chapter VIII

## THE TRANSFORMATION OF THE LEAGUE

The winds of change perceptible in the League politics since the latter part of 1910 gradually gathered momentum and by the end of 1912 swept the League into a new course, thus transforming its character and composition. This transformation was aided by various events that took place between September, 1911 and November, 1912.

In September–October, 1911, the Muslims of India were rudely shaken by Italy's aggression on the Turkish territory of Tripoli. A large majority of the Muslims of India had looked upon the Sultan of Turkey as their Khalifa. Their belief was considerably strengthened when the Treaty of Kuchuk Kaynarca (1774) recognised the Ottoman Sultan's position as the Khalifa of the Muslims even outside his territory.[1] By about the middle of the nineteenth century the influence of the Sultan-Khalifa over the Muslims of India had greatly increased due to the activities of the followers of Shah Waliullah and of the *ulama* of Deoband.[2] The British attempt to magnify the Turkish victory in the Crimean War (1854–6) and their invocation of a *fatwa* (religious pronouncement) of the Sultan-Khalifa asking the Indian Muslims to be loyal during the revolution in 1857 had also contributed to widening the Sultan's influence among the Muslims of the sub-continent.[3]

The outbreak of the Graeco-Turkish war in April, 1897, which was followed by anti-Turkish outbursts by the former British Prime Minister Gladstone and the British press, tended to deepen the sympathy of the Indian Muslims towards Turkey.[4] On this occasion they ignored Syed Ahmad Khan's advice that 'no Musalman ruler can be a Khalifa for those who do not live in his dominion'.[5] The *ulama* and the majority of middle class Muslims celebrated the Turkish victory over Greece by organising large-scale and spectacular demonstrations.[6] Another

---

[1] Aziz Ahmad, *Islamic Modernism in India and Pakistan 1857–1964*, p. 123.
[2] *Ibid.*, pp. 123–124.
[3] *Ibid.*, p. 124.
[4] The *Bombay Gazette Summary*, 4 August, 1906.
[5] Kazi Sirajuddin Ahmad, *The Truth About the Khilafat*, p. 14.
[6] The *Moslem Chronicle*, 5, 12 and 19 June, 1897.

immediate result of the Graeco-Turkish war was the outbreak of a serious uprising against the Government in the North-Western Frontier Province.[7]

During the first decade of the twentieth century the growing interest of the educated Muslims in the affairs of Turkey and other Muslim States gave birth to the Pan-Islamic Society in London. Leading members of this Society, including Abdullah Suhrawardy, Shaikh Abdul Qadir and Mushir Husain Kidwai, had toured several Muslim countries, thus establishing direct contact with their governments and prominent public figures.[8]  About this time, a few Muslim newspapers like the *Watan,* the *Vakil,* and the *Riyaz-ul-Akhbar* started collecting funds for helping Turkey to complete the Hejaz Railway which was to link Mecca, Medina and several other holy places of the Muslims. The venture was moderately successful. The *Watan* alone had collected and despatched 100,000 rupees to Turkey.[9]  In 1906, the British ultimatum to Turkey following the Turko-Egyptian boundary dispute and Lord Cromer's repression of the Egyptian nationalists, came in for stringent criticism in the Muslim press.[10]  The Government of India was warned that the Muslims of India could 'not bear any wrong done to the head of our spiritual world'.[11]  In May, 1906, a Muslim meeting held at Aligarh expressed its 'profound grief and alarm' at the British ultimatum to Turkey and requested the Government of India to persuade the British Government to avoid any Anglo-Turkish war.[12]

The increasing involvement of the Indian Muslims in the Turkish affair had caused great anxiety among the loyalist Muslim leaders. In July, 1906, Mohsin-ul-Mulk wrote an article in the *Aligarh Institute Gazette* and the *Bombay Gazette,* reiterating Syed Ahmad's arguments against the Ottoman Sultan's claim to the Khilafat and stressing the necessity of Muslim loyalty towards the Government.[13]  The article brought down upon him a storm of invective from the Muslim press. Some of these reproached Mohsin-ul-Mulk as a betrayer of the Muslim

[7]Hardinge to Crewe, 12 October, 1911. H.P. vol. 117.

[8]The *Pioneer Mail,* 21 December, 1906 and the *Gauhar-e-Shahwar,* September, 1906 (*vide* the *U.P. N.N.R.,* 1906).

[9]The *Pioneer Mail,* 27 May, 1907.

[10]The *Naiyar-e-Azam,* 12 May, 1906; the *Riyaz-e-Faiz,* 12 May, 1906, *vide* the *U.P. N.N.R.,* 1906; and the *Mihir-o-Sudhakar,* 3 August, 1906, *vide* the *Bengal N.N.R.,* 1906.

[11]The *Mihir-o-Sudhakar,* 27 July, 1906. The *Bengal N.N.R.,* 1906.

[12]The *Qasim-al-Akhbar,* 21 May, 1906. The *Madras N.N.R.,* 1906.

[13]The *Bombay Gazette—English News Supplement,* 14 July, 1906.

cause and repudiated him as a leader; whilst others thought that he was trying to curry favour with the Government.[14]  This restlessness of a large section of the Muslims over the question of the Khilafat was one of the reasons which had induced Mohsin-ul-Mulk to agree finally to the formation of the All-India Muslim League.  The same was the case with the Aga Khan, who told Chirol in 1910 that the undesirable prospect of a pan-Islamic movement in India was one of the considerations that had influenced his decision in favour of an all-India Muslim political party.[15]  The Aga Khan had hoped that with proper guidance through a political party, the danger of any pan-Islamic movement in India could be obviated.[16]

The first few years of the All-India Muslim League showed signs of the fulfilment of the expectations of the Aga Khan and other leaders like him.  From 1907 to the middle of 1910, the League had been able to persuade the Indian Muslims to devote more and more attention to their own problems than those of their co-religionists outside India. Nonetheless, the Muslim newspapers and journals all over the country had continued their interest in the course of events in Muslim States and noticed with uneasiness the signing of the Anglo-Russian Convention in 1907, which had brought southern and northern Persia under the respective influence of the two powers.  They grew anxious when in September–October, 1910, some British troops landed at Lingah– a Persian Gulf port.[17]  For the first time, the Muslim League was urged to give due consideration to the Persian question.[18]  The matter was promptly taken up by the London League, which requested the British Government to help preserve the independence and integrity of Persia.[19] It was also referred to generally in Nabiullah's presidential address at the Nagpur session of the All-India Muslim League held in December, 1910.[20]  These representations, however, had no effect upon the British Government and the Persian question continued to loom large in the eyes of the Indian Muslims.

In view of the Indian Muslims' continuous and growing interest in the affairs of Turkey, Persia and other Muslim countries, the sudden thrust

---

[14] The *Bombay Gazette Summary*, 4 August, 1906 and the *Jasus*, 14 July, 1906 (*vide* the *U.P. N.N.R.*, 1906).
[15] Chirol to Hardinge, 9 November, 1910. H.P. vol. 92.
[16] *Ibid.*
[17] The *Muhammadi*, 11 November, 1910. The *Bengal N.N.R.*, 1910.
[18] The *Zul Qarnain*, 14 October, 1910. The *U.P. N.N.R.*, 1910.
[19] The *Bengalee*, 4 November, 1910.
[20] *Proceedings of the Nagpur Meeting of the A.I.M.L.*, *op. cit.*, p. 33.

of Italy upon Tripoli could not but produce serious repercussions among them. Indeed, it created a ferment in the Muslim mind. Public meetings condemning the Italian aggression and seeking British intervention were held in Calcutta,[21] Dacca, Madras, Poona, Allahabad, Lahore, Karachi, Lucknow, Gorakhpur and several other towns all over the country.[22] The Muslim press in general denounced Italy as a hungry demon eager to devour Muslim lands.[23] Following in the footsteps of some Italian Bishops who had termed Italy's invasion of Tripoli as inspired by religious and civilising mission,[24] several Muslim newspapers sought to depict the war as an attack on Islam by Christianity.[25] The concern of the middle-class Muslims about the war was so widespread that it was proposed to issue Reuters messages as soon as they arrived in Calcutta in the vernacular for Muslim readers.[26]

The first attempt to help Turkey materially in her war against Italy was taken by the Muslims of Calcutta, who formed an Indian Red Crescent Society on 2 October, 1911. This Society aimed at taking steps for the prevention of hostilities and the collection of funds for the relief of sufferers. Among the leading members of its central committee were Ghulam Husain Arif, president, Haji Ahmad Abdul Latif, treasurer, and Abdullah Suhrawardy and Aga Moidul Islam (editor of the *Nama-i-Muqaddas Hablul Matin*), secretaries. Evidently, the Indian Red Crescent Society had been sponsored by Abdullah Suhrawardy and his supporters, who now included Mirza Shujaat Ali Baig, Persian consul-general and one of the vice-presidents of the Bengal League, and Aga Syed Husain Shustry, a leading Persian Muslim and another vice-president of the provincial League. Very soon, the Society became a powerful instrument of pan-Islamic activities within and outside Bengal and through its platform Abdullah Suhrawardy exercised considerable influence in shaping the course of Muslim politics in India.

---

[21] The *Pioneer Mail*, 6 October, 1911.

[22] See Political and Secret Department Papers (L/PS/10/196) and the *Pioneer Mail*, 6 and 13 October, 1911.

[23] The *Namai Muqaddas Hablul Matin*, 2 October, 1911 (*vide* the *Bengal N.N.R.*, 1911), the *Observer*, 4 October, 1911, etc., etc. (*vide* the *Punjab N.N.R.*, 1910).

[24] The *Namai Muqaddas Hablul Matin*, 9 October, 1909. The *Bengal N.N.R.*, 1911.

[25] The *Muhammadi*, 13 October, 1911 (*vide* the *Bengal N.N.R.*, 1911); the *Zamindar*, 5 October, 1911, etc. (*vide* the *Punjab N.N.R.*, 1911).

[26] The *Pioneer Mail*, 6 October, 1911.

The Muslim leaders of other parts of India did not immediately emulate the example of their counterparts in Calcutta. But in Madras the denunciation of Italy took the form of a boycott of Italian goods. At a largely-attended public meeting held at Madras on 5 October, 1911, under the presidentship of Abdul Quddus Badshah Saheb, vice-president of the provincial League and brother of Abdul Aziz Badshah Saheb, the Turkish vice-consul, a resolution was passed calling the Muslims all over the world to boycott Italian goods. The suggestion seems to have appealed to a considerable section of the Muslim politicians and was quickly taken up by the All-India League.

On 7 October, 1911, the council of the All-India Muslim League met at Lucknow to consider the situation created by the Italo-Turkish war. After prolonged discussion, the council adopted three resolutions which reflected the depth of Muslim feeling on the question. The first resolution, while expressing the League's 'deep abhorrence of Italy's unjustifiable and high-handed action in Tripoli and her flagrant and unprecedented outrage on international morality', cordially sympathised with Turkey and appealed to the British Government to exercise its influence in ending the war.[27] The second resolution advised the Muslims of India 'to keep a dignified attitude and place implicit confidence' in the benevolent and good intentions of the British Government and to raise subscriptions for the relief of sufferers. The third resolution asked the Muslims of India to boycott Italian goods.

The All-India League's decision to boycott Italian goods is significant. The Italo-Turkish war did not directly concern the Indian Muslims, whose interests it was the League's aim to serve. Moreover, boycott as a means of attaining political gains was anathema to several League leaders who had chastised the Hindus for boycotting British goods in Bengal. The acceptance of the principle of boycott by the League Council for an extra-territorial cause, therefore, indicated not only the strong pressure of public opinion on the leaders but also the growing influence of new elements as well as the pan-Islamists within the hierarchy of the League.

It is difficult to ascertain how far the League's appeal for the boycott of Italian goods was followed up in practice. The Government of India did not take any immediate note of the appeal and no reliable data are available on the matter. However, the boycott seems to have had some degree of success in different parts of the country. Despite the

[27]The *Pioneer Mail,* 6 October, 1911.

provincial government's hostile attitude, the boycott spread over a large area in Eastern Bengal. As the chief secretary to the Government of Eastern Bengal and Assam reported, 'attempts to produce a boycott of Italian goods have . . . led in some districts to an idea that it is the duty of good Muslims to boycott all European goods of whatever nationality.'[28] In Bombay through the efforts of men like Sir Currimbhoy Ibrahim, Baronet and Ibrahim Rahimtullah, who were taunted by non-Muslim journalists as 'Boycotter-in-Chief of Italian Goods', and 'Head Deacon of Italian Boycott', respectively,[29] the movement found considerable support among the Muslim merchants. The strong support for the boycott in the U.P.[30] and the Punjab[31] Muslim press suggests that it had obtained some success in these provinces as well.

While events abroad were thus agitating the minds of the League leaders, they were suddenly confronted with a startling development at home. On 12 December, 1911, the King (George V) announced at the Delhi Durbar the decisions for the absorption of Eastern Bengal and Assam into the Presidency of Bengal; the creation of a Lieutenant-Governorship for Bihar, Orissa and Chotanagpur; the formation of a Chief Commissionership in Assam and the removal of the seat of the Government of India from Calcutta to Delhi. The announcement was the outcome of the Government of India's proposals of 25 August, 1911, which had been approved by the Secretary of State in his despatch of 1 November, 1911.

Hardinge proudly claimed the Durbar announcement as a *coup d'état*.[32] Indeed, the announcement had certain characteristics of a *coup d'état*. It was conceived by one or two individuals, others being mostly persuaded or even manipulated[33] to acquiesce in it. It was kept a closely-guarded secret until the last moment; and was pronounced by

---

[28] From Le Mesurier, chief secretary to the Government of Eastern Bengal and Assam to the secretary, Home Dept., Government of India, J. & P. 5006/1911. Vol. 1058.

[29] The *Indu Prakash*, 3 November, 1911. The *Bombay N.N.R.*, 1911.

[30] The *Musafir*, 10 November, 1911; *Al-Mushir*, 11 November, 1911; *Al-Bashir*, 14 November, 1911, etc., vide the *U.P. N.N.R.*, 1911.

[31] The *Observer*, 11 October, 1911; *Zamindar*, 8 October, 1911, etc., *vide* the *Punjab N.N.R.*, 1911.

[32] Hardinge to Morley, 27 November, 1911. H.P., vol. 92.

[33] Butler and Carlyle were not in favour of the annulment of the partition of Bengal. On 11 August, 1911, Hardinge noted—'It received general approval except from Carlyle and possibly Butler'. Again, on 13 August, 1911, he recorded, 'Carlyle as usual is recalcitrant . . . Butler is also tiresome . . .' *Vide* Hardinge's

the King, whose words were irrevocable.[34]     While the decision to partition the former province of Bengal in 1905 had been the result of several years of official thinking and about two years of public considerations and discussions, it took Hardinge a few days of strictly confidential consultation with his executive councillors to undo it. Even the Lieutenant-Governors of the provinces concerned and the secretaries of the Government of India were not taken into confidence.

It has been rightly pointed out that the Durbar announcement was 'conceived of opportunism,' and that Hardinge made an about-face in recommending it to the Secretary of State.[35]     From February, 1911, until 15 June, 1911—three days before he received a note from Jenkins—Hardinge had consistently and vigorously opposed any revocation of the partition.  This persistent opposition is more significant when one considers the fact that the suggestion for such a reversal emanated from the King himself[36] and had the full support of the Secretary of State for India.  On 15 June, 1911, while commenting on a memorial submitted by Surendranath Banerjea demanding the annulment of the partition, Hardinge told Crewe: 'I shudder at the thought of any attempt to modify the present system as being likely to produce administrative chaos and to expose us to the charge of indecision of purpose and of treachery to the Mahomedans.'[37]     Earlier, on 4 May, 1911, while informing Crewe that Bhupendranath Basu (a prominent Congress leader) was on his way to England, Hardinge had observed that Basu had never raised the question of the partition of Bengal to him, 'probably because he knew that I would not listen to him, nor was the word partition mentioned once during the whole course of last Legislative Session . . . I therefore regard the question as practically dead, and I hope that no M.P.s will be so foolish as to listen to him if he tries to agitate for the reversal of that policy'.[38]     Still earlier, the Viceroy had

diary, August, 1911. H.P. Carlyle and Butler were brought round by Jenkins and Wilson respectively. *Vide* Wilson to Hardinge, 14 August, 1911, and Hardinge to Crewe, 24 August, 1911. H.P., vol. 113.

[34] Speeches of Lansdowne, Asquith, Bonar Law and Curzon, 12 December, 1911 and 21–22 February, 1912.  Parl. (Commons) Debates, vol. XXXII, columns 2154–5 and Lords Debates, vol. II, columns 138–234.

[35] S. Z. H. Zaidi, The Partition of Bengal and its Annulment—a Survey of the Schemes of Territorial Redistribution of Bengal (1902–1911), London University, unpublished thesis, p. 261.

[36] See pp. 234–235.

[37] Hardinge to Crewe, 15 June, 1911. H.P., vol. 117.

[38] Hardinge to Morley, 4 May, 1911. H.P., vol. 92.

noted that the 'feeling about the partition has almost entirely disappeared',[39] that its reversal would create 'the most profound anarchy in the administration of the two Bengals',[40] that any such suggestion 'is quite impracticable',[41] and that 'it is very desirable that not a whisper of such a possibility should be heard'.[42] Hardinge would have hardly used such strong words so many times had he had any doubt in his mind about the advantages of the continuation of the existing arrangements.

But on 18 June, 1911, Hardinge received 'a bombshell' from Jenkins[43] which the latter had prepared on the previous day. Following this note, Hardinge talked to Jenkins on 19 June, 1911, over the question of the annulment of the partition.[44] The same day he resolved to 'take up *his* [Jenkins'] idea'.[45] On 20 June, 1911, Hardinge drew up a note settling the main points of the plan for the undoing of the partition.[46] This note seems to have been based on Jenkins' memorandum. The memorandum, however, is not traceable, and one has to depend mainly on Hardinge's own comments on and quotations from it. In his *My Indian Years*, Hardinge admits the crucial importance of Jenkins in the matter.[47] But here Hardinge claims that Jenkins' memorandum of 17 June, 1911, merely 'caused *my* views on the question to materialise into a definite policy'.[48] It is rather hard to accept this claim of the Viceroy. There is not a shred of evidence either in the Government records or in Hardinge's own papers to suggest that prior to Jenkins' note, Hardinge had any thought except that of preserving the existing arrangements in Bengal.

Once converted to the idea of the revocation of the partition, Hardinge did not find it difficult to advocate it forcefully, though most of the arguments he put forward went against his earlier and repeated assertions. Previously he had attended to the benefits of the partition to the people of Eastern Bengal and Assam,[49] but now he thought

---

[39]Hardinge to Crewe, 16 February, 1911. *Ibid.*, vol. 117.

[40]Hardinge to Crewe, 25 January, 1911. *Ibid.*

[41]Hardinge to Arthur Bigge, private secretary to the King, 26 January, 1911. H.P., vol. 114.

[42]*Ibid.*

[43]Hardinge's diary, dated, 18 June, 1911. H.P.

[44]Hardinge's diary, dated, 19 June, 1911. H.P.

[45]Hardinge's diary, 19 June, 1911. H.P. Italics mine.

[46]Harding's note, 20 June, 1911. H.P., vol. 113.

[47]Hardinge of Penshurst, *My Indian years*, p. 37.

[48]*Ibid.* Italics mine.

[49]Hardinge to Crewe, 22 February, 1911. H.P., vol. 117.

that the measure had not been justified by its results.[50]   His earlier statement that the anti-partition agitation was 'almost wholly factitious' and 'engineered by politicians and journalists'[51] was now replaced by his condemnation of the partition on grounds of 'grave injustice' done to the Bengalis.[52]   The 'practically dead' agitation[53] was now considered 'as strong as ever'.[54]

The disappearance of Jenkins' note from the Government records as well as from Hardinge's papers has made it difficult to come to any definite conclusion about the Home Member's and the Viceroy's motives behind the abrupt decision for the undoing of the partition. Doctor Zaidi's suggestion that the idea 'came under consideration simply because the Government had failed to get a boon'[55] seems to be an over-simplification of the problem.  Doubtless, the proposition for the annulment of the partition had become very much tied up with the question of the King's granting a boon to the people of India. The liquidation of the province of Eastern Bengal and Assam was obviously a boon to the Bengali Hindus.[56]   But what was a boon to the Hindus was a bane to the Muslims.  The Government of India knew it.  It could, therefore, have arranged for some more generally acceptable boons.  If any particular phenomenon could be held responsible for Hardinge's instantaneous decision for the undoing of the partition, it was the King's visit to India.  But for that, neither the boon question nor the suggestion for the annulment would have arisen.  This conclusion becomes almost irresistible when one notes that 'the august author' of the scheme was none other than the King in person.[57]

The King had thought that the measure 'would flatter the Bengalis very much, allay discontent and stop sedition'.[58]   But as Crewe put it, 'more than anything else he [the King] had set his heart upon doing something which would, to some extent, satisfy that section of opinion in India which regarded partition as a mistake'.[59]   Thus, the King's

[50] Hardinge to Crewe, 6 July, 1911. *Ibid.,* vol. 113.

[51] Hardinge to Crewe, 22 February, 1911. *Ibid.,* vol. 117.

[52] Hardinge to Crewe, 13 July, 1911. *Ibid.,* vol. 113.

[53] Hardinge to Morley, 4 May, 1911. *Ibid.,* vol. 92.

[54] Hardinge's note, 20 June, 1911. *Ibid.,* vol. 113.

[55] S. Z. H. Zaidi—The Partition of Bengal, etc., *op. cit.,* p. 261.

[56] The *Hindi Bangavasi,* 1 January, 1912; the *Basumati,* 30 December, 1911, etc., *vide* the *Bengal N.N.R.,* 1911 and 1912.

[57] Morley to Hardinge, 24 March, 1911. H.P., vol. 92.

[58] The King to Hardinge, 16 December, 1911. *Ibid.,* vol. 79.

[59] Crewe to Hardinge, 27 January, 1911. *Ibid.,* vol. 117.

intention to flatter the Bengali Hindus appears to have been the outcome of his concern for securing a dignified, ceremonial and peaceful
visit to India which could have been marred by the anti-partition agitation. His experience of the Indian visit as the Prince of Wales in 1905,
when the agitation was strong, had probably made him more anxious
about the need to appease the anti-partitionists. Furthermore, some of
his advisers like W. Lawrence had been constantly inspiring him to undo
the partition of Bengal.[60] Even Crewe became a convert to this idea
and like a faithful courtier passed it on to Hardinge.[61]

Despite his undoubted loyalty and devotion to the King and the
Secretary of State, Hardinge found it impracticable to acquiesce in the
revocation. Politically, it would be a reversal of the policy of the past
few years.[62] Administratively, the reunited province would be far more
unwieldy.[63] On the other hand, the idea of the creation of a Governor-
ship with two commissioners for the two Bengals was impossible
because 'the danger would be that the post of Governor would be a
*sinecure* and he would feel uncomfortable in Calcutta being overshadowed by the Viceroy'.[64] The King's suggestion, therefore, was
rejected more on the grounds of lack of a suitable alternative administrative arrangement rather than on any political consideration.

The novel and vital feature of Jenkins' proposition for a 'revision of
the partition of Bengal' was his linking of the change with 'the creation
of an Imperial enclave at Delhi'.[65] The suggestion was romantic and
politically fascinating. In the first place, this would associate Hardinge's
name with one of the oldest and most celebrated capitals in the world.
Jenkins himself had pointed out that the transfer of the capital to Delhi
would be 'a bold stroke of statesmanship', and that it would 'mark a
new era in the history of India'.[66] Secondly, it would spare the
Viceroy from sharing the capital with a Governor or a Lieutenant-
Governor. Thirdly, the undoing of the partition would mean the carrying out of the cherished desire of the King. Fourthly, this would
appease the Hindus by removing the potent cause of their agitation
which had been menacing the administration for about six years.[67]

[60]Crewe to Hardinge, 16 December, 1910 and 27 January, 1911. *Ibid.*
[61]Crewe to Hardinge, 27 January, 1911. *Ibid.*
[62]Hardinge to Arthur Bigge, 26 January, 1911. *Ibid.,* vol. 104.
[63]*Ibid.*
[64]*Ibid.*
[65]Hardinge's note, 20 June, 1911. H.P., vol. 113.
[66]*Ibid.*
[67]There is no evidence either in the Government records or in contem-

The most important point against the annulment of the partition of Bengal was the question of breach of pledges to the Muslims. But there is such a thing as political expediency, and consideration of Muslim interests could not be expected to influence the expediency of Indian administration. Moreover, the reaction to the revocation of the partition of the weak and loyal Muslim community was not likely to be as violent as that of the anti-partitionists. Consequently, a little attention to Muslim sentiment by pointing out Delhi's importance as the old seat of Muslim rule in India, a vague promise of safeguarding Muslim interests after the liquidation of Eastern Bengal and Assam, and the bestowal of a few titles and honours on some Muslim leaders seem to have been deemed sufficient to allay the discontents of the Muslims.[68]

It is perhaps not surprising that the Government should have under-estimated the strength of the Muslim opposition to the reversal of the partition. But their estimate of the Muslim feelings against the measure was nonetheless wrong. Few events exerted such a decisive influence in shaping the attitude of Muslims towards the Government as this annul-ment of the partition of Bengal.

As for the political justification of the measure, history has proved how unrealistic and short-sighted it was. In less than four decades, Bengal was re-partitioned and the fate of the remainder of the former province of Eastern Bengal and Assam—Assam including the Nagaland, Mizoram and other tribal areas—still hangs in the balance.

The impact of the annulment of the partition of Bengal on the All-India Muslim League was large and far-reaching. The dissolution of the Eastern Bengal and Assam deprived the League of one of its *raisons d'être*. However, the League was not in a position to challenge the royal announcement. The fact that the announcement came from the King's lips weighed very heavily with the League leaders.[69]     The

porary newspapers to suggest that the anti-partition agitation was any worse in 1911 than it was between 1905–10. On the contrary, as late as 14 August, 1911, Butler asserted that the movement had declined (*vide* Butler's note 14 August, 1911. H.P., vol. 113). Similarly on 24 October, 1911, C. Bayley, Lieutenant-Governor of Eastern Bengal and Assam, reported that 'all attempts to rekindle enthusiasm on the subject of the partition have merely served to show that the embers are stone cold' (*vide* Bayley to Hardinge, 24 October, 1911. H.P., vol. 84).

[68]While the Government of India's despatch of 25 August, 1911, promised to safeguard the Muslim interests in Eastern Bengal and Assam, the Government also took special care in awarding high honours to Muslim leaders like the Aga Khan and Salimullah.

[69]Aziz Mirza, *Report of the All-India Muslim League for 1911*, p. 3.

defiance of the King's words would have been regarded as a serious act of disloyalty and the League leaders could not embark upon such a course. Moreover, such a policy was diametrically opposed to the creed of the League and the tradition of its leaders. Consequently, the League took some time in formulating and pronouncing formally its views on the matter. But the reaction of the individual members of the League was sharp.

The League leaders present at the Delhi Durbar were thunderstruck at the announcement.[70] They could hardly believe their ears. To most of them, the annulment of the partition was not only a breach of solemn and oft-repeated pledges but one that had humiliated the entire Muslim community. Their grief was boundless. As Viqar-ul-Mulk observed: 'This policy of the Government is like artillery passing over the dead bodies of the Muslims without realising whether any life remained in the bodies and whether they would be hurt.'[71] Viqar-ul-Mulk was convinced that the Government had snatched away a 'morsel' from the Muslims 'in order to placate the obstinate opposition of a stronger community'.[72] Abdullah Suhrawardy thought that Crewe and Hardinge had strained the loyalty of the Muslims 'to the breaking point when they were already exasperated by the affairs of Tripoli and Tabriz'.[73] Commenting on the reactions of the Muslim leaders at the announcement, Suhrawardy further remarked: 'If we are silent and less vocal, our silence is the silence of anger and sorrow and not that of acquiescence. In proportion to our devotion to the person and Throne of His Majesty is the intensity of our resentment at the cowardly device of putting the announcement in the mouth of the King-Emperor and thus muzzling us effectively.'[74] Another Muslim leader held that if agitation could result 'in unsettling a fact over and over solemnly declared as settled', regardless of the consequence of such a reversal of policy to those who in loyally upholding the Government's action had incurred 'the bitter enmity of the "nationalist agitators" ', then it was high time for the Muslims to reconsider their policy towards the majority community.[75]

---

[70] *Ibid.*

[71] Quoted in A. H. Albiruni's *Makers of Pakistan and Modern Muslim India,* p. 111.

[72] The *Aligarh Institute Gazette,* 3 January, 1912. The *U.P. N.N.R.,* 1912.

[73] Abdullah Suhrawardy to Curzon, 28 February, 1912, C.P., vol. 434(a).

[74] *Ibid.*

[75] Enclosed with Ameer Ali to Curzon, 18 February, 1912, C.P., vol. 434(a).

The League leaders also saw through the Government's motive in offering honours to some of their colleagues in connection with the Durbar. They regarded the offer of a G.C.I.E. to Salimullah as 'a bribe'.[76] Salimullah himself was 'left broken-hearted' at the reversal of the partition. And although he had formally acknowledged the honour conferred on him with 'grateful thanks',[77] he privately remarked that it was like a 'Tawq-i-Lanat' (a chain or collar of disgrace).[78]

Among the League leaders, only the Aga Khan had intended to support the announcement. This immediately brought him faced with a threat of no-confidence from the League members.[79] Eventually the Aga Khan endorsed the announcement in his individual capacity and not as the president of the League.[80]

The resentment of a large majority of the League leaders at the annulment of the partition was so intense that they immediately set out to reconsider their policy towards the Government as well as the Hindu community. A section of them thought that the Muslims could no longer rely upon the promises of a Government which was not strong enough to withstand sustained agitation. They also believed that 'the "Swarajists" will, with greater persistence and elated by this victory, presently begin to agitate for other things', and eventually attain self-government.[81] In the event, they held that unless the League leaders entered into some understanding with the Hindu leaders the future of the Muslim community would be gravely endangered. Some members of this section even suggested that the Muslim League should be abolished and that all Muslims should join the Congress.[82]

The other, and numerically larger section of the League leaders, however, disagreed with this view. They contended that although the Government had betrayed the Muslims, the latter would derive no benefit from joining the Congress. Viqar-ul-Mulk, one of the chief spokesmen of this group, pointed out that the Muslims did not dissociate themselves from the Congress because of any desire to remain faithful to Government, but because 'some of its important pretensions were detrimental

[76] Abdullah Suhrawardy to Curzon, 28 February, 1912. *Ibid.*

[77] Salimullah to Hare, 2 January, 1912. *Ibid.*

[78] Abdullah Suhrawardy to Curzon, 28 February, 1912. *Ibid.*

[79] Jenkins to Hardinge, 18 December, 1911. H.P., vol. 82.

[80] *Ibid.*

[81] Enclosure with Ameer Ali to Curzon, 18 February, 1912. C.P., vol. 434(a).

[82] The *Aligarh Institute Gazette,* 20 December, 1911 and the *Leader,* 24 December, 1911. *Vide* the *U.P. N.N.R.,* 1911.

to their interests'.[83]   He noted that the suggestion of the Muslims joining the Congress was the 'result of despondency for which Government
is particularly responsible, but no one should advise any man to commit
suicide'. As for loyalty towards the Government, Viqar-ul-Mulk thought
that 'it is not an "essence" it is only an "accident". It rests on some
foundation and it is weakened whenever that foundation is shaken.' He
therefore advised the Muslims to stand on their own feet and to make
best possible use of the worst situation by strongly and persistently
pressing their claims before the Government. The same views seem to
have been held by Salimullah and several other prominent members of
the League.

That a considerable number of League leaders present at Delhi desired
to follow the line of least resistance to the Government's decision,
became evident from Salimullah's letter of 20 December, 1911, to
Hardinge. Salimullah had before writing the letter consulted 'the leading Mahomedans now at Delhi'.[84]   The letter contained eight demands,
the fulfilment of which were considered to have been necessary to safeguard the Muslim interests and to reassure those Muslims who had
viewed 'the reversion of the Eastern districts of Bengal with feelings of
consternation'.[85] The demands were: the Governor of the newly constituted Bengal Presidency should spend equal time 'in the two capitals,
Calcutta and Dacca'; the Muslims of the Presidency should be provided
with separate and proportionate representation in the Legislative
Council and local self-governing bodies; either a separate annual budget
should be prepared for Eastern Bengal or arrangements should be made
to spend the revenue raised in the eastern districts on the administration
and development of those districts only; measure should be taken for
the appointment of more Muslims in the government service; alternately,
a Muslim member should be appointed to the executive council of the
new presidency; one officer with experience of administration in
Eastern Bengal and Assam should find a place in the executive council
of the presidency and two such officers should be employed as commissioners of the Dacca and Chittagong divisions; a Muslim Joint
Director or Assistant Director of Public Instruction should be appointed
for the purpose of supervising education in Eastern Bengal and Assam;
special grants should be made for higher education of Muslims and the

[83] The *Aligarh Institute Gazette,* 20 December, 1911. *Ibid.*
[84] Salimullah to Hardinge, 17 December, 1911, and Salimullah to Hardinge,
20 December, 1911. H.P., vol. 82.
[85] Salimullah to Hardinge, 20 December, 1911. *Ibid.*

recommendations of the Madrasa Reforms Conference held under the auspices of the Eastern Bengal and Assam Government should be implemented.[86]    While advancing these demands, Salimullah urged the Viceroy to give him and other Muslim leaders of Eastern Bengal an opportunity to place before him their needs and wants in detail.

Salimullah's demands were moderate and perhaps the minimum that could reassure the Muslims of Eastern Bengal and Assam. Of the eight demands, those concerning Muslim representation in the elective bodies and the government service were vitally necessary for the progress of the community. But these were either rejected off-hand or set aside by the Viceroy. On 21 December, 1911, Hardinge noted that the Muslims had already been provided with separate electorates in the Council.[87] Obviously, the Viceroy ignored the fact that the seats allotted to the Muslims in the provincial council (only four) fell far short of the representation their numerical proportion justified: Hardinge's comments on the question of the extension of separate electorates to the local bodies were even more unsympathetic. He observed that the matter would have to be settled for India as a whole, and 'not for any province or part of a province or any special denomination'.[88] Evidently, he did not think that the liquidation of Eastern Bengal and Assam provided any special ground for a consideration of the electoral problems facing the Muslims of the province. Hardinge, it may be noted here, suppressed his own views on the merits of the demand itself. He had come to India with the pre-conceived notion that the partial separate electorates granted to the Muslims were injurious to the Hindus. Immediately on his landing at Bombay in November, 1910, Hardinge had bluntly told a deputation of the Bombay League that 'special privileges to one community mean disabilities to another'.[89] Furthermore, in his private correspondence, the Viceroy was never tired of deprecating separate electorates,[90] thus tending to influence official opinion on the subject.

As regards the Muslim demand for more employment in the state service, Hardinge considered it impractical because appointments must depend on the capability of the various candidates.[91]    He could only

[86]*Ibid.*
[87]Hardinge's memorandum, 21 December, 1911. H.P., vol. 82.
[88]*Ibid.*
[89]The *Times of India Mail,* 26 November, 1910.
[90]Hardinge to the Maharaja of Bikanir, 19 December, 1910. H.P., vol. 82.
[91]Hardinge's memorandum, 21 December, 1911. *Ibid.*

ask the Governor of Bengal to see that Muslims 'with necessary qualifications' received a proper share in the service. Similarly, the Viceroy left the Muslim claims regarding educational matters to the consideration of the Education Member of the Government of India.[92] However, in this connection he asked the members of his executive council to consider the creation of a university at Dacca because 'this would be an undeniable proof' of the Government's intention to encourage Muslim education.[93] Here Hardinge seems to have deliberately withheld the information that C. Bayley, Lieutenant-Governor of Eastern Bengal and Assam, had already in October, 1911, proposed the establishment of a university and a High Court at Dacca.[94] Hardinge's motive in suppressing the proposal of the Lieutenant-Governor and in presenting it as his own suggestion was to project the university question as a compensation for the undoing of Eastern Bengal and Assam. But, as Abbas Ali Baig, member, India Council, rightly pointed out, the foundation of a new university at Dacca was one of the measures which would have been carried out 'if the development of Eastern Bengal under a separate Government had not been affected' by the annulment of the partition.[95]

The demand for a separate budget or special arrangements for the economic development of the eastern districts of Bengal was considered to have been 'impossible' by the Viceroy.[96] He thought that the Governor of the Presidency 'would naturally see that the administration and development' of these districts were not neglected. Hardinge could not have been ignorant of the fact that although the eastern districts of Bengal were rich in natural resources, prior to the creation of Eastern Bengal and Assam they had been utterly neglected and that Calcutta and its suburbs were developed mostly at the cost of these districts. The Viceroy had himself on 22 February, 1911, told Crewe that the reversal of the partition 'would mean the return of the new province to its former state of stagnation'.[97] Consistency was not Hardinge's virtue in so far as it concerned Eastern Bengal and Assam. He was, indeed, somewhat indifferent to the interests of its people. Even after the undoing of the province, Hardinge did not find it necessary to ask the Government of Eastern Bengal and Assam to suggest any

[92] *Ibid.*
[93] *Ibid.*
[94] C. Bayley to Hardinge, 28 October, 1911. *Ibid.*
[95] Abbas Ali Baig's note, 12 February, 1912. J. & P. 615/1912 with 667/12, vol. 1135.
[96] Hardinge's note, 21 December, 1911. H.P., vol. 82.
[97] Hardinge to Crewe, 22 February, 1911. H.P., vol. 117.

measure for safeguarding the interests of its people, nor did he refer
Salimullah's letter to the provincial Government. Of the demands
already raised, he could consider favourably only those relating to the
Governor's occasional staying at Dacca, the appointments of a Muslim
and a former Eastern Bengal and Assam official to the Governor's
executive council and the posting of two officers of the disappearing
province as commissioners of the Dacca and Chittagong divisions.[98]
These were 'practical and desirable' from the administrative point of
view and would at the same time serve the interests of the eastern
districts. The Viceroy also decided to give the Muslim leaders of the
province a hearing, as this 'would have a good effect' and provide him
with an opportunity to explain his views to them.[99]

Even before Hardinge's views on safeguarding the Muslim interest in
Eastern Bengal and Assam were known, a section of the League leaders
had come out with a call for an end to the Muslims' reliance on the
Government. The initiative in this respect was taken by Abdullah
Suhrawardy, who on 16 December, 1911, convened a meeting of the
Muslim leaders from all over India to discuss the situation created by the
Delhi declaration.[100] The hurriedly convened meeting was held at
Calcutta on 24 December with Syed Muhammad as its president.[101] It
was not well attended, but several letters and telegrams conveying
opinions of individual Muslim leaders were read at the meeting.
Abdullah Suhrawardy urged an immediate change in Muslim policy and
pleaded for a rapprochement with the Hindu community.[102] After
prolonged discussion, the meeting passed a resolution to the effect that
'the time has come for the Mussalmans to change their policy towards
other communities, but considering the importance of the question, it
is desirable that the line of policy to be adopted should be determined
after further deliberation'.[103] The resolution was proposed by Abdul
Majid, member, Eastern Bengal and Assam Legislative Council, and a
leading member of the provincial League, seconded by Aga Moidul
Islam, and supported by Ghulam Husain Arif and Wahed Husain,
pleader. While the proposer of the resolution was a man of moderate

---

[98] Hardinge's note, 21 December, 1911. *Ibid.*, vpl. 82.

[99] *Ibid.*

[100] G. H. Arif's speech at the Bengal Presidency Muslim Conference. *Vide* the *Bengalee*, 3 March, 1912.

[101] The *Englishman Weekly Summary*, 28 December, 1911.

[102] *Ibid.*

[103] *Ibid.*

but anti-Congress views, the seconder and one of the supporters (Arif) were pan-Islamists, and the other supporter a pro-Congress moderate. The resolution thus reflected the views of a cross-section of the League members in Bengal. The importance of the resolution can hardly be exaggerated. It marked the advent of a new era in Muslim politics which, in a year's time, was to transform the All-India Muslim League itself. Coming as it did within less than a fortnight of the Delhi announcement, the Calcutta resolution articulated the instantaneous reaction of a large section of the Muslims of Bengal to the annulment of the partition.

On 30 December, 1911, the Muslim leaders of the two Bengals attended a meeting held at Dacca at the invitation of Salimullah.[104] Salimullah himself was very ill but still he participated at the meeting, which was presided over by Nawab Khawaja Muhummad Yusuf. After a long and animated discussion the meeting adopted four resolutions, three of them unanimously. The first resolution, proposed by Nawab Ali Choudhury, seconded and supported respectively by Hemayetuddin Ahmad and Hossam Haider Choudury, both members of the Eastern Bengal and Assam Legislative Council, recorded a 'deep sense of regret and disappointment at the announcement of the annulment of the partition of Bengal in utter disregard of Mahomedan feeling and specially of the interests of Mahomedans of Eastern Bengal'.[105] The resolution, however, added that since the announcement had been made by the King-Emperor himself, 'the Mahomedans out of their loyalty to and profound respect and regard for the Throne, feel that they have no other alternative but to desist from entering a protest' against it. Only Abdullah Suhrawardy dissented from the resolution. Abdullah Suhrawardy's reasons for dissenting are not available but considering his very strong views on the matter, it may be presumed that he advocated an agitation against the announcement.

The second resolution of the meeting, proposed by Muhammad Ismail, seconded by Amiruddin Ahmad and supported by Abdul Majid, noted that since the interests of the Muslims were likely 'to be seriously affected' by the revocation of the partition of Bengal, the Viceroy should provide the Muslim leaders with an opportunity of waiting upon him in a deputation to present their views as to how the Muslim interests could be safeguarded. The third resolution, proposed and seconded by Khawaja Atiqullah and Abdul Jabbar respectively, demanded that in

[104] The *Englishman*, 1 January, 1912.
[105] *Ibid.*

the redistribution of provincial boundaries, the district of Sylhet should be included within the Bengal Presidency. The fourth and the last resolution, proposed by Abdul Rasool and seconded by Abdur Rahman, declared that, in view of the recent administrative changes, it was desirable to set up one strong and representative organisation for the whole of Bengal, with headquarters at Calcutta and branches in all the districts and sub-districts, 'to promote the advancement and welfare' of the Muslims of Bengal.

The resolutions were the handiwork of Salimullah. Exactly five years ago the same day, Salimullah had from the same spot at Shahbagh, Dacca, proposed the formation of the All-India Muslim League, with a view mainly to counteract the anti-partition agitation. Today, he had to surrender himself to the irrevocable decision of the King. Besides, the odds against a sustained agitation were indeed formidable. The Muslims of Eastern Bengal and Assam were too backward economically, politically and educationally to confront the combined strength of the Government and the Hindu community. In the hour of his most agonising disappointment Salimullah showed a remarkable sense of realism by adopting an attitude of least resistance to the annulment and by formulating demands necessary to safeguard the interests of the dissolved province in the altered situation.

After some murmurings,[106] the Dacca meeting's resolutions were accepted generally by the Muslims of Bengal,[107] but the bitterness and frustrations caused by the undoing of Eastern Bengal and Assam continued to torment the educated section of the community.[108] A substantial number of them now thought that their loyalty towards the Government had brought them nothing but humiliation and contempt and that they should follow the example of the Hindu community in strengthening their position as well as pressing their demands upon the authorities.[109]

The indignation of the Muslims of Bengal and Assam at the annulment of the partition of Bengal was equally shared by educated Muslims in other parts of India. Muslim newspapers and journals all over the country deprecated the Government's measure in undoing (as

[106] The *Mussalman,* 26 January, 1912. The *Bengal N.N.R.,* 1912.

[107] The Anjuman-i-Islamia, Faridpur; the Islamia Association, Noakhali; the Chittagong Islam Association; the Anjuman-i-Islamia, Manikganj (*vide* the *Englishman,* 9 January and 19 January, 1912) passed resolutions on the line of the Dacca meeting of 30 December, 1911.

[108] The *Mussalman,* 12 January, 1912. The *Bengal N.N.R.,* 1912.

[109] *Ibid.*

the *Zamindar* put it) 'an Islamic province' by 'one stroke of the pen'.[110]
The consensus of opinion in the Muslim press was that the Government
had sacrificed the interests of the Muslims in order to placate the
Hindus.[111]   A section of the Muslim press was convinced that unless
the Muslims of India started an agitation, their rights would continue to
be trampled upon.[112]   One journal even noted that it was impossible to
make any Indian believe 'today that "clamour and agitation" do not
pay in Indian politics. Some are even inclined to think that agitation
gains rather than loses if it has a slight flavour of force.'[113]

A majority of the Muslim press, however, agreed that since the Delhi
announcement was made by the King himself, the Muslims, instead of
agitating against it, should seek to safeguard the interests of their co-
religionists in Eastern Bengal through persistent representations. They
argued that the Muslims lacked the organisation, political training and
financial resources required for a sustained agitation and that if they
resorted to an agitation the result would be tumult and disorder.[114]

Within about six weeks of the undoing of the partition of Bengal and
less than four weeks of the Calcutta meeting organised by Abdullah
Suhrawardy, a large number of League members recognised the necessity
for a reappraisal of the Muslim policy. Prominent among them were
Ameer Ali,[115] Viqar-ul-Mulk,[116] Nawab Ali Choudhury,[117] Muham-
mad Ali,[118] Syed Raza Ali,[119] Samiullah Baig[120] and Abdul Aziz.[121]
The clamour for a new policy was, in fact, so widespread that the
*Punjabee,* a Hindu newspaper, rightly remarked: 'Almost everybody

[110]The *Zamindar*, 6 February, 1912. The *Punjab N.N.R.*, 1912.

[111]The *Waqt*, 23 December, 1911;   the *Vakil*, 6 January, 1912 (*vide* the *Punjab N.N.R.*, 1912);   and the *Al-Bashir*, 2 January, 1912;   the *Tajir*, 4 January,
1912;   the *Zulqarnain*, 14 January, 1912, etc. (*vide* the *U.P. N.N.R.*, 1912).

[112]The *Millat*, 2 February, 1912;   the *Curzon Gazette*, 23 January, etc. (*vide*
the *Punjab N.N.R.*, 1912).

[113]The *Comrade*, 23 December, 1912. The *Bengal N.N.R.*, 1911.

[114]Letter to the *Mussalman*, 26 January, 1912 (*vide* the *Bengal N.N.R.*, 1912).

[115]Ameer Ali to Curzon, 4 January, 1912. C.P., vol. 434(a).

[116]The *Aligarh Institute Gazette*, 3 January, 1912. The *U.P. N.N.R.*, 1912.

[117]Nawab Ali Choudhury's telegram to the London League, enclosed with
Ameer Ali to Curzon, 4 January, 1912. C.P., vol. 434(a).

[118]The *Comrade*, 3 February, 1912. The *Bengal N.N.R.*, 1912.

[119]Syed Raza Ali's letter to the *Pioneer Mail*, 5 January, 1912.

[120]Samiullah Baig's letter to the *Pioneer Mail*, 19 January, 1912.

[121]Abdul Aziz's views on the reappraisal of Muslim policy were pro-Congress
and during the last week of December, 1911, he joined the Congress party. *Vide*
the *Bengalee*, 30 December, 1911.

who is anybody in the Muslim League camp—who, on the eve of the Coronation Durbar, would have boxed your ears if you had asked him for a new policy—loudly advocated a change of policy, even to the extent of embracing the Hindus, as soon as the Royal announcement modifying the partition of Bengal was made.'[122]　A most significant aspect of this demand for a reconsideration of the Muslim policy was that it was pressed chiefly by the younger members of the party, but it was so overwhelming that no League leader, not even the Aga Khan, dared to raise his voice against it.

Muslim discontent against the Government policy in reversing the partition of Bengal increased further when on 31 January, 1912, Hardinge, in his reply to a memorial submitted by a deputation headed by Salimullah, evaded or disregarded most of the demands for safeguarding the interests of the people of East Bengal in general and the Muslims in particular. These demands were on the lines of Salimullah's eight points put forward to Hardinge on 20 December, 1911. The only significant difference between the two sets of demands was that while Salimullah's letter was silent about the extent of Muslim representation in the Legislative Council of the new presidency of Bengal, the deputation's memorial asked for a proportional representation for the Muslims in that body.[123]

Hardinge's reply to the Salimullah deputation followed the lines of his memorandum of 21 December, 1911, with some slight verbal modifications. The only positive notes in the reply were the intimation that he had recommended the appointment of a Muslim (Shams-ul-Huda) and a former Eastern Bengal and Assam official for membership of the executive council of the Governor of Bengal, and that he intended to recommend the constitution of a university at Dacca and the appointment of a special officer for education in East Bengal.[124]

True to his way of treating important decisions concerning the administration as confidential, Hardinge had kept his reply to Salimullah's deputation a 'secret'.[125]　But this time it did not work. On 1 February, 1912, the vigilant and influential *Bengalee* published the gist of

[122] The *Punjabee*, 20 January, 1912. The *Punjab N.N.R.*, 1912.

[123] The memorial submitted to the Viceroy by a deputation led by Salimullah J. & P. 4543/1912, vol. 1201. The memorial is dated 3 February, 1912, but the deputation was received by Hardinge on 31 January, 1912. *Vide* the *Englishman*, 1 February, 1912.

[124] Hardinge's reply to the Salimullah deputation. *Vide* J. & P. 4543/1912, vol. 1201.

[125] The *Englishman*, 1 February, 1912.

Hardinge's reply to the deputation. Immediately afterwards a storm was created by the Hindu press all over India over Hardinge's alleged attempt at cultural and linguistic partition of Bengal by creating a university at Dacca.[126] Consequently, the Government of India was compelled to publicly affirm the decision for the establishment of a university at Dacca.[127] At the same time Hardinge received a Hindu deputation to assuage their overflowing anger.

To the Muslims of India Hardinge's reply to the Salimullah deputation was like adding insult to the injury caused by the liquidation of Eastern Bengal and Assam. While generally welcoming the proposed university at Dacca, they refused to consider it an adequate compensation for the annulment of the partition of Bengal. Once again, the Muslims felt that the Government had neglected the interests of the Muslims of East Bengal and that agitation was the only way to make the Government accept their just demands. As the *Comrade* (whose editor Muhammad Ali had come to be regarded as the leader of the 'Liberal' section of the League) put it, 'agitation is acknowledged by the Government to be the only effective method of converting them; we trust the Mussalmans, who are by tradition a proselytising community, will preach this doctrine on the roadside and in the market-place till His Excellency and his colleagues are converted'.[128]

By March, 1912, the Bengal League leaders seem to have formally acknowledged the failure of their policy of quiet and peaceful representation to the Government. On 3 March, 1912, while presiding over the Bengal Presidency Muslim Conference held at Calcutta, Salimullah declared that the days had gone by when the Muslims were content to sit moping in a corner and allowed others to play with their interests.[129] 'We are now full of the vivifying spirit of the times, and are determined to have our voice heard in the Administration of the affairs of the country.'[130] The Bengal Presidency Muslim Conference was in itself a manifestation of the Muslim leaders' earnestness to work for the regeneration of their community. The conference was jointly convened by Salimullah, Nawab Ali Choudhury, Hossam Haider Choudhury, Seraj-ul-Islam, Ghulam Husain Arif, Abdullah Suhrawardy, Abdul

[126]The *Bengalee*, 2, 4, 6 and 7 February, 1912.
[127]The Government's press note, dated 2 February, 1912. *Vide* the *Bengalee*, 3 February, 1912.
[128]The *Comrade*, 3 February, 1912. The *Bengal N.N.R.*, 1912.
[129]The *Bengalee*, 3 March, 1912.
[130]*Ibid.*

Rasool, Abul Kasem and a few other prominent leaders of the two Bengals.[131]   It was attended by delegates from the twenty-five districts of the newly created Bengal Presidency.[132]   Most of these delegates had been elected at public meetings held at the respective district head-quarters[133] and were representative of the educated section of the community.   A considerable proportion of·them belonged to the pro-fessional classes and were connected with local self-governing bodies. The enthusiasm of the delegates for vigorous political activities was the most striking feature of the conference.

The Bengal Presidency Muslim Conference was mainly concerned with the formation of a political association for the Muslims of the presidency.   The chairman of the reception committee, Ghulam Husain Arif, however, took this opportunity to discuss the situation created by the annulment of the partition of Bengal and by the Italo-Turkish war. Arif had no doubt that the partition of Bengal of 1905 was a blessing to the Muslims of Eastern Bengal.[134]   He thought that in rescinding the partition, the Government had treated the Muslim public opinion with contempt and that the Muslims had been greatly shocked by this unfair and unjust measure.   He was convinced that the outrageous conduct of the Italians in Tripoli and the ill-treatment of the Persians by Russia had roused the indignation of the Muslims of India.   He was glad to note that the Muslims of India had generously responded to the appeal for funds for the Indian Red Crescent Society.

As regards the future policy of the Muslims of Bengal Arif thought that the Delhi declaration had thrown their minds into confusion. Some Muslim leaders were inclined to join the Congress, others wanted to strengthen the All-India Muslim League and a third group desired to have a strong and independent provincial organisation.   Without giving his personal comments Arif left the matter to the decision of the conference.

Unlike Arif, Salimullah devoted a considerable portion of his address to discussing the course of action to be pursued by the Muslims of Bengal.   He wanted the formation of a representative body of the Muslims of Bengal to work in co-operation with the All-India Muslim League.   The organisation should be as broad-based as possible but it

[131]The *Englishman,* 24 January, 1912.
[132]The *Bengalee,* 3 March, 1912.
[133]The *Englishman,* 31 January, 14 February, 15 February, 16 February, etc., 1912.
[134]The *Bengalee,* 3 March, 1912.

must harmonise its activities with those of the Muslims of other parts of India. To start with, Salimullah suggested the amalgamation of the Eastern Bengal and Assam and the West Bengal Muslim Leagues into the Bengal Presidency League.

Salimullah's suggestion was taken up by Wahed Husain, who formally proposed the merger of the Eastern Bengal and Assam and the West Bengal Leagues into one body. It was seconded by Nawab Ali Choudhury. There was a counter-proposal from Gauhar Ali, barrister and a supporter of Abdullah Suhrawardy. Gauhar Ali proposed the formation of a Bengal Presidency Muslim Association which should be free from 'the autocratic control' of the Muslim leaders from outside Bengal.[135] He did not consider the All-India Muslim League necessary.

Gauhar Ali's motion created an uproar in the meeting. There were demands for its withdrawal from all corners. But Muhammad Roshan Ali, a young delegate, seconded the proposal and another young delegate remarked that the country could no longer hold on 'to toadyism'. After the confusion was over, Muhammad Akram Khan, editor of the *Muhammadi*, made an eloquent speech saying that differences of opinion were not bad and that the matter should be settled by vote. Abul Kasem, secretary of the reception committee, also appealed for peace between the supporters of the two motions. Abdul Rasool, and Dr. Abdul Ghaffur spoke in favour of Wahed Husain's proposal and when put to vote, this was carried amid loud and lusty cheers.

The proceedings of the Bengal Muslim Conference reflected the general line of cleavage among the Muslim politicians of Bengal. Most of the prominent leaders including the conservatives, moderates and pro-Congress ones, favoured a broad-based Bengal League, while a section of the pan-Islamists and a few extremists sought to set up a radical Association. The advocates of the Association were few in number and young in age and political experience. But their agitating mood on the annulment of the partition of Bengal as well as issues of pan-Islamic interest, and their slogan against toadyism, posed a challenge to the established leaders. The established leaders were fully aware of the threat and their concern for wider public contact and more pragmatic policy appear to have been to some extent influenced by a desire to render the extremists ineffective as a political force.

The reactions of the All-India Muslim League towards the revocation of the partition of Bengal and other issues confronting the Muslims of India in general and those of East Bengal in particular were voiced at

[135]*Ibid.*

the League's fifth annual session, held at Calcutta on 3 and 4 March, 1912. The fifth annual session of the League had been scheduled to be held at Delhi in December, 1911, with Sahms-ul-Huda as president. But due to the Government's objection to holding any political meeting at Delhi on the eve of the Royal Durbar, it was deferred until March, 1912. Meanwhile, in February, 1912, Shams-ul-Huda was appointed member of the Executive Council of the Governor of Bengal and Salimullah was elected president of the session.

As could be expected, Salimullah's presidential address at the League meeting centred round the revocation of the partition of Bengal and of the existing state of Muslim feeling in East Bengal. His comments on the Government's neglect of the aspirations of the people of East Bengal were frank, forthright and to some extent bitter. He urged his audience to believe that the Muslims of the eastern districts of Bengal had supported the partition not out of enmity towards the Hindus, nor at the bidding of the Government, but because they were convinced that the measure would afford them ample opportunities for self-improvement.[136] 'Our ill-wishers at once perceived that the Partition would necessarily bring to the fore the long-neglected claims of the Mussalmans of East Bengal, and although we never got more than what was justly our due, what little we gained was so much loss to them.'[137] The real cause of the anti-partition movement was to deprive the down-trodden Muslims of East Bengal from enjoying equal rights of citizenship. Those who knew the utter helplessness of the Muslims 'at the hands of their Bengalee landlord, lawyer or creditor' would have an idea of the tremendous sacrifices which the Muslims had to make in rallying to the side of law and order.[138] But after six years of struggle, the Muslims had been left in the lurch. Suddenly the Government of India had reversed the partition for the sake of expediency.[139]

Salimullah thought that the annulment of the partition had 'all the appearance of a ready concession to the clamours of an utterly seditious agitation. It has appeared to put a premium on sedition and disloyalty, and created an impression in the minds of the irresponsible masses that even the Government can be brought down to its knees by a reckless and persistent defiance of constituted authority.' The Muslims of

---

[136] *Speech delivered at the Fifth Session of the A.I.M.L. held in Calcutta on 3 and 4 March, 1912 by Nawab Salimullah*, p. 5.
[137] *Ibid.*, p. 6.
[138] *Ibid.*, p. 7.
[139] *Ibid.*, p. 8.

Eastern Bengal were greatly distressed at the reversal of the partition, as well as by the manner in which it had been brought about without their being consulted. However, the King's involvement in the matter had made it impossible for them to defy it.

Salimullah was sorry to note the 'Bengalee' leaders' opposition to the proposed university at Dacca. The Muslims of East Bengal welcomed the decision for the creation of a university at Dacca because this would give a great impetus to the cause of higher education in that part of Bengal. No doubt, the benefits of the Dacca University would be shared by the Muslims who formed a majority of the people of East Bengal, but this was a contingency which could not be avoided. 'We cannot cease to be a part and parcel of the population of that part of the country simply to please the fancy of a set of politicians who would eternally penalise the whole of East Bengal for the sin of having harboured so large a Muslim majority.'[140] Salimullah, however, feared that neither the establishment of a university at Dacca nor the appointment of a special education officer would provide any appreciable benefits to the Muslims, unless sufficient funds were allocated for the exclusive advancement of Muslim education.[141] In this connection he also laid special stress on the appointment of an adequate number of Muslim teachers and inspecting officers for the advancement of education in the areas where the Muslim population preponderated.[142]

Salimullah strongly reiterated the Muslim demands for the extension of separate electorates in the local bodies and for larger employment of Muslims in various branches of the public service. He was firmly convinced that without the provision for separate representation, Muslim interests in the municipalities, district boards and local boards would never be safeguarded. Minto and Morley had in unambiguous terms pledged separate representation of the Muslims in the local bodies. The fulfilment of the pledges would not only be 'an act of bare justice' to the Muslims but would also be productive of the utmost harmony between Hindus and Muslims by removing all chances of controversy and rivalry for the acquisition of membership of the local bodies.[143] Salimullah thought that the Muslim claim for employment in state service had not met with indulgent consideration. Statistics showed that even in Eastern Bengal and Assam, where Muslims were

[140]*Ibid.*, p. 13.
[141]*Ibid.*
[142]*Ibid.*, p. 14.
[143]*Ibid.*, p. 18.

alleged to have been favoured in the government employment, there were far more Hindu officers without any university qualifications than there were Muslims.[144]  Justice and fair play to the Muslims demanded that, provided Muslim candidates satisfied 'the minimum test required for efficiency', they should get preference over the candidates of the advanced communities, till such time as their proportion in the services came up to their proportion in the population.[145]

Salimullah urged the Indian Muslims to become more vigilant in politics and to place their grievances before the Government in a constitutional manner. They should follow the examples of the Hindu community who had on occasions worked fearlessly for the benefit of the country.[146]  Muslim youths should be 'manly and self-reliant, for a spirit of servile dependence on others is repugnant to the best traditions of Islam'.[147]

Towards the close of his address Salimullah announced his withdrawal from active politics on grounds of ill-health.[148]  He felt satisfied to note that the League which he had initiated barely five years ago had grown into a representative body of the Muslims of India and that his co-religionists had proved themselves capable of withstanding challenges from any quarter.  He was convinced that the leadership of the League would pass on 'to stronger arms and stouter nerves', thus initiating the Muslims of India to a prosperous future.[149]

The Calcutta session of the League met in the midst of an organisational crisis. Barely a week before the session, Aziz Mirza, the secretary of the League had died.[150]  Consequently, Syed Wazir Hasan, the young joint secretary, was appointed acting secretary of the League.[151]  About the same time the Aga Khan, who had visited Calcutta in February, 1912,[152] and whose name was proposed for the presidentship of the annual session,[153] found his position as president of the League 'untenable'.[154]  On the eve of the Calcutta meeting, the Aga

[144] *Ibid.*, p. 20.

[145] *Ibid.*, pp. 20–21.

[146] *Ibid.*, p. 22.

[147] *Ibid.*, p. 23.

[148] *Ibid.*

[149] *Ibid.*, p. 25.

[150] The *Madras Weekly Mail*, 29 February, 1912.

[151] The *Bengalee*, 29 February, 1912.

[152] The *Times of India Mail*, 10 February, 1912.

[153] *Ibid.*, 27 January, 1912.

[154] Lovat Fraser to Curzon, 4 March, 1912. C.P., vol. 434(a).

Khan resigned from the presidentship of the League. The reasons given for the resignation were various, 'some private and personal', others connected with the reorganisation of the central office of the League by the appointment of two additional joint presidents at his behest.[155] But as Lovat Fraser of the *Times of India* and a friend of the Aga Khan wrote, the real cause of the resignation was the 'resentment [among the League members] about his attitude towards the Delhi business'.[156] The Aga Khan's support for the annulment of the partition of Bengal had made him a target for severe personal attack from the Muslim press. His leadership was strongly repudiated and he was told to mind his own business and that of the Ismaili community and to leave Muslim politics to others.[157] About a year later the Aga Khan himself admitted that the public and private criticism of his colleagues had become 'unbearable' and that he had thought it wise to withdraw from the League leadership.[158] The election of Salimullah as president of the Calcutta session in preference to him was possibly too much of a public renunciation of the Aga Khan by the League.

The Calcutta session of the League, however, wanted the Aga Khan to continue as the president of the League at least for the time being. The anti-Aga Khan section was not yet fully prepared to seize the leadership, while other moderate leaders, despite their resentment over the annulment of the partition of Bengal, were reluctant to part company with him. In the event, on the motion of Muhammad Shafi, seconded by Abdul Majid and supported by Rafiuddin Ahmad and a few others, the Aga Khan was re-elected president of the League.[159] This expression of confidence in him seems to have pleased the Aga Khan, who withdrew his resignation forthwith.[160]

While re-electing the Aga Khan as president of the League, the Calcutta session made it abundantly clear that his views on the Delhi announcement, on the Dacca University scheme (which he had disapproved) and the appointment of joint presidents of the League were not acceptable. Significantly enough, the League resolutions on the revocation of the partition of Bengal and the Dacca University were initiated by the younger and liberal members of the League. In moving the resolution

[155] The *Englishman*, 6 March, 1912.
[156] Lovat Fraser to Curzon, 4 March, 1912. C.P., vol. 434(a).
[157] The *Al-Bashir*, 30 January, 1912; the *Muslim Gazette*, 12 February, 1912 (*vide* the *U.P. N.N.R.*, 1912).
[158] The Aga Khan to Butler, 25 April, 1913. B.P., folio 57.
[159] The *Madras Weekly Mail*, 7 March, 1912.
[160] The *Englishman*, 5 March, 1912.

expressing the League's 'deep sense of regret and disappointment at the annulment of the partition of Bengal in utter disregard of Muslim feeling', and trusting that the Government would take 'early steps to safeguard Muslim interests' in the Bengal Presidency, Muhammad Ali observed that it might seem strange that he, not being born a Bengali, introduced the proposition.[161] But, as he considered the whole Muslim community of India as a single unit, he thought that when one portion of the community suffered, the remaining portions shared its grief. The Muslims had learnt the lesson of unity in this matter from the Hindus, who had made the subject of distribution of provincial boundaries in Bengal an all-India issue. Muhammad Ali remarked that the undoing of the partition of Bengal was a great blunder. It might shake the belief among the people that the King could do no wrong. It had established the fact that nothing could be regarded as 'a settled fact' if agitation against it could be persisted in. Muhammad Ali thought that the present moment was one of patience for the Muslims and trial for the Hindus. The latter should not be carried away by a feeling of triumph into a feeling of indifference towards the interests of the Muslim community. The resolution was seconded by Shaikh Zahur Ahmad, formerly secretary of the London League. In supporting the motion, Syed Wazir Hasan, the acting secretary of the League, said that the reversal of the partition was a 'slap' to the Muslims which they received in the spirit of Christians rather than Muslims.[162] They received this slap on one cheek and were prepared to turn the other. He called upon the Muslims not to consider the Dacca University scheme as compensation for the irreparable loss of the liquidation of Eastern Bengal and Assam. The resolution was carried unanimously.

In another resolution, moved by Nawab Ali Choudhury and seconded by Wasi Ahmad, barrister, Patna, the League, while welcoming the Dacca University scheme and the appointment of a special education officer for East Bengal, urged that the proposed university should be empowered to control and supervise the educational institutions in the Chtitagong, Dacca and Rajshahi divisions; that the special education officer should be independent of the Director of Public Instruction at Calcutta and should have the power of initiative and control with adequate funds at his disposal; and that the measures initiated by the

---

[161] The *Englishman*, 4 March, 1912.
[162] The *Madras Weekly Mail*, 7 March, 1912.

Government of Eastern Bengal and Assam for the progress of Muslim education should continue without any hindrance.[163]

The League session took serious note of the Italo-Turkish war and of the situation in Persia by passing two resolutions unanimously. On the motion of Muhammad Shafi, seconded by Sarfaraz Husain Khan, the League strongly deprecated the Italian invasion of Tripoli and hoped that the European powers would not fail to persuade Italy to withdraw from Turkish territory.[164] The resolution on Persia, proposed and seconded respectively by Ghulam Husain Arif and Samiullah Baig, sympathised with the Persians in their efforts to save their country from Russia and urged the British Government to ensure the independence and integrity of Persia.[165]

The League session passed several resolutions reiterating the demands for the extension of separate electorates to the local bodies; for the fixing up of a minimum of educational qualifications for various public services and the appointment of a larger number of Muslims under the government until their proportion was adequate from the point of view of their numerical strength; for instituting an enquiry into the management of public *waqfs*; for the creation of executive councils in the U.P. and the Punjab; and for putting an end to the system of recruiting Indian labour under indenture.[166] The session also passed two resolutions repeating the League's protests at the discrimination against Indians in South Africa and against the reduction of the age-limit in the Indian Civil Service examination.[167]

On two important resolutions passed at the session, the League members had strong differences of opinion among themselves. One of them concerned Muhammad Ali Jinnah's bill on the revalidation of *Waqf-ala'l-Aulad*. Several League members did not agree with the bill in its details but a majority expressed agreement with it and urged the Government to pass it into law.[168] The other controversial resolution proposed by Samiullah Baig, accepting in the main, the principles of Gokhale's elementary education bill and demanding that elementary education should be free and that Muslim interests in the matter should be adequately safeguarded, caused a tumultuous scene in the conference.

---

[163] The *Bengalee*, 5 March, 1912.
[164] The *Englishman*, 4 March, 1912.
[165] The *Bengalee*, 5 March, 1912.
[166] The *Englishman*, 4 March, 1912 and the *Bengalee*, 5 March, 1912.
[167] *Ibid.*
[168] The *Englishman*, 4 March, 1912.

The resolution was seconded by Mazhar-ul-Haque but Muhammad Shafi opposed it vehemently.[169]

Shafi argued that the principle of compulsion was repugnant to the spirit of Islam, that compulsion could not be introduced unless there was one school in each village, that the implementation of the bill would facilitate the spread of Hindi at the cost of Urdu and that it would give an effective weapon in the hands of the Hindus to dominate further over the Muslims and other minorities. Muhammad Ali, Shibli Nomani, Zahur Ahmad and Wahed Husain, supported the resolution and sought to answer the objections raised by Shafi. When Muhammad Ali was speaking, Shafi made several attempts to oppose him, but was ruled out of order. On rising to support the resolution, Abul Kalam Azad tauntingly remarked that 'only titleholders and members of the council' were opposing the bill' in order to show their loyalty to the Government. This observation created a pandemonium in the meeting. A number of delegates rushed to the dais while several others attempted to speak simultaneously. After some time, peace was restored and Azad's remarks were declared out of order. The members of the League then retired to an ante-room to record their votes but since the opponents of the resolution declined to vote, it was announced as passed unanimously.[170]

On the eve of the Calcutta session, a section of the Muslim press had threatened that unless the League reconsidered its policy, 'a more courageous party' would be brought into existence which would 'start constitutional agitation' for safeguarding the Muslim interests.[171] Within the League, Mujibur Rahman (editor, the *Mussulman*) had given notice of a motion that the 'whole question of the constitution' of the all-India and the provincial Leagues should be referred to a committee with instructions to make certain specific changes which would widen the membership as well as the activities of the party.[172] The Calcutta meeting, however, instead of passing any decision on these demands, asked the League secretary to ascertain formally the opinion of the different units as well as individual Muslim Leaders on the questions of changes in the policy and the constitution of the League. Accordingly, in April, 1912, Wazir Hasan issued a circular letter to all members of the

[169]The *Bengalee*, 5 March, 1912.
[170]*Ibid.*
[171]The *Muslim Gazette*, 5 February, 1912. The *U.P. N.N.R.*, 1912.
[172]The *Bengalee*, 1 March, 1912.

All-India Muslim League and leading Muslims seeking advice on these matters.[173]

Thus, while the All-India Muslim League was on the threshold of a transformation, a remark by Montagu in the House of Commons on 26 April, 1912, pushed it further along that road. Montagu had, in the course of the second reading of the Government of India Bill (which was to carry out the Delhi announcement), observed that the Muslims of East Bengal 'are the descendants of Hindu converts or are Hindu converts themselves, and have little or no relation except that of religion with those three-fifths of the Mahomedan population of India outside the limits of Bengal, who constitute so largely the fighting races of the north'.[174] This statement gave rise to a storm of protest from the League leaders and Muslim press all over India. The Madras Presidency League considered the remark as historically inaccurate and politically irrelevant. They asserted that the Muslims of India irrespective of their origin had 'by reason of their common religion, traditions, usage and Government' become welded in the course of ages 'into a solid and homogeneous mass of people with distinctive features of their own'.[175] The Bengal and the Bombay Leagues expressed alarm and surprise at Montagu's comment and emphatically declared that the Muslims of India formed 'a homogeneous nationality'.[176] The council of the All-India Muslim League strongly resented Montagu's attack on the solidarity of Muslim 'nationality' and urged the Under-Secretary of State to desist from misrepresenting the distinct political identity of the Indian Muslims.[177]

One of the strongest and most indignant protests against Montagu's remark came from Wazir Hasan who accused him of deliberately inflicting a second blow (the first being the revocation of the partition) on the Muslims of India as a whole and of East Bengal in particular. He reminded the Under-Secretary of State that although the Muslims, in deference to the King had not agitated against the undoing of Eastern Bengal and Assam, their disapproval and resentment against the measure was indeed very strong.[178] Wazir Hasan thought that Montagu's

---

[173]Wazir Hasan's speech at a meeting of the London Indian Association held on 11 October, 1913. *Vide* the *Comrade,* 8 November, 1913.

[174]Parl. Debates, Commons, Fifth Series. Vol. XXXVII, c. 807.

[175]The *Madras Weekly Mail,* 23 May, 1912.

[176]The *Madras Weekly Mail,* 23 May and 6 June, 1912.

[177]The *Pioneer Mail,* 4 June, 1912.

[178]The *Pioneer Mail,* 31 May, 1912.

aspersions on the 'homogeneous nationality' of the Indian Muslims betrayed his 'colossal ignorance' of conditions in India. The Muslims had already united together to safeguard their 'national interests against the rapidly growing Hindu domination'. However galling the dissolution of Eastern Bengal and Assam might have been to the Muslims, they did their utmost to accept the position. 'Why then add insult to injury and indulge in gratuitous flings at our nationality and our rights? Let us alone. We have learnt enough to rely upon our own strength and resources in the future.'[179]

The Muslims of India were, indeed, rapidly learning to depend on none but themselves. The cry of Muslim nationality had never been so loudly and emphatically proclaimed by such a large section of the educated Muslims. Montagu's statement had not only strengthened the growing solidarity among the Muslims of different parts of India but also invigorated the concept of Muslim nationality as a political creed. Henceforward, we find the 'Liberal' or the alleged 'young Turk'[180] group of League leaders more frequently interpreting the aspirations of the Indian Muslims in terms of a nationality. The leader of this group, Muhammad Ali, considered Indian Muslims as forming the greater Ulster in India.[181] He favoured a federation or confederation of a united states of India in which the boundaries of the states should be demarcated not on the basis of geographical area but on that of religious denominations.[182] Prominent members of this group, like Wazir Hasan, Syed Hasan Bilgrami, Shaukat Ali and Musa Khan, played significant parts in developing the concept of Muslim nationality as one of the constituent British-Indian nationalities.

The large-scale Muslim protests had been noted by Crewe, who, on 18 June, 1912, asked Montagu to 'take a casual opportunity to correct the misunderstanding' created by the statement.[183] Montagu agreed.[184] On 20 June, 1912, in reply to an interpellation from Macullum Scott, M.P., drawing attention to the Muslim disapprobation of his remark, the Under-Secretary of State regretted that the reference should have

---

[179] *Ibid.*

[180] Report from the Secretary to the Government of the U.P. to the Education Secretary, Government of India on the condition of the Aligarh College, 13 February, 1913. *Vide* Proc. Education, vol. 9196.

[181] *Supra,* p. 99.

[182] The *Comrade,* 4 January, 1913.

[183] J. & P. 2163, vol. 1159.

[184] *Ibid.*

given rise to misunderstanding and misapprehension.[185] His object in making the observation was to point out that to a great extent the Muslims of East Bengal were not descendants of those with whose history Delhi was so intimately connected. But he recognised and affirmed that the Muslims were 'animated by a religious feeling which produces a unity making them independent of geographical and racial separation'.

Montagu's explanation and his recognition of Muslim solidarity soothed Muslim feeling. At the same time it lent force to their faith in agitation. The extremists among them claimed Montagu's correction as the result of their protests and urged the Muslims to become more vocal and persistent in pressing their demands.[186]

In June, 1912, another ministerial pronouncement of a different nature considerably influenced the formulation of the future creed of the All-India Muslim League. In their despatch of 25 August, 1911, the Government of India had, in justification of the proposed transfer of capital from Calcutta to Delhi, spoken of the gradual devolution of power from the Imperial Government to provincial governments. It was noted that in the course of time, the Government of India would 'give the provinces a larger measure of self-government, until at last India would consist of a number of administrations, autonomous in all provincial affairs, with the Government of India above them all, and possessing power to interfere in cases of misgovernment, but ordinarily restricting their functions to matters of Imperial concern'.[187] This statement was widely interpreted in India as a pledge by His Majesty's Government of eventual self-governing provinces on federal and colonial lines.[188] This idea had gained further strength from a speech of Montagu, stating that 'we have endeavoured to look ahead, to co-ordinate our changes in Bengal with general lines of our future policy in India, which is stated now for the first time in [the] Government of India's despatch . . .'[189] The Tory politicians had become furious at such prospects. Consequently, on 17 June, 1912, pressed by Curzon,

[185] Parl. Debates, Commons, Fifth Series. Vol. XXXIX, c. 1822.

[186] The *Observer*, 3 July, 1912. The *Punjab N.N.R.*, 1912.

[187] The Government of India's Despatch, 25 August, 1911. *Vide* J. & P. 3500A/1911 with 2285/1912, vol. 1162.

[188] Speeches of Abdul Rasool and Surendranath Banerjea at the Bengal Provincial Conference held at Chittagong in April, 1912. *Vide* the *Statesman Weekly*, 11 April, 1912.

[189] Quoted by Curzon in the House of Lords. *Vide* Parl. Debates, Lords, Fifth Series, Vol. XII, c. 144.

Crewe categorically repudiated that His Majesty's Government ever intended to create autonomous provinces in India.[190]

Crewe's interpretation of the Government of India's despatch was the signal for a strong protest from the Indian press and particularly from the Muslim press. Even the conservative *Rohilkhand Gazette* asserted that 'British rule can not continue permanently in India unless England treats India as an integral part of the Empire and repose confidence in her . . . When the partition of Bengal was annulled after the Bengalis committed anarchist outrages and boycotted British goods there is no reason why Crewe's pronouncement about the political future of India should be treated as a settled fact.'[191]. The *Aligarh Institute Gazette* maintained that 'now that there is no such thing as a settled fact Lord Crewe's words will not bind his successors'.[192] The *Al-Mushir*,[193] the *Kaiser-e-Hind*,[194] the *Mussalman*[195] and the *Muhammadi*[196] wrote in the same vein and asked the Muslims to work for eventual self-government. As the *Comrade* correctly pointed out, Crewe's statement 'turned all vague hopes [of self-government] into a sharp, insistent desire'.[197] No wonder that while framing the League's creed in about six months' time men like the editor of the *Comrade* should insist on self-government as the ideal.

By about the first half of 1912, Muslim mortification at the events in the Italo-Turkish war and the activities of Russian troops in Persia had risen to a new peak. On 30 March, 1912, the Russians bombarded and considerably damaged the shrine of Imam Ali-al-Riza[198] —one of the holy shrines of the Muslims—at Meshed. Among the casualties were fifty unarmed pilgrims and worshippers. The Muslims of India in general and the All-India Muslim League and its branches in particular profoundly regretted the incident and once again urged the British Government 'to prevent by effective intervention [with the Russians] further arousing of Musulman feeling [which had] already [been]

[190] *Ibid.*, c. 155.

[191] The *Rohilkhand Gazette*, 12 July, 1912. The *U.P. N.N.R.*, 1912.

[192] The *Aligarh Institute Gazette*, 3 July, 1912. *Ibid.*

[193] The *Al-Mushir*, 18 July, 1912. *Ibid.*

[194] The *Kaisar-e-Hind*, 11 July, 1912. *Ibid.*

[195] The *Mussalman*, 28 June, 1912. The *Bengal N.N.R.*, 1912.

[196] The *Muhammadi*, 12 July, 1912. *Ibid.*

[197] The *Comrade*, 29 June, 1912. *Ibid.*

[198] Telegram from G. Barclay to E. Grey, Tehran, 31 March, 1912. Political and Secret Dept. Paper. L/PS/10/270.

deeply stirred'.[199] This time a succession of indignant Muslim meetings led Hardinge to plead with the India Office and the Foreign Office to 'at once dissociate ourselves from Russian action. This occasion following upon the execution of principal Mujtahid of Tabriz appears to necessitate serious protest to Russia . . .'[200] Moved by the appeal from the Government of India and by several representations from the London League,[201] the Foreign Office took up the matter with Russia[202] but failed to influence the latter's expansionist policy in Persia.

One effect of the Russian high-handedness in Persia and alleged Italian atrocities in Tripoli had been the active participation of the *ulama* in Muslim politics. Hitherto, the *ulama* had occasionally supported certain demands of the League. Now, through the Indian Red Crescent Society[203] and such other philanthropic and semi-political organisations, they came to the forefront of anti-Russian, anti-Italian and to some extent anti-European propaganda. The *ulama* of Deoband and Lucknow[204] together with those of Calcutta and Lahore became allies of the pan-Islamists within the League. Their organs, the *Namai Muqaddas Hablul Matin,* the *Muslim Gazette* (Lucknow) and the *Zamindar,* became highly effective advocates of a determined, vigorous and bold policy. Very soon a large number of vernacular newspapers, notably the new-born *Al-Helal* (editor, Abul Kalam Azad), sided with the *ulama* and the pan-Islamist politicians, thus making them an important force in Muslim politics.

The pan-Islamists, particularly of Bengal, successfully joined together the Muslim grievances over the revocation of the partition of Bengal, the government's negative attitude towards the demands for the extension of separate electorates and more employment in the state service with the sad plight of their co-religionists outside India. Similar sets of grievances had, in 1906, hastened the birth of the All-India

[199] From Abdullah Suhrawardy to Home Secretary, Government of India, 5 April, 1912 and from Wazir Hasan to private secretary to the Viceroy, 5 April, 1912, etc. Political and Secret Dept. Paper, 1776/1912. *Ibid.*

[200] Telegram from the Viceroy to the Secretary of State, 4 April, 1912. Political and Secret Dept. Paper, 1310/1912. *Ibid.*

[201] From the London League to the Secretary of State for India, 10 April, 1912. Political and Secret Department Paper, 1517/1912. *Ibid.*

[202] L. Malet of the Foreign Office to the Secretary, London League, 16 April, 1912. *Ibid.*

[203] The *Bengalee,* 26 March, 1912.

[204] The *Madras Weekly Mail,* 25 July, 1912.

Muslim League and in 1912, helped quicken its metamorphosis. As in 1906, when the initiative for the formation of the League came from Bengal, so in 1912 the transfiguration of the party started with the establishment of the Bengal Presidency League.

The undoing of the province of Eastern Bengal and Assam had forced the conservative and older members of the Bengal and the Eastern Bengal Leagues into the background. Consequently, early in 1912 there was no opposition to organising the Bengal Presidency League with delegates elected at public meetings. As regards the leadership of the party, the pro-Congress moderates of the Bengal League had, up to March, 1912, continued to co-operate with the 'exclusive' moderates as against the pan-Islamists. The 'motto' of the pan-Islamists, or as the government officials called them, the 'unconstitutional party', was 'No agitation—no concession'.[205] They aimed at converting the League into a strong political body in order 'to extort from Government all rights and privileges due to Muhammadans'. They were against 'the Aga Khan or any person who echoed the wishes of Government'. The 'exclusive' moderates, on the other hand, recognised the necessity for a change in the policy of the League but would not agitate against the Government. They were also against the Congress and concerted action with the Hindus. The pro-Congress moderates held a middle position between the two groups. They were not as radical as the pan-Islamists but favoured constitutional agitation and an understanding with the Congress moderates. None of these groups, however, agreed to dissolve or merge the League with the Congress or any such party.

By April—May, 1912, the pro-Congress moderates led by Abdul Rasool made their peace with the pan-Islamists headed by Abdullah Suhrawardy. This alliance seriously disturbed the exclusive moderates, whose position had already been weakened by Shams-ul-Huda's withdrawal from politics. At the time of the election of office-bearers of the Bengal Presidency League, Nawab Ali Choudhury, leader of the exclusive moderates, persuaded Salimullah to accept the presidentship of the party and thus avoided a direct clash with the Suhrawardy-Rasool combination. In the event, however, the key post of the secretary of the Bengal League went to Zahid Suhrawardy, barrister and lecturer of the Calcutta University. Zahid Suhrawardy was a newcomer in politics but like his younger brother, Abdullah Suhrawardy, he too was a staunch pan-Islamist.

[205] History Sheet No. 719. Proc. Education, 1913, vol. 9196.

Unlike that of Bengal, other provincial Leagues did not undergo any transformation. But in every province the pan-Islamists supported by pro-Congress moderates had become a factor to reckon with. In northern India the leadership of the pan-Islamists was provided by Maulana Shibli Nomani, principal, *Nadwat-ul-Ulama*, Lucknow, and a former lecturer of the Aligarh College. Shibli Nomani was a reputed scholar on Islamic subjects, having spent several years at Constantinople and having won an 'order' from the Sultan-Khalifa.[206] He had also come in contact with Muhammad Abduh, the co-worker and disciple of Jamaluddin Afghani.[207] Back in India he had maintained his contacts with Constantinople, Cairo, Damascus and other centres of Islamic learning. He had associated himself fully with the movements for separate electorates and the Muslim University. In 1912 he became a strong advocate of a radical change in the policy and the constitution of the League. He criticised the Aga Khan and several other League leaders for lack of courage in ventilating Muslim feeling on various issues.[208] He also urged the liberal members of the League to purge the party of the Zamindars and *taluqdars* and to separate themselves from the established leadership.[209]

Shibli Nomani's views were strongly supported by, among others, Syed Wahiduddin and Zafar Ali Khan, editors, respectively of the *Muslim Gazette* and the *Zamindar*. But it was his disciple, Abul Kalam Azad, editor of the *Al-Helal*, who had propounded Shibli Nomani's pan-Islamic radicalism in political jargon. Abul Kalam Azad had had his apprenticeship in journalism as the editor of *Al-Nadwa* under the direct guidance of Shibli Nomani.[210] But, as the editor of *Al-Helal*, Azad surpassed his guide and philosopher in pungent expression, metaphor and skilful handling of political issues. In 1912 the *Al-Helal* had limited circulation[211] but its influence was wide. It may be noted here that in contrast to his latter-day advocacy of Indian nationalism, in 1912, Azad considered the political creed of Islam as the only

[206] Porter to Du Boulay (regarding Shibli Nomani), 25 July, 1912. H.P., vol. 84.

[207] A. Ahmad, *Islamic Modernism in India and Pakistan 1857–1964*, p. 77.

[208] The *Muslim Gazette*, 3 April, 1912 and the *Kaisar-e-Hind*, 4 April, 1912. *Vide* the *U.P. N.N.R.*, 1912.

[209] The *Muslim Gazette*, 3 April, 1912; the *Ittehad*, 1 and 8 May, 1912 and the *Mashriq*, 14 May, 1912. *Ibid.*

[210] A. H. Albiruni, *Makers of Pakistan and Modern Muslim India*, p. 133.

[211] In December, 1912, *Al-Helal's* circulation was 1,000. *Vide* the *Bengal N.N.R.*, 1912.

panacea for the Indian Muslims. He thought it humiliating that the Muslims should 'ape the Hindus for the formulation of their political policy'.[212] There could not be 'a greater shame for the Muslims than to bow their heads before others for political education'.[213]

The influence of Shibli Nomani and his followers with the League leaders in northern India was limited, but through Muhammad Ali he had some success with the young liberals in different parts of the country. The liberals largely shared Nomani's pan-Islamic views but were more concerned with the problems facing the Muslims of India. They stood for a change in the policy and constitution of the League but as realists put aside Nomani's suggestion for separation with the established leadership. Moreover, their concern for a satisfactory charter for the proposed Muslim University had precluded them from starting any anti-Government agitation. Soon, however, their disappointment with the Government was completed with the latter's unwise and inconsistent handling of the Muslim University question.

Hardinge never liked denominational universities.[214] At the same time he had thought it 'extremely dangerous to discourage this Moslem undertaking which has been received with great enthusiasm by the Mahommedan community all over India'.[215] This would have led 'the whole of the Musalmans of India against us'.[216] Hardinge had decided 'to arrange with the Aga Khan that Government should have complete control' over the proposed university.[217] Together with Butler he had drawn up a set of conditions which was communicated to the Aga Khan 'most confidentially'.[218] The Aga Khan having agreed to these conditions,[219] the Viceroy asked Butler to continue private negotiations with the Muslim leader as regards the details of the university scheme. Personally, however, Hardinge was still indecisive on the project. In April, 1911, he had told Butler that there was some opposition against the Aga Khan from the two Bengals and that 'I had only to hold up my little finger to encourage the Mahommedans of Eastern Bengal and Bengal to have nothing to say to it and to wreck the Aga Khan's scheme.

[212] Quoted by Hafez Malik in his article 'Abul Kalam Azad's Theory of Nationalism' published in the *Muslim World*, vol. LIII, p. 34.
[213] *Ibid.*
[214] Hardinge to Morley, 9 March, 1911. H.P., vol. 117.
[215] *Ibid.*
[216] Hardinge to Morley, 29 March, 1911. *Ibid.*
[217] Hardinge to Morley, 11 March, 1911. *Ibid.*
[218] *Ibid.*
[219] Hardinge to Morley, 11 March, 1911. *Ibid.*

Of course I would never do anything of the kind—certainly not without consulting you—and it would, I think, have been a very dangerous step to take.'[220]

Hardinge's policy towards the Muslims did, however, contain elements of the unscrupulous. In January, 1911, he refused to receive a deputation from the Mahomedan Literary Society, which had welcomed and bade farewell to several Viceroys before him, on grounds of it being a non-political body.[221] After a few days, when the Central National Mahomedan Association—a political body—offered a similar deputation, the Viceroy turned it down on the plea of being immersed in public business.[222] During the same month, however, he received two deputations—one from the Indian National Congress and the other from the Indian Association. In fact, Hardinge never bothered about the inconsistency of his dealings with the Muslims. He was strongly opposed to separate electorates and had declined to introduce the system in the local bodies but while recommending the annulment of the partition of Bengal, he did not hesitate to argue that the provision for separate electorates in the legislative council was a guarantee to Muslim interests.[223] In the case of the undoing of the partition, he had also conveniently forgotten his earlier advocacy in defence of the *status quo*. He did exactly the same thing in respect to the Muslim University question. Failing to get the university sanctioned by the Secretary of State, he was now prepared to retract his own acceptance of its main features[224] and poured vials of wrath upon the Muslim leaders for their refusal to surrender.

On being approached by a deputation consisting of the Raja of Mahmudabad, Viqar-ul-Mulk, Dr. Ziauddin and Aftab Ahmad Khan, in May, 1911,[225] the Government of India had, on 31 July, 1911, told the Muslim leaders that the Secretary of State was ready to sanction the establishment of the university provided, first, that they could produce adequate funds, and second, that the constitution of the said university was 'acceptable in all details' to the Government of India

---

[220]Hardinge to Butler, 19 April, 1911. H.P., vol. 81.

[221]The *Mussalman,* 3 February, 1911. The *Bengal N.N.R.,* 1911.

[222]*Ibid.*

[223]The Government of India's despatch of 25 August, 1911. *Vide* J. & P. 3500A/1911 with 2285/1912, vol. 1162.

[224]See below p. 267.

[225]Butler to the Raja of Mahmudabad, 31 July, 1911. Enclosure No. 1 of the Government of India's despatch No. 258 of 1911, to the Secretary of State. Proc. Education, vol. 8942.

and to the Secretary of State himself.[226]  Consequently, in August, 1911, a draft constitution of the proposed Muslim University, together with a financial statement, was submitted to the Government.[227]  In September, 1911, some members of the university constitution committee, headed by the Raja of Mahmudabad, met Butler for a detailed discussion on the constitution. Butler insisted on stringent Government control over the university and 'conveyed the threat of "our terms or no university" in a gentle way'.[228] The Muslim leaders, on their part, were prepared to accept most of the conditions. The Government of India was satisfied that 'on nearly every point we are in agreement with the [Muslim University constitution] committee'.[229]  Therefore, in a despatch on 2 November, 1911, they strongly recommended the creation of the proposed university to the Secretary of State.[230] The despatch noted that the scheme for the university contained 'the results of considerable discussion and of somewhat long negotiation'. The Secretary of State, however, in his despatch of 23 February, 1911, expressed his inability to accept the Government of India's proposal.[231] At this stage the Viceroy realised the difficulties confronting the fulfilment of the Government's part of the agreement with the Muslim leaders.

The Secretary of State's main objections to the Government of India's recommendation for the Muslim University were directed, first, to the term 'Muslim' in the nomenclature of the university; second, to the proposed university's power of affiliation over institutions outside the Aligarh district; third, to the wide powers assigned to the university court; and fourth, to the proposal for the Governor-General to become the Chancellor of the university.[232]  These objections seem to have arisen because of administrative difficulties in controlling the affairs of an all-India Muslim University, as well as from Crewe's disliking for 'quasi-religious institutions'.[233]

The Government of India thought that the Secretary of State's

---

[226]*Ibid.*

[227]Enclosure Nos. 2 and 3 of the Government of India's despatch No. 258 of 1911. *Ibid.*

[228]Butler to Hardinge, 25 September, 1911. H.P., vol. 82.

[229]Government of India's despatch No. 258 of 1911, to the Secretary of State. Proc. Education, vol. 8942.

[230]*Ibid.* .

[231]Despatch from the Secretary of State to the Governor-General-in-Council, 23 February, 1912. *Ibid.*

[232]*Ibid.*

[233]Crewe to Hardinge, 5 September, 1912. H.P., vol. 118.

objections, if upheld, would create insuperable difficulty. They trusted that in view of the practical considerations and 'the grave political embarrassment which we anticipate from the adoption of Your Lordship's decision, Your Lordship will be prepared to reconsider the question and allow us to proceed on the lines of the proposals which we reached after prolonged and careful discussion'.[234]

The Secretary of State was not impressed by the Government of India's pleadings. He firmly pointed out that he had already reserved full discretion in regard to every detail of the university scheme. 'The freedom so expressly reserved can not be compromised by any action taken in India without my consent. Otherwise it will be impossible for me to exercise the control vested in me by statute.'[235]

The Secretary of State's decision was regretted by the Viceroy. But he bowed before it and immediately set the entire government machinery to exert 'strongest pressure through every possible channel, public and private, to check agitation, and hope that we may prevent outbreak of feeling [among the Muslims]'.[236]   Hardinge himself induced the Nawab of Rampur to do his utmost to prevent any agitation by the extremist leaders.[237]   He told the Nawab that if the Muslims 'behaved nicely, we shall look after their special interests', but if they agitated then the Government would turn their face against them and would deal with them firmly.[238]  On Butler's advice,[239] the Viceroy's private secretary telegraphed the Governors and Lieutenant-Governors of all the provinces to use their 'influence to stop any agitation' by the Muslims.[240]   Furthermore, Hardinge exerted pressure on the Nizam of Hyderabad and the Begum of Bhopal (two prominent contributors to the Muslim University funds) to use their good offices in favour of the Government's decision.[241]

[234] The Government of India's despatch of 28 March, 1912, to the Secretary of State. Proc. Education, vol. 8942.

[235] The Secretary of State's despatch to the Governor-General-in-Council, 12 July, 1912. Proc. Education, vol. 9195.

[236] Telegram from the Viceroy to the Secretary of State, 6 August, 1912, Proc. Education, vol. 9195.

[237] Hardinge to Butler, 30 July, 1912. H.P., vol. 84.

[238] *Ibid.*

[239] Butler to Hardinge, 22 July, 1912. *Ibid.*

[240] Private secretary to the Viceroy to private secretaries to the Governors of Bombay, Madras and Bengal; and the Lieutenant-Governors of Burma, Punjab, Bihar and Orissa, 22 July, 1912. *Ibid.*

[241] Private secretary to the Viceroy to Agent to Governor-General, Central India and to Resident Hyderabad. *Ibid.*

The difficulties of administering a Muslim University at Aligarh with powers of affiliation over Muslim institutions throughout India were obvious. Hardinge ought not to have accepted such a proposition when it was first laid before him. But once he had accepted the proposal, he owed it to the Muslim leaders to persuade the Secretary of State to sanction it or, in the alternative, to offer some compromise formula which would have been acceptable to the Home Government and the Muslim leaders alike. In fact, Butler had suggested that the Government should conciliate Muslim opinion by undertaking special measures for their educational advancement.[242]   But Hardinge thought that such measures would make the Muslims feel that 'we make concessions to them owing to pressure applied' upon us.[245]   Since the annulment of the partition of Bengal, Hardinge had become over-cautious about yielding to agitation.[244]   He was confident that the steps he had taken to 'suppress' any agitation on the Muslim University question would succeed[245] and that 'the older members would gain the upper hand and that the firebrands will loose such momentary influence as they now enjoy' among the Muslim leadership.[246]   He therefore tried hard to encourage the Muslim moderates to throttle down the influence of the progressives or the 'extremists' as he called them.[247]

The chief burden of the operation to curb the influence of the advanced Muslim leaders was carried by Butler.   Butler sent the

[242] Butler to Hardinge, 22 July, 1912. H.P., vol. 84.

[243] Hardinge to Butler, 30 July and 6 August, 1912. *Ibid.*

[244] On 12 August, 1912, Hardinge told Roos-Keppel: 'The young Turk party among the Mahomedans think that they can squeeze Government by agitating. They will, however, find in the end that they have made a mistake.' *Vide* Hardinge to R. Keppel, 12 August, 1912. *Ibid.*

[245] Hardinge to Chirol, 7 August, 1912. H.P., vol. 84.

[246] Hardinge to Crewe, 9 September, 1912. H.P., vol. 118.

[247] Hardinge to Crewe, 30 July, 1912. *Ibid;* and Hardinge to Butler, 16 August, 1912. H.P., vol. 84. Hardinge's concern about the ascendancy of the progressive elements in Muslim politics was so deep that he was 'glad' to note that Roos-Keppel, Chief Commissioner of N.W.F.P. had 'induced the Peshawar Committee [of the Muslim Educational Conference] to decline the honour of a visit from the Moslem Educational Congress'. (*Vide* Hardinge to R. Keppel, 12 August, 1912). H.P., vol. 84. Hardinge was particularly anxious about the activities of Muhammad Ali and Wazir Hasan whom he considered 'fire-brands and agitators'. (*Vide* Hardinge to Crewe, 11 September, 1913. H.P., vol. 119). In September–October, 1913, when Muhammad Ali and Wazir Hasan went to London in order to place Muslim grievances before the Home Government, Hardinge prevailed upon the Secretary of State not to grant them any interview. *Ibid.*

Maharaja of Durbhanga to work upon the Raja of Mahmudabad and a few other leaders of the U.P. to prevent them joining in any agitation.[248] He advised Hardinge to write to the Government of the U.P. to ask that access to Aligarh be denied to Muhammad Ali.[249] He considered Muhammad Ali a dangerous man and was determined to check his influence with the students of the Aligarh College. Presumably at his instance, the Government of the U.P. tried 'to encourage quietly the growth of a reaction amongst the respectable trustees [of the Aligarh College] against the domination of Muhammad Ali...'[250] Butler also sought to utilise his friendship with the Raja of Mahmudabad to persuade him not to create a row over the Government's decision on the University question. Addressing him as 'My Dear Bhai Saheb [elder brother]', Butler begged the Raja not to take action 'under the stress of disappointment'.[251] At the same time Butler's threat to his elder brother was undisguised: 'If this movement for a University is to end in a political agitation, then I think that it is very doubtful if you will get a University at all ... I warn you most solemnly that you must use all your influence to stop agitation.'[252]

But the Raja of Mahmudabad and most of the Muslim leaders refused to be browbeaten or cajoled. Their consternation at the Government's decision was profound.[253] Once again they felt betrayed. They could have hardly expected the Government of India's going back upon their words and asking them to sacrifice the most important characteristics of the proposed university, particularly its name and the power to affiliate outside institutions, which were so dear to the Muslims of India.[254] Their reply to Butler's official communication of 11 August, 1912, to the Raja of Mahmudabad conveying the Government's decision on the matter contained an indignant protest and a prayer for reconsideration.[255]

---

[248] The Maharaja of Durbhanga to Hardinge, 15 July, 1912. H.P., vol. 84.

[249] Butler to Hardinge, 3 November, 1912. *Ibid.*

[250] Secretary to the Government of the U.P. to the Education Secretary, Government of India, 13 September, 1913. Proc. Education, vol. 9196.

[251] Butler to the Raja of Mahmudabad, 22 July, 1912. Enclosed with Butler to Hardinge, 22 July, 1912. H.P., vol. 84.

[252] *Ibid.*

[253] Telegram from the Viceroy to the Secretary of State, 6 August, 1912. Proc. Education, vol. 9195.

[254] Telegram from the Viceroy to the Secretary of State, 24 June, 1912. H.P., vol. 83.

[255] The *Madras Weekly Mail,* 22 August, 1912.

The Muslim reply was drafted by a committee consisting of Muhammad Ali, Muhammad Shafi, Mazhar-ul-Haque, Abdul Majid and Nawab Ishaq Khan, the newly-elected secretary of the Aligarh College.[256] It was then approved by the Muslim University constitution committee at its meeting held on 11 and 12 August, 1912.[257] At the meeting, a letter from the Nawab of Rampur counselling acceptance of the Government's decision was read, but it had little effect. The younger members of the committee, particularly Muhammad Ali and Mazhar-ul-Haque, were all set for an agitation.[258] The general argument adopted by them 'was "look at what happened in Bengal, and the result of agitation in regard to the partition" '.[259] However, pending the Government's reply to their letter, the constitution committee deferred the final decision on the subject till October, 1912.[260]

In October, 1912, when the Muslims of India were already in a ferment over the repeated somersaults by Hardinge's Government, the Balkan States declared war upon Turkey. The news of the war convulsed Indian Muslims. Hundreds of indignation meetings were held, and Red Crescent Societies sprang up in almost every important town all over India.[261] At the beginning of the war the Muslims demanded intervention by the British Government for the restoration of peace. But when Asquith, the Prime Minister of Britain, and several of his colleagues openly encouraged the enemies of the Turks, they saw the Balkan war as a manifestation of European hostility towards Islam.[262] Gradually the agitation against the war took an anti-European and to some extent an anti-British turn. As the All-India Muslim League and its branches were in the forefront of the agitation,[263] their attitude towards the Government had changed even before the proposed reconsideration of their creed and constitution.

[256] *Ibid.*

[257] *Ibid.*

[258] Hewett to Hardinge, 13 August, 1912. H.P., vol. 84.

[259] *Ibid.*

[260] The *Madras Weekly Mail*, 22 August, 1912.

[261] The *Times of India Mail*, 5 and 12 October, 1912; the *Madras Weekly Mail*, 14, 21 and 28 November etc., 1912; and Political and Secret Department Papers 4238, 4334, 4422, 4553, 4613, etc., etc. *Vide* L/PS/306; and Political and Secret Department Papers 4115 etc. *Vide* L/PS/11/35 and L/PS/10/270.

[262] Telegram from the Assistant Secretary, the Bihar League to the Home Secretary, the Government of India: Political and Secret Dept. Paper 128. L/PS/10/306.

[263] Political and Secret Dept. Paper No. 4209. *Ibid.*

It so happened that the sixth annual session of the All-India Muslim League scheduled to be held at Lucknow under the presidentship of Ameer Ali in December, 1912, fell a victim to the Balkan war. Immediately at the outbreak of the war, Ameer Ali was seized with enthusiasm for organising relief works for Turkey. At his initiative a British Red Crescent Society was formed in London and a medical mission was despatched to Turkey.[264] Ameer Ali and the London League were also busy in memorialising the British Government for intervention in the war.[265] Therefore, on 29 October, 1912, Ameer Ali and the Aga Khan jointly telegraphed the secretary of the All-India Muslim League urging postponement of the League session as a 'token [of] mourning [at the] grave peril [of] Islam'.[266]

Meanwhile, preparations for the League session had been in progress. Wazir Hasan had toured various parts of the country consulting the leading Muslims as regards the future policy and constitution of the League.[267] In the light of these consultations and what he had gathered from the replies to his letter of April, 1912, Wazir Hasan had also prepared a draft of the revised constitution of the League which was to be presented at the annual session.[268] He now put the joint telegram of the Aga Khan and Ameer Ali to the consideration of an emergency meeting of the League council. After prolonged discussion the council telegraphed back to London: 'Most important questions [are] awaiting solution for next League Sessions . . . consider postponement unjustified and fatal to Indian Moslem interests. Turkey may still succeed otherwise League Sessions in mourning [would be] much better than no Session . . .'

In reply to the League council's telegram, on 5 November, 1912, the London League wired that Ameer Ali's absence would mean irreparable loss to relief and other important works undertaken by them and that if he was to preside, the League session must be postponed that year. Consequently, a meeting of the League council held at Lucknow on 12 November, 1912, decided finally by a majority of votes to postpone the session *sine die*.[269] The meeting also passed a resolution deeply regretting Asquith's remarks that the victors of the Balkan War should be allowed to retain the fruits of their conquest.

[264] Political and Secret Dept. Paper 4115. L/PS/11/35.
[265] Political and Secret Dept. Papers 3899, 3995 etc. *Vide* L/PS/10/306.
[266] Quoted in Wazir Hasan's letter to the Pioneer Mail, 13 December, 1912.
[267] Wazir Hasan's letter to the *Pioneer Mail,* 13 December, 1912.
[268] *Ibid.*
[269] The *Madras Weekly Mail,* 5 December, 1912.

A section of the Muslim leaders had taken serious objection to the postponement of the League session. They held the Aga Khan responsible for this action and urged the League leaders to break off with him.[270]    Sensing the disappointment of a considerable section of League members at being deprived of the opportunity of expressing their feelings on several issues, Wazir Hasan convened an extended meeting of the League council on 31 December, 1912.[271]  The agenda of the meeting included discussion on the existing political situation, Hindu-Muslim problems, relief to Turkey, as well as the constitution and creed of the All-India Muslim League.

The meeting of the All-India Muslim League council held at Lucknow on 31 December, 1912, under the presidentship of the Aga Khan was well-attended.[272]    Several non-members attended the meeting at the special invitation of the secretary.  The temper of the meeting was 'unusually Radical'.[273]  From the beginning it was dominated by the younger and liberal members.  The discussion centred mainly on the revised draft of the creed and constitution of the League presented by Wazir Hasan.  The revised draft proposed the objects of the League to be, first, to maintain and promote among the people of India feelings of loyalty towards the British crown;  second, to protect and advance the political and other rights of the Muslims of India;  third, 'to promote friendship and union' between the Muslims and other communities of India;  and fourth, 'without detriment to the foregoing objects, attainment under the aegis of the British crown, of a system of self-government suitable to India, through constitutional means, by bringing about, amongst others, a steady reform of the existing system of representation, by promoting national unity, by fostering public spirit among the people of India and by co-operating with other communities for the said purposes'.[274]

The proposed objectives greatly differed from the existing creed of the All-India Muslim League.  Instead of the promotion of loyalty of the Indian *Muslims* towards the British *Government*,[275] the League's

---

[270]The *Muslim Gazette,* 4 December, 1912 and the *Zulqarnain,* 7 December, 1912.  *Vide* the *U.P. N.N.R.,* 1912.

[271] The *Times of India Mail,* 14 December, 1912.

[272]The *Bengalee,* 3 January, 1913.

[273]The *Comrade,* 4 January, 1913.

[274] *The Draft Constitution and Rules of the A.I.M.L.,* approved by the Council of the League at its meeting held on 31 December, 1913, pp. 1–2.

[275]*Rules and Regulations of the A.I.M.L.,* 1910, p. 1.

members now proposed to concern themselves with the promotion of *Indian* loyalty towards the British *crown*. The deletion of the term Muslims and the substitution of British crown for the British Government were significant. They were intended to emphasise the wider outlook and independent character of the League. The proposed first objective had also eliminated the League's aim of removing 'any misconception that may arise [among the Muslims] as to the intentions of the Government with regard to any of its measures'.[276] Similarly, the proposed second objective had quietly dropped the League's existing motto of placing the Muslim 'aspirations before the Government in temperate language'. Evidently, the makers of the revised draft objective had no faith in petitioning the Government for the redress of Muslim grievances. The proposed third objective was equally significant. Its authors were not satisfied in keeping the promotion of concord and harmony between the Mussalmans and other communities dependent upon their loyalty to the Government and to the protection of Muslim political rights. Indeed, they would not restrict their aim to promotion of concord and harmony. They stood for more specific and higher aims, i.e. the promotion of 'friendship and unity' with other communities. The proposed fourth aim was entirely an innovation. It was also the most momentous. Its adoption was bound to change the character of the League completely.

The participants at the meeting seemed prepared for far-reaching changes in the League creed. The proposals regarding the second and the third objectives were carried without any opposition. The suggestion for the first aim was, however, opposed as not radical enough. Mazhar-ul-Haque asked why, of all the people in India, the Muslims should make a speciality of expressing their loyalty.[277] He thought that the League should give up declaring its own chastity. Mazhar-ul-Haque's objection was supported by Muhammad Ali Jinnah, who, though not yet a member of the League, had been taking keen interest in its activities.[278] Jinnah pointed out that the Muslim claim for loyalty reflected on the loyal feelings of other people in India.[279] The objection, however, was rejected by a large majority and the objective was adopted as proposed.

The suggestion for the fourth aim of the League was strongly objected

[276]*Ibid.*
[277]The *Times of India Mail,* 4 January, 1913.
[278]Muhammad Ali Jinnah had attended the Calcutta session of the A.I.M.L., held in March, 1912.
[279]The *Times of India Mail,* 4 January, 1913.

to by two opposing groups. Muhammad Abdullah thought that the demand for self-government in any form was unjustified and should not form part of the League creed.[280] Mazhar-ul-Haque, on the other hand, took objection to the word 'suitable' attached to self-government. He proposed to substitute for the word 'suitable' the words 'on colonial lines'.[281] The amendment was opposed by Jinnah who strongly supported the original proposal. Although a Congressman, Jinnah admitted that the Congress ideal for colonial self-government was wrong and that some day it would proclaim the ideal suggested by the League.[282] Conditions in India were different from those in other British colonies. What was applicable in other colonies was not necessarily applicable in India. Moreover, since self-government was to be an ideal to be achieved in the future, it was only practical that the League should not commit itself to a definite form of self-government now.[283]

Mazhar-ul-Haque's amendment was also opposed by Muhammad Ali. Muhammad Ali's speech at the meeting is not available but since he seems to have been one of the chief architects of the revised creed, his arguments in defence of 'suitable' self-government as put forward in the *Comrade* of 4 January, 1913, is worthy of special attention. Muhammad Ali agreed with Jinnah that due to differing conditions between India and other British colonies, the colonial form of self-government would not be practical for India. But he laid special stress on other factors. He thought that British India was an artificial creation lacking religious, political and historical cohesion.[284] Furthermore, British India differed greatly from the Indian States. The future constitution of India could therefore be modelled only on the lines of the German Confederacy or of the United States of America with the exception that the lines of demarcation in India should be religious rather than territorial.[285]

After prolonged and heated discussion in which several speakers took part, the objective as proposed was adopted by an overwhelming majority of votes.

Certain sections of the revised rules and regulations of the League adopted at the meeting were as important as the metamorphosis of its

---

[280] The *Naiyar-e-Azam*, 19 January, 1913. The *U.P. N.N.R.*, 1913.
[281] The *Times of India Mail*, 4 January, 1913.
[282] *Ibid.*
[283] *Ibid;* and the *Bengalee*, 3 January, 1913.
[284] The *Comrade*, 4 January, 1913.
[285] *Ibid.*

creed. These were the reduction of the membership fee from twenty rupees to five rupees per annum; the replacement of the educational qualification, i.e. the capability of 'reading and writing with facility' by that of literacy, which meant the capability of writing one's name in any language; the increase in the maximum number of members of the council from forty to one hundred and fifty; the provision for any Muslim association within or outside British India to be affiliated to the League;[286] and the elimination of the clause fixing the maximum number of members of the all-India League at 800. While thus leaving the membership of the all-India League wide open to all literate Indian Muslims throughout British India and abroad and making its controlling body as representative as could be practicable, the revised constitution of the League also, for the first time, imposed control over its component units. The council of the League was required to bring the activities of the various branches of the organisation in line with those of the parent body. It was further authorised to impose limitations and conditions, to the extent of affiliating and disaffiliating any provincial and district League or branch association.[287]

The revised aims and constitution transformed the All-India Muslim League into a liberal and progressive body of the Muslims of British India. The most significant characteristic of the meeting that adopted these changes and the one that ratified them in March, 1913,[288] was that despite strong differences of opinion held by several members on certain points, these were accepted without any threat of a split in the party. Indeed, this transformation was followed by greater co-operation and unity among the rank and file of the League members.

---

[286] *The Draft Constitution and Rules of the A.I.M.L., op. cit.,* pp. 1–5 and 12.
[287] *Ibid.,* p. 12.
[288] The draft constitution of the League was finally adopted at the sixth annual meeting of the A.I.M.L., held at Lucknow on 22 and 23 March, 1913, under the presidentship of Muhammad Shafi. *Vide* the *Pioneer,* 24 March, 1913.

## Chapter IX

## CONCLUSION

The All-India Muslim League was born at a time when the Muslims of India were passing through a period of considerable uneasiness, caused by the anti-partition agitation and by the imminence of constitutional reforms. The founders of the League had decided to protect and advance Muslim interests by respectful representations to the Government.

The makers of the League had recognised signs of Muslim ill-feeling towards the Hindus and aimed to prevent their exacerbation. In December, 1907, however, the League's attitude towards the Hindus was changed, prevention of ill-feeling being replaced by the cultivation of harmony and good relations. Five years later the League aimed at promoting unity between the Muslim and other Indian communities. Thus the evolution of the League's policy towards non-Muslims followed a consistent course. This evolution was quickened by four factors. Firstly, a majority of the League leaders were anxious to conciliate the other communities and particularly the Hindus. Secondly, the League leadership, being mostly from upper India, could not evaluate properly the depth of Hindu-Muslim tension in the two Bengals. Thirdly, the Government deliberately encouraged an accord between the moderates among Hindu and Muslim leaders. Fourthly, the liquidation of Eastern Bengal and Assam convinced a considerable number of League members that the Government was both unwilling and unable to safeguard the Muslim interests in the face of Hindu opposition and that unless they entered into an understanding with the Hindu leaders their future would be greatly imperilled.

The development of the League's attitude towards the Government followed a different pattern. Until the Durbar announcement of December, 1911, the League leaders never felt any need for reconsidering their policy of loyal reliance on the Government. It was the undoing of the partition of Bengal that proved to be the turning point. The dissolution of Eastern Bengal and Assam was not only a hard blow to the Muslim interests, but also a demonstration of the Government's scornful indifference to Muslim public opinion. To a large section of League

276

members its lesson was obvious—agitation was the only way to success. So, on the fifth day after the Delhi announcement the Rubicon was crossed with Abdullah Suhrawardy's public call for a change in the Muslim policy towards the Government.

The course of events during the following ten months moved the League leaders swiftly towards the pursuit of self-government through constitutional means as their ideal. The resentment at the alleged British acquiescence in the dismemberment of Muslim countries, the disappointment with regard to the extension of separate electorates to the local bodies and the apportionment of appointments in the government service, the indignation at the Viceroy's bungling over the question of the Muslim University, as well as the prospect of eventual provincial self-government as adumbrated in the Government of India's despatch of 25 August, 1911, affirmed the immediate need for a change in the League policy.

The above factors, however, could by themselves have hardly induced the League to effect a revolutionary change in policy unless it had been internally prepared for it. By 1912 the younger members of the League—most of them belonging to the professional classes and supported by the growing body of western educated Muslims—had attained great influence in the League. Of them, Nabiullah, Muhammad Ali, Wazir Hasan, Zahur Ahmad, Shaukat Ali, Raza Ali, and Samiullah Baig of the U.P.; Abdullah Suhrawardy, Abdul Rasool, Mujibur Rahman, Abul Kasem, Sultan Ahmad, Abul Kalam Azad, and Fazlul Haque of Bengal; Mazhar-ul-Haque and Fakhruddin Ahmad of Bihar; Fazl-i-Husain and Muhammad Iqbal of the Punjab; G. M. Bhurgri of Bombay and Yakub Hasan and Hameed Hasan of Madras were most energetic and vocal. Although they differed amongst themselves as regards the particular form of self-government to be sought, they shared a longing for an autonomous status for India. The elevation of Wazir Hasan as secretary of the League following the death of Aziz Mirza had provided these young activists with a degree of control over party affairs which could not be contained by the older leaders. The older leaders, in their turn, were completely demoralised and some of them had already joined the chorus for a new and vigorous policy.

A most significant factor that quickened the transformation of the policy and the constitution of the League was the rapid growth of political consciousness among the Muslims of the sub-continent. This unique phenomenon can be gauged from the fact that between 1907 and 1912 the circulation of the Muslim newspapers and journals increased by over one hundred per cent.[1]  The Muslims exhibited their growing interest in political matters by forming queues before the newspaper offices and by joining public meetings in their hundreds.  By the end of 1912 it had become difficult for the League to ignore the clamour for changes in its policy and constitution without risking loss of support and sympathy from the Muslim public.

During the period of our study the League had worked under several limitations.  Until 1910 it had no full-time secretary.  Its president was a weather-cock whose religious and sporting interests had led him to spend most of his time abroad.  From his election as president of the League in March, 1908, till December, 1912, the Aga Khan had stayed in India for a total of about thirteen months only.  Of these thirteen months at least seven months were devoted to the cause of his spiritual followers i.e. the Ismaili community.  The absence of a full-time president to guide the destiny of the League was aggravated by the paucity of educated and financially solvent party workers at the provincial level. The Muslim middle class had not yet reached that stage of educational and economic progress when any appreciable number of them could afford to choose politics as a vocation.  Another predicament which had greatly impeded the activities of the League during this period was the absence of a party organ and particularly of a daily newspaper.  Doubtless several Muslim journals assisted the cause of the League but they were owned by individuals often with commercial motives and could not have been substitutes for a party paper.

Contrary to the wholly untrue but widely held view that the League was 'the favourite [and] pampered child of British imperialism'[2] from its very birth, the party, during the period under review, had worked under the vigilant and sceptical eye of the Government.  We have seen how Minto had sought to utilise some League moderates against a majority of their colleagues.  Minto had revealed himself fully when he 'entirely' agreed with R. H. Craddock (Chief Commissioner of C.P.) in his estimation of the League.[3]  Craddock thought that although the League had been 'actuated by entirely loyal motives, there is no guarantee that this will always continue to be the case. As the organisation

[1] This has been calculated on the basis of the number of subscribers of the Muslim newspapers and journals in 1907 and 1912.  An exact figure is not possible because in several cases the native newspaper reports for the various provinces do not mention the number of subscribers of the particular paper.

[2] N. V. Rajkumar, *Indian Political Parties*, p. 102.

[3] Private secretary to the Viceroy to Craddock, 22 August, 1910.  Min. P. Corr. India, 1910, vol. 2.

grows in influence it will no doubt press demands upon the Government which the Government could not concede, with the consequent result of a considerable abatement in the loyalty of their attitude towards the Government.'[4]    Similar anxiety about the League's motives had prompted Hewett to take steps to curb the influence of Muhammad Ali and his group in the U.P. George Clarke of Bombay was openly hostile to the League.[5]   He had considered the Bombay League 'a fiction invented by a single individual'.[6] The League had received tougher and more unsympathetic treatment from Hardinge and his Government. Hardinge's dealings with the League leaders were marked by a determination to discourage and even suppress the more advanced amongst them.[7]   His chief adviser on Muslim affairs, Butler, reported that the 'Moslem League has ceased to be regarded as a responsible body' by the Government.[8]

Judging from its practical gains, the achievements of the All-India Muslim League between 1906 and 1912 were really impressive.  The attainment of separate electorates was an event of singular importance to the Muslims of India. This recognition of a separate political identity of the Muslims greatly facilitated the eventual birth of the separate Muslim state.–Pakistan.   Again, it was the League's constitutional agitation that had persuaded the Government of India to rectify the verdicts of the Privy Council in regard to the validity of *Waqf-ala'l-Aulad.* The Waqf Revalidation Act of 1913 had saved a large number of Muslim families from the verge of ruination.  The League had also a major share in the phenomenal progress of the Muslims of India in the field of elementary and higher education. Between 1907 and 1912 the number of Muslim students increased by 97.3% in the Arts Colleges; by 41.0% in the Professional Colleges; by 81.1% in the Secondary Schools; by 29.9% in the Primary Schools; and by 315.3% in the Special Schools.[9]

---

[4] Craddock to private secretary to the Viceroy, 16 August, 1910. *Ibid.*

[5] Minto conceded that Clarke was 'somewhat anti-Mahomedan'. *Vide* Minto to Morley, 14 August, 1909. Mor. P., vol. 22.

[6] Clarke to Morley, 25 June, 1909. *Ibid.*, vol. 42(f).

[7] The dismissal of Abdullah Suhrawardy and Abdul Rasool as lecturers of the Calcutta University;   the forfeiture of the security and proscription of several Muslim newspapers including the *Comrade,* the *Zamindar* and the *Al-Helal;* the internment of Muhammad Ali and Shaukat Ali were among the measures adopted to gag the advanced section of the League leaders.

[8] Butler to the Aga Khan, 26 March, 1913. B.P., folio 57.

[9] *Progress of Education in India, 1907–12: Sixth Quinquennial Review,* p. 246.

However, the League's greatest success during the first six years of formation was in the sphere of political organisation. Within a short time it had galvanised the Indian Muslims into a political force second only to the Congress. Henceforward both the Government and the Congress were compelled to consider the Muslim viewpoints before embarking on any measure affecting the Indians in general. The political course charted by the League during this period continued to be the guide for the Indian Muslims till the thirties of the present century. Even the two-nation theory that led to the partition of the subcontinent into India and Pakistan in 1947 was largely influenced by the League's concept at this early stage of a homogeneous Muslim nationality.

# BIBLIOGRAPHY

A. *PRIVATE PAPERS*

I. *Harcourt Butler Papers (India Office Library, London, MSS.EUR.F.116)*
Vol. 4. Correspondence with Sir W. Holderness, 1912–1924.
39. Correspondence with Sir V. Chirol, 1910–1922.
42. Foreign Office and Political Department, 1910–1911.
49. Aligarh University and Sundry Letters, 1911–1920.
51. Correspondence with Minto, 1910–1914.
53. Correspondence with Hardinge, 1911–1927.
57. Mohammedans: Troubles with in 1906, 1913 and 1921; Correspondence with the Aga Khan thereon.

II. *Lord Curzon Papers (India Office Library, London, MSS.EUR.F111)*
Vols. 426–428. Letters received from various people in India, 1907–1912.
433. Miscellaneous Correspondence about Indian Matters, 1904–1911.
434. Correspondence about the new capital at Delhi and reversal of the Partition of Bengal, 1909–1912.
435. Notes by Curzon on the Scheme to make Delhi Imperial Capital and on the proposal to reconstitute the Province of Bengal.
436. Official Papers relating to the new capital at Delhi and to the reconstitution of Bengal.

III. *Lord Hardinge (Baron Charles Hardinge of Penshurst) Papers. (University of Cambridge Library)*
Vol. 79. Correspondence with the King-Emperor (Original), 1910–1916.
104. Correspondence with the King-Emperor (Printed), 1910–1911.
105. Correspondence with the King-Emperor (Printed), 1912–1916.
80. Transfer of capital (Original).
81–86. Correspondence with persons in India (Printed), 1910–1911.

92. Correspondence with persons in England and Abroad, 1910–1911.

113. Transfer of the Seat of the Government of India from Calcutta to Delhi and the creation of a new Lieutenant-Governorship at Patna, 1911.

117–120. Correspondence with the Secretary of State for India, 1910–1914.

IIIa. *Lord Hardinge Papers (Kent Archives Office, Maidstone).*

U927. Administrative Papers.

VP2. Diary including an account of Lord Hardinge's voyage to India and preparations for the Durbar, November, 1910–December, 1911.

VP3. Diary including the events of the Durbar, 1912.

Vab-Vaq. Correspondence with persons in India, 1911–1913.

VC8–VC9. Telegraphic Correspondence with the Secretary of State, 1910–1912.

IV. *Lord Minto (Fourth Earl of Minto) Papers. (National Library of Scotland, Edinburgh)*

M968–977. Correspondence with persons in India (Original), 1905–1910.

M978–987. Letters and Telegrams, India (Printed), 1905–1910.

M995–996. Correspondence with persons in England and Abroad (Printed), 1905–1910.

M998. Correspondence with the King-Emperor, 1905–1910.

M999–1004. Correspondence with the Secretary of State for India and Sir A. Godley, 1905–1910.

M1050–1051. Reports of Council Committee.

M1079–1082. Correspondence Regarding Council Reform.

M1107–1109. Newspaper cuttings.

V. *Lord Morley Papers. (India Office Library, London, MSS.EUR.D.573)*

Vols. 1–5. Copies of Letters from Morley to Minto, 1905–1910.

7–25. Letters from Minto to Morley, 1905–1910.

28–29. Public Telegrams: Secretary of State to Viceroy and Viceroy to Secretary of State, 1905–1910.

32–35. India: Council Reform, 1906–1909.

42a–42h. Correspondence between the Secretary of State and the Governor of Bombay, 1907–1911.

B. *OFFICIAL RECORDS AT THE INDIA OFFICE LIBRARY, LONDON*

I. *Judicial and Public Department Papers:*

*1906*
File 2876, vol. 773.

*1907*
File   275, vol. 793.
     614,     796.
    1164,    803.
    1540,    807.

*1908*
File 2755 with 2896, vol. 881.
    3141 with 3094, vol. 882.
    3612 with 3722, vol. 889.
    3757,          890.
    3855,          893.
    4264,          898.

*1909*
File    70, vol. 909.
      83,     909.
    184,     912.
    298,     914.
    798,  ·919.
    893,     920.
   1949,    935.
   3594,    960.
   3568,    960.
   4067,    966.

*1910*
File   202, vol. 979.
   1046,    991.
   1166,    992.
   1636,    998.

*1911*
File  ·664,    vol. 1058.
    770,       1061.

*1911 cont.*
Files  864,
    1656 and
    2647,     1066.
Files 4776
   and 4924,   1071.
File  4508,     1116.
    4616 with
    71/1912,   1127.
File  2077 with
    1303/1912  1146.

*1912*
File   415 with 466, vol. 1132.
    1178 with 1176,   1144.
Files  443, 2263, 2938,
    3024, 3273 and 3757
    with 1303,      1146.
File 1528 with 1833,   1154.
File 2080 with 2163,   1159.
    652 with 2285,   1162.
Files   63, 654, 844,
    918, and 1218 with
    1260/1911,     1071.

*1913*
File   377, vol. 1131.
   3675 with
    727, vol. 1137.
    1855, vol. 1232.
    1956,     1232.
    1658 with
    2198,     1236.
    1211 with
    3589, vol. 1261.
    3327 with
    3672, vol. 1262.
    4056,     1267.
    4456,     1278.
    4558,     1278.

II. *Political and Secret Department Papers:*

| | |
|---|---|
| L/PS/10/196 | L/PS/11/61 |
| L/PS/11/18 | L/PS/11/63 |
| L/PS/11/27 | Subject File 4287/1912. |
| L/PS/11/35 | 2672/1912. |
| L/PS/11/39 | 617/1913. |

III. India: *Education Proceedings.*
vols. 8154, 8155, 8432–8434, 8698, 8699, 8942, 8943, 9193–9196.

VI. India: *Education Department General Proceedings.*
vols. 8452, 8700, 8944, 9197.

V. India: *Home (Public) Proceedings.*
vols. 7311–7313, 7587, 7588, 7872–7874, 8150–8152, 8427–8429, 8716, 8960–8962, 9213.

VI. India: *Legislative Proceedings.*
vols. 8217–8219, 8498–8501, 8755–8757, 9009–9013.

VII. *Public and General Letters from India and Bengal.*
vols. 34–43.

VIII. *Bengal: General Proceedings.*
vols. 7576, 7577, 7859–7861, 8137–8139, 8416, 8417, 8676, 8677, 8923.

IX. *Bengal: Municipal Proceedings.*
vols. 7578–7580, 7862–7864, 8140–8142, 8418–8420, 8684, 8686, 8934, 8936.

X. *Bombay: Legislative and Legal Proceedings.*
vols. 8588, 8837, 9082.

XI. Bombay: *Local Self-Government Proceedings.*
vols. 6235, 8030, 8304, 8584, 8832, 9077.

XII. *The U.P. Local Self-Government Proceedings.*
vols. 7549, 7833, 8111, 8392, 8659, 8900.


C. *OFFICIAL PUBLICATIONS*

I. *The Parliamentary Debates (Authorised Edition). Fourth Series.*
vols. 152–198.

II. *The Parliamentary Debates. Official Report. Commons.* vols. I–LI.

III. *The Parliamentary Debates. Official Report. Lords.* vols. I–XII.

IV. *Proceedings of the Council of the Lieutenant-Governor of Bengal, 1906–1912.*

V. *Proceedings of the Council of the Governor of Bombay, 1901, 1907–1912.*

VI. *Legislative Council Debates, Eastern Bengal and Assam,* 1906–
   1912.

VII. *Proceedings of the Council of the Governor-General of India,*
   1906–1913.

VIII. *Proceedings of the Council of the Governor of Madras,* 1909–
   1912.

IX. *Proceedings of the Council of the Lieutenant-Governor of the
   Punjab,* 1908–1912.

X. *The U.P. Legislative Council Proceedings,* 1907–1912.

XI. *Report on Indian Constitutional Reform, 1918 (London).*

XII. *Sedition Committee Report, 1918 (Calcutta).*

XIII. *Selections from Native Newspaper Reports for Bengal, Bombay,
   Madras, the Punjab,* and the U.P., 1906–1912.

## D. *NEWSPAPERS AND PERIODICALS*

The *Bengal Times* (weekly), Dacca, 1906–1908.
The *Bengalee* (daily), Calcutta, 1906–January, 1913.
The *Bombay Gazette* (daily), Bombay, 1906–1910.
The *Bombay Gazette English News Supplement,* Bombay, 1908.
The *Bombay Gazette Overland Summary* (weekly), Bombay, 1906–
   1912.
The *Civil and Military Gazette* (daily), Lahore, 1907–1912.
The *Comrade* (weekly), Calcutta, 1913.
The *Contemporary Review* (monthly), London, 1907, 1909.
The *Eastern Bengal and Assam Era* (weekly) Dacca, 1909–1912.
The *Englishman* (daily), Calcutta, 1906–March, 1913.
The *Englishman Weekly Summary,* Calcutta, 1906–January, 1913.
The *Hindustan Review* (monthly), Allahabad, 1909–1912.
The *India* (weekly), London, 1906–1912.
The *Indian Review* (monthly) Madras, 1906–1912, 1916.
The *Madras Weekly Mail,* Madras, 1906–1912.
The *Morning Post* (daily), London, 1907–1909.
The *Moslem Chronicle* (weekly), Calcutta, 1897, 1905.
The *Nineteenth Century* (monthly), London, 1882, 1905–1912.
The *Pioneer* (daily) Allahabad, 1888, 1896, 1903, 1906–1912.
The *Pioneer Mail* (weekly), Allahabad, 1906–January, 1913.
The *Quarterly Review,* London, 1906, 1909.
The *Rangoon Gazette* (weekly), Rangoon, 1907–1910.
The *Spectator* (weekly), London, 1907, 1909.
The *Statesman Weekly,* Calcutta, 1907–1912.
The *Times* (daily), London, 1907–1912.
The *Times of India Mail* (weekly), Bombay, 1906–January, 1913.

E. *INDIAN PARTY PROCEEDINGS, REPORTS AND ADDRESSES AND THE INDIA OFFICE LIBRARY TRACTS.*

The All-India Muslim League:   *Proceedings of the Annual Meeting of the All-India Muslim League held at Amritsar on 30th and 31st December, 1908.*

- *Proceedings of the Third Annual Sessions of the All-India Muslim League held at Delhi on the 29th and 30th January, 1910.* Allahabad, 1910.

- *Proceedings of the Annual Meeting of the All-India Muslim League held at Nagpur on the 28th and 29th December, 1910.* Allahabad, 1910.

- *Report of the All-India Muslim League for 1910.* Allahabad, 1910.

- *Report of the All-India Muslim League for 1911.* Allahabad, 1911.

- *Presidential Address of Adamjee Peerbhoy at the Karachi Session of the All-India Muslim League:* Appendix E of the *Surat Congress and Conferences* by G. A. Natesan, Madras.

- *Speech at the All-India Muslim League Session at Amritsar by Syed Ali Imam.* Bankipur, 1908.

- *Speech at the Fifth Session of the All-India Muslim League* held at Calcutta by Nawab Sir Salimullah. 1912.

- *Rules and Regulations of the All-India Muslim League, 1909.* Aligarh.

- *Rules and Regulations of the All-India Muslim League, 1910.* Allahabad.

- *The Draft Constitution and Rules of the All-India Muslim League, 1913.* Lucknow.

- *The Constitution and Rules of the All-India Muslim League, 1913.* Lucknow.

| The London Branch of the All-India Muslim League: | *Report of the Inaugural Meeting of the All-India Muslim League, London Branch*, 1908. London. |
|---|---|
| | - *The Indian Mahomedans and the Government*, 1909. London. |
| | - *The Indian Councils Bill, 1909*, London. |
| | - *The Second Annual Report of the London Branch of the All-India Muslim League*, 1910. London. |
| The National Mahomedan Association: | *The Rules and Objects of the National Mahomedan Association with a List of the Members.* Calcutta, 1882. |
| The Central National Mahomedan Association | *The Rules and Objects of the Central National Mahomedan Association with the Quinquennial Report and List of Members.* Calcutta, 1885. |
| | - *Report of the Committee of the Central National Mahomedan Association, 15 April, 1883. Calcutta, 1883.* |

*Reports of the Indian National Congress for the years 1885–1895, 1906, 1908–1912.*
*The Partition of Bengal—An open Letter to Lord Curzon, 1905* by 'One of the People'. Dacca. Tract 995.
*The Unrest in India Considered and Discussed, 1907,* by S. A. Khan. Bombay. Tr. 1001.
*All About Partition.* Calcutta, 1905. Tr. 1037.
*The Congress Split, 1908: The Surat Congress, 1908,* Madras. Tr. 1042.

## F. LONDON UNIVERSITY UNPUBLISHED THESES

| Ahmad, Sufia. | 'Some Aspects of the History of the Muslim Community in Bengal, 1884–1912.' Ph.D., 1961. |
|---|---|
| Jones, I. M. | 'The Origins and Development to 1892 of the Indian National Congress.' M.A., 1947. |
| Khatoon, Latifa. | 'Some Aspects of the Social History of Bengal, with Special Reference to the Muslims, 1854–1884.' M.A., 1960. |

McLane, J. R.　　　'The Development of Nationalist Ideas and Tactics and the Policies of the Government of India, 1897–1905.' Ph.D., 1961.

Zaidi, S. Z. H.　　　'The Partition of Bengal and its Annulment—a Survey of the Schemes of Territorial Redistribution of Bengal (1902–1911).' Ph.D., 1964.

Zakaria, R. A.　　　'Muslims in India: A Political Analysis, 1885–1906.' Ph.D., 1948.


## G. PUBLISHED ARTICLES

Ali, Ameer.　　　*Memoirs of the Right Honourable Syed Ameer Ali. The Islamic Culture.* vol. V. No. 4; vol. VI. Nos. 1–3.

Barrier, G. N.　　　'The Arya Samaj and Congress Politics in the Punjab, 1894–1908. *The Journal of Asian Studies.* vol. XXVI. No. 3. May, 1967.

*The Punjab Government and Communal Politics, 1870–1908. The Journal of Asian Studies.* vol. XXVII. No. 3. May, 1968.

Islam, Z. and Jensen, R.　　　*Indian Muslims and the Public Services, 1871–1915. Journal of the Asiatic Society of Pakistan.* vol. IV. 1964.

Lebra, J. C.　　　*British Official and Unofficial Attitudes and Policies Towards the Indian National Congress 1885–1894. The Indian Historical Quarterly.* vol. XXXI. No. 2. 1955.

Malik, Hafeez.　　　*Abul Kalam Azad's Theory of Nationalism. The Muslim World.* vol. LIII. No. 1. 1963.

Moore, R. J.　　　*John Morley's Acid Test: India, 1906–1910 (Review Article). The Pacific Affairs,* vol. XL. Nos. 3 and 4, Fall and Winter, 1968.

Parel, Anthony.　　　*Hume, Dufferin and the Origins of the Indian National Congress. Journal of the Indian History.* vol. 42. 1964.


## H. PUBLISHED BOOKS

Ahmad, A.　　　*Studies in Islamic Culture in the Indian Environment.* London, 1964.

—　　　*Islamic Modernism in India and Pakistan.* London, 1967.

Ahmad, B.　　　*Justice Shah Din, His Life and Writings.* Lahore, 1962.

Albiruni, A. H.　　　*Makers of Pakistan and Modern Muslim India.* Lahore, 1950.

Ali, A. Y.　　　*A Cultural History of India During the British Period.* Bombay, 1940.

| | |
|---|---|
| Ali, M. | *Thoughts on the Present Discontent.* Bombay, 1907. |
| (editor A. Iqbal) | *My Life: A Fragment.* Lahore, 1942. |
| Ambedkar, B. R. | *Pakistan or the Partition of India.* Bombay, 1946. |
| Andrews, C. F. and Mukherjee. | *Rise and Growth of the Congress in India.* London, 1938 |
| Azad, A. K. | *India Wins Freedom.* Calcutta, 1959. |
| Aziz, K. K. | *Britain and Muslim India.* London, 1963. |
| Bahadur, Lal. | *The Muslim League: Its History, Activities and Achievements.* Agra, 1954. |
| Bagal, J. C. | *History of the Indian Association, 1876–1951.* Calcutta, 1953. |
| Baljon, J. M. S. (Jr.). | *The Reforms and Religious Ideas of Sir Sayyid Ahmad Khan.* Lahore, 1964. |
| Banerjee, A. C. | *The Indian Constitutional Documents.* 2 vols. Calcutta, 1948. |
| Banerjea, S. N. | *A Nation in Making.* London, 1925. |
| Bartarya, S. C. | *The Indian Nationalist Movement.* Allahabad, 1958. |
| Bilgrami, S. H. | *Addresses, Poems and Other Writings.* Hyderabad, Deccan, 1925. |
| Blunt, W. S. | *India Under Ripon: A Private Diary.* London, 1909. |
| | *My Diaries.* London, 1919. |
| Bombay Govt. | *Source Material for a History of the Freedom Movement in India.* Bombay, 1958. |
| Bose, N. S. | *The Indian Awakening and Bengal.* Calcutta, 1960. |
| | *The Indian National Movement.* Calcutta, 1965. |
| Butler, Sir Harcourt. | *India Insistent.* London, 1931. |
| Chaudhuri, B. M. | *Muslim Politics in India.* Calcutta, 1946. |
| Chaudhuri, N. C. | *Autobiography of an Unknown Indian.* London, 1951. |
| Chaudhury, R. C. | *The Congress Split.* Calcutta, 1908. |
| Chintamani, C. Y. | *Indian Politics Since the Mutiny.* London, 1940. |
| Chirol, V. | *Indian Unrest.* London, 1910. |
| Clarke (Sir G. Lord Sydenham). | *My Working Life.* London, 1925. |
| Coupland, Sir R. | *Report on the Constitutional Problem of India.* London, 1942. |
| Cumming, Sir J. | *Political India, 1832–1932.* London, 1932. |
| Curzon, Marquis of. | *British Government in India,* 2 vols. London, 1925. |
| Das, M. N. | *India Under Morley and Minto.* London, 1964. |
| Desai, A. R. | *Social Background of the Indian Nationalism.* Bombay, 1956. |

| | |
|---|---|
| Dufferin, Marquis of Dufferin and Ava. | *Speeches Delivered in India, 1884–1888.* London, 1890. |
| Elliot, Murray K. (G.J.) 4th Earl of Minto. | *Speeches by Minto (1905–1910).* Calcutta, 1911. |
| Farquhar, J. N. | *Modern Religious Movements in India.* New York, 1918. |
| Faruqi, Zia-ul-Hasan. | *The Deoband School and the Demand for Pakistan.* London, 1963. |
| Fraser, Lovett. | *India under Curzon and After.* London, 1911. |
| Fuller, J. B. | *Some Personal Experiences.* London, 1930. |
| Ghose, P. C. | *Indian National Congress.* Calcutta, 1960. |
| Gilbert, M. | *Servant of India.* London, 1966. |
| Grover, B. L. | *A Documentary Study of British Policy Towards Indian Nationalism 1885–1909.* Delhi, 1967. |
| Gopal, Ram. | *Indian Muslims—A Political History (1858–1947).* London, 1959. |
| Gopal, S. | *The Viceroyalty of Lord Ripon.* London, 1953. *British Policy in India, 1858–1905.* Cambridge, 1965. |
| Gore, J. | *King George V: A Personal Memoir.* London, 1941 |
| Graham, G. F. I. | *The Life and Work of Sir Syed Ahmed Khan.* London, 1909. |
| Griffiths, P. | *The British Impact on India.* London, 1952. |
| Gupta, A. (edited). | *Studies in the Bengal Renaissance.* Jadavpur, 1958. |
| Hardinge, First Viscount Hardinge of Penshurst. | *My Indian Years, 1910–1916.* London, 1918. *Speeches of Lord Hardinge, vol. I.* Madras (n.d.) |
| Heimsath, C. H. | *Indian Nationalism and Hindu Social Reform.* Princeton, 1964. |
| Hunter, W. W. | *The Indian Musalmans.* London, 1884. |
| Husain, A. | *Fazl-i-Husain—A Political Biography.* Bombay, 1946. |
| Husain, S. A. | *The Destiny of Indian Muslims.* Bombay, 1965. |
| Jackson, S. | *The Aga Khan: Prince, Prophet and Sportsman.* London, 1952. |
| Jain, M. S. | *The Aligarh Movement: Its origin and Development 1858–1906.* Agra, 1965. |
| Kabir, H. | *Muslim Politics, 1906–1942.* Calcutta, 1943. |
| Khaliquzzaman, C. | *Pathway to Pakistan.* Longmans Pakistan Branch, 1956. |
| Khan, A. M. | *The Communalism in India—Its origin and Growth.* |
| Khan, the Aga. | *Memoirs.* London, 1954. |

| | |
|---|---|
| Khan, Sir Syed. | *The Present State of Politics.* Allahabad, 1888. |
| Khan, S. S. A. | *The Life of Lord Morley.* London, 1923. |
| Krishna, K. B. | *The Problem of Minorities or Communal Representation in India.* London, 1939. |
| Lovet, Sir V. | *History of the Indian Nationalist Movement.* London, 1921. |
| Low, D. A. | *Soundings in Modern South Asian History.* London, 1968. |
| McCully, B. T. | *English Education and the Origins of the Indian Nationalism.* New York, 1940. |
| Mahmud, Syed. | *Hindu-Muslim Cultural Accord.* Bombay, 1949. |
| Major, E. | *Viscount Morley and Indian Reform.* London, 1910. |
| Majumdar, A. K. | *Advent of Independence.* Bombay, 1963. |
| Majumdar, B. B. | *History of Political Thought from Rammohun to Dayananda (1821–84).* vol. I. Calcutta, 1934. |
| - | *Indian Political Associations and Reform of Legislature (1818–1917).* Calcutta, 1965. |
| Majumdar, R. C. | *Glimpses of Bengal in the Nineteenth Century.* Calcutta, 1960. |
| - | *History of the Freedom Movement in India.* Calcutta. vol. I, 1962. vol. II, 1963. |
| Mallick, A. R. | *British Policy and the Muslims in Bengal, 1757–1856.* Dacca, 1961. |
| Mary, Countess of Minto. | *India, Minto and Morley (1905–1910).* London, 1934. |
| Masani, R. P. | *Dadabhai Naoroji: The Grand Old Man of India.* London, 1939. |
| Mehta, A. and Patwardhan, A. | *The Communal Triangle in India.* Allahabad, 1942. |
| Metcalf, T. R. | *The Aftermath of Revolt: India, 1857–1870.* Princeton, New Jersey, 1965. |
| Misra, B. B. | *The Indian Middle Classes: Their Growth in Modern Times.* London, 1961. |
| Morley, Viscount John. | *Recollections.* 2 vols. London, 1917. |
| Mujeeb, M. | *The Indian Muslims.* London, 1967. |
| Mukherjee, H. & U. | *The Growth of Nationalism in India (1857–1905).* Calcutta, 1952. |
| Mukherjee, P. | *Indian Constitutional Documents.* Calcutta, 1918. |
| Natesan, G. | *Congress Presidential Address.* 2 vols. Madras. |
| Nehru, J. L. | *Discovery of India.* London, 1956. |
| Nevinson, H. W. | *The New Spirit in India.* London, 1928. |
| Noman, M. | *Muslim India: Rise and Growth of the All-India Muslim League,* Allahabad, 1942. |

Pal, B. C.              *Nationality and Empire,* Calcutta and Simla, 1916.

Panikkar, K. M.        *Indian Nationalism: Its Origin, History and*
(and an Indian          *Ideals.* London, 1920.
Student).

Philips, C. H.         *Historians of India, Pakistan and Ceylon.*
                        London, 1961.

        -              *The Evolution of India and Pakistan,* 1858–
                        1947. London, 1962.

Prasad, R.             *India Divided.* Bombay, 1946.

Rajkumar, N. V.        *Indian Political Parties.* New Delhi, 1948.

Rajput, A. B.          *Muslim League, Yesterday and Today.* Lahore,
                        1948.

Ronaldshay, Lord       *The Heart of Aryavarta.* London, 1925.

Seal, A.               *The Emergence of Indian Nationalism: Com-*
                        *petition and Collaboration in the Later Nine-*
                        *teenth Century.* Cambridge, 1968.

Sen, S.                *The Birth of Pakistan.* Calcutta, 1955.

Singh, G. N.           *Landmarks in Indian Constitutional and*
                        *National Development, vol. I. 1600–1919.*
                        Delhi, 1950.

Singh, H. L.           *Problems and Policies of the British in India,*
                        *1885–1898.* Bombay, 1963.

Smith, W. C.           *Modern Islam in India.* London, 1946.

Smith, W. R.           *Nationalism and Reform in India.* New Haven,
                        1938.

Spear, T. G. P.        *India, Pakistan and West.* London, 1958.

        -              *A History of India (a Pelican original).* vol. I.
                        Middlesex, England, 1966.

Thompson, E. and       *Rise and Fulfilment of British Rule in India.*
Garret, G. T.           London, 1934.

Tyabji, H. B.          *Badruddin Tyabji: A Biography.* Bombay, 1952.

Waley, S. D.           *Edwin Montagu: A Memoir and an Account of*
                        *His Visits to India.* London, 1964.

Wasti, S. R.           *Lord Minto and the Indian Nationalist Move-*
                        *ment, 1905–1910.* Oxford, 1964.

Wedderburn, W.         *Allan Octavian Hume, C.B.* London, 1913.

Wilson, S. G.          *Modern Movements Among Muslims.* London,
                        1916.

Woodruff, P.           *Men who Ruled India, vol. II.* London, 1954.

Wolpert, S. A.         *Tilak and Gokhale: Revolution and Reform in*
                        *the Making of Modern India.* Berkeley, Los
                        Angeles, 1962.

        -              *Morley and India, 1906–1910.* Berkeley, Los
                        Angeles, 1967.

Zacharias, H. C. E.    *Renascent India, from Ram Mohun Roy to*
                        *Mohandas Gandhi.* London, 1933.

# APPENDIX I

# THE FIRST DRAFT OF THE MEMORIAL OF THE SIMLA DEPUTATION

### 'Strictly Prohibited

'Draft Memorial drawn up for private perusal and approval of Members only by Nawab Imad-ul-Mulk, Bahadur (Syed Hosain Bilgrami).

'To

## HIS EXCELLENCY THE RIGHT HONOURABLE

## THE EARL OF MINTO,
### P.C., G.M.S.I., G.M.I.E., G.C.M.G.,
### Viceroy and Governor General of India.

'MAY IT PLEASE YOUR EXCELLENCY:

Availing ourselves of the permission graciously accorded to us, we, the undersigned Nobles, Jagirdars, Talukdars, Merchants, and others, representing a large body of the Mohamedan subjects of His Majesty the King-Emperor in different parts of India, beg most respectfully to approach Your Excellency with the following Memorial for your favourable consideration.

'2. We have no need to be reminded of the incalculable benefits conferred by British rule on the teeming millions belonging to divers races, and professing divers religions, who form the population of the vast Continent of India. Nor can we forget the chaos and misrule from which British arms extricated us when the country was a prey to an innumerable host of adventurers bent on rapine and plunder. We have good reason to be grateful for the peace, security, personal freedom, and liberty of worship that we now enjoy; and, from the wise and enlightened character of the Government, we have every reasonable ground for anticipating that these benefits will be progressive and that India will, in the future, occupy an increasingly important position in the Comity of Nations.

'3. One of the most important characteristics of British policy in India is the increasing deference that has, so far as possible, been paid from the first to the views and wishes of the people of the country in matters affecting their interests, with due regard always to the diversity of race and religion which forms such an important feature of all Indian problems.

'4. Beginning with the confidential and unobtrusive method of consulting influential members of important communities in different parts of the country, this principle was gradually extended by the recognition of the right of recognised Political or Commercial organisations to communicate to the authorities their criticisms and views on measures of public importance; and, finally, by the nomination and election of direct representatives of the people in Municipalities, Local Boards, and—above all—in the Legislative Chambers of the country. This last element is, we understand, about to be dealt with by the Commission appointed by Your Excellency at the initiative of His Majesty's Secretary of State for India, with the view of giving it further extension; and it is with reference mainly to our claim to a fair share in such extended representation that we have ventured to approach Your Excellency on the present occasion.

'5. The Mosulmans of India number, according to the Census taken in the year 1901, over sixty-two millions, or more than one-fifth of the total population of His Majesty's Indian Dominions; while if the Native States and Burmah were excluded from the computation and a reduction made for the uncivilized portions of the community enumerated under the heads of Animists and other minor religions, the proportion of Mosulmans to the whole population of British India would be found to be approximately one-fourth. In these circumstances, we desire to submit that, under any system of representation, extended or limited, a minority amounting to a quarter of the population—and in itself more numerous than the entire population of any first class European power, except Russia—may justly lay claim to adequate recognition as an important factor in the State. We venture, indeed, with Your Excellency's permission, to go a step further than this and urge that the position accorded to the Mosulman Community in any kind of representation, direct or indirect, and in all other ways affecting their status and influence, should be commensurate not merely with their numerical strength, but also with their political importance; and that, in estimating the latter, due weight should be given to the position which they occupied in India a little more than a hundred years ago, and of which the traditions have naturally not faded from their minds.

'6. The Mosulmans of India have hitherto placed implicit reliance on the sense of justice and love of fair dealing that has always characterised their Rulers, and have in consequence abstained from pressing their claims by methods that might prove at all embarrassing; but earnestly as we desire that the Mosulmans of India should not in the future depart from that excellent and time-honoured tradition, recent events have stirred up feelings, especially among the younger generation of Mohamedans, which might, in certain circumstances and under certain contingencies, easily pass beyond the control of temperate counsel and sober guidance.

'7. We, therefore, pray that the representations we herewith venture to submit, after a careful consideration of the views and wishes of a large number of our co-religionists in all parts of India, may be favoured with Your Excellency's earnest attention.

'8. We hope Your Excellency will pardon our stating at the outset that representative institutions of the European type are entirely opposed to the genius and traditions of Eastern Nations, and many of the most thoughtful members of our community look upon them as totally unsuitable to the social, religious, and political conditions obtaining in India. Since, however, our Rulers have, in persuance of their own immemorial instincts and traditions, found it expedient to give these institutions an increasingly important place in the Government of the country, we Mohamedans cannot any longer, in justice to our own national interests, hold aloof from participating in the conditions to which their policy has given rise. We must therefore acknowledge with gratitude that such representation as the Mosulmans of India have hitherto enjoyed has been due to a sense of justice and fairness on the part of Your Excellency and your illustrious predecessors in office, and the heads of Local Governments by whom the Mohamedan Members of Legislative Chambers have with scarcely one exception been invariably nominated; but we venture to submit that the representation thus accorded to us has necessarily been inadequate to our requirements and has not always carried with it the approval of those whom the nominees were selected to represent. This state of things has, in existing circumstances, been unavoidable; for while, on the one hand, the number of nominations reserved to the Viceroy and Local Governments has necessarily been strictly limited, the selection, on the other hand, of really representative men has, in the absence of any reliable method of ascertaining the direction of popular choice, been far from easy. As for the results of election, it is most unlikely that the name of any Mohamedan candidate will ever be submitted for the approval of Government by the electoral bodies as now constituted, unless he is prepared to forego the right of private judgment and undertake to vote with the majority in all matters of importance. We submit that a Mohamedan elected on these terms necessarily ceases to represent his own community and becomes a mere mandatory of the Hindu majority. Nor can we, in fairness, find fault with the desire of our Hindu fellow-subjects to take full advantage of their strength and vote only for members of their own community, or for persons who, if not Hindus, are pledged to vote for the interests of the Hindu community. It is true that we have many and important interests in common with our Hindu fellow-countrymen, and it will always be a matter of the utmost satisfaction to us to see these interests safeguarded by the presence in our Legislative Chambers of able supporters of these interests, irrespective of their nationality. We Mosulmans have, however, additional interests of our own which are not shared by other communities, and these have hitherto suffered grievous loss from the fact that they have not been adequately represented. Even in the Provinces in which the Mohamedans constitute a distinct majority of the population, they have too often been treated as though they were inappreciably small political factors that might without unfairness be neglected. This has been the case, to some extent, in the Punjab; but in a more marked degree in Sindh and in Eastern Bengal, where Mohamedan interests have suffered, owing partly to the backwardness of the community in education, for which they are not wholly to blame, but still more to their ignorance of the arts of self-assertion and political agitation.

'9. Before formulating our views with regard to the election of representatives, we beg to observe that the political importance of a community to a considerable extent gains strength or suffers detriment according to the position that the members of that community occupy in the service of the State. If, as is unfortunately the case with the Mohamedans, they are not adequately represented in this manner, they lose in the prestige and influence which are justly their due. Our first prayer, therefore, is that Your Excellency will be graciously pleased to issue strict orders that, both in the Gazetted and the Subordinate and Ministerial services of all Indian Provinces, a due proportion of Mohamedans—to be locally determined—shall always find place. Orders of like import have, at times, been issued by Local Governments in some Provinces, but have never, unfortunately, been strictly enforced, on the ground that qualified Mohamedans were not forthcoming. This allegation, however true it may have been at one time, is no longer tenable now, and wherever the will to employ them is not wanting, as is often the case in offices manned mostly by Hindus, the supply of qualified Mohamedans, we are happy to be able to assure Your Excellency, is greater than any possible demand.

'10. As Municipal and District Boards have to deal with important local interests, affecting to a great extent the health and comfort of the inhabitants, we shall, we hope, be pardoned if we solicit, for a moment, Your Excellency's attention to the position of Mosulmans thereon before passing on to higher concerns. These institutions form, as it were, the initial rungs in the ladder of Self-Government, and it is here that the principle of representation is brought home intimately to the intelligence of the people. Yet the position of Mosulmans on these Boards is not at present regulated by any guiding principle capable of general application, and practice varies in different localities. The Aligarh Municipality, for example, is divided into six wards, and each ward returns one Hindu and one Mohamedan Commissioner; and the same principle, we understand, is adopted in some other Municipalities, but in many localities the Mosulman tax-payers are not adequately represented. We would, therefore, respectfully suggest that Local Authority should, in every case, be required to declare the number of Hindus and Mohamedans entitled to seats on Municipal and Local Boards, such proportion to be determined in accordance with the numerical strength, social status, and local influence of either Community—in consultation, if necessary, with their leading men.

'11. We would also suggest that the Senates and Syndicates of Indian Universities might, so far as possible, be similarly dealt with: that there should, in other words, be an authoritative declaration of the proportion in which Mohamedans are entitled to be represented in either body, whether by election or nomination or both.

'12. We now proceed to the consideration of our share in the Legislative Chambers of the country. Beginning with the Provincial Councils, we would suggest that, as in the case of Municipalities and Local Boards, the proportion of Mohamedan representatives entitled to a seat should be determined and declared with due regard to the important considerations which we have ventured to point out in paragraph 5 of this Memorial; and that the Mohamedan Members of District Boards and Municipalities, and the Registered Graduates of Universities, should be formed into Electoral Colleges, and be authorised, in accordance with such rules of procedure as Your Excellency's Government may be pleased to prescribe in that behalf, to return the number of members that may be declared to be eligible.

'13. With regard to the Imperial Legislative Council, whereon the due representation of Mohamedan interests is a matter of the utmost importance, we would solicit:—

 (1) That in the cadre of the Council, at least, one member out of every four should always be a Mohamedan.
 (2) That, as far as possible, appointment by election should be given preference over nomination; and that in any case the majority of members should be appointed by election.
 (3) That for purposes of choosing Mohamedan representatives, Mohamedan members of the Provincial Councils and Mohamedan Fellows of Universities should be invested with electoral powers to be exercised in accordance with such procedure as may be prescribed by Your Excellency's Government in that behalf.

'14. The methods of election we have ventured to suggest are necessarily tentative: they may even be found, in certain respects, defective; but they are the simplest and the least complicated of the two or three that have occurred to us in the very limited time at our command. But, provided the choice be left free and unhampered in the hands of respectable and educated Mohamedans, we shall have no hesitation in accepting any other method that may be considered more practicable.

'15. We have reason to believe that the generality of Mohamedans in all parts of India feel it a grievance that Mohamedan Judges are not more frequently appointed on the High Courts, and Chief Courts of Judicature. Since the creation of these Courts only three Mohamedan lawyers have held these honourable appointments, all three of whom have happily justified their elevation in a most signal manner. It is not, therefore, an extravagant request on their behalf that, whenever possible, a Mohamedan Judge should be given a seat on each of these Courts. Qualified lawyers, eligible for these posts; can always be found—if not in one Province, then in another; and seeing that a Bengalee Judge sits on the bench of the Punjab Chief Court, there should be no objection to a Mohamedan, provided he is qualified, being translated from one Province to another.

'16. There has lately been some talk, we understand, of the possible appointment of one or more Native members on the Executive Council of the Viceroy and the India Council in England. Should such appointments be contemplated, we beg that the claims of Mohamedans in that behalf may not be overlooked. More than one Mohamedan, we venture to say, will be found in the ranks of the Covenanted and Uncovenanted Services fit to serve with distinction in either of these august Chambers. We have, at this moment a retired Judge of the High Court of Calcutta, domiciled in England, who, by his ability as a lawyer, his standing as a scholar, and his reputation as an experienced and versatile man of the world, cannot fail to be an ornament to the India Council: we mean Mr. Syed Amir Ali, in whom the Mohamedans of India repose the fullest confidence.

'17. In conclusion, we beg to assure Your Excellency that in assisting the Mosulman subjects of His Majesty at this crisis in the directions indicated in the present Memorial, Your Excellency will be strengthening the foundations of their unswerving loyalty to the Throne and laying the foundation of their political regeneration and national prosperity, and Your Excellency's name will be remembered with gratitude by their posterity for generations to come.

'We have the honour to subscribe ourselves

Your Excellency's

Most Obedient Humble Servants,

# APPENDIX II

## Lord Minto's Reply to the Simla Deputation

In reply to the memorial submitted by the Muslim deputation at Simla on 1 October, 1906, Lord Minto said:

'Your Highness and gentlemen,—allow me, before I attempt to reply to the many considerations your address embodies, to welcome you heartily to Simla. Your presence here today is very full of meaning. To the document with which you have presented me are attached the signatures of nobles, of Ministers of various States, of great landowners, of lawyers, of merchants, and of many other of His Majesty's Mahomedan subjects. I welcome the representative character of your deputation as expressing the views and aspirations of the enlightened Muslim community of India. I feel that all you have said emanates from a representative body basing its opinions on a matured consideration of the existing political conditions of India, totally apart from the small personal or political sympathies and antipathies of scattered localities, and I am grateful to you for the opportunity you are affording me of expressing my appreciation of the just aims of the followers of Islam, and their determination to share in the political history of our Empire. As your Viceroy I am proud of the recognition you express of the benefits conferred by British rule on the diverse races of many creeds which go to form the population of this huge continent. You yourselves, the descendants of a conquering and ruling race, have told me today of your gratitude for the personal freedom the liberty of worship, the general peace and the hopeful future which British administration has secured for India. It is interesting to look back on early British efforts to assist the Mahomedan population to qualify themselves for the public service. In 1782 Warren Hastings founded the Calcutta Madrassah, with the intention of enabling its students 'to compete on more equal terms with the Hindus for employment under Government'. In 1811 my ancestor Lord Minto advocated improvements in the Madrassah and the establishment of Mahomedan Colleges at other places throughout India. In later years the efforts of the Mahomedan Association led to the Government Resolution of 1885 dealing with the educational position of the Mahomedan community and their employment in the Public Service, whilst Mahomedan educational effort has culminated in the College of Aligarh, that great institution which the noble and broad-minded devotion of Sir Syed Ahmed Khan—(applause)—has dedicated to his co-religionists. It was in July, 1877, that Lord Lytton laid the foundation-stone of Aligarh, when Sir Syed Ahmed Khan addressed these memorable words to the Viceroy: 'The personal honour which you have done me assures me of a great fact, and fills me with feelings of a much higher nature than mere personal gratitude. I am assured that you who upon this occasion represent the British rule have sympathy with our labours. To me this assurance is very valuable and a source of great happiness. At my time of life it is a comfort to me to feel that the undertaking which has been for many years and is now the sole object of my life, has roused on the one hand the energies of my own countrymen, and on the other has won the sympathy of our British fellow-subjects, and the support of our rulers, so that when the few years I may still be spared are over, and when I shall be no longer amongst you, the College will still prosper and succeed in educating my countrymen to have the same affection for their country, the same feelings of loyalty for the British rule, the same appreciation of its blessings, the same sincerity of friendship with our British fellow-subjects as have been the ruling feelings of my life. (applause).' Aligarh has won its laurels, its students have gone forth to fight the battle of life strong in the tenets of their own religion, strong in the precepts of loyalty and patriotism, and now when there is much that is critical in the political future of India the inspiration of Sir Syed Ahmed Khan and the teachings of Aligarh shine forth brilliantly in the pride of Mahomedan history, in the loyalty, commonsense, and sound reasoning so eloquently expressed in your address.

'But, gentlemen, you go on to tell me that sincere as your belief is in the justice and fair dealings of your rulers, and unwilling as you are to embarrass them at the present moment you can not but be aware that 'recent events have stirred up feelings amongst the younger generation of Mahomedans which might pass beyond the control of the temperate counsel and sober guidance'. Now I have no intention of entering into any discussion upon the affairs of Eastern Bengal and Assam, yet, I hope that without offence to any one I may thank the Mahomedan community of the new Province for the moderation and self-restraint they have shown under conditions which were new to them and as to which there has been inevitably much misunderstanding, and that I may, at the same time, sympathise with all that is sincere in Bengali sentiments. But above all what I would ask you to believe is that the course the Viceroy and the Government of India have pursued in connection with the affairs of the new Province—the future of which is now I hope assured—(applause)—has been dictated solely by a regard for what has appeared best for its present and future populations as a whole, irrespective of race or creed, and that the Mahomedan community of Eastern Bengal and Assam can rely as firmly as ever on British justice and fair play for the appreciation of its loyalty and the safeguarding of its interests.

'You have addressed me, gentlemen, at a time when the political atmosphere is full of change. We all feel it would be foolish to attempt to deny its existence. Hopes and ambitions new to India are making themselves felt; we can not ignore them, we should be wrong to wish to do so. But to what is all this unrest due? Not to the discontent of mis-governed millions—I defy anyone honestly to assert that; not to any uprising of a disaffected people. It is due to that educational growth in which only a very small portion of the population has yet shared, of which British rule first sowed the seed, and the fruits of which British rule is now doing its best to foster and to direct. There may be many taxes in the harvest we are now reaping, the Western grain which we have sown may not be entirely suitable to the requirements of the people of India, but the educational harvest will increase as years go on, and the healthiness of the nourishment it gives will depend on the careful administration and distribution of its product. You need not ask my pardon, gentlemen, for telling me that 'representative insti-tutions of the European type are entirely new to the people of India' or that their introduction here requires the most earnest thought and care. I should be very far from welcoming all the political machinery of the Western world amongst the hereditary instincts and traditions of eastern races. Western breadth of thought, the teachings of Western civilization, the freedom of British individuality, can do much for the people of India. But I recognise with you that they must not carry with them an impracticable insistance on the acceptance of political methods. (Applause).

'And now, gentlemen, I come to your own position in respect to the political future; the position of the Mahomedan Community for whom you speak. You will, I feel sure, recognise that it is impossible for me to follow you through any detailed consideration of the conditions and the share that community has a right to claim in the administration of public affairs. I can at present only deal with generalities. The points which you have raised are before the Committee which, as you know, I have lately appointed to consider the question of representation, and I will take care that your address is submitted to them. But at the same time I hope I may be able to reply to the general tenor of your remarks without in any way forestalling the Committee's report. The pith of your address, as I understand it, is a claim that in any system of representation—whether it affects a Municipality, a District Board, or a Legislative Council in which it is proposed to introduce or increase an electoral organisation—the Mahomedan Community should be rep-resented as a community, you point out that in many cases electoral bodies as now constituted can not be expected to return a Mahomedan candidate, and that if by chance they did so it could only be at the sacrifice of such a candidate's views to those of a majority opposed to his own community whom he would in no way represent; and you justly claim that your position should be estimated not merely on your numerical strength but in respect to the political importance of your community, and the service it has rendered to the Empire. I am entirely in accord with you. (Applause). Please do not misunderstand me, I make no attempt to indicate by what means the representation of communities can be obtained, but I am as firmly convinced as I believe you to be, that any electoral representation in India would be doomed

to mischievous failure which aimed at granting a personal enfranchisement regardless of the beliefs and traditions of the communities composing the population of this continent. (Applause). The great mass of
the people of India have no knowledge of representative institutions, I
agree with you gentlemen, that the initial rungs in the ladder of self-
government are to be found in the Municipal and District Boards, and
that it is in that direction that we must look for the gradual political
education of the people. In the meantime I can only say to you that
the Mahomedan Community may rest assured that their political rights
and interests as a community will be safe-guarded in any administrative
organisation with which I am concerned, and that you and the people
of India may rely upon the British Raj to respect, as it has been its pride
to do, the religious beliefs and the national traditions of the myriads
composing the population of His Majesty's Indian Empire. (Applause).

'Your Highness and gentlemen, I sincerely thank you for the unique
opportunity your deputation has given me of meeting so many distinguished and representative Mahomedans. I deeply appreciate the energy
and interest in public affairs which have brought you here from great
distances, and I only regret that your visit to Simla is necessarily so
short.'

# APPENDIX III

Some Prominent Delegates to the Inaugural
Session of the All-India Muslim
League, Dacca, December, 1906.

(In the absence of the original proceedings of the inaugural session of
the All-India Muslim League it has not been possible to compile a complete list of delegates or even the prominent delegates to the session.
The following list has been prepared mainly on the basis of a group-
photograph of a large number of delegates, and newspaper reports of
the proceedings of the Conference).

*Assam:* Abdul Majid, Rukunuddin, Abdul Karim, Shams-ul-
Ulama A. N. M. Wahed, Syed Abdul Majid, Abdul
Ahad Choudhury and Dewan Abdul Hamid.

*Bengal:* Mirza Shujaat Ali Baig, Syed Irfan Ali, Wahed Husain,
Naseer Husain Khan Kheyal, Abdullah-al-Mamun
Suhrawardy, Shahed Suhrawardy, Nawab Amir Husain,
Abdul Hamid and Abdur Rahman Siddiqi.

*Bihar:* M. Sharfuddin, Mazhar-ul-Haque, Sarfaraz Husain
Khan, Ali Imam, Shah Muhammad Sulaiman of
Phulwari Shareef and Muhammad Yusuf.

*Bombay:* Rafiuddin Ahmad and Khorshedji.

*Burma:* Abdus Salam Rafiqi and Anwar Ahmad.

*Dehli:* Hakim Ajmal Khan.

*Eastern Bengal:* Salimullah, Nawab Ali Choudhury, Nawab Yusuf
Khan, Nawab Abdus Subhan Choudhury, Nawab
Hossam Haider, Ali Nawab Choudhury, Syed Abdul
Jabbar, Khawaja Muhammad Azam, Choudhury
Ghulam Sattar, Choudhury Alimuzzaman, Aga Kazim
Shirajee, Mirza Faqir Muhammad, Hemayetuddin
Ahmad, Khan Bahadur Bazlur Rahman, Qazi Ziauddin,
Qazi Zahirul Haque, Muhammad Fazlul Karim, Mirza
Yusuf Ali, Emaduddin Ahmad, Altaf Ali, Mafizuddin
Ahmad, Muhammad Ismail, Dewan Abdul Hamid,
Abdul Khalique, Abdul Halim, Muzaffar Ahmad,
Abdul Aziz, Abdul Sattar and S. M. Taifoor.

*Punjab:* Khawaja Yusuf Shah, Khawaja Ghulam Sadiq, Zafar
Ali Khan, Waheduddin, Fazal Muhammad Khan and
Shamshad Ahmad Khan.

*The United Provinces of*
*Agra and Oudh:* Mohsin-ul-Mulk, Viqar-ul-Mulk, Raja Naushad Ali Khan, Nawab Muhammad Ali, Sahebzada Aftab Ahmad Khan, Syed Nabiullah, Shaukat Ali, Muhammad Ali, Syed Ghulam Hasnain, Shaikh Abdullah, Syed Wazir Hasan, Syed Baquer Hasan, Shah Mustafa, Zahur Ahmad, Syed Zahur Ahmad, Dr. Ziauddin Ahmad, Nisar Ahmad Khan, Khawaja Ghulam-us-Saqlain, Hamid Ali Khan and Abdullah Jan.

# APPENDIX IV

## MEMBERS OF THE PROVISIONAL COMMITTEE OF THE ALL-INDIA MUSLIM LEAGUE APPOINTED AT ITS DACCA SESSION 1906

Joint Secretaries:

Nawab Viqar-ul-Mulk.
Nawab Mohsin-ul-Mulk.

Members:

Eastern Bengal:

The Honourable Nawab Salimullah of Dacca.
The Honourable Chaudhry Nawab Ali (Mymensingh).
Moulvie Himayatuddin (Barisal).

Assam:

Moulvie Abdul Majid, B.A., B.L. (Sylhet).

Western Bengal:

Mr. Abdul Rahim, Bar.-at-Law (Calcutta).
Nawab Nasiruddin Khayal (Calcutta).
Nawab Amir Hossein Khan (Calcutta).
Mr. Shamsul Huda, *Vakil* (Calcutta).
Mr. Serajul Islam, *Vakil* (Calcutta).
Mr. Abdul Hamid, Editor, *Moslem Chronicle* (Calcutta).

Behar:

Mr. Ali Imam, Bar.-at-Law (Patna).
Mr. Mazhar-ul-Haque, Bar.-at-Law (Chhapra).
Mr. Hasan Imam, Bar.-at-Law (Patna).

Oudh:

Mr. Nabi-ullah, Bar.-at-Law (Lucknow).
Mr. Hamid Ali Khan, Bar.-at-Law (Lucknow).
Nawab Imad-ul-Mulk (Bilgram).
Munshi Ihtisham Ali, Rais (Lucknow).
Mr. Zahoor Ahmed, B.A., LL.B. (Lucknow).
Mr. Mahomed Nusim, *Vakil* (Lucknow).
Mr. Ghulamus Saqlain, B.A., LL.B. (Lucknow).
Raja Nowshad Ali Khan (Lucknow).

Agra Province:

Nawab Mohsin-ul-Mulk (Aligarh).
Nawab Viqar-ul-Mulk (Amroha).
Sahebzada Aftab Ahmed Khan, Bar.-at-Law (Aligarh).
Mr. Mohamed Ishaque, B.A., LL.B. (Allahabad).
Moulvie Kiramet Hussein, Bar.-at-Law (Allahabad).
Mr. Abdur Raoof, Bar.-at-Law (Allahabad).
Mohammed Raoof, Bar.-at-Law (Allahabad).
Haji Mahomed Moosa Khan (Aligarh).
Khan Bahadur Muhomed Mozammil-ullah Khan (Aligarh).
Mr. Abdullah Jan, *Vakil* (Saharanpore).
Mr. Abdul Majid, Bar.-at-Law (Allahabad).
Haji Ismail Khan (Aligarh).
Sheikh Abdullah, B.A., LL.B. (Aligarh).
Mr. Mahomed Ali, B.A. (Oxon.).

Punjab:

Mr. Mahomed Shafi, Bar.-at-Law (Lahore).
Mr. Fazle Hussein, Bar.-at-Law (Lahore).
Mr. Abdul Aziz, Editor, *Observer* (Lahore).
Khaja Yousoff Shah (Ludhiana).
Hakim Ajmal Khan (Delhi).
Sheik Gholam Mohammed Sahib, Editor, *Vakil* (Amritsar).
Mr. Ghulam Sadiq (Amritsar).

Frontier Province:

Mufti Fida Mahomed Khan, Bar.-at-Law (Peshawar).

Sindh:

Mr. A. M. Dehlavi (Hyderabad).

Kathiawar:

Mr. Ghulam Mohammed Munshi, Bar.-at-Law (Rajkote).

Bombay Presidency:

Nawabzada Nasir-ullah Khan, Bar.-at-Law (Bombay).
Mr. Rafiuddin, Bar.-at-Law (Bombay).

Madras Presidenoy:

Khan Bahadur Abdul Hadi Badshah.
Khan Bahadur Ahmed Mahi-uddin (Madras).
Mr. Yakub Hussein, Proprietor of the *Moslem Patriot* (Madras).
Nawab Gholam Ahmed (Coromandel).
Mr. Abdul Hamid Hasan, B.A., LL.B., Editor, the *Moslem Patriot* (Madras).

Orissa:

Mr. Naur-ul-Huq, Secretary, Mahommedan Association (Cuttack).

Central Provinces:

Khan Saheb Mahomed Amir Khan, Pleader (Nagpur).
Mr. H. M. Mullick (Nagpur).

Burma:

Mr. A. S. Rafique (Rangoon).

> *Proceedings of the Home Department (Public),*
> *January-April* 1907, vol. 7587 February 1907.

# INDEX